The West Indies

→ Prevailing Winds   ⇒ Ocean Currents

ATLANTIC OCEAN

SALVADOR

CAICOS
TURKS
GREAT INAGUA
TORTUGA
Navidad   Isabela
HAITI   DOMINICAN
          REPUBLIC
Port-au-Prince
          Santo
          Domingo
HISPANIOLA

MONA PASSAGE

San Juan
PUERTO RICO
ST. CROIX

VIRGIN IS.

ANEGADA PASSAGE

ANGUILLA
ST. MARTIN
SABA
ST. KITTS   BARBUDA
NEVIS   ANTIGUA
MONTSERRAT
GUADELOUPE

DOMINICA

MARTINIQUE

ST. LUCIA

ST. VINCENT
BARBADOS

SEA

ARUBA
CURAÇAO
BONAIRE

GRENADA

MARGARITA

TOBAGO

TRINIDAD

Marta

Maracaibo
Caracas
L. MARACAIBO

VENEZUELA

IA

0   Miles   300

palacios

Mainstream of the Modern World Series

EDITED BY JOHN GUNTHER

A FAMILY OF ISLANDS

Alec Waugh has also written

THE EARLY YEARS OF ALEC WAUGH (1963)

MY PLACE IN THE BAZAAR (1961)

FUEL FOR THE FLAME (1960)

IN PRAISE OF WINE (1959)

LOVE AND THE CARIBBEAN (1959)

ISLAND IN THE SUN (1956)

GUY RENTON (1952)

NO TRUCE WITH TIME (1941)

THE BALLIOLS (1934)

THAT AMERICAN WOMAN (1932)

HOT COUNTRIES (1930)

KEPT (1925)

THE LOOM OF YOUTH (1917)

The Mainstream of

DOUBLEDAY & COMPANY, INC.

A FAMILY

OF ISLANDS

A HISTORY OF THE WEST INDIES
FROM 1492 TO 1898,
WITH AN EPILOGUE SKETCHING
EVENTS FROM THE SPANISH-
AMERICAN WAR TO THE 1960'S

by Alec Waugh

Garden City, New York, 1964

Library of Congress Catalog Card Number 64–16202
Copyright © 1964 by Alec Waugh
All Rights Reserved
Printed in the United States of America

Contents

CONTENTS

Foreword

I went to the West Indies first in 1927; I have been there often since. They have never lost their fascination for me. They have a common background and a common lot. There they stretch, the peaks of a submerged mountain range between the tip of Florida and the Venezuelan coast. They are green and fertile; most of them are mountainous; their climate, considering that they lie within the tropic belt, is temperate. They are cooled by a northeast wind. They are subject to hurricanes and earthquakes. Five hundred years ago they were unknown to Europe. They were inhabited by two brown-skinned races; the gentle and indolent Arawaks in the north and the fierce cannibal Caribs who were advancing from the south, liquidating opposition as they went. The Caribs would presumably have eliminated and absorbed the Arawaks before very long, but Columbus' "doom-burdened caravels" got there first. Within sixty years the Arawaks had disappeared, the few surviving Caribs were entrenched in scattered strongholds, and a new labor force was being recruited on the Guinea coast.

The Vatican by Papal Bull divided the new world between Spain and Portugal, but that ownership was not long unchallenged. For two and a half centuries the Caribbean was the cockpit of Europe's navies: Britain, France and Spain contended there for mastery, with intermittent interventions from the Dutch. Most of the islands changed hands once at least. Europe had just discovered the delights of coffee, tea and cocoa. Sugar boomed. Fortunes were made and lost, the ports on the Guinea Coast were busy. The phrase "rich as a Creole" was in daily use. Then, after the Napoleonic Wars, the tide of prosperity receded. The conscience of the world was roused and the slaves were freed. It was discovered that sugar could be made from beet; one by one the white landowners went home, leaving their lands to the descendants of the slaves.

That, in synopsis, is the story of the West Indian Islands. The caprice of history and geography has decreed for each of them a somewhat different fate, so that I, reading their history and visiting them regularly, have come to recognize their separate identities. I have come to see them, in fact, as a family of islands, so that when I began to write their history, I felt that I was engaged upon a family saga that covered a succession of generations; that I was tracing the fortunes of the various branches of that family with first one branch in the ascendant, then another. I was working, in fact, upon a kind of novel with islands instead of individual characters as the protagonists.

One of the chief problems in the writing of that kind of novel lies in the decision of how and where it is to end. In a sense it cannot finish, it cannot do more than stop; the current of effect and cause continues after the word "finis." Any conclusion must be arbitrary. Yet there are landmarks. A family saga ends usually with a funeral or a marriage, with the closing of an individual chapter or the opening of a new one. And in this case the Spanish-American war of 1898 does provide a convenient curtain. It marks the end of four centuries of Spanish occupation. What Columbus started, ended when the red and gold flag was run down at Havana. Nor is it inappropriate that the Spanish general who handed over the reins of power should have sailed eastward on the first day of the twentieth century.

As I wrote this saga, I thought of myself, in the role familiar to me, as a novelist. And there are few novelists who do not, when they correct their proofs, suspect that however hard they have striven to avoid them, mistakes and misprints will have found their way into the text. A character with brown eyes in the first chapter will find their color mysteriously changed to gray in the seventeenth. On page seventeen a bedroom is described as facing east and on page 176 a heroine's siesta is disturbed by the afternoon sun shining in her face. The Le Havre boat train from Paris will start from the Gare du Nord instead of from the Gare St. Lazare. The reader is horrified at the author's carelessness, but it seems inevitable that such slips should occur. It takes, after all, a number of months to write a book, and most human beings in the course of a year manage to misdirect an envelope, to arrive on the wrong night for dinner, or to deposit a house guest at an airport station sixty minutes after the plane has taken off. Our concentration slackens. And one of the troubles about authorship is this—that if one has made that kind of slip in manuscript, one rarely spots it in revision. Nor do proofreaders; while editors, ready though they may be to amend one's grammar, rarely spot one's howlers.

If the author of a piece of fiction makes mistakes, how infinitely more vulnerable is the novelist who attempts a narrative of recorded fact.

I know that there will be many mistakes in the ensuing pages. I can only crave the indulgence of my readers, assuring them that I have tried my hardest to be accurate, and I would like to express my gratitude to those who have helped me with advice and guidance—I did most of my research in the Brigham Young University in Provo, the Library of Congress in Washington, the London Library, the New York Public Library, the Public Library in Peterboro, New Hampshire, and the Library of the London West Indian Committee; their staffs were very helpful. A number of officials and residents in the various islands have in the course of my visits assisted me, by their introductions and interpretations, to a better understanding of the problems of West Indian life. They are too many to recall by name, but I would like to express my especial gratitude to Charlesworth Ross, onetime Administrator of Montserrat and now a magistrate in Antigua, whom I have been meeting under the most friendly and congenial conditions for over thirty-five years, and who knows more about the Leeward Islands and Dominica than anyone has ever known. Finally, I would like to record my debt to the directors of the MacDowell Colony in Peterboro, who, while I was working on this book, extended to me once again the peace and hospitality of their quiet woods.

CHAPTER I

Spain Lights the Torch

At ten o'clock on the night of October 11, 1492, Christopher Columbus saw from the deck of his caravel, the *Santa Maria,* a light on the horizon. Four hours later a seaman discerned the outline of what is now known as Watling Island, and the ships were ordered to lie to.

Columbus has not put on record the thoughts that lit his mind as the swift dawn broke. But he would not have been human if his sense of triumph had not been quickened by the chuckle of the man who had been proved right. For many years he had himself been certain that, because the world was round, Asia could be reached by a western route; he had inferred, because the distance between the edge of the West and the edge of the East was very long, that the distance by sea between Spain and India must be very small. To his own mind this truth was evident. But he had argued to unheeding ears. Henry of England had been impressed but dilatory; John of Portugal had tried to cheat him; the council of Salamanca, while he had loitered in the courts of Spain, had dubiously weighed his testimony, deciding finally that his project was "vain, impracticable and resting on grounds too weak to merit the support of the government." Even when Queen Isabella of Castile had at last approved his plan, staking her jewelry upon her faith in him, the doubters had been more numerous than the believers; he had had the greatest difficulty in raising a crew in Palos.

Now it was all over. In a few hours he would set foot on the promised land. He would soon deliver into the hands of the great Khan a letter of introduction from his sovereigns. "We have heard," so the letter ran, "that Your Highness and your subjects entertain great love for us and for Spain. We are informed, moreover, that you and your subjects very much wish to hear news from Spain. We therefore send our admiral, Christopher Columbus, who will tell you that we are in good health and perfect prosperity." I told you so, Columbus must have thought. I told you so.

He was never to learn that the doubters were right and he was wrong; that his calculations had been at fault; that the group of islands that were to be known later as the West Indies were twelve thousand miles distant from Cathay and the mighty Khan; and that had not the continent of the Americas been interposed between Spain and China, his caravels would have assuredly perished in mid-ocean.

We do not possess the letter in which Columbus announced his achievement to his sovereigns, but the letter which he sent to the treasurer of Aragon can indicate its nature. "The Caribbean Islands," he wrote, "are as beautiful as any in the world, and no area is luckier in its climate; the land is fertile and mountainous and a trade wind cools its heat." Columbus spoke of the fruit, the birds, the flowers; of the towering mountains, the different kinds of palm; of trees so tall that they seemed to reach the skies and never lost their foliage. The rivers were full of gold, and the natives wore gold ornaments, which surely proved that he was within range of the riches which Marco Polo had described.

He was delighted with the appearance and behavior of the natives. They were very different from the coarse-featured Africans and the swarthy Moors with whom Europe was familiar. They were pale brown in color, their features were fine, their hair was coarse but not curly, and was worn short. They were Asians rather than Moors or Africans.

No trace remains of the Indians who welcomed him. They have since been named Arawaks, and there is abundant evidence that they were weak, charming, indolent, pleasure-loving. They bore, as far as we can gather, a spiritual resemblance to the Polynesians. They had broad faces and flat noses. They altered the shape of their heads, depressing their scalps in childhood with a wooden frame, a procedure that so strengthened the skull that the Spaniards were later to complain that a blow from a broadsword often broke the blade off at the hilt. They had fine dark eyes and friendly smiles. They were tall and they moved gracefully. They lived mainly upon maize. They had made no attempt to develop the resources of the soil, though they possessed some skill in the fashioning of domestic furniture, and presented Columbus with some handsome ebony chairs. They danced in groups for hours on end. They amused themselves with a fiber football, which they kicked over their shoulders with the backs of their heels, maintaining it in the air for long periods. They seemed to have no laws or priests, believing that power and goodness were in the sky. Their weapons were wooden spears. The women wore nothing but a small leaf-covering, while the men inserted birds' feathers in their hair.

Columbus wrote in his eventual report, "So lovable, so tractable, so peaceable are these people that I swear to Your Majesties that there is not in the world a better nation nor a better land. They love their neighbors as themselves and their discourse is ever sweet and gentle and accompanied with a smile."

Las Casas, Bishop of Chiapas, who visited the islands on a later expedition and is our most important witness to the period, though his testimony has to be accepted with reserve, since he was the Indians' most strenuous apologist, wrote of them as "naturally simple. They know not what belongs to policy and address, to trick and artifice, but are very obedient and faithful to the rightful governors. They are humble, patient and submissive. They are a weak, effeminate people, not capable of enduring great fatigues; they care not to be exposed to toil and labor, and their life is of no long continuance; their constitution is so nice that a small fit of sickness carries them off. . . . They are so poor that they live in the want of almost everything; they are very cool and indifferent in the pursuit of temporal advantages and seem not to be inclined to pride and ambition; their way of living is so frugal that the ancient hermits in the wilderness were scarce more sober and abstemious. They go naked, yet they have the modesty to wear a kind of apron about their waists."

Columbus' report went on, "These people are very simple in weapons, as Your Majesties can see from the seven of them whom I have brought over so that they may learn our language; we can send them back, though Your Majesties may, whenever you so wish, have them all sent to Castile; or you may keep them captives in the island, for with fifty armed men you will keep them all under your sway and will make them do all you may desire." He did not realize that though a people may be weak, it can be capable of preferring death to slavery.

Columbus returned home almost at once, landing in Palos in the following March. The court was in Barcelona, and his month's journey thither through Andalusia, through a countryside fresh with young grain, with the trees in full leaf and the fruit in blossom, was as rich a triumph as any man had known. Very few had expected him to be successful; the winter's storms had been exceptionally severe; after an eight months' silence his death had been presumed. In Seville and Cordova, in Valencia and along the coastal road through Tarragona, he was received with acclamation. At Barcelona, cavaliers and merchants and a thronging populace were at the gates to honor him.

Ferdinand and Isabella, with their throne set in public before the Cathedral, awaited him under a canopy of gold brocade. At the head of the procession marched six Indians; they were painted and befeathered, they were hung with ornaments, and they were very cold. The crew followed them, carrying live parrots, stuffed animals and examples of Indian furniture. Columbus rode upon a horse with a velvet bonnet on his head and a regal cloak about his shoulders. Ferdinand and Isabella rose from their seats to greet him, commanding him to sit beside them. He presented them with the log of his voyage; he expatiated on the wonders he had seen and even more upon those which he expected to see on his second voyage. When he had finished his story, his sovereigns and Prince Juan knelt with their hands raised in gratitude to heaven. The court knelt too; the choir of the royal chapel sang the *Te Deum* and a procession started through the city.

The welcome was appropriate to his achievement. But he had, in fact, brought back very little. His journey had not by any means paid its expenses. He had traveled with three ships, the *Santa Maria* of one hundred tons, with a crew of fifty-two men, the *Pinta* of fifty tons with eighteen men, and the *Nina* of fifty tons with eighteen men, and he returned with two, the *Santa Maria* having gone aground in Hispaniola, and a fort having been built out of its wreckage; the settlement had been called La Navidad and forty-four Europeans had been left in charge of it. Moreover, though he had brought back a certain amount of gold, he had discovered no sources of gold. Nor had he delivered his credentials to the Khan. He had not, however, been expected to show a profit on this one trip, but to indicate how profit could be made on a later one, and he could justifiably present a roseate account of his prospects. He never himself doubted that he was within a few miles of the fabulous fortunes of the East, and he convinced his audiences.

Tall, grayhaired, with clean-cut rugged features, he was an impressive figure. It is not surprising that for six months he was the most feted man in Spain. Nor is it surprising that Isabella should see her admiral's achievement as the symbol of the greatness that, under God, was soon to be conferred upon her country. Her life's work was coming to fruition. With Granada freed from the Moors, with the unconverted Jews expelled, she was free to concentrate upon her people's welfare, to restore the war-ravaged countryside, revive local industries, found universities and hospitals, assuming her role of patron of the arts and sciences. In Columbus' achievement, with its promise of new wealth and its prospect of spreading the Gospel among unenlightened peoples, she foresaw the fulfillment of her heart's dearest prayers. She promised to finance a second voyage, and this time there would be no difficulty in finding men for it.

The second voyage was to be a very different project from the first. Columbus had started on his first voyage as a missionary and an explorer, to make discoveries and to spread the Gospel. He was now setting out to found an empire. But before this could be done, the legality of the operation had to be determined. The Portuguese had been the initiators in discovery. Diaz had been the first man to round the Cape of Good Hope, and Portugal had established itself on the west coast of Africa. When King John learned of Columbus' discoveries, he claimed that Spain had trespassed upon his domains. Ferdinand and Isabella appealed to the Pope, who prudently adjudicated between the two nations by drawing an imaginary line from pole to pole a hundred leagues west of the Azores; everything east of this line belonging to Portugal, and everything west of it to Spain. This Papal Bull left Portugal in control of the African coast, which is one of the several reasons why Spain was never involved directly in the slave trade. It also explains why Brazil became a Portuguese colony.

The second expedition was very much larger than the first. Seventeen ships were assembled instead of three, and fifteen hundred men instead of eighty-eight. Many varieties of men were to make the crossing. The prospective colonists were not all of them, by any means, seamen under a captain's orders. Many were independent adventurers in search of gold and glory; there were also ecclesiastics, with very definite views as to their own importance, whose standards were not those of the admiral; neither faction would accept the admiral's authority without question. The group also included a number of recently released jailbirds who, once free from discipline, were likely to prove truculent.

The seventeen ships were provisioned not only for the voyage but for residence. The deficiencies in the diet of the islands were to be repaired with many kinds of seed, with wheat and barley, with sugarcane from the Canaries, with oranges, melons, lemons. They also took animals—cows, bulls, goats, horses, poultry. The descendants of the eight pigs that Columbus took with him on this voyage were later to provide the *conquistadores* of South America with their main source of nourishment.

The instructions given to Columbus were specific. It must be made clear on every occasion that authority derived from the King and Queen and from no one else. An oath of allegiance to the crown was to be taken by every man setting out on the expedition. Every judicial sentence had to be announced by the town crier as "the justice which is rendered by the King and Queen, our sovereigns," and all the orders issued by the admiral and viceroy had to be delivered in the name of Ferdinand and Isabella.

Yet, although these orders were given under the names of Ferdinand and Isabella, Isabella thought of herself primarily as Queen of Castile, rather than the joint occupant of the Spanish throne, and she regarded Columbus' expeditions as a Castilian operation; she decreed that the new territories should be administered from Seville, and formed a special department to deal with them. This decision was later to hamper the colonial machine, since Seville stands several miles up a river that is awkward for big shipping.

The day Columbus sailed upon this second voyage was the high point of his career. Never again was he to enjoy completely the confidence of his fellow men. It was a proud day for his country, too, the beginning of Spain's imperial greatness. Yet ironically enough, four hundred years later, historians were to wonder whether, in spite of Spain's achievements across the Atlantic, it might have been better for her if Portugal had accepted Columbus' proposal in the first place. Had Portugal discovered the New World, the most ambitious Spaniards would not have been lured to emigrate, nor would the sudden inflow of bullion have disorganized Spanish economy, causing inflation and, through a faulty appraisal of the reasons and consequences of that inflation, ruining the home industries that Isabella had been so anxious to foster. Little of the gold that came into Spain reached the Spanish people. It went to middlemen and to other countries; it enriched the Creole colonists and it financed the ruinous Flemish Wars. It might have been better for Spain if she had spread her power, as Ferdinand himself had wished, across the Mediterranean instead of the Atlantic, pursuing the Moors into Africa.

For his second voyage Columbus took a southern route, and his first landfall was the island that he called Guadeloupe. He made here the unwelcome discovery that it was inhabited by a race very different from the gentle Arawaks. He found human limbs hanging from the rafters, and the remains of a young man being boiled with the flesh of geese and parrots. These cannibals, who came to be known as Caribs, had been gradually advancing up the Lesser Antilles, exterminating opposition as they went. Adult men and women were killed; girls were kept to provide babies for the larder; boys were caponized.

This unsavory disclosure partially resolved one problem that had puzzled Columbus. Lack of a common language had proved a great hindrance in his dealings with the Indians. He had taken on board a few Arawaks whom he had instructed in the elements of Castilian, so that they might act as interpreters, but the Arawaks conversed largely in sign language. He had noticed on his first voyage that Indians in the bush often fled in terror at the first sight of a Spaniard, shouting, "Can, Can." He was convinced that the object of their terror was the armies of the great Khan, and instructed his men to shout after them, "No can. No can." He now realized that "can" was the Indian word for Carib territory; and that the Indians were terrified of a race that was perpetually raiding their coast for the replenishment of its larders.

On this second voyage Columbus discovered several of the islands that are known now as the Lesser Antilles—Antigua, Dominica, Montserrat, Puerto Rico. He found pineapples, rhubarb, cinnamon, cassava bread, yams, sweet potatoes; he also saw some excellent cotton rugs and earthenware vessels. But he found no gold. Its absence, coupled with the ferocity of the Caribs, convinced him that it was useless to attempt a settlement there, and he pushed on to Hispaniola. There he was to receive a second shock.

The Indians who welcomed him at La Navidad did their best to assure him that all was well, but indicated, as best they could by signs, that some of the garrison had died of sickness and others had quarreled among themselves. He was soon to discover that not one of his former comrades was alive. He was never to learn under what conditions they had met their end.

This second voyage was the first colonial expedition that Europe had undertaken, and the odds against its success can be appreciated readily today. In our estimate of its chances, we can be guided by the experience of four and a half centuries. Columbus was first in the field. He had no such guide. His second voyage was indeed to serve as a warning to his successors.

Setting out to build a new Spain across the water, he believed that culture, customs and faith could be transplanted easily, once the Atlantic had been crossed. He had no conception of the different way of life that was demanded by a different climate and by the demands of a different, if subject race. The Spaniards had to accommodate themselves to tropical conditions. Diseases to which the Indians were immune might well prove lethal. They had to discover what diet and clothes were most suitable to the climate, and what kind of house. They also had to live on terms of cordiality with a race speaking a different language, a race with different ideas, laws, customs.

Columbus landed at Watling Island dressed in the full regalia of a Spanish grandee, carrying the royal standard. The heat must have been overpowering, and it would appear from pictures that Spaniards dressed in the tropics just as they would in Spain, in satin and velvet, very often in armor and always carrying swords. They must have endured the greatest discomfort. The strain on their nerves must have been incessant. The pictures that illustrate early West Indian books always show Europeans dressed as though they were attending a court function in Madrid, Paris, or London.

Only an exceptional man could have conducted such an enterprise successfully. Columbus was an exceptional man; he was more than an exceptional man; he was a man of genius. But he was the wrong kind of genius for this particular undertaking. He was a man in conflict with his time. There are two types of man in conflict with their time—the reactionary who hankers for the past, and the visionary whose aim exceeds his grasp. Columbus had the faith and imagination to picture a Christian and Spanish empire beyond the seas, which would fill the coffers and heighten the prestige of Castile and Aragon; he could foresee a pattern of trade payments in which the colonies would provide raw materials for the home country's industries, in return for which the home country would supply finished products; he also visualized trade between the colonies and neighboring countries, to the home country's eventual profit. He saw the necessity of stocking a colony with the resources that a European population required. Many of the arrangements that were made for the second voyage were the outcome of Isabella's foresight, but Columbus must have made his own contribution. Considering that not only he and his sovereigns but Europe as a whole had no previous experience of colonial administration, it is remarkable that the expedition should have been fitted out so quickly, that allowances should have been made for so many contingencies. Columbus was far more than a navigator; he had the vision of a great proconsul. But he had not the temperament of one.

It has been said of the British Empire that it was founded by rebels, by men who put their telescopes to their blind eyes, but that it was organized from London by the very men against whom those rebels were in conflict. There was constant friction between the bureaucrats of Whitehall and the Warren Hastings' of India and the Stamford Raffles' of Singapore, but the two acted as balances for one another; they supplemented one another; for two centuries they created harmony out of disharmony. Columbus, however, was expected to combine within himself these two opposing factions. He was the rebel, the initiator, but he had to be also the cautioning counselor. It is not surprising that the result should have been unsatisfactory.

Columbus was authoritative, intolerant of opposition, distrustful of his fellows. On his first voyage he had managed to quarrel with his second-in-command and with the crew of his own ship, and had concealed from his crew the extent of the day's run, keeping two separate logs so that they should not know how far they were from Spain. He did not confide in his associates. He trusted only his family, although he must have known that his brother Diego was ineffectual. Like most ambitious men, he was ruthless and relentless in the pursuit of his ambition. He did not spare himself; why should he spare others? He never considered the feelings and interests of others. He was completely absorbed in himself and in his dream. He was not equipped for the role of colonial governor, and on this second instance he was rendered even more unsuitable by his overriding need to make contact with the mainland of Cathay.

Since La Navidad had been destroyed, he established a second settlement a few miles along the coast, which he called Isabela. The site for it was to prove unsuitable, and it was soon visited by an epidemic. The nature of this epidemic is unknown. Today the Caribbean area is one of the healthiest in the world, but more British troops died of yellow fever in the West Indies during the Napoleonic Wars than fell in action in the Peninsular campaign. It may have been that the colonists were the victims of influenza; it may have been that they were the victims of undernourishment and overwork. It is certain that the ill health among the settlers contributed to their intractability. The Hidalgos were indignant at being put to work on menial labors, on fencing, ditching, the raising and roofing of houses. They had been assured that gold was here; why could they not get at it?

Columbus also was sure that gold was there. His certainty that it was there heightened the unhappy atmosphere in the colony. Leaving the management of Isabela to Diego, he marched into the interior with a large portion of his troops to examine a section of the island where he believed gold to exist. He was away only two and a half weeks, but seventeen days is a long time in the tropics when tempers are strained, and he returned to find Isabela a hospital rather than a camp.

The colonists were starving; the food they had imported had deteriorated and the native food did not agree with their digestions. He had no flour with which to relieve their distress, but there was wheat and there was a river. He therefore ordered the building of saw mills. This was a further indignity to his Hidalgos.

Columbus was impatient with their trivial complaints. What did their petty dignities matter in comparison with the wealth that lay so near at hand? On his short trip into the interior he had reached, through a difficult mountain pass, a fertile valley with friendly natives, beyond which he had found a dry, rocky territory whose rivers contained gold. Surely any moment now he would stumble on the lands of treasure. His health was weakening; he had no time to waste.

He flung himself with spasmodic energy into his role as Viceroy: he founded another settlement on the north coast, then another on the south side of the island, calling it Santo Domingo; but all that was something that he did with his left hand, a sideshow. He was fretting to be away. The sense of urgency prevented him from paying the necessary attention to the needs and importunities of his subjects.

He was always impatient to be away, to explore the interior of Hispaniola and the coastline of Cuba. The word "can" again misled him. A native told him that there was gold in "Cubanacan." This meant to his Indian informant that there was gold in the center of Cuba, "nacan" being the Indian for middle, but Columbus believed that Cuba was part of the mainland and that he was actually in China. He was so convinced that Cuba was the mainland that he made his crew swear before a lawyer that it was a continent; he threatened them with fines if they would not sign. Each time he returned to Isabela he found the colony in a worse state. It was essential that a strong man should be continually on the spot, yet Columbus was forever absenting himself, delegating his powers to a council presided over by Diego.

On one of his excursions, an envoy whom he had sent into the interior with a letter of introduction to the great Khan returned with the letter undelivered but with the report that he had seen men carrying flaming branches with which they fumigated their homes and villages, placing the stalks in their mouths, inhaling the smoke, then blowing it out into the air. He had, in fact, discovered tobacco. But Columbus was not interested in this great source of wealth. It was not gold. The incident is typical of the whole Spanish adventure across the ocean. Spain was only interested in gold and silver, not the means to wealth.

Columbus discovered Jamaica, but found no gold there and was soon on his way back to Cuba. He sailed along its coast to within a hundred and fifty miles of its western tip. Had he continued his voyage he must have realized that Cuba was an island, and he might have learned that Yucatan and the mines of Mexico were across the water, but the claims of his double role intervened. He was short of food, the winds were high, the coastline was set with shoals.

He retraced his path, zigzagging among the islands, uncertain of his direction. After a five months' absence, he returned to chaos. He also returned in broken health, unfit to continue the administration of the city. He delegated his powers this time to his elder brother.

Commanders in the field complain that the bureaucrats directing their destiny from a desk in a capital cannot place themselves imaginatively in the position of someone who is "on the spot." The bureaucrats in their turn complain that the man on the spot does not appreciate that his problem is one of many, to be assessed in relation to those of others. During the thirty months that Columbus spent upon his second voyage, Ferdinand and Isabella had a great deal upon their hands, much of which must have seemed, particularly to Ferdinand, more important than an expedition of seventeen vessels to the West.

Ferdinand had always been more concerned with the Old World than the New. Now that the Moorish menace had been removed, he could concentrate upon his diplomatic role in the courts of Europe. He had at his disposal the veterans of the Moorish War, and he was confident that if he played his cards carefully he could establish Spain as a first-rank power. He was too busy recruiting and organizing an army, and manipulating political alliances, to give his full attention to the Caribbean. Isabella, for her part, was occupied with her children's marriages, that of her delicate and adored son, Juan, to Margaret of Austria, and that of her daughter, the infanta Juana, to the son of the Emperor Maximilian. These marriages would ensure the continuance of her own stock in Castile and Aragon and might lead to the union of Spain and Portugal. The progress of her empire across the seas had become momentarily of secondary importance.

Such news as she did receive had worried her. The reports of Columbus himself still glowed with optimism, but there was not as yet any very practical return for the considerable cost of the expedition. Very little gold had been sent home; and only small quantities of musk and cinnamon. Columbus insisted that the discovery of the rich gold and silver mines of Cathay was imminent, but his only concrete suggestion was to send home Carib cannibals as slaves, so that they could be cured of their taste for human flesh and be instructed in the faith. The returning caravels could bring out cattle. This, in his opinion, would prove a profitable trade and provide the crown with substantial dues.

The idea did not commend itself to Their Majesties, particularly to Isabella. She and Ferdinand had sponsored the baptism of the first Indians that Columbus had brought back. The role that she conceived for them in the social hierarchy, as attendants and servants to the Spaniards, was certainly a lowly one, but they were subjects and not slaves. In the instructions which he had taken on his second voyage, Columbus had been adjured to treat the Indians with affection. Their Majesties' reply to Columbus' suggestion was noncommittal. They must wait, they said, until they had consulted with their theologians.

Before a decision had been reached, four ships arrived in Seville, containing some five hundred Indian slaves. Isabella was at first under the impression that these slaves were prisoners of war, Columbus having sent her news of a battle in which three hundred Spaniards, with the help of bloodhounds, had routed 100,000 Indians. As it was the custom of the day to treat prisoners of war as slaves, Isabella, believing this to be the status of the Indians and believing them to be all male, authorized their sale. She was highly indignant when she learned that they were of both sexes, some little more than children. She commanded that they should be freed and returned to their homes. But before her orders could be carried out, the slaves had died. They had been brought over unclothed like cattle and they had been unable to withstand the cold. They had proved a highly unprofitable investment for their purchasers.

This shipment of slaves was the chief tangible return for the shareholders in the expedition, but the lack of material return was not the major cause of the Queen's concern. There was now a regular caravel service with an exchange of letters between the court and Hispaniola, and Isabella was in receipt of private reports from her new subjects. She read of quarrels between Columbus and his men, and complaints of his tyrannous behavior. Nor was she pleased to learn that when he had handed over the administration of the city to his elder brother, during his sickness, he had conferred on him the title of *adelantado*, a title which admitted the bearer to many privileges. He appeared to be usurping the royal authority.

In her concern, she decided to send out an envoy who would report back to her on the precise conditions that existed there. His credentials were ambiguous. "Gentlemen and Squires and others who are in the Indies at our behest, we send you thither Juan Aguado, our butler, who will speak to you on our behalf. We order you to have faith in him and believe what he says."

Columbus was puzzled and alarmed. He did not fail to notice that the document contained no reference to himself. Was his position no longer secure at court? He decided to return, to state his case and to have his authority confirmed. He took back the sick and any others who might be glad to get away. Two hundred and twenty colonists were delighted to leave the land of promise.

From the point of view of the colony's welfare, he could not have left at a more inconvenient time, and the man whom he appointed as mayor of Isabela in his absence was singularly ill-fitted for a post of such high responsibility.

The reception that was accorded to Columbus in Cádiz, in June 1496, was very different from that which had welcomed him at Palos thirty-nine months earlier. No balconies were decked with flags. No courtiers thronged to honor him. On the contrary, those who had invested in his enterprise were aggrieved. They felt they had been cheated, while those who had been jealous of his sudden elevation to the aristocracy and resentful of the signal honors that had been showered on him, were quick to sneer. What else could you expect from an Italian upstart!

Columbus, self-centered and imperious though he was, had the common sense to recognize that he had enemies at court. Self-confident and convinced though he might be of the ultimate value of his discoveries, he realized that the story he had to tell would not be popular. He returned ready to meet opposition, and with a keen sense of the dramatic he exchanged the velvet bonnet and gorgeous cloak in which, at Seville, he had crossed the stone Moorish bridge over the Guadalquivir, for the shabby gray robe of a Franciscan.

It was thus that he presented himself at court. His movements were slow with gout, his face was lined with sickness, but the Admiral of the Seas carried his head high, his eyes were bright; he spoke with the old eloquence. "Your Highnesses," he promised, "will win these lands which are in another world, where Christianity will have so much enjoyment and our faith in time so great an increase. All this I say with very honest intent and because I desire that Your Highnesses may be the greatest Lords in the world. Lords of it all, I say, and that all be with much service and satisfaction of the Holy Trinity." Once again Ferdinand and Isabella listened; and once again fate smiled on the great fanatic. He was given an unexpected chance to prove his skill as a navigator.

The court was awaiting at Burgos the arrival from England of Margaret of Austria to celebrate her betrothal to Prince Juan. The weather had been bad and the King and Queen had been worried by the fleet's delay. They had finally decided that it was no use waiting any longer. On a Saturday the court moved to Soria, the King and Queen staying on until Monday. On that night Columbus wrote to tell them that since the wind had changed, the fleet would sail in a day or two, and, if it did not stop at the Isle of Wight, would be in northern Spain on Monday. And indeed on Monday a ship that had not stopped at the Isle of Wight did arrive, at the very port that he had prophesied. Once again his stock stood high; and indeed Isabella's faith in him had never wavered. He had accomplished what he had promised. He had crossed the ocean, he had added vast territories to her dominions. He had not found the gold that he expected, but she was less interested in gold than he. She had an aristocratic, a regal attitude to money. She had, she said, spent more money on enterprises of less importance. She confirmed him in his authority and promised to fit him out on a third voyage, agreeing to the complicated conditions he demanded.

Two years were to pass, however, before he was ready to sail again, and during them much happened. In August 1496, Margaret of Austria landed in northern Spain, and within a week it was apparent that she and Prince Juan were ecstatically in love. She was eighteen, he was nineteen. It was like a fairy story. The wedding was celebrated in the following March with the utmost splendor. It seemed to Isabella that in this union of her new empire and the old empire of

Charlemagne the destiny of Spain had been confirmed. But Prince Juan was not only young and elegant, he was also delicate, and his doctors were soon warning the Queen that his constitution could not stand the strain placed on it by a marriage that was a love affair; they urged a temporary separation. Isabella could not agree that man should separate whom God had joined. Her theologians agreed with her. Within a year her son was dead.

She never recovered from this blow. As a Christian Queen she endured stoically the few sad years that lay ahead, but by the time Columbus was ready to sail on his third voyage she was no longer the young woman of dreams who had listened to a visionary.

There were further blows to fall. A year later, her daughter Isabel, Queen of Portugal, died in childbirth, and the son who should have inherited the throne did not long survive her. At a time when Isabella's patience and strength were strained to the limits of endurance, Columbus added an intolerable burden.

On the day of departure, on the docks, he lost his temper with the Bishop's adjutant, struck him, knocked him down and kicked him. It is probable that this act, more than any other, counted against Columbus with Isabella. What confidence could she have in a man who could lose his temper so completely, in public and against a person whom he should have held as sacrosanct? If he was to behave like this in Spain, what might he not be expected to do in far Hispaniola? She was ready to give credence now to the reports that reached her from those distant shores.

She had good cause to be exasperated. Once again he was to break her express command and send back Indian slaves. Convinced though she was of Columbus' skill as a navigator, she had come to feel grave doubts about his effectiveness as an administrator. She was herself an administrator of the highest order and could recognize the lack of essential qualities in others. Finally, her nerves stretched taut, her patience exhausted by the continual complaints about his brutality and highhandedness, she sent out Francisco de Bobadilla with instructions to adjudicate between the various disputants. She appointed him governor and chief magistrate of Hispaniola, and empowered him to send back to Spain anyone whose actions were endangering the national interest; Christopher was told to hand over to him all the property of Their Highnesses and "to believe him and do what he says."

On his arrival, Bobadilla found two Christians recently hanged swinging from the gallows. The enquiries he made convinced him that he had interrupted a condition of chaos which was very close to anarchy. He decided that the Admiral's presence was the chief deterrent to peace and ordered his arrest. Columbus returned from his third voyage neither in a velvet cap nor in a Franciscan gown, but in chains.

The colonial pattern that was to be repeated so often in the years ahead, among so many nations, was first established here, the man on the spot being misunderstood and condemned by the authorities at home. But though Bobadilla went beyond Isabella's intentions, if not beyond her instructions, which were vague and comprehensive, and though it is possible that Isabella's choice of Bobadilla was injudicious, there have been few criticisms of his honesty and rectitude.

In this, his darkest hour, Columbus behaved with great astuteness. His sense of the theater did not fail him. The master of the ship that carried him back offered to remove his chains, but he refused. The chains, he asserted, had been placed there under the orders of Her Majesty, Isabella of Castile, and by her orders only could they be struck off. He also was at pains to see that Ferdinand and Isabella received news of his disgrace through the friendly offices of the master of the ship before Bobadilla's official report reached them. Isabella, horrified that a man whom she had honored should suffer such indignities, instantly ordered his release and summoned him to court, sending money so that he could appear in clothes worthy of his station.

The magnetism of his personality bleached the formal bureaucratic testimony against him. He had a great capacity for self-pity, a great sense of his own importance. He was a superb figure of the Renaissance. In a letter to the infanta's governess he wrote, "They judge me as a governor who had gone to Sicily, or to a city or town under a regular governor, where the laws can be observed *in toto* without fear of losing all, and I am suffering grave injury. I should be judged as a captain who went from Spain to the Indies to conquer a people numerous and warlike, whose manners and religion are very different from ours, who live in sierras and mountains, without fixed settlements, and where, by divine will, I have placed under the sovereignty of the King another world whereby Spain, which was reckoned poor, is become the richest of countries."

Columbus, in ill health, tortured with gout but with his eyes ablaze, may well have been even more impressive at his fortune's lowest ebb than he had been in the pride and glory of his first return; and it was certainly of considerable feats that he had to tell. On this third voyage he had taken a southern route, reaching Trinidad and the Gulf of Paria. He was disappointed at not being received there by Chinese clothed in silk, but he was comforted to find that the natives of Venezuela had upon their arms pearls which might be a satisfactory substitute for gold. The Gulf of Paria contained fresh water, which surely proved the proximity of some great river. The Scriptures had laid down that in the earthly paradise grew the tree of life, from which flowed the four great rivers of the world, the Ganges, the Nile, the Tigris, and the Euphrates. The discovery of this fifth river suggested that he was near the earthly paradise. He was convinced that he was on a continent.

Their Majesties listened and were impressed. The man whom they had raised to such high honor still seemed worthy of it; they were prepared to confirm him in his rank; but they did not consider that Bobadilla had been at fault. Their envoy might have been overzealous, but he had not been mistaken. Columbus was the greatest navigator that the world had known, but he did not possess the qualities of a colonial governor. They would indeed have been happy to find for his old age a sheltered and honored sinecure at home, but the imagination of Columbus was still alight. Like that other great visionary of Spain's Golden Age, he inhabited simultaneously the world of truth and fantasy. He was still convinced that India was close at hand, and he had added now to his program, as a corollary, a scheme to liberate Jerusalem. He had calculated from a study of the Bible that the earth's course had only 155 years to run. Many prophecies were still unfulfilled. There was no time to waste.

Once again Their Majesties let themselves be persuaded. They agreed to finance a fourth voyage, but they stipulated that it was to be simply that of an explorer. Its primary object was the discovery of a sea passage through the Caribbean mainland to the farther seas. The expedition was to consist of four caravels, manned by 135 men and boys. On one point Their Majesties were adamant. He was not to visit Hispaniola, to which had been dispatched independently a colonizing expedition of thirty-two ships manned by two thousand five hundred men.

Columbus' last voyage was the most turbulent of the four—to him personally it was disastrous; to its sponsors it was unproductive, since he brought back no gold and did not discover the passage to the southern seas. Yet it served a purpose—coasting along Central America he touched on the sources of the New World's wealth and, in terms of the dramatic unities, it presented a fitting climax to his career.

From the start he was unlucky. His first objective was Jamaica, but a heavy storm battered him all the way from Dominica, and he was forced to take shelter under the lee of Hispaniola. He was short of supplies and one of his ships was no longer seaworthy. In spite of the injunctions of Isabella, he begged leave to put into harbor, but was refused. In harbor were the ships of the governor who had supplanted him, Ovando. They were about to return to Spain; their flagship was carrying not only Bobadilla but two of his own bitterest foes. There was also on board a vast store of gold, the largest that was ever returned from Hispaniola. A storm was threatening, and Christopher begged once again to be allowed to shelter in Santo Domingo. Again permission was denied him. So he moved down the coast under its protection, while the fleet that had ignored his warning sailed into the open seas, into the full rage of the storm. Twenty ships, including the flagship, were destroyed. Only one ship returned to Spain. An Aeschylean revenge had been accorded to Columbus.

For him the next eight months were a mounting torture. Sick, abandoned, threatened by hostile natives, with one ship helpless, he wrote despairingly to Isabella, "I came to serve Your Highnesses at the age of twenty-eight, and now I have no hair on me that is not white, and my body is infirm and exhausted. . . . Isolated in this pain, infirm, daily expecting death, surrounded by a million savages full of cruelty and our enemies . . . and thus separated from the holy sacraments of Holy Church, how neglected will be this soul if here it part from this body."

The letter is an astonishing mixture of self-glorification and self-pity. On his way westward he had reached the Central American coast. He glowed as he described it. Inland, he asserted, were deep veins of copper. He had seen cotton sheets, and farther on, in the Cathay which he always believed to be close at hand, were, he had been assured, sheets woven with gold. He was handicapped, he realized, by lack of an interpreter, but the much that he had seen, the little that he had been able to infer, convinced him that at last he was within reach of the long-fabled riches. "When I discovered the Indies, I said that they were the biggest and richest dominion in the world. I spoke of the gold, pearls, precious stones, spices, commerce and fairs, and as everything did not turn up at once, I was put to shame. This lesson makes me now say no more than what I hear from natives. Of one thing I dare speak, because there are so many witnesses, that is, that in this land of Voragua (Nicaragua), I have seen more signs of gold in the first two days than in Hispaniola in four years. The lands of the country could not be more beautiful nor better tilled, nor the men more cowardly; there are good harbors and beautiful rivers; it can be easily defended against the world. All this in safety for the Christians, with certainty of overlordship, with great hope of honor and growth for the Christian religion. . . . Your Highnesses are as much Lord and Lady of this as of Jerez and Toledo." It was on this voyage that he developed the theory that the earth was shaped like a pear.

His troubles multiplied. He had to face disaffection in his crew, treachery from the natives, he was sick and weak with fever. Only his will sustained him; the resolve to justify himself in the eyes of the world and of his sovereigns.

Isabella read his letters in the gardens of the Alhambra while her husband, who had lost interest in these costly sailings, developed his European schemes. She was ill and old and tired; she had lost the zest for living. She had just learned of the estrangement between her daughter, Doña Juana, and her husband, Philip of Burgundy, an estrangement that was to lead to the young Spaniard's mental break-down. Did she see a parallel between these despairing letters from Jamaica and her own deep-seated grief? Eleven years ago when she and Ferdinand had risen from their thrones in Barcelona, the dis-covery of the New World had symbolized the radiant future that awaited a Spain delivered from the infidel and purged of heresy; a Spain that would lead the world in the arts and sciences. How quickly those dreams had crumbled, as the marriages on which that future had been based had been dissolved by death. What would happen to Spain now?

Isabella was never to see her admiral again. Columbus landed at the mouth of the Guadalquivir early in November; he set out im-mediately for court, but before he could reach her, she had died.

During the eighteen months of life that still remained to him, Co-lumbus was persistent in his efforts to inspire Ferdinand's interest in his plans, but without success. Ferdinand had a great deal on his mind. His daughter, Juana, now Queen of Castile, was already men-tally deranged, and he was quarreling with his son-in-law. He had no male heir and the need for one was hurrying him into marriage with a young Princess. He was committed to the drama of European politics. He was free at last to follow his dream of an African empire, with the western Mediterranean a Spanish lake, and the Moslems driven back to their Eastern strongholds. He was busy with the training and the administration of the army that was to make the Spanish infantry, with their short swords, the most formidable and dreaded force in Europe. His life was reorientated and those dreams of the Great Khan's ransom had become as shadowy as many of the other dreams that he had shared with Isabella when they both were young. A new life was nourished by new ambitions.

And indeed, nothing of very immediate importance seemed to be happening across the ocean. Nicolas de Ovando, whom Isabella had sent out there before Columbus' last voyage, was proving an efficient administrator. He nourished no dreams about Cathay. He had a commission on hand, to organize a colony, and he set to work on it.

His expedition had been planned in the light of the mistakes that had been made on Columbus' second voyage. It contained less of the Hidalgo type of emigrant and a greater proportion of solid artisans and agriculturists who were anxious to develop the island and use Santo Domingo as a base for exploration. Ovando took with him vines, olives, oranges, lemons, figs and a certain amount of livestock, pigs, horses, cattle. He collected further recruits in the Canaries and took on there rice and bananas. He also exported a few Negro slaves. For many years Spain had been importing slaves in small quantities to work in the south, particularly in Andalusia. Slaves had also been imported into the Canaries, where it was forbidden to enslave the original inhabitants, though this was a technicality, since the Spaniards were allowed to enroll Indians to work on their estates. The distinction between a serf and a slave is not apparent to the toiler in the fields.

Ovando set to work briskly and effectively. On his arrival, he found three hundred quarrelsome, ill-nourished Spaniards on the brink of rebellion and despair. Within four years the population had risen to twelve thousand. Neither in the mines nor rivers was gold found in the quantities that the emigrants had hoped, but agriculture began to flourish. Ovando introduced the irrigation system that the Moors had initiated in Andalusia. The climate was unfavorable to the vine and olive tree, but oranges, figs and lemons flourished; so did rice, bananas and the sugarcane; pigs proliferated, though the culture of them had to be discouraged, because they devoured the sugar crop; on the other hand, the wild herds of cattle provided hides and tallow, which were returned very profitably to Spain.

On the surface, the colony was prospering, with the city of Santo

Domingo set out on the Spanish pattern, with a piazza, a cathedral and public buildings, but the problem of a labor force was insistent. On the death of Isabella, the system of *repartimentos* was established, by which land was made over to Spaniards, who were allowed to enroll Indians to work it on the system prevalent in the Canaries. But the Indians would not work. The Spaniards laid down a program and a time schedule. Every native of fourteen years and over was to furnish every three months a bell full of gold dust; the natives who lived in regions where no gold could be extracted from the rivers were to provide twenty-five pounds of spun cotton instead. Those who delivered their quota wore a stamped token round their necks. But the Indians refused to be coerced; they fled into the mountains, they starved themselves, they committed suicide rather than work for the Spaniards. They did not understand the religion in which the Spanish priests diligently and patiently endeavored to instruct them. Their new tormentors were not, they gradually gathered, cannibals, but that was the only difference they could detect between the Spaniards and the Caribs.

So insistent were the Spaniards in their demand for gold that one of the Cuban chiefs believed that the Europeans' god was gold, and that gold was responsible for their sins. This belief led him to the conviction that there would be no peace while the Spanish god existed. He told his followers to throw the gold into the sea. The Spaniards tied him to the stake; their priests besought him to accept conversion before the faggots were lighted, so that he could go to heaven. He asked if there were any Spaniards in heaven. Yes, he was told; there were a great many. "In that case," he said, "I would prefer not to go there."

The Spaniards were exasperated beyond the limits of control. They had crossed the Atlantic in danger and great discomfort, in the hope of making a speedy fortune. That fortune, they were convinced, was within their grasp, but they were prevented from reaching it by the apathy of these futile heathen. They were driven to desperate measures. To inspire industry in the survivors they would roast a few dozen over a slow fire, having gagged them first so that their screams should not disturb their master's siesta. The Indians, in retaliation, whenever they encountered a solitary Spaniard, slew him. The Spaniards retorted by burning and disemboweling a hundred Indians for every Spaniard killed. But still the Indians would not work.

Ovando tried to recruit labor in other islands, but the Indians from the Bahamas were no more tractable than his own. It is impossible to tell how many Indians there were in Hispaniola when Columbus landed. Las Casas' estimate is two million. This is almost certainly an exaggeration, but there were undoubtedly very many. Within twenty years hardly one remained. There was, in fact, no alternative to the importation of slaves from Africa. Many of them died on the journey over, but those who survived had strong constitutions that could resist the climate, and they were used to work. But they were no more patient of subjection than the Indians. There was always the danger of rebellion, and quite a number fled into the hills to join with the Indians and become known as "Maroons." In the meantime, the number of common-law marriages contracted between Spaniards and Indian women was rapidly creating what came to be known as the "Creole class"—Creole in its original use meaning "native, or indigenous to the soil." The stage was being set, indeed, for that long conflict between black and white, between brown and black that harries Caribbean civilization to this day.

Yet under Ovando progress was being made. Pearls were being shipped from the Gulf of Paria, a certain amount of gold was being found in Cuba, the supply of hides and tallow was proceeding calmly. The first European colony was putting down solid roots and would have come to fill a modest but useful place in the pattern of Spanish political economy had not the discoveries of Balboa, Cortés and Pizarro poured into the treasuries of Seville the wealth of Peru and Mexico during the first years of Ferdinand's successor's reign.

It has been said that the greatest misfortune that befell Spain was the death of Ferdinand and Isabella's son. Had Don Juan and his line survived, the destiny of Spain would have been Spanish, its ambitions directed toward the Mediterranean, toward Africa and Italy. But the son of Ferdinand and Isabella's demented daughter was not only their grandson but also that of the Emperor Maximilian. Charles V's grandeur as a monarch is to be matched only by that of Louis XIV. No European king has owned so much territory in his own right as opposed to possession by conquest. In addition to Spain itself, he had inherited Naples from Ferdinand, and Burgundy and the Netherlands from his father; when he secured the election as Holy Roman Emperor, the center of Europe and the Germanic principalities passed under his control. He is spoken of as Spain's greatest king, but he was scarcely a Spaniard at all. He was not, indeed, until the very end of his reign, King of Castile and Leon, but regent for his demented mother, in whose name he signed every proclamation. He spent only a quarter of his life in Spain. On his accession he spoke little Spanish. He was an Austrian, a Habsburg, and his thoughts and ambitions were focused north of the Pyrenees. He set less store by his Spanish than by his Austrian possessions. The Netherlands lay nearest to his heart. To consolidate his empire, he gave his eastern approaches in Hungary and Bohemia to his brother Ferdinand, and concentrated upon his rivalry with France.

Charles as a personality lacks the somber majesty of gloom that envelops his son Philip. He had little personal charm, but he had great qualities as a ruler; he was patient; in victory his demands were moderate; he took a long time to make up his mind, but when he came to a decision he carried out his purposes with pertinacity; his greatest strength lay in his capacity to assess the capabilities of his generals and ministers. His appointments were invariably wise. As an administrator he knew how to take a short view; he could recognize what was of immediate importance, and make the most effective moves to implement his decisions. He found it easier to take a short view because, as a Catholic, he intuitively took a long one. He was not as belligerently devout as his grandparents had been and his son was to become. His ultimate purpose was to strengthen the authority of the Church and to spread its teaching. But he had not, to the extent that his grandparents had had and his son was to have, the threat of heresy within his kingdom. Martin Luther was to start his campaign in the early years of his reign, but Charles did not hasten into action. He was prepared to temporize with the Reformation in its early years. If he had realized into how serious a danger it was to grow, he might not have bequeathed the Netherlands to Philip, thereby launching Spain upon a disastrous alien war, but it might well have been that he would have put the interests of his beloved Netherlands before those of Spain. He was always an Austrian at heart. And it was as an Austrian that he welcomed the doubloons that poured from the silver mines of Pitossi, as an aid to the fulfillment of his dynastic interests; he did not, as Isabella would have done, wonder what benefits through this sudden accretion of wealth would accrue to the Spanish people.

Charles accepted these successive miracles as acts of God, and in his methodical, painstaking way set about their administration. These new dominions were not colonies but parts of Spain. In Santiago, Cartagena, Lima, he built cities on the Spanish pattern, with a cathedral, a piazza and the appropriate public buildings. Their governors were directly responsible to the King. They were as powerful in their own setting as the King in his, except that complaints of bad management might lead to the sending out of a royal commission. Justice was administered through *audiencias*, by judges sent out from Spain. There was no popular control of the central government, but the municipalities had rights even as they had in Spain, and they could petition the crown. Charles drew up instructions on how trade was to be conducted and to what extent the resulting revenues were to be allotted to the crown. It was strictly ordained that no ships other than Spanish were to deal with the dependencies, that all goods were to be brought home to Seville, and that no Spaniard could trade without a license. The Pope had decreed that all lands lying west of a certain line belonged to Spain. The Papal Bull was not subject to alteration. It was a law transcending all other laws. Charles could not imagine that any Christian would question its validity. He did not foresee a time when the Papal authority would be flouted, not merely by pirates but by monarchs professing Christianity. He did not foresee that for nearly two hundred years the West Indies would become the focus of European politics and the cockpit of Europe's navies. European history during the seventeenth and eighteenth centuries has to be studied in relation to the West Indies. The fortunes of the islands were dependent on what was happening in the courts and on the battlefields of Europe, but at the same time Europe's destinies were shaped by the importance of the Sugar Islands.

CHAPTER II

The Spanish Main

When Charles V abdicated his throne, he gave to his son, Philip, two main instructions—to oppose heresy and keep peace with England. That was in 1556, when the man who was most responsible for making impossible the fulfillment of those instructions was a twenty-four-year-old seaman, busily and blithely plying his trade at Plymouth Hoe.

John Hawkins would have been astonished had he been told that such a fate awaited him. He had nothing but the friendliest feelings for Spain and for its monarch. Throughout his lifetime and for several years before, Spain had been his country's ally. There was no heritage of rancor. France was the traditional enemy of England; France with her twelve million inhabitants against England's four; France who could invariably rely on Scotland's support from across the border. When Philip married Mary Tudor, Hawkins was happy enough to think of him as his Royal Master; there are indeed reasons for believing that when Philip came to Southampton in 1553 for his marriage, Hawkins was able to render him certain services after a rough crossing.

Hawkins was a man of charm, with an easygoing nature, except when the discipline of the sea demanded ruthlessness. He was of medium height, erect and handsome; he was elegant in dress; he impressed strangers; he was persuasive in debate; but beneath his charm there was a hard rock of loyalty. He was his sovereign's servant. His own interests were subservient to that service. At sea he ordered the daily observances of the Church, but there is no reason to believe that he was exceptionally devout; he was certainly not a partisan Protestant as Drake was. He was presumably glad enough to see the authority of the Pope curtailed and church property dispersed, but he did not want any change of ritual. He was a professional seaman and his own life was not affected below the surface by the Reformation and the Counter-Reformation. He accepted with equanimity the dissolution of the monasteries, the reforms of Edward VI, the restoration of Mary Tudor and the established order of Elizabeth. That was other people's concern, not his. His business was the sea, and the trade of the sea, as it had been his father's. He was a Plymouth man, and the prosperity of Plymouth depended on the ships that anchored beyond the sound, in Sutton Pool.

His father, William Hawkins, was one of the most important city merchants, both a mayor of the city and a member of Parliament. He was also a fine navigator, who crossed the Atlantic more than once, and was one of the first to organize the triangle of trade—a home port, the Guinea coast, America—that was to form a pattern of commerce for two and a half centuries.

At first, he exported cloth and tin to western Europe, bringing back salt from La Rochelle, wines from Bordeaux, and, from Spain and Portugal, wine, sugar, olive oil and pepper. He traded with the Canaries, which, though Spanish possessions, were open to foreign traders; he also collected pepper from the Guinea coast. Later he decided to cross the Atlantic and bring back wood from Brazil, and the dyes that were so valuable in the cloth trade. Brazil belonged, as did the Guinea coast, to Portugal, but Portugal was unable to police two such long coastlines. Both coasts were, in fact, divided into two; Guinea by Cape Palmas, Brazil by Cape San Roque.

As early as 1530, two years before the birth of John, William Hawkins had equipped an expedition to sail from Plymouth to the Guinea coast, thence to Brazil. John Hawkins grew up in terms of the triangle of trade, a point to be remembered when one considers the conflicts in which he was to become involved in the Caribbean.

By the time that John Hawkins was ready to go to sea, the Caribbean situation had assumed a pattern. The Spaniards had been disappointed in hopes of bullion in Cuba and Hispaniola, and they had no labor with which to exploit the agricultural possibilities of the islands. Even when there had been Indians available to work the mines, the supply of gold had been minute. Their experiences in the Lesser Antilles had been so unfortunate that they had decided to leave them to the fierce and hostile Caribs. Most of the original settlers on Hispaniola had moved to the Pacific coast, and the few remaining Spanish settlements were at the mercy of French privateers. But though the islands were valueless in themselves, they were of great importance as bastions protecting the gold and silver caravans from South America. In 1524, a French corsair captured a Spanish galleon and was astounded by the richness of its cargo; for the greater part of this period France and Spain were at war, and the harrying of Spanish galleons became one of the chief activities of the French navy. English historians, when recounting the deeds of Hawkins and Drake, forget to remind their readers that France had several years' start in the arena. To combat the French corsairs, Charles V started and Philip II regularized a system of convoys that for over a century safeguarded the transportation of silver from the New World to Seville.

The current of the trade winds was the determining factor in West Indian history, until steam supplanted sail in the middle of the nineteenth century. Barbados, for example, never flew a French flag, because the French in Martinique and Guadeloupe could not attack against the northeast trades. For a westbound European ship the first natural port of call was Dominica, and the Gulf Stream would carry it back to Europe either by the Florida Channel, north of Cuba, or by the Windward Passage, past Jamaica, north of Hispaniola. A ship bound for Brazil could only return by coasting the Spanish Main.

The Spanish system was concentrated on two annual fleets, the *flota* and the *galleones*. The *flota*, the smaller fleet, took a northern route to Santo Domingo, Cuba, and New Mexico. The *galleones* served the Spanish Main, calling at Margarita to take on pearls. Both fleets assembled in Nombre de Dios Bay to collect the treasure that had been brought up the Pacific coast and carried by mules across the isthmus. Both fleets returned to Europe via Havana. Under this system Santo Domingo was valuable as an administrative center; Havana was important as a fort; while on the Spanish Main Margarita was important as a base for the pearl trade, and Cartagena as a port.

The convoy system was effective, but expensive. The costs of the convoy and the protection involved had to be borne by the local merchant, most of whose rewards were absorbed by the bureaucratic overheads of Seville; there was consequently an infinite scope for bribe and graft. Free trade would have been highly advantageous to the colonists. It was not surprising that the privateer was welcomed. Such was the situation when John Hawkins, in the early years of Elizabeth's reign, began to interest himself in the Caribbean.

His interest was practical and commercial. For a number of years he had been trading with the Canaries and the Guinea coast. His relations with the Spaniards were cordial, as were those of a great many Englishmen who had close links with Andalusia and had factories in Seville. English ships had helped the Spaniards in some of their expeditions, and Englishmen had been given grants of land as Spanish subjects. From his contacts with the Spaniards of the Canaries, Hawkins had come to appreciate the problems of the colonists on the Spanish Main and in the Antilles. There was a great shortage of manufactured goods and of labor. A few slaves had been imported, but the trade was so set about by restrictions, so many middlemen had to have their cut, that the cost to the colonists was excessive. Hawkins was convinced that he could supply slaves and goods at half the price. He was assured by his friends in the Canaries that he would be warmly welcomed.

Hawkins, like his father, was most anxious to ensure the legality of any expedition that he undertook. He was resolved not to be classed as a privateer. He recognized that the lands "beyond the lines" were Spanish possessions; and he knew that the Spanish monarchy considered itself to hold, under the Pope's approval, a monopoly of trade with them. But the Spaniards had always allowed foreign trade with the Canaries, and the man on the spot could usually be trusted to interpret liberally instructions that had been issued by a bureaucrat three thousand miles away. Moreover, the relations between England and Spain were cordial. Though Elizabeth had broken with the Pope, the bonds of self-interest remained. France was as great a menace to England as she was to Spain. Mary, Queen of Scots, had as strong a claim to the English throne as Elizabeth herself. Mary could rely on France to defend that claim. Spain was at war in the Netherlands; her troops had to be transported thither by sea. They were liable to be harried by the French; if England was to join with France, their transport would be grievously imperiled. The spectacle of a heretic England might be distressing to Philip II, and a time might come when England's apostasy might make a claim upon his crusading instinct, but first things first. The Netherlands stood at the head of the list.

Since the disasters of Hawkins' third voyage, "his troublesome voyage," as contemporary historians were to christen it, were to break this cordial atmosphere and to label Spain as the first enemy, it is pertinent to note the extreme caution that Hawkins displayed before making his first trip to the Antilles. For he suspected that his voyage would occasion complaints from several quarters, both Portuguese and Spanish.

He set out from Plymouth in October 1562, with three ships—260 tons—and a hundred men. The syndicate that backed this venture was based in London. He did not sail under the Queen's commission, but he had the backing of solid city magnates.

He paused at Teneriffe; a Spanish friend had sent news of his voyage to Hispaniola, and Hawkins was able to sail for Africa, fortified in the knowledge that he would be expected in Santo Domingo. He was to state in his subsequent report that he acquired three hundred slaves on the Guinea coast; the Portuguese claimed that he took on nine hundred; the Spanish estimate was four hundred. It was in no one's interest to be precise. He probably took on around five hundred.

From the Guinea coast, he picked up the northeast trades. He proposed to conduct his business in Hispaniola. Santo Domingo was the seat of government, and the officials and merchantmen of the city were awaiting him. But he knew that he would be likelier to sell his cargo away from the scrutiny of officialdom. He also knew that the planters on the north side of the island were in more urgent need of slaves. He sailed therefore for the minor seaports, Isabela, Puerto de Plata and Monte Cristi.

He encountered there the chicanery and double-dealing that is usually attendant on a dubious enterprise. He had to have the coverage of a license to trade. The colonists wanted his wares, but everyone insisted on his cut and a veneer of respectability had to provide an alibi for the bureaucrats of Seville, who would need to be persuaded that Hawkins' concessions had only been granted at the pistol's point. As a result of these negotiations, Hawkins agreed to send one of his caravels back to Lisbon, another to Seville.

This curious conduct exemplifies his desperate anxiety to appear as an honest trader. He may have conducted business with a finger on the trigger, but he could produce bills of lading, and Negroes left in bond stood to his credit as a proof that he had paid customs dues. Moreover, he had had the good sense to store the most valuable part of his cargo in the ship in which he sailed back to England, so that even if the ships that he sent to Lisbon and Seville were confiscated by the Portuguese and Spaniards—as they were—the expedition would show a substantial profit. Hawkins was running a justifiable risk. Philip's policy was not yet certain. And not only Hawkins, but the Queen was hoping to get his trade recognized as legitimate. If the cargo sent back to Seville had not been confiscated, a precedent would have been established. And indeed, seventy odd years earlier, Henry VII and Ferdinand and Isabella had agreed that there should be free trade between their subjects and each other's dominions. But that was three years before Columbus discovered the New World, and before England had renounced the authority of Rome. It was, in legal terminology, "a pretty point."

Hawkins returned to England in August 1563. In the following summer he began to fit out a second voyage. The success of his first voyage had increased his reputation. His first voyage had been sponsored by city magnates, but the court and "the establishment" were concerned with his second. Leicester, Pembroke, and Clinton, the Lord Admiral, had shares in it. Sir William Cecil denied to the Spanish that he was an investor, but he was behind the scenes. Moreover the Queen herself was a participator, and allowed Hawkins the right by charter of one of her own large ships.

Hawkins' second voyage was of crucial importance in the relations between Spain and England, and it is reasonable to assume that, although it was a joint stock company venture which was expected to make a profit for its shareholders, it was also a *ballon d'essai*. Spain was having great difficulty with the French privateers in the Caribbean. She had more upon her hands than she could cope with. English seamen, if allowed to trade freely with the Spanish colonists, might solve many of her colonial problems. Hawkins' voyage was, in part, an experiment to find out whether it was possible for England, which was Protestant, to do business with Catholic Spain on terms of mutual self-interest. Religion was the testing point. Philip had been instructed by his father to oppose heresy and to remain friends with England. Were these instructions contradictory? Hawkins' second and third voyages resolved these questions.

Hawkins started out with three Plymouth ships and the *Jesus of Lubeck,* seven hundred tons, one of the largest ships in the Royal Navy. She had been purchased by Henry VIII nearly twenty years earlier, but now, owing to neglect at the hands of Edward VI and Mary Tudor, she was barely seaworthy. The other three ships were of 130, fifty and thirty tons respectively. Of the 150 seamen who manned the expedition, eighty were in the *Jesus*. There were also some gentlemen adventurers and their servants, twenty or so in all. They set sail under Hawkins' habitual instructions, "Serve God daily, love one another, preserve your victuals, beware of fire and keep good company." By "keep good company" he meant "Don't lose touch with your fellow vessels."

The journey was attended by the minimum of secrecy. He called at Teneriffe, to interview the friend there who would advise him as to his procedure and alert his friends in Hispaniola. He then moved down the Guinea coast, collecting slaves. To the Portuguese this was officially an act of piracy. The English excuse was the casual policing of the African coast and the readiness of the Africans to trade. We can assume that the Portuguese too welcomed the opportunity of profitable if surreptitious business, although they sent to Lisbon self-pitying dispatches explaining how the slaves had been taken from them at the pistol's point.

As always, Hawkins was careful at every stage to maintain the legality of his transactions, and formal bills of lading were exchanged. With a cargo of six hundred slaves, he sailed to Dominica, watered there and, crossing to Margarita, presented his compliments to the governor. The governor, who did not receive him, warned Hispaniola that Hawkins was on his way.

The situations that proceeded to develop are complicated, and do not need to be recorded here in detail. Hawkins presented himself everywhere as a legal trader. He informed the Spanish authorities that his fleet belonged to the Queen, and that he was sailing under her orders. He further added that he was "a great servitor of the majesty of King Philip, whom I served when he was King of England." He asked for a license to trade, adding that if he did not receive the license he would do as well as he could without it. He knew that the Spaniards were as anxious to trade with him as he was to trade with them.

Luck was with him. Sailing along the Spanish Main, he traded as he went, selling Negroes, linen, wines and food, taking on gold, silver and various precious metals, and booking orders for a return visit; from the treasurer of one of the colonies he obtained a testimony to his good behavior. He sailed northward on the best terms with the authorities, who proceeded in self-defense to draw up reports that they had been forced into this trade against their will.

He had hoped to call in at Hispaniola and take on hides. But he was unlucky with his pilot. The weather was bad. He failed to find a satisfactory port in the Greater Antilles, and eventually landed in Florida, where the French had established a colony whose existence was causing the Spanish considerable concern, since it commanded the return route of the convoys. The colony was in a desperate condition and Hawkins hoped by persuading the Frenchmen to return with him that he would ingratiate himself with the Spaniards and encourage them to take a tolerant view of his activities, as indeed they might have done had he been successful.

The presence of a French settlement on the east coast of Florida was a typical corollary to the Spanish system of colonialization, which needs to be included here, even if in a parenthesis. As it has been already pointed out, the Spanish noblemen and gentry, who found themselves at a loose end when the Moorish War was ended, were swordsmen and crusaders who despised trade and labor. They crossed the Atlantic in search of gold that was to be won in battle. Let them conquer the chiefs and let the slaves work in the mines. In the early years of the immigration Florida had appeared to offer a tempting spoil. Rumors of the fountain of Bimini, whose waters restored youth to the aged bather, were in circulation among the Indians of Hispaniola and Cuba; and it was the legend of this fountain, as much as the lure of gold, that enticed Ponce de Leon thither. He launched two expeditions; from the first he returned looking much older than he had when he set out; from the second he returned wounded by the fierce Seminole Indians and on the verge of death. He did not find gold and he did not find the waters of Bimini, but he did discover the Bahama Channel which was later to provide the homeward route for the silver fleet. When he made his first expedition he believed that Florida was an island. He landed there in early April, 1513; took formal possession and christened it Florida, some say because it was covered with spring flowers, others because he landed on Resurrection Day, the *Pascua Florida* of the Spanish Catholics.

Ponce de Leon's expeditions failed, but the legend of Bimini and its surrounding gold mines lingered. Just as Pizarro and Raleigh were later to believe in an El Dorado and a golden lake, so did the early followers of Columbus believe that there existed somewhere beneath the sun a fountain of eternal youth. Where was it likelier to exist than in this magical universe they had discovered? Eighteen years later another expedition sailed, this time under Hernando de Soto. The news of the expedition fired the imagination of the Spaniards. Noblemen sold their estates and jewelry so that they could enroll, and there assembled in Seville many more volunteers than de Soto's fleet of nine small vessels could accommodate. Eventually he set sail with six hundred handpicked warriors.

The campaign lasted for three and a half years; of the six hundred swordsmen who set out, barely three hundred returned; they bore neither gold nor jewels, they were blackened by the sun, they carried their packs, they were clothed in deerskins. De Soto was not one of the survivors. The story of their disastrous and courageous treks, "high failure towering o'er low success," has been recorded by a contemporary historian, the Inca Garcilaso de la Vega, and has been issued recently in an excellent translation under the auspices of the University of Texas. De Soto's failure convinced the Spaniards that there was no point in attempting any further experiments in Florida. They did not realize that the deerskins which the survivors wore on their return, and the mantle of marten and beaver skin in which de Soto's body was wrapped before being buried in the river, were evidences of a wealth no less great than that provided by the ingots of Peru. For more than two centuries, the fur traders of the Mississippi were to enrich the English and French markets.

The Spaniards were prepared to dismiss Florida from their accounts, and in September 1561, Philip II definitely decided that no further attempt would be made to found a settlement, but he had not at that point reckoned with the menace that the French and later the English privateers were to present, and he was highly disconcerted to learn that a colony of French Huguenots under Jean Ribaut had been dispatched from Dieppe to the very spot, Port Royal in South Carolina, where a Spanish attempt had failed. He was even more put out, two years later, when Admiral Coligny, a Huguenot and a foe of Spain, founded a second colony on St. Johns River at Fort Caroline, under René de Laudonnière.

Ribaut's first colony had failed, and Laudonnière's was in a far from prosperous condition. He had not picked his men wisely; they were for the most part ex-soldiers, and as such, a mixture of Huguenots and Catholics who had recently been at war with one another. He had brought out no farmers; and his artisans could not overnight convert themselves into tillers of the soil; while the soldiers found employment not only more lucrative but far more in tune with their tastes and temperament in raiding the Spanish treasure ships in the Bahama Channel.

This was the colony which Hawkins visited. It was in dire straits. Only ten days' supply of food remained when his ships appeared on the horizon. Laudonnière must have been sorely tempted by his offer, but he was uncertain whether England and France were still at peace and doubted if he could trust the engaging slave trader; moreover, siren voices were whispering in his ears. One of his scouts had actually seen and talked with men who had drunk from the fountain of youth and were congenially enjoying their third century of existence. He decided to stay on, and he must have felt reassured when Ribaut returned from France with supplies and reinforcements to

extent of three hundred men. But in addition to supplies and reinforcements, Ribaut brought disquieting news. He had been warned by
Coligny that Don Pedro Menéndez was leaving Spain for the coast of
"New France," and ordered "not to suffer him encroach upon you
any more than he would you should encroach upon him."

Menéndez's expedition was Philip's retort to the establishment
of a fort so close to Havana. His representative in Mexico had sent
a serious warning: "The sum of all that can be said in the matter is
that they put the Indies in a crucible, for we are compelled to pass
in front of their port, and with the greatest ease they can sally out
with their armadas to seek us and easily return home when it suits
them." Philip was urged to take action before the colonists reached
St. Augustine. "Seeing that they are Lutherans, it is not necessary to
leave a man alive, but to inflict an exemplary punishment, that they
may remember it forever."

Menéndez—the man whom Philip chose to expel the French and
protect the Bahama Channel—was an aristocrat from Asturias, experienced in naval warfare. Menéndez was given what has been
described as a typical conquistador's contract. Apart from a small loan
from Philip, he had to bear all the expenses of the venture. In return,
he was allowed considerable privileges and the opportunity of making
ample profits. He was given a grant of land and a couple of fisheries
—one of pearls. He could draw a salary from the customs sheds. He
could trade with the other islands. He was relieved of certain customs
duties, and for five years he was allowed to keep whatever loot he
might capture from privateers. His title of *adelantado* of Florida was
hereditary. His fleet consisted of a six-hundred-ton man-of-war, six
fifty-ton sloops and four small boats for the shallows. He took out
a hundred soldiers, a hundred sailors, and three hundred officials, artisans and farmers, of whom two hundred had to be married. Four
Jesuit priests and twelve friars were to complete the colony, along
with five hundred Negro slaves, half of whom were to be women.
He was instructed to divide the land between the settlers and to
build two towns, each protected by a fort. Each town was to start
with a population of a hundred citizens. The fact that he was able to
invest such a large sum in the gamble of this new colony is a proof
of the efficiency he had previously displayed in harrying pirates. The
final roll call of his company was 2,646, and not a Jew, heretic or
mendicant among them. He sailed from Cádiz two months after
Ribaut had left France. He anchored on August 28 in a river's mouth;

he named it in honor of the saint whose day it was—St. Augustine.
It was destined to fill an honored role in history.

After a week's pause he sailed northward in search of the French.
Our knowledge of what transpired is mainly based on Woodbery
Lowery's "researches in Spanish settlements within the present limits
of the United States 1513–1561." Menéndez found four of Ribaut's
ships by the St. Johns River; he directed his ships among them.
It is reported that the following conversation ensued. The Spaniard
addressed them with "courtly foreign grace":

"Gentlemen, whence this fleet?"

"From France."

"What are you doing here?"

"We bring artillery, infantry and supplies for a fort owned by the
King of France."

"Are you Catholics or Lutherans?"

"Lutherans, and our General is Jean Ribaut."

Similar questions were set to the Spanish flagship.

"I am the General," Menéndez answered. "My name is Pedro
Menéndez de Avilés. This is the Armada of the King of Spain. I am
instructed to burn and hang any Lutherans who may be found here.
In the morning I shall board your ships. If there are any Catholics
among you, they will be respected."

Silence fell; then the French cut their cables and sailed through
the Spanish ships. They were faster than the Spaniards.

Next morning Menéndez returned to the river's mouth. Three
French ships were anchored within the bar, and soldiers were massed
upon the bank. Menéndez decided to withdraw to St. Augustine,
where he converted a large Indian house into a fort. He now had a
base for troops and for supplies. The French watched him from a
distance and then returned to St. Johns River. At this point the two
French commanders disagreed. Ribaut was nominally in command
and he decided to launch an attack on St. Augustine with four
hundred of his troops. Laudonnière argued that of the 240 men left
behind in Fort Caroline many were sick, and that he would be helpless should Ribaut's ships be delayed at sea, thus giving the Spaniards
an opportunity to attack by land. Ribaut refused to be deterred, but
Laudonnière's qualms were justified. Ribaut was held off by violent
winds and Menéndez, guided by Indians and a French prisoner, surprised the Frenchmen at Fort Caroline in their sleep. Only twenty-
six members of the garrison, including Laudonnière, escaped into
the woods and were rescued by Ribaut's ships.

On his return to St. Augustine, Menéndez learned that 140 refugees from two French ships were in the neighborhood. Two hundred of their fellows had been drowned or killed by savages, and they themselves were helpless without supplies. They begged him to spare their lives, but he retorted that he was "waging a war of fire and blood against all who came to settle these parts and plant in them their evil Lutheran sect." That is the Spanish account of the incident.

According to one French record, Menéndez promised the castaways that if they surrendered their arms and ammunition he would spare their lives. Both accounts are agreed on what subsequently transpired. The men surrendered; the ten Catholics among them were set apart; the remainder were fed and wined, then told that because they were so numerous they must march to St. Augustine with their hands bound behind them. Menéndez gave instructions to his officers, then went ahead. A certain distance away, behind a hillock, he drew a line with his spearhead in the sand. When the procession reached the spearline, the Spaniards set upon and decapitated their prisoners. The spot is still known as *Las Matanzas* (The Massacre).

A little later, Menéndez learned that Ribaut and two hundred Frenchmen had been cut off by an inlet, as their compatriots had been, in an attempt to reach Fort Caroline by land. The Spaniard followed a similar procedure. Ribaut and his men were promised their lives if they surrendered. Their hands were bound and they were led to the spearline that was now littered with the decaying corpses of their friends. Seventeen Catholics were set aside; then the Lutherans were slaughtered. Menéndez wrote in his report:

"I put Jean Ribaut and all the rest of them to the knife, judging it to be necessary to the service of the Lord our God and of Your Majesty, and I think it a very great fortune that this man be dead . . . he could do more harm in one year than another in ten; for he was the most experienced sailor and corsair known, very skilful in the navigation of the Indies and the Florida coast."

Philip noted on the back of this dispatch:

"As to those he has killed he has done well, and as to those he has saved, they shall be sent to the galleys," and to Menéndez he wrote:

"We hold that we have been well served."

Barrientos, a contemporary historian, considered that Menéndez was merciful to his prisoners, since he was legally entitled to have them burned alive. "He killed them, I think, rather by divine inspiration."

According to French reports, a certain number of the prisoners were hanged and an inscription was set above them: "I do this not as to Frenchmen but as to Lutherans." There is no reference to this hanging in Spanish reports, but the story was believed in France, and two years later, revenge was taken by Dominique de Gourgues who, in the late summer, crossed the Atlantic with a body of 150 men. After a winter's trading, he sailed north to Florida, made friends with an Indian chief, and with Indian allies and guides effected a raid upon the encampment at San Mateo. Menéndez was away, and it is reported that the guards in the first blockhouse were contentedly picking their teeth after dinner when they were startled by Gourgues' cry: "Yonder are the thieves who have stolen this land from our King. Yonder are the murderers who have massacred our French. On! On! Let us avenge our King! Let us show that we are Frenchmen."

Most of the soldiers in the first two blockhouses were killed, but as many as possible were taken prisoner. The French then attacked the fort itself, their wrath having been increased by the discovery of French cannon in the blockhouses. The Spaniards made a sortie, but they had not seen the Indian allies who were hidden behind trees, and were caught between two fires. Again, as many of them as possible were taken alive so that they should receive the same fate as the French. Above the branches of the same trees from which his friends had swung, Gourgues inscribed on a pine tablet with a hot iron: "I do this not as to Spaniards, not as to Marranos (secret Jews), but as to traitors, robbers and murderers."

On his way back he captured three Spanish treasure ships and tossed their crews overboard. He was welcomed home as a hero.

Menéndez is chiefly remembered by American, French and English historians as the butcher of *Las Matanzas*, but in Spanish history he is honored as one of her greatest colonial administrators. Much of his work survived for many years, and that part of it that survived is significant in the story of the West Indian Islands. He was a man of vision. His fortification of the Peninsular was intended to protect the Bahama Channel. He would then drive the French out of Santa Elena and out of the Bay of Santa Maria (Chesapeake Bay), which might contain, who knew, the Northwest Passage in which all believed. Florida might be the gateway to Cathay. Spain would, through Florida, have a direct link with the Philippines. He had dreams of a Florida rich in silk and pearls, in sugar, in wheat, in rice, in timber. He saw the New World as a whole. He said, with what Herbert E. Bolton has called "a twentieth-century contempt for distance and a Spanish disregard of time":

"Florida is but a suburb of Spain, for it does not take more than forty days' sailing to come here, and usually as many more to return."

During the nine years he spent there, he established a line of posts between Tampa and Santa Elena, established three permanent settlements at St. Augustine, San Mateo and Santa Elena, and garrison posts in northern Georgia, at Tampa and Charlotte Bays on the west coast, at Biscayne Bay and the St. Lucie River on the east. For two and a half centuries these posts were to play an important role in Caribbean strategy.

Eventually Menéndez was recalled to Spain to assist in the preparation of Philip's great Armada. He did not live, however, to see it sail. He was a great seaman. Had he lived longer its fate might have been different. It is also possible that if he had never had to cross the Atlantic, if Hawkins had been able to persuade Laudonnière to abandon his French settlement, English and Spanish relations would not have been forced to deteriorate and Philip might have been able to follow for a little longer his father's instructions to stay friends with England.

Hawkins' second voyage had not realized all his hopes for it. He had failed to collect hides from Hispaniola, and he had not evacuated the French colony, but he brought his ships home safe, and the syndicate received a sixty percent dividend on its investment. He had again proved that triangular trade with the Guinea coast was a profitable enterprise.

Back in England, he informed the Queen that he had always been a help to all Spaniards and Portuguese that had come his way, "without any harm or prejudice by me offered to any of them, although many times in this tract they have been under my power." In honor of his achievement Elizabeth granted him a coat of arms. But in Madrid the news of his return was received with anything but satisfaction. Philip took a long time to make up his mind, but once he had done so he was inflexible, and he had now decided that the monopoly of the Caribbean had to be preserved. Of the two Spanish governors who had had dealings with Hawkins, one was brought back to Spain as a prisoner, and the treasurer of another colony was subjected to a cross-examination that left him in no doubt that on a future occasion he would have to show greater resolution.

On an official level, the traditional cordiality between the two countries was maintained, and it was on courtly terms that the Spanish ambassador, da Silva, presented to Elizabeth his interest in Hawkins. Da Silva was, indeed, sufficiently accommodating to invite Hawkins to dinner, an occasion which proved that Hawkins was regarded as an honest man. Hawkins was careful to impress on the Spaniard the legality of the transactions and, producing his licenses, spoke of the cargo of hides that had been confiscated after his first voyage. Hawkins was still unable to believe that Spain would continue to oppose a trade that was so obviously in her interest. He imagined that these inquiries had been instigated merely "for the form," and he gave da Silva his assurance that he would never again visit the King's West Indian possessions without the King's permission.

He had no intention of keeping this promise, and da Silva was aware of this. What could be expected of a Plymouth seaman when the Queen of England was equally ready to prevaricate?

Within a few weeks of Hawkins' return, preparations were under way for a third voyage; Elizabeth knew that its main object was trade between Africa and the Caribbean; indeed, through her contribution of two ships of the navy, she became a shareholder in the expedition. Yet she and Cecil gave da Silva their assurance that the fleet was bound for the Guinea coast, to exact reparation for a ship sunk in the previous year. To complete the "make-believe," she made the other members of the syndicate swear that Hawkins was not bound for the Spanish west. She too could not believe that Philip would remain insensible to the dictates of common sense. His colonists were short of labor and supplies, his convoys were harassed by French and Turkish privateers. Surely he could not be blind to the advantages of Anglo-Spanish amity. Indeed, Hawkins went so far as to offer da Silva his own assistance in clearing the Mediterranean of Turkish pirates. But the English reckoned without Philip's obstinacy and sense of mission as a Christian prince. In Philip's eyes, the old pattern of European diplomacy had changed; the main issue was ceasing to be the rivalry between Spain and France, between the Habsburgs and the Valois, but the conflict between the true faith and heresy. And England had now become a country of heretics.

Hawkins had not realized this when he set out on his third voyage in October 1567, the voyage that was to be labeled "troublesome" and was to determine the course of West Indian history for half a century.

This third fleet was considerably his largest; six ships with a tonnage of 1,333, manned by four hundred seamen, including the *Jesus*, now far from seaworthy, and whose leaking seams were to be responsible for the final calamity of the voyage. In this expedition was sailing Hawkins' cousin, Francis Drake.

From the start, difficulties were encountered. Four days out of Plymouth, they were attacked by so fierce a gale that Hawkins expected the *Jesus* to sink. The Portuguese on the Guinea coast were resolved to protect their trading rights. The Africans resisted their invaders with poisoned arrows, which resulted in several deaths. At one point so few slaves had been acquired that Hawkins wondered whether it was worthwhile crossing the Atlantic with so negligible a cargo; and he had finally, in Sierra Leone, to fight a pitched battle and sack a town before he had his holds well stocked.

This action set a pattern for one of the most deplorable aspects of the future slave trade, the encouragement and instigation of tribal wars that would produce prisoners. On his arrival at the Gold Coast, Hawkins found that the King of Sierra Leone and one of the chiefs were besieging a town of eight thousand inhabitants. The King and chief promised Hawkins prisoners in return for his assistance; Hawkins accepted the proposition, and after two days' hard fighting, captured and destroyed the town. The victors organized a cannibal banquet in the ruins, and there were very few survivors except for the prisoners that Hawkins took on board.

On this third voyage, Hawkins was in the position of a first-class golfer playing a round when the putts "won't drop." On his second voyage he had crossed the Atlantic in five and a half weeks; the "troublesome voyage" took seven weeks. When he arrived at Borburata, the governor was up-country. The letter which he sent to the governor is indicative of Hawkins' attitude. "I know," he wrote, "that the King of Spain, your master, unto whom also I have been a servant and am commanded by the Queen, my mistress, to serve with my navy as need requireth, hath forbidden that you should give license for any stranger to traffic. I will not therefore request any such thing at your hand, but that you will license me to sell sixty Negroes only and a parcel of my wares, which in all is but little, for the payment of the soldiers I have in my ships. In this you shall not break the com-

mandment of your Prince, but do him good service and avoid divers
inconveniences which happen oftentimes through being too precise in
observing precepts without consideration."

No letter could be more diplomatic or more definite. It is polite,
yet it is a threat. It recognizes the other man's point of view, and
offers him an alibi. Hawkins knew that the colonists wished to trade
with him, and while he awaited the governor's answer he set up
booths on shore. Trade proceeded briskly, and by the time the governor's letter of refusal arrived, the immediate needs of the colonists
had been satisfied. Hawkins proceeded confidently along the coast.

In Borburata, the civilities of evasion had been observed, but at
his next port of call, Rio de la Hacha, the opposition was definite;
there was no "sham fighting," there were actual casualties, but eventually the demands of self-interest prevailed; a fraudulent letter was
written to Madrid, and Hawkins, with his store of Negroes lessened
and his supply of bullion increased, proceeded to Santa Marta, where
the governor asked him to go through the drill of capturing the town
by force, so that he could explain to his sovereign that against his
will he had been forced to do business with the heretic. Cartagena,
however, was so strongly fortified that subterfuge was impossible. The
strength of the city prevented its governor from pleading *force ma-
jeure*, so Hawkins turned the corner and made for the Gulf Stream.

Up to this point, the trip, though hazardous, though it had involved more casualties than had been expected, had not been unsuccessful. Hawkins had sold much of his merchandise and he had
taken on a satisfactory cargo of pearls and gold. Had he now encountered favorable winds, and made his journey straight home to
England, the syndicate would have declared a handsome dividend;
but from this point luck turned against him. In terms of weather,
August and September are the worst months in the Caribbean. Hawkins did not strike a hurricane, but he met seas stronger than the
Jesus of Lubeck could surmount. She was forced to turn her back
upon the wind, and by the time the winds had dropped she was no
longer fit to cross the Atlantic until she had been repaired. Hawkins
would have been wise to accept her as a liability. As far as his voyage
was concerned, she had served her purpose. She had, with her height
and weight, impressed and intimidated his adversaries, and she had
been invaluable for the transportation of his merchandise, but most
of the slaves were sold, and the cargo with which he was returning was
of small bulk. He did not expect to go into action again. It was
unlikely, even if he got her back to England, that the *Jesus* could

be refitted for a major voyage; but she was the Queen's ship, and he was resolved that "she should not perish under his hand." He decided to take her into port.

The nearest harbor was San Juan de Ulúa, the port for Mexico City. The captain of a Spanish ship, who was carrying cargo thither from Santo Domingo, offered to guide him there, at the same time warning him that the Spanish convoy was due at the end of September to collect the annual store of treasure. There was nothing that Hawkins was less anxious to encounter, but he believed he could repair the *Jesus* in twelve days, so with the royal standard on the topmast of the *Jesus* he sailed into San Juan.

For the moment the Englishman's luck held good. The colors of the Queen's arms had been so dimmed by bad weather that the Spaniards who were expecting the arrival of the convoy did not recognize the lions and fleur-de-lis and sailed out to welcome Hawkins in the belief that he was the convoy. San Juan de Ulúa was a ramshackle port, practically uninhabited except during the weeks when the silver fleet was stationed there, the residents of the area living for the greater part fifteen miles up the coast at Vera Cruz, which had no harbor, but from which a road ran inland direct to Mexico City. The shipping of San Juan was protected by the shore guns of a small island. When the residents of the port realized their mistake, the panic was so uncontrolled that Hawkins was able to capture this island without firing a shot. He was thus able to dictate terms. He must, he insisted, have opportunities for repair, and he must replenish his larder, for which he would pay the appropriate price. He prepared with the officials a report to the authorities in Mexico, explaining that his capture of the island was not an act of war. A number of Spanish merchantmen which he presumed to be laden with treasure were in port, but he respected their neutrality. As at all other points, he scrupulously obeyed his Queen's commands. If only he could get her ship repaired before the arrival of the convoy, all might still be well. But the gales that had hampered his own journey eastward had favored the convoy on its westward passage; the Spanish fleet arrived on the following day. Eleven large merchantmen were accompanied by two men-of-war, and on board was the Viceroy of New Spain, Don Martin Enriquez, son of the Marquis of Alcanizes.

Hawkins was now in a most difficult position. As an honorable and peaceful trader, he could scarcely deny a Spanish port to a Spanish fleet, yet if he allowed the fleet to enter, he would be at its mercy. He opened negotiations. Don Martin was furious and indignant. He, a grandee of Spain, to discuss terms with a Plymouth sailor! At first he vowed that he would force an entry, but his military and naval advisers assured him that this was impossible. He decided therefore to come to terms, with the mental reservation that he would break those terms as soon as might prove convenient.

Don Martin's subsequent behavior was to blacken his country's reputation in the eyes of Englishmen for many years, and was to convince Englishmen that they could do no business with the Spaniards, yet Don Martin did not regard himself as having behaved dishonorably. As long as he was serving his God and his King, he was convinced of his own virtue; any act was justified that advanced the glory of his King and the interests of the faith. Don Martin regarded Hawkins' insistence on the legality of his transactions as contemptible hypocrisy, an attempt to find a different name for piracy.

The terms suggested by Hawkins were reasonable. The English were to complete their work upon their ships and were to occupy the island until their departure. No armed Spaniard was to land upon the island. Each side was to hand over ten gentlemen as hostages. Don Martin accepted the proposal, assuming that as long as his men went onto the island without arms they would be allowed free passage. "And I am very confident," he concluded, "that when we meet, friendship will increase between these fleets, since both are so well disciplined."

Although he was already preparing his attack upon the English, he signed this letter as a viceroy. "When," Hawkins was later to report, "I questioned certain movements of his men, he replied that he, in the faith of a viceroy, would be our defense from all villainies."

The Spanish surprise attack was carefully worked out. Troops were to be embarked onto a merchantman; the fraternizing Spanish troops upon the island were to attack the Englishmen with hidden weapons. The English ships were to be captured and boarded; one of the hostages was to murder Hawkins.

The English were taken unawares. They were outnumbered and outgunned. On shore they collapsed quickly, and the island and its guns were soon in Spanish hands, but on board they fought with skill and valor. Indeed, the Spanish second-in-command stated that had the English fought as well on land as they did at sea, the result might have been different. Hawkins encouraged his gunners with his customary gusto. He had his page bring him a measure of beer in a silver mug and drank their healths in it. As he set the mug down, a shot shattered it. "Fear nothing," he cried, "for God, who hath preserved me from this shot, will also deliver us from these traitors and villains." By now the *Jesus* was immobile, but Hawkins could not leave her until he had transferred to another and stouter ship, the *Minion,* the gold and pearls that were the profit of his trading. Only one other ship was fit to sail, the *Judith,* a fifty-ton ship under the command of Francis Drake. Hawkins fought till none of his Spanish adversaries was fit to follow him. At dusk he sailed out of range. In the morning he found that the *Judith* had "forsook him in his great misery."

When the Spaniards took over the *Jesus,* they found in its holds, in addition to fifty Negro slaves and a certain amount of merchandise, the ten hostages sent to Hawkins by the viceroy. Hawkins had left them there, in the hope that the viceroy would show a similar clemency to the English hostages. His hopes were ill-founded. In addition to the hostages, Don Martin held Robert Barrett, whom Hawkins had sent under a flag of truce with a message to the Spaniards, before the outbreak of hostilities. Barrett and the hostages were subjected to the same treatment that was accorded to the prisoners taken in the action. Most of them were examined by the Inquisition; Barrett was burned at the stake in Seville, some were so ill-used in prison that they died of hunger; others ended their lives as galley slaves. Only one of the hostages returned safe to England, in 1590.

Hawkins continued eastward in the *Minion* with some two hundred men aboard. In the heat of the action he had had no time to transfer provisions from the *Jesus;* he had thought of his booty first. There was not nearly enough food aboard to feed the crew. They lived on stewed hides, on rats, cats and parrots. Some of the men asked to be set ashore, to try their fortune with the Indians and the Spaniards. Over a hundred were, some of them to be killed by the Indians, others to fall into the hands of the Spaniards and be subjected to the exactions of the Inquisition. The records of their interrogations remain, including that of the various punishments to which they were condemned at a Mexican *auto-da-fé.* A certain leniency was shown to those who had come to manhood after Elizabeth's accession and had therefore not had the opportunity of instruction in the true faith during the reign of Mary Tudor, and it is known that Hawkins' nephew Paul, who was captured at San Juan, was allowed to settle in New Spain and marry there. For the most part, the rest is silence.

Hawkins' bad luck continued. Winds were contrary. His men died of ill nutrition, and the survivors had scarcely enough strength to work the ship. Eventually, on the last day of December, he arrived at Vigo. It was risky for him to land, but unless he had supplies he would be unable to reach England; and he had the money with which to make his purchases. Relying on the good sense and good will of the average man, he decided to "put on an act." Half dead of hunger though he was, he dressed himself in his finest clothes, breeches of crimson velvet, a jacket of scarlet leather trimmed with silver braid, a silken cloak and a gold chain. The Spaniards, with their love of pomp, of color and of breeding, could not resist a handsome man endowed with the grand manner. To the fury of King Philip, his demands were granted.

To his crew the sudden plenty was to prove disastrous, as in 1946, Europeans crossing to America after years of semistarvation found that their withered stomachs could not contain an unrestricted diet. In addition to the men that had died on the voyage, over forty more died in Vigo Bay. Hawkins found a few recruits for his ship. But the Spanish ambassador in England reported that there were not more than fifteen survivors of the hundred who had sailed from Mexico.

Life was accounted cheap in those days, and the gold and pearls that Hawkins brought back represented a profit for the syndicate that had financed the enterprise. But far more had happened on "that troublesome voyage" than the loss or profit on the sale of six hundred slaves or the death of four hundred seamen; the fate of the West Indian Islands had been cast; the possibility of an Anglo-Spanish alliance had been destroyed. From now on, it was to be war to the death "beyond the lines"; the way lay open to the buccaneers; what Spain could not hold, France and England would possess; and as the glory of Spain receded, the Caribbean was to become increasingly the arena in which the rivalry of France and England was renewed from one reign to the next.

CHAPTER III

Beyond the Lines

Hidden from the world, I rule with a little piece of paper the destinies of the hemispheres." So wrote His Most Catholic Majesty, Philip II of Spain, in the last years of his life, at the close of the sixteenth century. He wrote it at his desk in the Escurial, the fantastic edifice with which he commemorated his victory over the French at Saint-Quentin on August 10, 1537, a day sacred to Saint Lawrence.

Philip II has often been compared with Louis XIV of France, and the basic differences between them cannot be more easily appreciated than in a comparison between Versailles and the Escurial. Versailles is the playground of a pleasure-loving monarch, known as "the Sun King," who strove to dazzle the world with his achievements. The Escurial is a convent, a church, a palace and a mausoleum. It was not built, as was Versailles, in a spirit of self-glorification, but to make manifest the glory of God.

Set on the southwestern slopes of the Guadarramas so as to be visible from the greatest range of viewpoints, surrounded by rocky hills and thin, stunted vegetation, three and a half thousand feet above the sea, exposed to the cold winds of the sierras, it took twenty-one years to build. It was built in the form of the gridiron on which St. Lawrence suffered. The cloisters and its courts were its bars, the towers at the corners of the monastery were its inverted legs, and the palace which extended its length was its handle. The ground plan indicates an area of four hundred thousand square feet. It has seven towers, fifteen gateways, more than twelve thousand doors and windows. The diameter of the dome is sixty feet, its height at the center over three hundred feet. The style is Doric, bold and simple, which provides a dramatic contrast with the bronze, marble and pictures of the High Altar, and with the Royal Mausoleum, a sumptuous octagonal chamber with twenty niches, filled with black marble urns for the ashes of kings and of their mothers. Here were to lie his own ashes beside his father's, and those of all the successors to the throne for two hundred years, except Philip V and Ferdinand VI. It was constructed mainly of granite, which was hewn from a nearby quarry, and some of the stones were so huge that fifty yoke of oxen were needed to drag them up the hill. The resources of the New World and the old were ransacked for the rich materials that its adornment needed, jasper from Burgo de Osmer, damask and velvets from Granada, gold and silver from Peru. Its library, which contained the King's own collection, was among the most valuable in Europe. The Escurial is one of the great masterpieces of the Renaissance, and it was here, in a small cell-like room, that Philip labored over his files.

Nothing escaped the scrutiny of his relentless industry. He combined in his person the portfolios of half a dozen ministries, and not even his father had exerted wider powers. In 1580, when the strain on his relations with England was growing keener, he annexed the throne of Portugal, which brought him not only the great port of Lisbon, but Brazil, the Guinea coast and trading posts in the Far East; an annexation which created difficulties for the Portuguese economy, closing Lisbon to the Netherlanders and opening the Far East to Holland and to Britain.

Philip had the perpetual problem of France's growing power; he had to keep France encircled, through his ownership of Milan and Naples. Italy was the corridor between Vienna and Madrid. His brother was the Emperor. Flanders was equally important; it covered France's eastern flank. Without it, Spain would cease to be a European power. He could, if opposition became too great, dispense with the Dutch provinces, but he must hold Belgium. He was oppressed by the claims of power politics, but he saw those claims in terms not of self-aggrandizement but of his mission to extend and to defend the faith. He had to limit the rising power of France. He had to keep her weak, but he also had to keep her Catholic. He could only fulfill the various claims upon him through the wealth of the New World. A large portion of his time in that chill comfortless room was devoted to the dispatches from his governors and the reports from the Ministry in Seville.

In England, in Holland and in parts of France, the name of Philip II is one of the most hated in modern history. By the Spaniards he is deeply loved. He was their first real king. His father had spoken Spanish badly and had spent less than a quarter of his life in

Spain. Charles V's affiliations were with Austria and Flanders. He spoke Flemish; he enjoyed the heavy drinking and eating and the coarse jesting of the Belgians. Philip was a Spaniard in heart and training. He was the kind of man the Spaniards most admire—dignified, austere, devout; passionate in his youth and avid of entertainment, but in middle age conscientious, industrious, a family man. He was a considerate husband; his wives adored him and his servants were devoted to him; he was scrupulous in honesty and his sense of duty. Moreover, he shared the ambitions of his fellow countrymen. They too were insistent on a Spain free of foreigners and unbelievers. They were intensely nationalistic. They had lived under the chains of Islam long enough. They distrusted the *Moriscos*, the converted Moors; they believed that they were not only secretly continuing to perform Moslem rites but were in correspondence with the Moors in Africa, aiding the Barbary pirates and ready to welcome an invasion. They were also distrustful of the Jews who had assisted the original invasion by acting as guides and spies, who as Orientals were closer in sympathy with the Moors than with the Spaniards. If the label "fifth columnist" had existed then, it would have been attached to the *Moriscos* and the Jews. The Spanish people applauded and approved the Inquisition.

One of Philip's first public acts on his accession was to attend an *auto-da-fé* (an act of faith) at Valladolid. It was the type of ceremony dearest to the Spanish heart. It combined the pomp of a Roman triumph with the terrors of the Day of Judgment. The *auto-da-fé* was the apotheosis of the Inquisition. After months of imprisonment, torture, interrogation, the heretics were brought into the open to confess their guilt and suffer the penalties that were to be exacted of them. It was a day of celebration. At one end of the square, on a richly carpeted platform, were the seats of the Inquisitors, with the arms of the Holy Office set above them. Opposite a large scaffold was the royal gallery. At six on a May morning, every bell in the capital began to toll, and the procession started from the prison. The condemned were attended by two familiars of the Holy Office; those who were to be burned, by two friars in addition. Those who were to be reconciled wore sable; those who were not to be forgiven were draped in a loose yellow sack, with a conical pasteboard cap embroidered with figures of flames that were fed by devils. Many of the prisoners limped as a result of torture. One such—a man of noble birth—paused before Philip's throne. "Is it thus," he asked, "that you allow your innocent subjects to be persecuted?" The King replied, "If it were my own son, I would fetch the wood to burn him, were he such a wretch as thou art."

The cortege that followed these unlucky wretches glittered with Renaissance pageantry. There were the magistrates of the city, the judges of the court, the ecclesiastical orders, the nobles of the land on horseback. The members of the tribunal carried the standard of crimson damask, the arms of the Inquisition and the insignia of the founders. There was a long train of familiars. It was a brilliant spectacle on that bright May morning.

A sermon was delivered. The Grand Inquisitor administered an oath. The populace on its knees swore to maintain the purity of the faith and to inform against unbelievers. Philip too took the oath; he rose from his throne; his sword flashed from its scabbard.

The secretary of the tribunal read out the crimes and sentences. For the reconciled there was loss of property and civil rights; an imprisonment that might well be lifelong. The condemned, with cords round their necks, in their hands a cross or inverted torch, were handed over to the *corregidor* of the city to be dealt with "in all kindness and mercy." The place of execution lay outside the city. Those who had admitted their guilt were, as an act of grace, garroted before being burned. The Spaniard's delight in ceremonial had been indulged, his relish of cruelty had been assuaged, and it was to this tribunal that the English and French sailors captured in the Caribbean were brought for judgment.

Philip, seated in the Escurial, reading the reports of his governors, his ambassadors and spies, had no illusions as to the extent and depth of the hatred that was mounting against him across the Channel. But he was in many ways a patient man. He had so many obligations, so many responsibilities, that he could endure minor irritations. He was, moreover, very much in debt. Declared insolvent as early as 1557, he had, through a bankruptcy in 1572, ruined an Augsburg banker with a debt of four million florins. He could only obtain loans at usurious rates of interest, and always working against him behind the scenes were the Jews whom his ancestors had expelled. He had to proceed slowly. English historians tend to present his reign in terms of his conflict with Elizabeth. But actually, to him, his conflict with the crescent was more important, and it could be argued that in the light of Christendom's longer story, the victory of Lepanto was more significant than the defeat of the Armada.

Philip was a patient man. During his brief period as consort of the English crown, he had urged moderation upon Mary Tudor. He had

instructed his confessor to preach against the burning of Hooper, his
view being that action against the crown should be treated as treachery, not as heresy. "In England," so Sir Charles Petrie explains in his
biography of Philip, "there was every reason to avoid making religious
martyrs and there was not the slightest need to do so, for the same
end could be achieved by different means. A large number of the
Protestants burned by Mary could easily have been punished by death
in the ordinary way for murder, breach of the peace, high treason
or some other criminal offense, for most of them were engaged in
subversive activities which could have been construed as treasonable
by any sixteenth-century government."

Time, he believed, was on his side. He had the main strategy of the
New World planned. Hispaniola, Cuba, Puerto Rico, which had
seemed so important on their discovery, had become now unimpor-
tant except as bastions for his silver fleet, but as that they were of
supreme importance. No interference, no interlopers could be allowed. The Pope's bestowal of the Caribbean was a sacred trust. His
temper rose when he learned of each new flaunting of his authority.
As the months went by, his wrath became concentrated upon one
figure, *El Draqui,* the Plymouth pirate, Francis Drake.

When Hawkins set sail on his "troublesome voyage," his cousin
Francis Drake was in his middle twenties. Drake's conduct, in command of the *Judith* at San Juan de Ulúa, when he withdrew his ship
from the action and left Hawkins to face the consequences of Spanish treason, has caused his biographers some concern. Hawkins described himself as "forsaken in our great misery," but Hawkins was
given to self-pity, as his final letter to his sovereign shows, and there
is no indication that the Hawkins family felt any resentment toward
Drake. In afteryears Hawkins was ready to serve with Drake and
under him. They were both Plymouth men; the same town continued
to hold them both, and Drake's expedition six years later against
Nombre de Dios, a private enterprise launched from Plymouth,
could have hardly been undertaken without family approval. Hawkins'
accusation was a permanent entry on Drake's record, and was later
brought up against him by Frobisher, but at this distance of time,
and with scanty records at our disposal, it may be assumed that it
was generally believed he had acted as a good sailor should in bringing his ship home safe. Certainly that episode is the one unfavorable
entry in his record.

In character Drake was very different from his cousin. He had not
Hawkins' happy-go-lucky nature. His upbringing had been hard. At

Gillingham Reach on the Medway, the Tudor navy's home port, his father had been a Bible reader to the ships. It was a bare existence. From his father he acquired a hatred of Popery and a faith in a personal God little less intense than Philip's. As Philip did, he accepted his reverses as the will of God. As a boy of ten he had seen, after the failure of Wyatt's rebellion against Mary Tudor, corpses swinging from gibbets along the Medway. That rebellion had been a protest against Mary's Spanish marriage. From the very start he had thought of the Spaniards in terms of cruelty. He never went to school. Such learning as he had came to him from his father. He learned to read and write. He never expressed himself easily on paper, but he acquired a knack for oratory that stood in greater stead one who had to command men face-to-face. He could preach a vigorous sermon and in his later years he was an effective Parliamentarian. But his real education came from the hulk that was his home. As a boy, the sound of washing water was in his ears, and his cot rose and fell with the tides. It was said of the Spaniards who manned Philip's galleons that they were not sailors, but soldiers afloat. Drake was a seaman first.

His feats are common knowledge. Every English schoolboy is familiar with the voyage of *The Golden Hind*, the first English ship to sail round the world, and with his raiding of the mule train between Panama and Nombre de Dios. Both stories read like a serial in a boys' magazine; all the ingredients are there.

Before embarking on his first adventure, on the isthmus, he reconnoitered the ground, making two explorer's voyages on which he sought no trade, and attacking no ship or city. In a small ship of thirty tons, he searched for a small unsuspected harbor near Nombre de Dios which he could use as a base for operations. With the help, presumably, of Spanish refugees, he found one which was such a favorite breeding ground for pheasants that he called it Port Pheasant. He cleared the ground near the beach, he cut paths through the woods, he buried provisions. He also made friends with the local Indians and with a number of escaped slaves known as Cimaroons, who lived as nomads in the bush and were ready to befriend any enemy of Spain. Drake has been called an opportunist, and his success in action was largely due to his instinct for recognizing the psychological moment for swift and bold attack, but he laid his plans carefully, loading the dice in his own favor. When he sailed from Plymouth in May 1572, with the *Swan* and the *Pasha*, a seventy-ton ship, he was justified in feeling that he deserved success.

Students in courses of creative writing are taught that there are formulas for the writing of best sellers. For the romantic novel it is, "Boy meets girl, boy loses girl, boy finds girl." For the western, for the adventure saga, a hero starts out with courage, resolution and the sense of a just cause. He meets adversity, his luck deserts him, but his courage does not falter. Eventually fortune "turns its wheel" and victory is his. Drake's voyage to Nombre de Dios fulfilled this formula in every detail. As he landed at his secret harbor, he noticed that the trunk of one of the trees was glittering in the sunlight. A metal plate had been nailed to it. On the plate had been cut the message: "Captain Drake. If you fortune to come to this port make haste away. For the Spaniards which you had with you here the last year have betrayed their place and taken all that you left here. I depart from hence this present 7th of July 1572. Your loving friend John Garret." Drake read this message on July 12. We know nothing of John Garret or of the Spaniards who betrayed him, but that warning notice is the prelude to a sequence of adverse events.

In addition to the two ships, Drake had brought three small pinnaces, made in parts, to be assembled quickly. In them he sought another harbor. He encountered two small frigates from Nombre de Dios. The slaves who were loading timber warned him that a garrison of soldiers was shortly expected, to protect the city against the Cimaroons. Drake had to act quickly.

On the night of July 28, he was within striking distance of Nombre de Dios. The attack would be made at dawn, he told his men. But as the night wore on he realized that his young crew was feeling the nerve strain of its long trek down the coast. Inactivity might prove more than they could stand. The moon began to rise. The sky was cloudless and he grasped his chance. "There comes the dawn," he cried. "Get under way."

The attack was a complete surprise. The town was protected against land attack from the Cimaroons, but not against a sea attack. Only one gunner guarded the shoreside battery. He fled in terror. The town was waked by his cries and by the tolling of the bells from the church tower. With his drums beating, his trumpets sounding, his fire-pieces lit, Drake marched down the street toward the marketplace. The militia and the inhabitants under arms were already mustered. They fired, but they fired low and only one man, a trumpeter, was killed. Drake answered promptly—musket fire, arrows, then a charge. The Spaniards, still in a daze, broke and fled.

The town lay at Drake's mercy. But he had to work fast. The

pinnaces were threatened. He had to man them before daybreak. He found a storeroom stacked with bars of silver, but Drake wanted the gold and jewels that were kept in the King's treasure-house by the waterside. During his reconnaissance he had discovered where it was. But luck at that point deserted him. A tropical storm burst upon the town, the matches of his muskets were put out, the powder ruined and the bowstrings loosened. By the time the storm was over it was apparent that Drake was badly wounded in the leg. He had concealed his injury so as not to frighten his raw recruits, but the spot where he had sheltered from the storm was drenched with blood. His men insisted that he return on board where his wounds could be properly dressed. He was more than their leader, he was their navigator. Without him they were helpless. Weak with loss of blood, he let them carry him to the pinnace. He sailed from his harborage with no richer plunder than a cargo of Canary wine which was to have been landed on the following morning. He had failed at the very moment when success was within his grasp. But he did not abandon hope. He had no intention of returning to Plymouth empty-handed.

For six months Drake played the pirate along the Spanish Main. First he discovered near Darien a harbor concealed from view that was never used by Spanish vessels. Here he established a camp which he called Port Plenty; he built houses and a clubroom for his men. He trained them in archery. They played bowls and quoits; they were well fed with fish and deer and hogs. They recovered their health and spirits. He organized a series of raids. He captured on the high seas a number of frigates laden with wheat, poultry and live hogs. At the mouth of the Magdalena River was a settlement where the Spaniards replenished their ships on the homeward journey; it contained a consignment of a country cheese that was highly prized in Spain. That winter the Hidalgos of Seville and Madrid were deprived of that special delicacy. He sailed for Curaçao and captured a ninety-ton ship with a cargo of well-salted food.

The Spaniards never knew where he was; he was here, he was there, striking suddenly, then slipping away like a panther in the jungle. And all the time he was weighing his new, second raid on the stores of treasure. Nombre de Dios was warned and guarded, but he had another project; to raid the mule train that crossed the isthmus between Panama and Vera Cruz. Herein lay the cause of his five months' wait. He had learned from the Cimaroons when the great stores on the Pacific coast would be unbarred and the mules assembled. Many of his men were sick with fever, and several had died, including his brother Joseph, but on February 3, with eighteen of his own men and twenty-five Cimaroons, he set out across the isthmus.

The journey took eleven days. They marched from dawn till ten o'clock, rested while the sun was high, then marched till four o'clock. Each night the Cimaroons built a camp out of palmetto boughs with a thatching of plantain leaves. Finally they reached a ridge. The guide led Drake to a tree in whose trunk had been cut steps. An arbor in which ten men could sit had been constructed at the top. Drake was the first Englishman to look on the Pacific. He knelt and prayed to God to let him sail on that ocean in an English ship. He then summoned his crew to stand beside him and listen to his repetition of the prayer. As he descended from the ridge, he felt that he was entering another universe. In the place of the wet, cool woods, he tramped through an open savannah; over its high pampas grass he caught glimpses of the church towers of Panama.

This change of scenery determined the tactics of his ambush. Owing to the heat of the open savannah the first stage of the journey was made by night; the later stage was made by day through the cool woods. Drake planned to make his attack by night. He dressed his men in white so that they should not attack each other in the dark. He divided them into two groups.

He had been told that the mules would be in harness, one behind the other, and that if the first mule was held it would lie down, and those behind would follow its example. Drake therefore set his men fifty yards from the road, spaced so that the first mule of the last train would reach his second group at the same time that the first mule of the first train reached the other.

They waited, their eyes strained; at last, after an hour, they heard the tinkle of bells along the path, but once again Drake was to be disappointed. A drunken member of his crew was overhasty and warned the Spaniards. The mule train that they captured was merely the commissariat of provisions. Only two of the mules were laden with ingots, and those with silver ones. Once again Drake was forced back to his pinnaces, but not even then did he abandon hope.

The formula of the adventure serial was being followed to the final detail. He assured his men that the attack would be repeated, this time with greater strength; to be repeated, though, under different conditions. This time the attack was to be launched on the Atlantic side of the ridge, and this time they had the assistance of a French ship, which had been met by chance and whose captain would be clearly of greater use as an ally than as a competitor or adversary. The Frenchman was not welcome as a partner but there was no alternative.

This time everything went to plan. Two caravans, one of fifty mules and one of seventy, weighed down with gold and silver, stumbled into the ambush. In the short battle that ensued the French captain was seriously wounded, but the Spaniards were outmanned and outgunned; within a few minutes Drake's men were busy with the unloading of the mules; a little of the silver was buried in holes dug by land crabs under the roots of trees, but they carried the greater part on their own shoulders, along with the boxes of jewels and the gold. For two days they struggled under the weight of their plunder toward the river where they had left the pinnaces.

At last they saw it, glittering between the trees in the morning sunlight, and then, at that final moment, Drake came very near despair. He saw, instead of his own two pinnaces, seven Spanish pinnaces patrolling the mouth of the river. He imagined that his crews had been captured, and had revealed under torture the secret anchorage where the frigates awaited him.

Drake watched, concealed from view. At length the Spaniards abandoned their patrol and made for Nombre de Dios. The English were still in a desperate plight, marooned on a foreign shore, but Drake had recovered his composure. The pinnaces might have been captured, but it would take some time for the Spaniards to interrogate the sailors and plan their course of action. There was possibly still time to get to the ships, by water if not by land. Let them make a raft, and he for one would sail in it.

Trees were felled, a sail was made out of a biscuit bag; an oar and rudder were made out of a sapling. With one of his crew and two Frenchmen, Drake climbed aboard. "If it pleases God," he said, "that I should put my foot in safety aboard my frigate, I will, God willing, by one means or another, get you all aboard, despite all the Spaniards in the Indies."

It was a hazardous journey. The sea was rough, the waves washed over them, the heavy tropical sun beat down; but the wind was at their backs, and at last, after they had struggled for nine miles down the coast, they saw their own pinnaces. There had been no cause for alarm. A head wind had delayed Drake's two pinnaces and forced the Spanish pinnaces to shelter in the Rio Francisco.

Drake saw the pinnaces before they saw his raft, and at this last moment his warm, full-blooded Devonian sense of humor inspired him to the playing of a practical joke. The swift dusk of the Caribbean was falling fast; the pinnaces were sheltering for the night. Drake landed out of sight, then ran round the spur of land as though he were being chased by Spaniards. He and his three companions stumbled aboard breathless and gasping. The crew of the pinnaces were convinced that disaster had befallen the expedition. How had things turned out, they asked. Drake replied with the cold monosyllable, "Well," as he invariably did when he was the victim of misfortune; then, with a laugh, he pulled out from under his shirt a bar of gold.

From now on the voyage was relatively simple. He recovered a part of the silver he had buried and made for home. He sailed past Cartagena with the cross of St. George flying from his maintop. He captured a frigate that was loaded with food and honey, the latter a very useful medicine for the sick. In Cuba he acquired a great store of turtles. He sailed through the Bahama Channel, leaving behind a reputation not only for audacity and skill but also for gentleness. As Nichols, the official historian, relates, there were at that time upwards of two hundred frigates active in the Spanish Main, "the most of which during our abode in those parts we took, and some of them twice or thrice each; yet never burned nor sunk any, unless they were made out men-of-war against us or laid snares to entrap us. And of all the men taken in these several vessels, we never offered any kind of violence to any, after they were once come under our power; but either presently dismissed them in safety or kept them with us some longer time, provided for their sustenance as for ourselves and secured them from the rage of the Cimaroons."

Drake landed in Plymouth in early August on a Sunday morning, and the news of his arrival emptied the churches. The priests finished their sermons to vacant benches. The congregation was assembled on the quay "to see the evidence of God's love and blessing toward our gracious Queen and country by the fruit of our captain's labor and success."

He had been away fifteen months. Of the seventy-three men and boys who had sailed with him, less than half returned, but that was a reasonable quota in Elizabethan days, when disease was as lethal as the Spaniards' muskets, and in compensation the holds of his ship were crammed with jewels and gold and silver. It was the first great voyage for plunder in the Caribbean. It set the pattern for piracy for a hundred years, until Henry Morgan brought the curtain down with his sacking of Panama.

During the next thirteen years, achievements even greater were to be credited to *El Draqui*. On his return from the West Indies he furnished at his own expense three frigates which he put with his own services under the command in Ireland of the Earl of Essex. He achieved high distinction in battle both on sea and land, and it may be assumed that this service was a recognition of the Queen's clemency in allowing him to keep his treasure, for at this time England was officially at peace with Spain, and it is undeniable that his exploits complicated her policy of appeasement.

That policy was to be further complicated by the mighty voyage of circumnavigation on which he embarked in the autumn of 1577, a voyage, however, that was undertaken with the Queen's connivance. When he had looked from that high tree at Darien he had prayed that one day he might be allowed to sail his own ship on those far waters. On his return to England, his imagination had been fired by the prospect of plundering the Spanish galleons on their way up the Pacific coast to Panama. Within three years he had begun to organize his plans, and Elizabeth was in a mood to offer him protection. She was aware that Philip II's illegitimate brother, Don John of Austria, was planning to marry Mary, Queen of Scots, and share the throne of England with her. An expedition to attack Philip on the Pacific coast, where his harbors were unguarded, and the ships that brought the treasures of Peru to Panama were unarmed, fancying that they enjoyed complete immunity, might well provide the needed counterirritant. Philip was again near to bankruptcy. Elizabeth saw a chance of teaching him that he could not carry out his plans in Europe unless he kept the peace with her. She informed Drake that she "would be gladly revenged on the King of Spain for divers injuries that I have received." But she instructed Drake that he was to keep his plans a secret. So complete indeed was the security observed that when Drake's fleet of five ships sailed out of Plymouth Sound, the Spanish ambassador in London believed that he was bound for the Levant.

The voyage he undertook may well be regarded as the greatest ever made by an English seaman. Drake was not only the first Englishman to sail round the world, but he was the first sea captain to insist on equality before the mast under his command. He was accompanied by a number of gentleman adventurers such as had harassed Columbus' second voyage; young men of birth and wealth who were ready to fight the Spaniard but who expected their share of the plunder in return for the financial aid they had given to the expedition, and who were not prepared to undertake menial tasks. Columbus' Hidalgos were indignant at being forced to hew wood and build houses. Drake insisted that his young men of fashion should scrub decks and man the pumps. On this score alone, his voyage is one of the most important in the history of the sea; yet it lies outside the scope of a history of the West Indies. He never in the course of it sailed in the Caribbean. He made south for Mogador, called at the Cape Verde Islands, captured a Portuguese caravel and acquired from it a Portuguese pilot who knew the Brazilian coast. He rested in the mouth of the River Plate, sailed southward through the Straits of Magellan, then, working up the coast, began his series of raids on Spanish ports and shipping that led as much as anything to the delay of the "invincible Armada."

When he sailed from Plymouth, he had hoped after his attacks on the Spanish ships to return to England by the Northwest Passage. He had believed that there was some route through into the Caribbean. He sailed into San Francisco Bay. He planted the Queen's standard in what now is Canada, but he found no Northwest Passage. He had, therefore, to turn westward and sail round the world if he would once again see Plymouth Sound. When he set out he had no idea that this expedient would be forced on him. He did not know to what extent he would be making history.

He returned to Plymouth in the autumn of 1580. He had been away for close upon three years. He had the vaguest idea of what had been happening in his absence. As *The Golden Hind* swung into the Sound, one of his crew shouted to an astonished fisherman, "Is the Queen alive?" Had the Queen not been alive, had Mary, Queen of Scots, been ruling in her stead, the situation might have been ominous for Drake, whose holds were filled with plunder from a nation that was, in diplomatic usage, friendly. But Queen Elizabeth was very much alive and very ready to appreciate the tangible results of her seaman's enterprise. Though the English merchants in Seville, fearful for their property and status, besought her to disavow the pirate, though members of her council were insistent that the treasure should be returned to Spain, Elizabeth was too avaricious, too tenacious of her own authority to resign her share of half a million pounds. On New Year's Day, wearing the emerald crown that Drake had given her, she announced that in the spring she would visit *The Golden Hind* in person and there dub its general a knight. She was already walking the road that led to the bonfires on the downs and to the fire ships in the Straits of Dover. But they lay seven and a half years away, and three years later it might well have seemed that Drake's days at sea were over.

He had made a fortune while comparatively a young man. The Queen had granted him a country house. He acquired land. His first wife had died and he remarried. He served on a royal commission, a highly important one, that was to decide the future strategy of naval war. Which was the more effective, the big ship or the little ship? Frobisher, Carew and Raleigh sat with him on the commission. He must have considered his work on it as important as a voyage to distant islands. He entered Parliament. He made speeches, he sat on committees, one of which considered the clauses of a bill "for the better and more reverent observancing of the Sabbath day." His second marriage was only a few months old, his bride was young and beautiful. Everything seemed calm and peaceful, but in the spring of 1585 an English ship called the *Primrose* sailed into Plymouth with a grim tale to tell.

In the previous year Spain had endured an unlucky harvest. Galicia and Andalusia were faced with starvation. Philip II, to meet the situation, suggested that English ships bring wheat to Spain. He assured them that they could sail into Lisbon Harbor with immunity. He gave his personal guarantee that their persons and property would be safe. But he instructed his authorities in Lisbon to capture by surprise every English boat, confiscate the cargo and imprison the crew. Eleven ships were stolen in this way; the captain of the *Primrose* alone, suspecting deceit, was on his guard, and in the ensuing battle killed twenty-seven of the raiders, the *Primrose* herself escaping with the loss of three men only.

Philip did not consider his conduct treacherous any more than his viceroy had in San Juan de Ulúa twenty years before. The end justified the means, and Philip had the absolute certainty that his goal was sacrosanct. But in England the news of his double-dealing roused the country's wrath. No one, incidentally, appeared to think that the captain of the *Primrose* had behaved treasonably in carrying food to a fleet that was shortly to invade England.

English merchants were indeed as late as this trading briskly with the enemy. Bristol supplied guns cast in the Forest of Dean. A Sussex ironmaster sold Philip a hundred pieces of cannon. In 1587 nine shiploads of light shotted and long-range guns with powder, shot and muskets crossed the Channel, while Spanish sailors were nourished by west country butter and cornish pilchards. Business was business, and war had not been declared. The country clamored for revenge and Drake had no difficulty in obtaining authority to fit out a punitive expedition. In terms of profit it was not his most successful voyage, but the damage to Spain's prestige was incalculably great.

He began by stealing a Spanish ship loaded with salt fish. When its captain expostulated, he retorted, "If we are not at war, why have English merchants been arrested?" Failing to intercept the Silver Fleet, he made for Santiago; one of his crew was murdered, so he sacked the city. Philip, when the news reached him, offered a reward of £40,000 for Drake's head or person. Worse news was soon to follow. Drake landed at Santo Domingo. He sent a young Negro with a message to the governor. A Hidalgo who was standing by considered this an insult and ran the boy through with his sword. Drake proceeded to the spot where the murder had been committed and had two friars hanged. He told the governor that he would hang two more friars every day until the murderer had been executed. After due deliberation the governor agreed to hand over his officer. But Drake was not satisfied with that. The Spaniards must hang him themselves.

Santo Domingo was at this moment at the peak of its beauty and renown. An earlier Spanish report of it had said:

"As touching the buildings, there is no city of Spain that is to be preferred before this, generally. The houses are for the most part of stone. The situation is much better than that of Barcelona, by reason that the streets are much longer and plainer and, without comparison, more direct and straightforth. For being builded now in our time, besides the commodity of the place of the foundation, the streets were also directed with cord, compass and measure, wherein it excelleth all the cities I have seen. It hath the sea so near, that on one side there is no more space between the sea and the city than the walls. On the other part, hard by the side and at the foot of the houses, passeth the River Ozama, which is a marvellous port, wherein laden ships rise very near to the land and in manner under the houses' windows. In the midst of the city is the fortress and castle; the port or haven is so fair and commodious to defreight or unlade ships as the like is found in few places of the world. The chimneys that are in this city are about five hundred in number and such houses as I have spoken of before, of the which some are so fair and large that they may well receive and lodge any lord or nobleman of Spain with his train and family, and especially that which Don Diego Colon, the viceroy under Your Majesty, hath in this city is such that I know no man in Spain that hath the like, by a quarter. Likewise the situation thereof on being above the said port, and altogether of stone and having many large and fair rooms with as goodly a prospect of the sea and land as may be devised, seems to me so magnifical and princelike that Your Majesty may be as well lodged therein as in any of the most exquisite builded houses of Spain. There is also a cathedral church builded of late where as well as the Bishop according to his dignity, as also the canons are well indeed. The church is well builded of stone and lime and of good workmanship. There are furthermore three monasteries which are well builded, although not so curiously as they of Spain. There is also a very good hospital for the aid and succour of poor people. . . . To conclude, this city from day to day increaseth in wealth and order, as well for the said admiral and viceroy with the Lord Chancellor and council appointed there by Your Majesty have their abideage here as also that the richest men of the island resort hither for their most commodious habitation and trade of such merchandise as are either brought out of Spain or sent thither from this island which now so aboundeth in many things that serveth Spain with many commodities as it were with usury requiting such benefits as it first received from thence."

The importance of Hispaniola had waned since that report was sent, but the city itself had waxed in charm and substance. Drake's destruction of it was not an easy project. "We spent," the record runs, "the early part of the mornings in firing the outmost houses, but they being built very magnificently of stone with high lofts gave us no small travail to ruin them. And albeit for divers days together, we ordained each morning by daybreak until the heat began at nine of the clock that two hundred mariners did nought else but labor to fire and burn the said houses, whilst the soldiers in a like proportion stood forth for their guard, yet did we not or could not in this time consume so much as one third part of the town, and so in the end, wearied with firing, we were contented to accept of five and twenty thousand ducats of five shillings and sixpence the piece, for the ransom of the rest of the town."

In the town hall where he collected this sum hung the city's coat of arms. Its motto ran, Non Sufficit Orbis. The world is not enough. He made contemptuous mock of this. They had better, he suggested, send it back to Spain and have the motto changed, or else have the Caribbean properly policed.

Philip complained to Elizabeth in Latin:

Je veto ne pergas bello defendere Belgas;
Quae Dracus eripuit nunc restituantur oportet;
Quas Pater evertit, jubeo te condere cellas;
Religio Papae, fac restituantur ad unguem.

[I forbid you to continue to defend the Low Countries by war; what Drake seized must now be restored; what monasteries your father overthrew I order you to refound; see that the religion of the Pope is restored in every way.]

To which Elizabeth replied:

Ad Graecas, Bone Rex, fiant mandata Kalendas.

[My good King, your commands will be obeyed at the Greek Kalends.]

That is to say, never, since there are no Kalends in the Greek calender.

A year later Drake was sailing into Cádiz Harbor. He captured the *San Philip* and brought back papers which proved the value of the East India trade and led to the founding of the East India Company. But the raid did not give Elizabeth much satisfaction, since it did not declare a dividend. She was concerned with what Drake brought back in plunder, not in what he had destroyed. But, in fact, the burning of many casks, seventeen hundred tons in weight, which could each hold thirty thousand tons of liquid, and which had been intended for the watering of the Armada, was a very serious blow to the Spanish administration. Seasoned staves were in short supply, and Philip was very heavily in debt. Elizabeth and her ministers never appreciated how poor Spain was. And the lack of fresh water because of faulty and leaking casks was one of the great handicaps under which the Armada travailed.

"God blew and his enemies were scattered." The galleons of the "Invincible Armada" were broken on the Scottish shoals and the Irish coasts; barely half of them limped back to Spain. Philip received the news in Barcelona. He could not believe that it had happened, that the fleet whose banners had been blessed should have been destroyed, that the fleet that had sailed to fulfill God's will had sailed in vain. For a week he shut himself away in prayer and agony. He emerged tired and drained, but with the old assurance, the old self-confidence. If it was God's will, he must accept it. God, in His own time, in His own way, would reveal the mysteries of the divine intention. Meanwhile, his work awaited him. There was the endless accumulation of dispatches and reports, the long rows of figures. There was the war in the Netherlands to be prosecuted. He must strengthen the security of the Silver Fleet, fortify the harbors where it was collected, so that the raids of *El Draqui* could be beaten off; institute a fast messenger service—*avisos*—so that news of an English or French sailing could set the governors on their guard. The cargoes of gold were taken on board small, fast cruisers at Havana. God must have had His own good reasons for the winds that had fallen on His fleet. Himself, he must wait and watch and be on his guard.

A mighty victory, an utter rout, a defeat whose very completeness gave it the high dignity of tragedy—so that for the vanquished as much as for the victors, for Philip as much as for Elizabeth, for the Spaniards as much as for the English, the preparation, the sailing and the destruction of the Armada can be seen in retrospect as "their finest hour." It was the climax of thirty years of plotting, planning and high endeavor. The years that followed were, in many respects, gray with anticlimax for many of Elizabeth's greatest seamen, for Drake and Hawkins, for Frobisher and Martin, and most of all, in spite of an occasional flash of the old magic, for Sir Walter Raleigh.

Raleigh, in many ways, stands apart from his contemporaries. He crossed the Atlantic in a different spirit. Whereas Hawkins had gone there as a merchant, Drake as a privateer, the Spaniards in search of gold and the conversion of the heathen, Raleigh had had the imperial vision. He was the first Englishman to see the value of a "New England" which would send back raw materials, purchase English woolens, offer a home to a surplus population and provide an army when danger threatened. He never visited North America, and his colony in Virginia did not succeed in his lifetime, but it was the first stage in the building of the British Empire.

In his last great adventure, however, he did imitate the Spaniards, setting out deliberately in quest of gold. In the same way that Ponce de Leon had believed in the fountain of eternal youth, so did a great many Spaniards believe in the existence of an El Dorado in the center of South America. They held that after Pizarro conquered Peru, a number of Indians fled inland and refounded their empire in the vast plains eastward of the Andes. The gold of Peru, they argued, must have come from somewhere. Surely, somewhere inland lay Peru's heart of gold; surely, its wealth flowed through the veins of Guiana. This was the legend that fired Raleigh's imagination.

In 1594 Raleigh's personal stock stood low, his favor, in his own words, "declining and falling into a recess." He had only intermittently enjoyed public popularity. He was arrogant; he had risen too fast; as the Queen's favorite, he had made too much money. He was one of those to be accused, as Marlowe was, of atheism, and he had now lost the Queen's good will by conducting an intrigue with one of her ladies-in-waiting, even though he subsequently atoned with marriage. He spent several months in prison, and on his release was banished from the court to his estate at Sherborne. He needed to restore his status. "I did therefore in the winter of my life undertake these travels, fitter for boys less blasted with misfortunes, for men of greater abilities, for minds of better encouragement."

A year earlier one of his privateers had captured the report prepared for the Governor of Trinidad, Don Antonio de Berreo, by the head of a mission of thirty-five men that had been sent up the Orinoco to find and annex the capital, Manoa. The report encouraged Raleigh to send one of his servants, John Whidden, who had served with him during the cruise to the Azores in 1586, to examine the coast of Guiana. Berreo invited some of his men ashore and had them murdered. This action confirmed Raleigh's resolve, and in the following February he sailed for Trinidad with a commission from Elizabeth "to discover and subdue heathen lands not in possession of any Christian prince or inhabited by any Christian people." He was empowered "to offend and enfeeble the King of Spain" and instructed "to resist and expel anyone attempting to excel within the place he chose for his colony."

He was six weeks at sea, but he did not find the journey irksome. He traveled with a box of books and studied for several hours a day. He needed only five hours sleep. He set sail with five ships, only two of which reached Trinidad. He found the island scantily settled and was able to make a thorough reconnaissance. First casting anchor in the southwest of Curiapan, he followed the coast for five days. He found a salt river with oysters growing on its trees. He discovered a lake with "such an abundance of stone pitch that all the ships of the world might be laden from them." He trimmed his ships with the pitch and found it excellent; it did not melt in the sun as Norwegian pitch did. He proceeded to what is now San Fernando. The island, he reported, "hath the form of a sheephook and is but narrow: the north part very mountainous, the soil excellent, will bear sugar, ginger, or any other commodity which the Indies yield, . . . a store of deer, wild pigs, fruits, fish and fowl, . . . for bread there are maize and cassava and divers roots: there are many wild beasts such as are not found in the Indies." There were several different tribes of Indians. The Spaniards had found gold in the rivers but neglected it because they were more interested in Guiana.

Such Spaniards as he met were "friendly, more for doubt of their own strength than for aught else." They came on board to buy linen, and Raleigh "entertained them kindly and feasted after our manner. . . . These poor soldiers having been many years without wine, a few draughts made them merry, in which mood they vaunted of Guiana and all the riches thereof and all what they knew of the ways and passages, myself seeming to purpose nothing less than the entrance or discovery thereof, but bred in them an opinion I was bound only for the relief of those English whom I had planted in Virginia."

The governor was an elderly man, the son-in-law of the powerful *adelantado* Gonzola Ximenes, from whom he had inherited considerable wealth. He did not interfere with Raleigh's activities, but ordered the hanging and quartering of any Indians who befriended him. This decided Raleigh on offensive action. He felt genuine sympathy for the Indians; he also remembered Berreo's treatment of Whidden's sailors. He recognized that it would be highly dangerous for him to enter Guiana by small boats, traveling four hundred miles from his ships and leaving behind a hostile garrison that was interested in the same enterprise. Had he done so, he "should have savored very much of the ass." So he sacked the Spanish settlement of St. Joseph and took Berreo prisoner.

In Berreo he recognized and appreciated a fellow aristocrat. He described him as "very valiant and liberal, a gentleman of great assuredness and of a great heart. I used him according to his estate and worth in all things I could, according to the small means I had." From Berreo he received what seemed to him a firsthand account of the Spanish officer, Martinez, who as a punishment for unsoldierly conduct was marooned on the Orinoco. Discovered by Indians, he was taken as a curiosity to their Emperor, who lived in Manoa. He was blindfolded during his journey, which lasted for two weeks. His bandages were removed when he entered the city. That was at midday; he traveled on till nightfall before he reached the Emperor's palace. It was Martinez who invented the name El Dorado, because it was the custom of the chiefs to strip naked, anoint their bodies with a kind of white balsam, and have their servants blow powdered gold on them through hollow canes. They would then sit aglitter from head to foot, feasting and drinking for a whole week on end. Martinez stayed among these golden men for seven months; he was then blindfolded once again and led outside the city.

Raleigh lingered longer than he should have done in Trinidad because he wished to obtain as much information as possible from Berreo. He found Berreo companionable, but was deeply shocked by his treatment of the Indians. He showed their chiefs the Queen's portrait, explaining to them that he was the servant of a queen who was the great *cacique* of the north and a virgin, who had more *caciques* under her than there were trees on the island, who was an enemy of the *Castellanos* in respect to their tyranny and oppression, and had sent him to free them and withal to defend the country of Guiana from their invasion and conquest. Raleigh learned that the resentful Indians had driven the Spaniards out of Guiana and that there remained only a small garrison on an eastern branch of the Orinoco delta, which would not interfere with the exploration he planned to undertake up the western channel.

Raleigh was now ready to start upon that expedition. It lasted a month and its discomforts provided one of the grimmest experiences of his service. He "carried 100 persons and their victuals for a month, driven to lie in the rain and weather, in the open air, in the burning sun and upon the hard boards and to dress our meat and carry all manner of furniture in them, that what with the victuals being mostly fish, with the wet clothes of so many thrust together and the heat of the sun, I will undertake there was never any prison in England that could be found more unsavory and loathsome, especially to myself, who had for many years before been dieted and cared for in a sort far differing."

Yet he did not lose his faith in the Golden City, and he believed that had he started ten days earlier, before the rivers were flooded, he would have reached Manoa. An Indian chief told him that if fifty Englishmen were left to defend his province against the Spaniards, he would show the others the road to Manoa. Everywhere Raleigh showed the Indians courtesy and kindness, and 180 years later another traveler was to discover that the legend still lingered of an English *cacique* who had urged them "to persevere in enmity against the Spaniards" and who had promised to return with forces that could defend them.

He undertook no belligerent action. "It would have been agreeable," he wrote, "to have sacked a city or two and brought back gold, but it would have been in my opinion an utter overthrow to the enterprise, if the same should be hereafter by Her Majesty attempted, for then, whereas now they have heard we were enemies to the Spaniards and were set by Her Majesty to relieve them, they would as good cheap have joined with the Spaniards at our return, as to have yielded unto us, when they proved that we came both for one errand and that both sought but to sack and spoil them, but as yet our desire for gold or our purpose of invasion is unknown to them and it is likely that if Her Majesty undertake the enterprise, they will rather submit themselves to her obedience than to the Spaniards of whose cruelty they have already tasted, and therefore until I had known Her Majesty's pleasure, I would rather have lost the sack of one or two towns, although they might have been very profitable, than to have defaced or endangered the future hopes of so many millions and the great good and rich trade which England may be possessed of thereby."

There were, of course, no cities available for him to have sacked, but his faith in the wealth of El Dorado was unbounded. He amplified Martinez' description of the palace. "All the vessels of the Emperor's home were of gold and silver and the meanest of silver and copper for strength and hardness of the metal. He had in his wardrobe hollow statues of gold which seemed giants, and figures in proportion and bigness of all the beasts, birds, trees and herbs that the earth bringeth forth and all the fishes that the sea of waters of his kingdom breedeth. He had also ropes, budgets, chests and troughs of gold and silver, heaps of billets of gold that seemed wood, marked out to burn. Finally, there was nothing in this country whereof he had not the counterfeit in gold. . . . a garden of pleasure where they went when they needed the air of the sea, which had all garden herbs, flowers and trees of gold and silver—an invention and magnificence till then never seen."

His imagination embellished every rumor. The mountains were so filled with precious metals that they dazzled the eyes. The resources of Peru and Mexico would be soon exhausted, but Guiana was "the very magazine of all rich metals," a country "that hath yet her maidenhead; never sacked, burned or wrought: the face of the earth hath not been torn nor the virtue and salt of the soil spent by manurance: the graves have not been opened for gold, the mines not broken with sledges nor their images pulled down out of their temples. It hath never been entered by any army of strength and never conquered or possessed by any Christian prince."

He accepted also the rumor of a tribe that had eyes in their shoulders, their mouths in the middle of their breasts, and from between whose shoulders grew backward a great mane of hair; a description that was perhaps responsible for Desdemona's reference to

men whose heads
Do grow between their shoulders . . .

And indeed the belief in this tribe was to persist late into the century, Hartsinck talking in 1770 of a black race in Surinam with forked hands and feet like a lobster's, with only a thumb and forefinger.

Raleigh was away seven months, and the book in which he recorded his adventures was received with derision by his fellow courtiers. It reflected more doubt upon his truthfulness "than all the questionable acts of his life put together." There were not lacking those who wondered whether he had made the trip at all. Perhaps he had been in Cornwall all the time. The detail that amused the court more than any other was that of the oysters, "very salt and well tasted," that he claimed to have found growing on the mangroves of Trinidad. "Oysters on trees indeed, how could you believe anything of the man who presented a report like that."

But Raleigh was to remain haunted till the end by the legend of Guiana, whose "great unspoiled city Geryon's sons call El Dorado."

While Raleigh was upon these travels, Philip, crouched over his files in his bleak cell, racked by gout and arthritis, was to learn that Drake was planning another trip to the West Indies. For six years Drake had been ashore. Soon after the Armada, he had led a raid on Cádiz that had proved unsuccessful, and he was out of favor with the Queen. In a desultory way, England was still at war with Spain. But Philip had now turned his attention to Huguenot France. This was a welcome relief for Elizabeth, though she did not welcome the establishment of a fortified strongpoint across the Channel. She was content to let Drake return to Devon, build Plymouth up into an important naval station, and later, as a member of Parliament, busy himself upon committees. If another Armada were to be launched, she would have him in reserve. It was slowly that the tide of events drove her to reconsider the value of her old servant. Henri IV now sat upon the throne of France. The man who had thought Paris worth a mass was adept at playing one party off against another. Elizabeth sent an expedition to the defense of Brest. The English losses were heavy; Frobisher died of his wounds, but Brest was relieved and a threat to England passed.

Philip's difficulties mounted. He was short of money and his signature on a bill had been dishonored too often in Genoa and Augsburg for anything but bullion to be accepted there. Now, surely, so it seemed to Drake, was the time to strike a final and conclusive blow. A return to Nombre de Dios, a march across the isthmus, the sacking of Panama, the plunder of its treasure—why not? Drake longed to be at sea again, and this time Elizabeth listened sympathetically.

If the first raid upon the mule train contained all the best-seller ingredients of a boys' adventure story, his last voyage contains the Aeschylean unities of Attic tragedy. It is an eternal theme, the man of fifty trying to relive his youth, to recapture youth, to disprove the evidence of time. Drake's scheme in itself was sound, just as the scheme of his Cádiz adventure had been sound, but he was no longer thirty. Napoleon said after Austerlitz, "A general has twelve years, I have seven left." Ten years later, at Waterloo, immobile upon his horse, he was unable to summon a flash of that inspiration which had once been his and might have carried a day that was, as Wellington said afterward, "nearest run thing you ever saw."

At fifty, after six years ashore, Drake, without knowing it, had lost his suppleness, not so much in body as in mind. His responses were no longer swift, and his early success had been won by the rapidity, the sureness, the confidence with which he struck, allied with the careful, methodical preparation of his plans.

Elizabeth too was aging, and her counselors were timid. She made difficulties, she laid down conditions. She insisted that another admiral should sail with equal authority, and she chose as that other man John Hawkins, who was now sixty-three, who had always disagreed with Drake on points of naval strategy; Hawkins, under whom Drake had sailed as a junior on "that troublesome voyage"; Hawkins, who had reported unfavorably on Drake, and later had been outshone by Drake in terms of fame and wealth. Elizabeth could not have chosen worse.

Worse was to follow. The news that Drake was to sail again brought volunteers in thousands to his command, and when the rumor of it reached Spain, nine thousand soldiers deserted and the inhabitants of Lisbon took to the hills. A swift blow at this point, in spite of the handicaps that had been imposed on him, might have succeeded. But Elizabeth procrastinated. She was afraid that Philip was planning a second Armada; and indeed, four Spanish galleons which had intended to raid the Channel Islands lost their direction and landed by mistake in the charming Cornish fishing village of Mousehole, among whose inhabitants today can be detected a trace of Spanish ancestry, and burned Newlyn and Penzance.

Elizabeth, in her alarm, insisted that Drake and Hawkins, before sailing for Nombre de Dios, should reconnoiter the south of Ireland and the coast of Spain, then cruise in the Atlantic in the hope of intercepting the gold fleet on its way from Havana. She even fixed a date by which they must return, and was incensed when her admirals explained that it was impossible to make such promises, and that as large a force as it was proposed to send to Panama could not be maintained on board for such a length of time. In her anger she would probably have canceled the expedition had she not been informed that the chief ship of the Mexican gold fleet had been crippled in a storm and had taken refuge at Puerto Rico, with bullion worth two and a half million pounds aboard. It was too great a prize to be resisted. So, at the end of August, twenty-seven ships manned by twenty-five hundred men, the biggest expedition that England had ever launched, set sail from Plymouth.

Within a few days trouble had begun. A dual control can never be satisfactory, particularly when the two leaders hold contrary views, but in this case there was the latent lack of harmony that had always lain between the cousins. They began to quarrel over the kinds of incident that feed the flame of disunion in families. Drake protested that he was carrying too large a share of the armed force. Hawkins retorted that he should have been "entreated," not ordered, to take over Drake's surplus. Then came their first big disagreement. It was Drake's habit to plunder some fort or other on his way to the West Indies; he now chose the Grand Canary. Hawkins disagreed. In his opinion they should make first for Puerto Rico. There was a hot argument at the war council and Hawkins was overruled, but the outcome proved that he was right.

It was ten years since Drake had sailed these waters, and during that period Philip had strengthened his defenses. If Drake had followed the tactics that had proved successful years before at Santiago, Santo Domingo and Cartagena, and landed his troops in the dark, he might have had the town at his mercy. But he waited till daylight and in full view of the fort looked for a suitable landing beach; the sea was rough, however, and the beach which he had selected was heavily protected. He could not risk a landing, and was forced to cancel the operation. He sailed away without the firing of a shot. Never had *El Draqui* withdrawn before. His soldiers felt ashamed. Their morale went down.

Luck now turned against him. He made for Dominica and reached his anchorage on the leeward side by the northern route. Hawkins went southward through the channel between Dominica and Martinique. Two of his ships were slower than the rest and fell behind. Ninety-nine times in a hundred this lack of speed would have made no difference. The two ships would have arrived at their rendezvous in Guadeloupe a day late and that would have been all. But this was the hundredth time. Philip had sent five of his fast new frigates to bring back the treasure of the galleon stranded in Puerto Rico. To their astonishment they saw ahead of them two small English ships; they attacked and captured one of them. Ninety-nine times in a hundred this capture would not have been of great importance, but once again this was the hundredth time. Hawkins had imprudently told his officers that their first objective was Puerto Rico. The rumor had spread through the ships. The five fast frigates discovered the purpose of the expedition and made full speed to warn the governor there.

Drake realized instantly the full implications of this disastrous news; a surprise attack was now impossible, yet it might still be possible to attack before the defenses of the town were completely organized. Only one course was open—to attack at once. Hawkins, however, opposed this plan. He insisted that the ships must be watered first and the batteries placed in position. He was old and he was ill; he was weary rather than wary. He refused to commit his squadron to an action that seemed to him haphazard. At Grand Canary, Drake had got his way and events had proved that Hawkins' advice had been the sounder. Now, when he should have insisted on his point of view, Drake yielded to the older man. Had he lost his confidence as a result of his retreat at Grand Canary? Had the war council lost its faith in him? Did family feeling at the last assert itself? How could he quarrel with a kinsman desperately sick? Drake yielded and the enterprise was doomed. There was a delay of three days in Guadeloupe, then of another day in the Virgin Islands. At Virgin Gorda, in the hope of a surprise, he sailed through a channel that had never been used before and that is known today as Drake's Channel.

During that last day's sail John Hawkins died. It has been suggested that his illness was aggravated by his disagreement with his cousin. Certainly during his last hours he was in a bitter mood. "Sir John Hawkins on his deathbed," so ran the message that eventually reached Elizabeth, "willed me to use the best means I could to acquaint Your Highness with his loyal service and good meaning toward Your Majesty, even to his last breathing. And forasmuch through the perverse and cross-dealings of some in that journey who, preferring their own fancy before his skill would never yield but rather overrule him, whereby he was so discouraged and as himself then said, his heart even broken that he saw no other but danger of ruin likely to ensue of the whole voyage, wherein in some sort he had been a persuader of Your Majesty to hazard as well some of your good ships as also a great quantity of treasure; in regard of the good opinion he thought to be held of his sufficiency, judgment and experience in such action willing to make Your Majesty the best amends his poor ability would then stretch into, in a codicil as a piece of his last will and testament, did bequeath to Your Highness £2,000 if Your Majesty will take it."

In the view of the bitterness, injustice and self-pity of this message, it is possible to acquit Drake of the strictures laid upon him by Hawkins after the action in Vera Cruz.

The death of Hawkins inevitably dispirited the crews. Drake, however, went into action with restored self-confidence, knowing that he was in sole command; but he was soon to realize that the capture of his ship at Dominica was not the only piece of bad luck to intercept him. Before the five frigates had brought the news of his exact destination, a fast ship from Grand Canary had warned the governor of Puerto Rico that Drake was on his way to the West Indies. Philip in the spring had told the governor that Drake was reported to be preparing an expedition, but the governor had not considered that Puerto Rico was a likely object of it, and had taken no particular precautions. If Drake had not visited Grand Canary, the slow ships would not have encountered the fast Spanish frigates, nor would an *avizo* have brought news of his presence in the Atlantic; he would have found San Juan unprepared. But now he found the approaches to the city guarded by guns that had been dismounted from the frigates and sited advantageously along the cliffs. As Drake was dining in his flagship on the eve of attack, a battery opened fire on him and a cannonball crashed into his cabin, killing two of his three chief officers. In that disastrous moment he recognized that the chances of a surprise attack had disappeared.

The tourists who today pour into San Juan by ship and plane would find it difficult to reconstruct the terrain of the action that Drake launched during the next two days, but the walls of the fort of El Morro, with the waves dashing against them, look as formidable now as they did to Drake three and a half centuries ago. San Juan has spread and its lagoon has been enlarged. In Drake's day it was clustered on a bulge of ground, linked to the mainland by a narrow neck. He planned to take his fleet into the harbor and land his men under the covering fire of his guns. But the entrance was very narrow, guarded partially by the anchored frigates. He decided to burn them out; he would have been wiser to cut them out. He made the attack by night, and though eventually he managed to set the biggest of the ships alight, the success was to his disadvantage. The flames lit the scene so clearly that the guns and the muskets of the forts had an excellent target. The English were beaten off with heavy losses.

Next day he made a second attempt, this time by getting to windward of the island and sailing past the forts through the channel, but the governor had anticipated his plan, and the narrow entrance was blocked by sunken ships. Drake was too experienced a sailor not to recognize that his chance had gone. He told his officers not to be despondent. "I will bring you," he said, "to twenty places far more wealthy and easier to be gotten." After all, had not his first plan been an attack on Panama? Once again a triumphant close would settle the account of the disappointments along the way. He was thinking himself back twenty years. He had not realized the extent to which Philip had learned his lessons, how the harbors had been fortified, and how the system of *avisos* guarded those towns against surprise. He did not realize with how much greater speed he would have to strike if he was to achieve success. He did not recognize how much he had lost the capacity for speed in twenty years.

The Drake of thirty would have been horrified by the course followed by the Drake of fifty during the next six weeks. He sailed southward across the Caribbean to where he could pick up the trade wind, but instead of making with crowded sails for Nombre de Dios he made for Rio de la Hacha. He met no opposition but he found a wily governor. The inhabitants had fled to the woods, burying their valuables. Drake demanded a ransom. Negotiations were delayed. The governor played for time; the longer he could keep Drake at anchor the longer would be the time at the disposal of his colleagues along the coast. Finally, when his warnings had been acknowledged, he told Drake that he was at liberty to burn the town. Drake did so, and little good it did him.

He proceeded to Santa Marta. The story was repeated. There was no resistance, there were no inhabitants to plunder. He went on to Nombre de Dios, to discover that it was no longer a large port, that it had been superseded by Porto Bello, twenty miles away, which had a better climate. He was tempted to move westward to this new city, but he was back to his old hunting ground. Surely it would be wiser to strike on a course that was familiar. The old mule trail still led into the jungle, but there was the alternative of the Chagres River, which was partially navigable. A council of war was summoned, and it was decided to attempt the mule train.

A Captain Baskerville, with 750 picked men and a Captain Maynarde as his second-in-command, was assigned the task. Within five days they were back, with depleted forces, the men half-starved, exhausted, their shoes worn through, their spirit broken. The path was half-covered now by jungle; there were no friendly Cimaroons; on the high ridge from which Drake had looked onto the Pacific a stockade had been constructed. There was no way round it through the jungle. Baskerville made three assaults but they were beaten off. During the march thither it rained continuously; the powder was ruined. Baskerville was convinced that this stockade was the first one of a series. He turned his back on Panama. "I am persuaded," Maynarde wrote, "that never army great or small undertook a march through to unknown places so weakly provided and with so small means to help themselves, unless it might be some few going covertly to do some sudden exploit before it was thought of by the enemy and so return unspied."

Why, one wonders, did not Drake make contact with the Cimaroons before he ordered the march? They had been his friends. They could not have forgotten him. They must have been somewhere. They could have given him the information that he needed. They could have lent him guides. He had gone out of his course to attack Grand Canary. He had wasted nineteen days at Rio de la Hacha and Santa Marta, yet at Nombre de Dios he acted without forethought. Had he forgotten how carefully he had planned that earlier raid, how much he had depended then upon the Cimaroons? Yet even with their help, with all that planning, it was only at the third attempt he had succeeded.

His heart was heavy. How was he to face Elizabeth? She had invested seventy thousand pounds in the venture, and he was bringing her back a consignment of pearls worth a few paltry hundreds. But he did not despair. From prisoners and escaped slaves he had learned what he had indeed already suspected, that news of his presence was known throughout the Caribbean; every Spanish port was manned and ready. Drake spread his maps and books upon his cabin table. He must find new worlds to conquer. What of that great city they spoke of in Honduras, and the streets by the Lake of Nicaragua that were paved with gold? He addressed his officers with such confidence that they recovered their lost faith. Which of the two would they prefer, Honduras or Nicaragua? Baskerville leaped to his feet. "Both," he cried. "One after the other. And all too little to content us if we took them."

Drake burned Nombre de Dios, sank a number of small frigates, and confiscated a little gold and some twenty bars of silver. He captured on his way north one of Philip's *avisos*, and learned from it that the towns by the Lake of Nicaragua were impoverished groups of shacks and that the approach to them was strewn with reefs. The wind turned against him and he ran short of food. The Bay of Nicaragua was the unhealthiest area along the coast. The men fell sick; a number of them died, including two senior officers. Drake was sick with dysentery. The wind still blew against him and he decided to return to Porto Bello. He was now so weak that he could not leave his cabin. Maynarde grumbled at him for having brought him out of England on false pretenses. Drake shook his head. "I know no more of the Indies than you do. I never thought a place could be so changed, as it were, from a delicious and pleasant arbor into a vast and desert wilderness."

Never had he encountered such vexatious winds. He was astonished that on this long voyage he had not seen a single ship worth chasing. But sick and enfeebled though he was, his courage did not abate. "God hath many things in store for us, and I know many means to do Her Majesty good service and to make us rich. For we must have gold before we return to England."

But Drake was never again to see the steeples of the churches that he had emptied on that far August morning; his fever mounted and he died as his flagship came within sight of Porto Bello. Baskerville took command, buried the mighty admiral in Nombre de Dios, then returned to Porto Bello. He burned every house of it, but found no treasure to take home. The greatest expedition that England had ever launched had failed. The fleet returned, through the Florida Channel, fighting the Spaniards as they went, more than holding their own.

Philip said, when the tidings of Drake's death reached him, "This should cure my sickness," but his sickness lay beyond the limited knowledge of his day. For a number of years he had been tormented by gout, and now his whole body was afflicted by decay. In contrast to his father, who had been a glutton, he had lived abstemiously in terms of food and drink, but his death was to be a greater torture than any that had been executed by the Holy Office. His last journey, when he was carried in a litter to the Escurial, took seven days because the least jolt caused him the acutest agony. He had sores that would not heal, sores that spread. He could not bear to be touched. His sheets could not be moved. A man exquisitely fastidious in his comportment, he was exposed to the most humiliating revenges of our mortal nature. So that his physical functions could continue, an aperture was cut beneath him in his bed. The stench of the room was nauseating. To the nurses and priests attending him, the process of decomposition appeared to have begun already. But he never complained. His eyes shone; a slot that may still be seen was opened in the wall so that he could watch the service of the Mass. He was existing on a level of the highest spiritual exultation. To his son and heir he said, "I should have wished to spare you this trial, but I want you to see how the monarchies of the earth end. . . . You are young as I too have been. My day draws to a close; the time of yours God alone can see, but it must end like mine."

His agony in the Escurial lasted for forty-seven days. No man has met the approach of death more nobly.

CHAPTER IV

The Brethren of the Coast

Elizabeth survived Philip by five years; the stage was then occupied by lesser mortals. James I, "the wisest fool in Christendom," was a shambles of a man and Philip III was agreeably indolent. Each realized that war between them was wasteful and unrewarding, and James readily guaranteed that his ships would not trade in the New World. Within a few weeks of his accession, Raleigh was in the Tower.

James' treatment of Raleigh provides the best example of the changed atmosphere at the English court. James held Raleigh responsible for the execution of Essex, whom he had thought of as a partisan. Raleigh had been the favorite of the Queen, who had ordered the execution of his mother. Raleigh was the foe of Spain. The trial on a flimsy charge of treason was conducted shamefully and brutally, and Raleigh was condemned to death. The sentence was not, however, carried out, and Raleigh was left in prison.

He was there for thirteen years, but even in prison he was a source of irritation to the King. Henry, the Prince of Wales, a young man of charm and character, who, had he lived, might well have changed the road of history, became his friend. Foreign guests paid calls on Raleigh. The success of Raleigh's *History of the World* nettled James' pride, and he tried to get it suppressed on the grounds that it did not pay sufficient respect to the sanctity of monarchy, but too many copies were in circulation for the fiat to have much effect. The royal vanity was hurt. James was constantly being made to feel that the most significant man in England was not on the throne but in the Tower. He itched to be rid of Raleigh.

He was also desperately anxious for an alliance with Spain. He hoped for a marriage between his son Charles and one of Philip III's daughters. He was abjectly under the influence of the Spanish ambassador, the Count of Goldimar. He was ready to do anything to placate Spain. Spain hated Raleigh, and all the time Raleigh, from the Tower, was pleading for permission to sail once again in search of that golden city which still haunted his imagination. Raleigh was aging fast; he had had a stroke, he shivered with ague, he limped from the wound he had received at Cádiz. Yet during his lonely pacings of the battlements, he yearned that "something ere the end, some work of noble note, might yet be done." Finally James yielded. He did not pardon Raleigh. Raleigh was still "a man dead in law." He was only released so that he could make another attempt upon the gold mines of Guiana. The commission which empowered him to search heathen territories, but forbade him to trespass on the possessions of the Spanish King, did not contain the words "trusty and well-beloved." Raleigh was warned that if he committed any acts of piracy he would be beheaded on his return.

James was a devious creature; his motives were mixed. He was avaricious and would have welcomed gold, yet he hoped for Raleigh's failure and he did his best to ensure that failure by informing Goldimar in detail of his subject's plans. It was impossible to tell at that time where the Spanish possessions began and ended, and indeed two and a half centuries later the Venezuelan boundary line was still in dispute, but it was certain that the Spanish, now that they had been put on their guard, would offer opposition. James had, in fact, hedged his bet. If Raleigh succeeded, his coffers would be full. If Raleigh failed, he would be quit of a tiresome rivalry. He could not lose. Raleigh, no doubt, suspected this, but he was prepared to run the risk; he knew that if he returned with his holds full James would overlook a little letting of Spanish blood.

Raleigh took a year assembling a fleet of seven ships of war and three pinnaces, manned by ninety gentlemen adventurers and a sorry assemblage of 318 cutthroats. He sailed from Plymouth in May 1617. His own ship was ironically called *Destiny*. Luck was consistently against him. Gales drove him back, first into Falmouth, then as far north as Cork. Sickness broke out among his crew. The best summer days were lost and he did not reach the Canaries until early in September. Here the Spanish governor set upon the men whom he had sent ashore to search for supplies and murdered fifteen of them. On the way westward fever struck his fleet. On *Destiny* alone, forty-two men died and Raleigh himself was prostrate for a month. When at last they reached Trinidad on New Year's Eve, he was too sick to join the landing party. He instructed its leader to avoid hostile encounters with the Spaniards and he himself remained aboard. He read, met his old Indian friends, repelled a few feeble Spanish attacks and studied local plants and flowers. While he was thus peacefully employed, the news reached him that the alerted Spaniards had harassed his party, manned a tiny settlement from which they had delivered an attack, and that in the ensuing action his own son had lost his life. This was, he knew, the end.

He could, had he wanted, have taken his ships and men to France, but he preferred to fulfill his promises to the friends who had stood surety for him. He sailed back to Plymouth, to arrest and to a retrial on the original grounds of treason. A few weeks later, James I handed his head to Goldimar on a charger, as a proof of his loyal intentions and good faith.

Philip accepted the gift complacently, as he had accepted his father's legacy—in a way that his father had foreseen. Philip II had created a system that his son could not continue; Philip II had the soul of a bureaucrat, his son had not. It was inevitable that his son should delegate that vast body of paper work to an adviser, to a series of advisers. The fate of Philip II's system depended on the quality of those advisers, and the system itself was built upon a false economy.

With the Silver Fleets arriving regularly twice a year, with the cities of the New World growing in wealth and stature, it was impossible for the Spaniards to recognize that their country was impoverished. At Madrid, in terms of the arts and sciences, Spain's golden century was in flower. Cervantes was writing *Don Quixote*; the plays of Lope de Vega, Calderon, Tirso de Molina, Montalban, Mouto were producing in profusion the plots that were to embellish the French stage a century later. Quevedo was publishing his satires. Philip III himself was a *littérateur* of considerable merit. He and his successor were the patrons of Velazquez, Zurbaran, Murillo and Rebena; they adorned the Escurial with the pictures of Titian and Tintoretto. They bought the pictures of Charles I of England which the commonwealth put upon the market. They added to the library of the Escurial the spoils of the Moroccan Emperor. They built the palace of Buen Retevo. The life of the court under Philip III was so formal that the French ambassador reported jocularly that the King had been killed by the heat of a brazier because the appropriate official was not at hand to move it; yet the life of the court was no less sumptuous for being formal. Ladies of gentle birth walked masked in the streets. There was an ostentatious parade of carriages. The lure of wealth had drawn a large section of the population across the water, and there was no incentive to ambition. The *alcabala*—the tax on every sale—was raised under Philip III from 10 percent to 14 percent, and in addition, a further tax was levied, through a series of custom-houses, on goods in transit. The need for quickly realizable taxation led to the burdening of transactions in food and manufactures, which strangled both agriculture and industry. It is an axiom of colonial administration that the colonies should supply raw materials and that the mother country should supply manufactured goods in return, but Spain did not produce manufactured goods. She had to obtain them from abroad. She insisted that no ships other than Spanish should deal with the Spanish colonies. The centralization of this commerce in Seville enormously increased the cost of goods to the colonists; it is not surprising that the colonists welcomed the Dutch, British and French privateers who could supply them not only with manufactured goods but also slaves at a much smaller cost. Gold and silver flowed continuously across the Atlantic, but very little of it reached the Spanish treasury.

During the sixteenth century the population of Spain was reduced by half, by wars and emigration. In Philip III's reign it was further reduced by the expulsion of the remaining *Moriscos* from Andalusia. There were political reasons for this step. The *Moriscos'* sympathies lay across the Mediterranean; but nonetheless their removal was a liability. They were mainly employed in agriculture, since other professions were barred to them. Andalusia is one of the most fertile territories in the country, and Spain could not afford the loss of so many peasants.

Step by step during the seventeenth century Spain's power diminished. She could no longer retain her hold on her possessions. Philip III made a truce with the Dutch Protestants; his son recognized their independence. In 1643 at the battle of Rocroi, the dreaded Spanish infantry was routed by the French; the Spanish square, the solid phalanx of pikemen, had been considered invincible, but Condé proved that once it was broken it was helpless. Spain's prestige, however, still stood high. It was as hard for Europe as for Spain to recognize that bullion was not necessarily wealth. Madrid basked in a florid luxuriance. The Spanish heart was rigid still with pride, even though it had lost faith in pretensions which it could not enforce. Spain sustained her self-importance with a sulky opulence and with contempt for labor; across the water, the hardier northerner took what she could not hold.

Spain's needs in the Caribbean were now confined. She needed fortified bastions for her treasure fleets, but she had no use for the smaller islands. She considered them as hers, but she could not enforce her claim to them. She could not be bothered to occupy the western section of Hispaniola. It was mainly populated now by wild horses and the descendants of the bloodhounds that had been imported to chase the resistant Indians.

Puerto Rico also was neglected. It had been discovered on Columbus' second voyage, and when Ponce de Leon sailed into San Juan Harbor he exclaimed, "*Que puerto rico*" ("What a rich port"), and the name stuck.

Juan Ponce de Leon was a native of Santervas de Campos in Leon. He served for fifteen years as a shield bearer to a Knight Commander in the Moorish Wars, and he fought so well against the Indians that Ovando made him a captain and sent him to prospect the area round San Juan, where he was subsequently installed as the island's first governor. His name is remembered for his discovery of Florida, for his vain quest for the fountain of eternal youth, and also because of his ruthless gallantry in battle. With a hundred men he routed a force of five or six thousand Indians. His crossbowmen were particularly effective from behind an entrenched camp. The Spaniards, who were wounded, exhausted and hungry, wanted to attack the Indians and get it over, but Ponce would not let them. He told his best archers to wait till the chief who wore a disc of gold round his neck came within range. As soon as he did, he was shot. The Indians at once retreated, and armed resistance was at an end.

The Indians were distributed among the conquerors. But Ponce de Leon never succeeded in subduing the Caribs, and there were not enough troops available to pacify Puerto Rico. The Spaniards quarreled among themselves. The islanders took to the hills; the Caribs constantly raided the southern and eastern sections of the island. Smallpox struck the island; there was a plague of ants. The news of Cortés' achievements in Mexico attracted the adventurous. The death penalty was imposed on the Spaniards who tried to leave the island, but there was no adequate authority to implement the order. The island became a jungle. There were a hundred or so stone houses in San Juan, but in 1536, crown officers were writing that no ship from the Peninsular had entered its port for two years. Negroes and Indians escaped into the hills, from which they conducted raids upon their former masters, who abandoned the search for gold and developed agriculture in a desultory fashion. The first settlement at San Germán disintegrated and disappeared. Probably San Juan would

have, too, if the French corsairs had known that it was undefended.
When at last desultory attacks from English and French privateers
forced Spain to defend it, the King made an assignment on the royal
treasury of Mexico for nearly half a million pesos. This levy—a *situados*—continued till the Mexican revolution. Eventually, in 1600,
San Juan became a penal settlement, a presidio with four hundred
inhabitants, black, white and mongrel. Spain neglected Puerto
Rico, but she had even less use for the Lesser Antilles, the group
of islands that curved, green and mountainous and fertile, from the
tip of Florida to South America. They held no gold or silver, and the
Caribs were fierce and hostile. No race, indeed, could have been more
different from the gentle Arawaks. Most of our knowledge of it comes
to us from Père Labat, the French priest who spent a dozen years
in the islands at the end of the seventeenth century. The Caribs,
according to him, were tall and brown, with shining, long black hair
which they dressed carefully every day and only cut short when they
were in mourning. Eight days after its birth, a child's ears, lower lip
and the cartilage between the nostrils were pierced, strings passed
through them and pendants attached. The Arawaks flattened the
heads of their children with boards, but it was the Carib mother who
was responsible for this operation. Seated during the day, she would
put one of the child's legs on one of her thighs with its head on the
other thigh. When the child was asleep she would open her right
hand and put it on the child's forehead. Leaning her left elbow on
it, she would recline her head against it. She would often sleep this
way.

The Caribs attached great importance to personal appearance. They
scarred their cheeks with deep incisions which they painted black.
They inscribed black and white circles round their eyes. They were
beardless, removing all superfluous hair. In the perforated dividing
cartilage of their nostrils they inserted a fishbone or piece of tortoise-
shell. The teeth of their dead enemies provided bangles for their arms
and ankles; shinbones supplied them with arrowheads. Their children were taught the use of the bow and arrow by having their food
suspended out of reach from trees and having to go hungry till they
could shoot it down. When a male child was born, he was sprinkled
with drops of his father's blood. The father suffered considerably
during the ceremony by which this blood was produced, but he submitted stoically, believing that the courage he displayed would be
transmitted to his son. A young man suffered an extremely painful
initiation ceremony before he was admitted to the rights of manhood.

He was gashed with the saw-like leaves of the pineapple; it was called "being passed by the lances." A man who wished to lead his fellows into battle had to endure even more excruciating tests, suffocation being one of them. The courageous and successful warrior was highly honored. He could change his name, taking that of the most formidable enemy who had fallen by his hand. His countrymen offered for his choice the most beautiful of their daughters. Polygamy existed as a status symbol. Wives took their turn by the month in polygamous households. Pregnant wives did not have marital relations with their husbands. Marital fidelity was axiomatic. According to Rochefort, there was no punishment for adultery because the crime was unknown. When the white man introduced adultery, the injured husband became his own avenger. Men could desert wives, but wives could not desert their husbands.

In times of peace there was no exercise of authority, no ruled or rulers. The Caribs set great store by independence. There was no division of land, everyone cultivating as much land as he needed. Theft was considered a great crime, and was rarely committed. There were no judges; there was no law; private property did not exist. They understood exchange, but not the value of articles. The French at one time started a war with them, because they took a hammock in exchange for pork. The men ate their meals in common, the women feeding apart. They were formal in their social observances. They showed great hospitality to strangers, and had their own ways of showing a stranger how fully he might partake of that hospitality. If the cassava bread was unfolded he could eat as much as he liked, but if it was folded he was expected to leave some. When Caribs met each other after a separation, they embraced, their heads on each other's shoulders, one knee on the ground. They had three different languages—one for women among themselves, one for general use, and a third which was exclusively masculine and was employed only when the men were engaged in serious discussions. The men learned the women's language but never deigned to use it. Labat believed that the women's language was Arawak in origin, the female prisoners after their menfolk had been slaughtered continuing to talk among themselves in their familiar tongue. But this is guesswork. Labat's guesses were not always accurate. He believed, for instance, that the Caribs originally came from Florida. It is now generally held that they came from South America. Labat also doubted if they were cannibals. He believed that they cooked the limbs of their dead enemies so that they could preserve them as trophies. On this point no one is in agreement with him.

Fighting was their passion. "Frown on a Carib and you must fight him," so the legend ran. "Fight him and you must kill him or be killed." They brought oystershells from South America, which they crushed into a powder for the carvings on their clubs. Their clubs were so heavy that they sank in water. They never needed to force volunteers to battle. When the men set out to battle they took one woman with them, to cook for them, paint them and comb their hair. In Guadeloupe, when an early governor saw the Caribs send away their women he guessed that they were preparing to attack. They rarely attacked at night, for fear that they would kill each other. They waited till dawn, when they delivered themselves of a grisly shriek before they charged. They had few relaxations when they were not fighting, beyond wrestling in their own style, without body holds, grasping each other by the arm above the elbow and striving to throw the other by means of a jolt. They were idle. They are reported to have had melancholy dispositions.

They were punctilious about what they ate. They made stews out of tomalley; crabs were their favorite delicacy; certain foods, such as eels, turtles, Mexican hogs and sea cows, they avoided as unclean. They did not eat poultry or cattle. They disliked fat and made their elderly male prisoners starve before they killed them. At feasts they would rub their bodies with gum from the trees and fix feathers into it. They had a kind of beer which they brewed from trees, and they fermented fruit juice. Like the Romans, they forced themselves to vomit so that they could consume more. Calabashes served as crockery. They had their gardens in the hills, where they fished for tadpoles, crayfish and small snails. Manioc was their staple diet. They cooked in manioc water. They possessed the art of baking clay, and the ruins of their kilns were found in Barbados during the seventeenth century. When they drew their bows they had three arrows in their fingers. The Arawaks did not at first believe a Spaniard could die. A half-breed, to prove that they were mortal, drowned one. But not until he began to putrefy did the Arawaks believe that he was dead. The Caribs had no such illusions.

Though they believed in an afterlife, they were filled with remorse at death. The corpse was painted red, with the hair carefully arranged; it was then wrapped in a cotton hammock; bread and wine were buried with it, and a fire was set round the grave. At the end of a year, the body was uncovered and earth was thrown upon it and trampled down. The mourners drank for twenty-four hours.

Labat said that they were naked but modest, hiding the "shameful parts," but not all the witnesses are agreed on this. Bryan Edwards notes that clothing was not considered necessary to personal comfort in a climate where there was no winter, adding that women on reaching the age of puberty wore a half boot made of cotton, a privilege that was denied to women who had been captured in war. They had ornaments but that was all. To them, hair was the greatest beauty, and they mocked bald men. They had as much culture as was necessary for their way of life. Christopher Columbus' men saw a canoe for the first time when they landed in Hispaniola, and the French learned the art of the canoe in Guadeloupe. The Caribs could count as far as they needed, up to five but no further. To express ten they would say, "All the fingers." To express twenty, "All the fingers and all the toes." They had four colors—yellow, red, black and white. They had no organized religion. Their priests were witch doctors. They knew the right remedy for their own complaints. When Drake on his last voyage put into Dominica, fever was raging in his ships; three hundred men had died, but the Caribs provided a cure. There are still doubts of the origin of syphilis, which many maintain was brought back to Europe after Columbus' first voyage; there is evidence that the Caribs had a cure for yaws, a form of gonorrhea, out of sandalwood.

In only one island today can you find any survival of the Caribs. On the windward coast of Dominica there is a Carib reservation. Their faces have a Mongolian cast, their black hair is straight, their lips are soft and full, their cheeks less brown than yellow.

They have abandoned their old language. Nearly all of them are Roman Catholics. They enjoy cricket. Once they built a special kind of cabin, with a second floor under the roof, on which they slept, but they have now adopted the conventional style. They are very pacific. The corporal in charge of the local police post has little trouble with them. They enjoy their rum as much as the next man does, but they keep their squabbles to themselves. When a Carib feels the need to "let off steam," he calls a friend across and exchanges a couple of punches with him, without rancor or ill temper. That, and no more than that, and he feels a great deal better.

They still make canoes. I saw one under construction. Long and narrow, scooped from a single trunk, it was being dried over a fire, with the inside filled with boulders to prevent the wood from shrinking. I also saw a local craftsman at work on one of the baskets that are in universal use throughout the island. They are made in two layers, with large leaves arranged between to make them waterproof. The cover is decorated by the weaving of different-colored fibers. Their only disadvantage to the northerner is the weakness of the handle, but this is no disadvantage to the islander, who carries his luggage on his head. I tried to talk to the man who made it, but he spoke only the local patois. I was only a little more successful with the councilor to whom the corporal introduced me. A short, dapper little man with a drooping black mustache, he looked like a Maupassant character out of the original Albin Michel edition. He spoke some English, and I could understand what he said to me, but his vocabulary was small and I could not be sure that he was understanding what I said. He was a courtly, gracious man who appeared to be in agreement with me. His replies, however, rarely bore much relation to my original enquiries.

It was difficult to realize that the ancestors of this quiet man were cannibals, but it is equally difficult to reconstruct their life from the fragmentary and prejudiced accounts that have come to us from those who arrived in their territory with the intention of enslaving them. "Our knowledge of them," wrote Bryan Edwards, "is limited within a narrow circle. Of a people engaged in perpetual warfare, hunted from island to island by revenge and rapacity, few opportunities could have offered, even to those who might have been qualified for such researches, of investigating the natural dispositions and habitual customs with minuteness and precision. Neither indeed could a just estimate have been formed of their national character from the manners of such of them as were at length subjugated to the European yoke; for they lost together with their freedom many of their original characteristics, and at last even the desire of acting from the impulse of their own minds."

Rochefort wrote: "We discern a wonderful change in the dispositions and habits of the Caribs. In some respects we have enlightened, in others, to our shame be it spoken, we have corrupted them. An old Carib once addressed one of our planters on this subject. 'Our people,' he complained, 'are become almost as bad as yours. We are so much altered since you came among us that we hardly know ourselves, and we think it is owing to so melancholy a change that hurricanes are more frequent than they were formerly. It is the evil spirit who has done all this; he has taken our best lands from us and given us up to the dominion of the Christians.'"

Since there were no precious metals in the Lesser Antilles, the Spaniards had no inducement to undertake the subjugation of this warlike race, but there were others, French, English, Dutch, to whom the possibilities of the Caribbean were an irresistible magnet and who were not to be so easily deterred.

The first settlements took place between 1625 and 1635. The French were the first in the field, in colonization as in piracy, and they had the pick of the islands—Martinique, Dominica, Guadeloupe, St. Lucia, Grenada; and even in those islands that have changed their allegiance since, the French influence remains. Dominica and St. Lucia are still predominantly Catholic, and the bush peasants speak a patois that contains more French than English words. The Dutch and English took the islands which the French did not want. The Dutch got Curaçao, which was excellently situated for trade with the northern coast of South America; they also had Saba and St. Eustatius. England took Antigua, Montserrat and Barbados, a flat dry island which they found uninhabited except by some pigs which had been left there by the Portuguese. Two islands were in dispute; St. Martin between the French and Dutch, St. Kitts between the French and English. St. Kitts, after many battles, passed eventually into British hands, but St. Martin has continued to be divided. At a certain point in its history it was decided to send a Frenchman and a Dutchman walking round the island in opposite directions; the point at which they met should mark the boundary between the two nationalities.

The second quarter of the seventeenth century was a period of experiment and establishment. England, France and Holland were actively concerned with their home affairs; they saw colonial problems in terms of the national interest. They did not know how important the West Indies were to prove. The imperial pattern of colonization had not yet grown clear to them. Men of a classical education, they were aware of the nature of the Pax Romana and of the system of tributary tribes and nations that had maintained the vast edifice of its administration, but they did not yet see themselves as inheritors of that system.

The colonization of the Caribbean was at this time a haphazard day-to-day affair; the colonists were not even certain of their tenure. Spain still felt it had a right to all territory west of the line. She raided St. Kitts, for instance, in the early days of its colonization by the French and British, massacred a large number of the colonists, and drove others to seek shelter in Antigua and Montserrat, but she established no settlement to take their place, and the refugees returned. The same thing happened later in Hispaniola, but it soon became apparent that Spain would not bother to attack ports that could defend themselves. She had enough concerns of her own. Well-defended colonies were immune except during the periods when their mother countries were at war, but this was not so serious a problem, since European countries tended to confine their campaigns to their own frontiers.

During the sixteenth century the waters "beyond the lines"—south of Cancer, west of the meridian of the Azores—had always been independent of legislation. Monarchs had officially disowned their subjects, although they had given them their tacit approval and even invested money in their enterprises. There had been always a state of war in the Caribbean. It was not till the eighteenth century that the islands became so rich and prosperous as to be determinant factors in European foreign policy. They were a sideshow in the early years of the seventeenth century, minor investments that might prove valuable one day. In the meantime, it was useful to own a place where rebel prisoners could be sent and loyal subjects could be rewarded with grants of land.

The French were the first to undertake serious colonization, first with the Company of St. Christophe, which was changed by Richelieu to the Company of the Islands of Amerique, and which undertook the colonization not only of Martinique but also of Guadeloupe, which the Spaniards had finally decided to relinquish because of the fierceness of the Caribs. The company promised to do its best to convert the heathen, and undertook to introduce four thousand white colonists of mixed sexes. The King would appoint the governors. The company was also authorized to colonize any island unoccupied by a Christian prince. That was in 1635; it was not for thirty years that an organized regulation of colonial life and trade was undertaken. Colbert was then Louis XIV's Chancellor of the Exchequer, and history has confirmed his claim to be reckoned one of the great economists. He made mistakes, one of his chief being to regard all men as his enemies, and in consequence to consider that the strength of a country could be assessed by the poverty of its neighbors. He did not envisage the possibility of a universal prosperity, with countries exchanging their own goods. "We have no need of anybody and our neighbors have need of us"—that was his maxim. One of the most important functions of peace was in his

eyes the establishment of trade. He was anxious to create new industries. France must not seek from foreigners the goods which were
essential to her existence. He revived the cloth trade, bringing over a
Dutch expert to Abbeville. At the Gobelins in Paris, under the direction of Lebrun, and at Beauvais, he ordered the creation of tapestries
superior to the Flemish ones. He brought Venetian workers for the
glass factories of St.-Gobain and Tourlaville. He forbade the importation of the Venetian point with which the great lords and ladies
trimmed their dresses; lace was to be made all over France. The manufacture of soap, tin, arms and silk provided work for thousands who
had been on the edge of starvation. The Habsburgs had impoverished
Spain by destroying local industries. Colbert did not repeat their mistake. The Habsburgs had restricted local trade by the sales tax. Colbert suppressed a number of inland duties. Isabella had realized the
necessity of establishing local trade, but her successors had followed a different practice. Isabella recognized that the roads were so
bad because mules were so common, and she made it a criminal
offense to ride a mule. But her successors had allowed her law to pass
into desuetude. Colbert put the roads in order.

He was a ruthless man. When he needed sailors for his galleys he
instructed judges to condemn minor culprits to them. Madame de
Sevigné described him as being like the North Star, "cold but stead-
fast." He knew what he wanted, and he devised schemes for bringing about the fulfillment of his plans. He was alarmed by the power
of the Dutch navy and the weakness of the French. Most of the
trade with Martinique and Guadeloupe was carried in Dutch bottoms. This Colbert forbade, pleading as an excuse that a pest was
raging in Amsterdam. He sent a squadron of French ships to patrol
the Caribbean. He ordered his justices that in all cases where there
was any doubt, the case must go against the foreigner. He armed
the Caribs and incited them to attack the Dutch, who, he said, must
lose the habit of West Indian trade. A few years later he opened a
factory on the Guinea coast.

The colonists were indignant. They found themselves without the
necessities of existence. They were short of slaves; there were not
enough French ships to bring them the goods they needed; but Colbert was adamant. The colonist must be prepared to suffer in the
ultimate interests of France. He did not care if the womenfolk were
short of shoes. Eventually they would get their reward. In his view,
as in that of most contemporary European administrators, colonies
existed solely for the benefit of the mother country. He refused, for

instance, to allow the planters to barter their rum in Boston for the salt meat and livestock that they badly needed, because the trade would be of advantage to a rival's colonies. At the same time, he would not allow rum to be sold in France because it might prove more popular than brandy. Bordeaux exported wine, brandy, slaves, flour, salt beef in return for sugar and small quantities of indigo, ginger, cotton, tobacco, hides. Bordeaux, Nantes and La Rochelle were the ports used in France for the Caribbean trade, the Norman and Breton ports being endangered by European wars. Up to a point, tobacco was an important export and served as currency. But overproduction sent down the price. Colbert made tobacco a state monopoly. This ruined the tobacco trade in the French West Indian colonies, but it helped the sugar industry. Colbert organized imports so that each colony should make its own contribution. The heavy duties imposed made it very difficult to make any profit. When the islands turned to the cultivation of sugar, sugar was refined in Holland. Colbert stopped this and started a refining industry in France. He also allowed refineries to be built in the islands, but not on such a scale as would damage the refineries in France. The colonists were often in a desperate state. It was more profitable to grow sugar than to raise food, but they had to have salt beef. A three-cornered trade with Canada was a yearlong operation, and the Boston market was closed to them. The slaves, they complained, could not support long hours in the sun on a diet of yams, potatoes and cassava bread. They needed food, livestock, staves and lumber, which they could have obtained from New England in return for rum and molasses, but this Colbert forbade.

Colbert, up to a point, made the same mistake that Philip II did of overconcentrating the trade of the West Indies. He insisted, for example, that Irish beef should be transshipped at Nantes; he made goods more expensive for the planters than they need have been; he checked the prosperity of the islands by preventing foreign traders from importing the goods which France did not herself produce. The population of the islands did not increase as rapidly as it might have done. He was no doubt right in being more interested in the Far East trade, and the Caribbean company that he had founded did, in fact, go into bankruptcy, so that finally the islands were returned to the King. At the same time, he had a vision which Charles V and Philip II never had had, of a self-supporting, self-sufficient colonial empire. Realizing that Temperate Zone colonies produced the same articles that Europe did, he recognized the value of the West Indies as a middleman. He delayed the advancement of Guadeloupe and Martinique, but their ultimate prosperity was largely due to him; as also was the efficiency and power of the French marine. In 1664 there was not a French ship trading with the islands; ten years later there were over 130, and in 1683 there were three hundred. He was a great man.

The restrictions that he placed upon his colonists undoubtedly encouraged smuggling, and it was during his period of rule that there flourished in the Caribbean that wild group of lawless men known as the Brethren of the Coast, who, from their strongholds in Jamaica and Hispaniola, plundered the trade of the area. These men were known as buccaneers, an anglicized version of the French word *boucanier*, meaning one who cures meat over an open fire by the *boucan* process. The French, on the other hand, adapted the English word "freebooter" into *filbustier*, which later became reanglicized as "filibuster." There are those, however, who maintain that the word comes from the Spanish *filibote* (fee-lee-bote), English flyboat, a small, swift sailing vessel with a large mainsail that could pursue merchantmen in the open sea, but avoid men-of-war in the shoals and shallows.

They were, these men, the riffraff of seven nations and the seven seas; they were homeless, rootless, with families long since forgotten. They were mutineers, escaped prisoners, shipwrecked pirates; they had no country, they owed no allegiance to anyone except themselves. They settled originally in the western section of Hispaniola. Potentially one of the richest islands in the Caribbean, it had been abandoned by the Spaniards in their quest for gold. The Indian population had been reduced to a few thousands; only a meager number of scattered plantations and villages remained, and the untamed jungle was infested by wild horses, the descendants of the dogs whom the Spaniards had brought out to chase the Indians, and herds of pigs and oxen. The Spaniards had tried to reduce the menace of the dogs by strewing the savannahs with the carcasses of poisoned horses, but the horses were outnumbered by the hounds. It was here that the refugees of tyranny made their homes.

They had first come here from St. Kitts, whence they had been expelled by the Spanish raid. At the beginning their life was relatively pacific. They had plenty to eat, they enjoyed a free and easy existence; they enjoyed hunting, and they went out in parties of five or six, with their muskets. They chose pork for their staple diet. They cut the meat in long strips and laid it over open fires (*boucans*).

Gratings were constructed of green sticks, a form of barbecue; the meat was exposed to the smoke and saturated with the fat, bones and offal of the carcass and the trimmings of the hides. This method of cooking left the meat with a bright red color and gave it an appetizing flavor, preferable in that damp climate to the jerked beef that was prepared in Chile, Peru and on the River Plate by drying the meat in the sun.

The buccaneers might have been well enough content to lead their life in the bush if they had been left alone. They lived so prosperously, indeed, that the French governor-general of St. Kitts decided to change his seat of government to Tortuga, an island off the north coast of Hispaniola, in 1634, the year after the colonization of Guadeloupe and Martinique had started. Four years later the Spanish attacked Tortuga and cleared out its inhabitants. It was the last gesture of the old Spanish imperialism, but it lit a flame of wrath that was to harry the Caribbean for thirty years.

The Spaniards could not hold what they had taken. Within a few months the buccaneers had returned, this time in a far from pacific mood. They had been twice dispossessed by the Spaniards; they were ready for revenge, and they were to be joined in the months immediately following by sea beggars—*gueux de la mer*—from the revolted Netherlands, by French Huguenots, and by traders whose ships had been intercepted by the Spanish revenue cruisers, the *guarda costas*, who regarded every foreign ship as contraband; all of these new arrivals were to have a hatred of Spain as one of their most insistent instincts. They were not only bent on self-support, on mere subsistence. They were set on plunder.

They were a motley crew, from many stocks, from many ways of life, but they managed to achieve in their exile an indistinguishable similarity of appearance. They wore a common uniform, a small close-fitting cap, a jacket of cloth with breeches that came halfway to their knees. One had to look carefully to tell whether this garment was of cloth, so stained was it with blood. They wore a belt, set with a bayonet and four knives. There were few of them that were taller than their musket. On their feet, like the Indians, they wore moccasins, made out of oxhide or pigskin. As soon as the animal was dead they would cut away the skin that had covered it. Setting the big toe where the knee had been, they would bind it with a sinew. The rest of it was taken a few inches above the heel and tied there till the skin had dried, when, having taken the impress of the man's foot, it would keep its shape.

They had neither family nor children. There was scarcely a woman on the island. Each was constrained to take one of his fellows to himself, to help him in the ordinary business of life, to tend him when he was sick. They lived together, sharing their possessions; he who lived the longer inherited them. They divided their work. The one would hunt, while the other would protect the hut and cook.

Food was plentiful in Tortuga. There was a profusion of fruit, of yams, pineapples and bananas, and on the mainland there were herds of wild boar, and flocks of pigeons which in certain seasons of the year were admirable but after the season, because they fed on a bitter seed, were as rough as gall upon the palate. They sold beef to home-bound vessels.

Every so often boredom, lack of money and a need of adventure and revenge would send them out to sea. Their expeditions were carefully planned. They held a meeting to decide when they should attack, to raise funds and to elect officers who would be allowed an extra share of the plunder.

In spite of their lawlessness, the Brethren of the Coast showed in regard to one another a very precise observance of the law. Their motto was "no prey, no pay." The articles of their code established the principle of equality. Each brother was entitled to a vote on matters of policy and to an equal share of the plunder. An exact scale of penalties was agreed upon. Death was the punishment for the brother who brought a woman in disguise on board. Whoever stole from a comrade had his ears and his nose slit and was disembarked on the handiest strip of beach with no other provisions than a fusee, some shot, a bottle of gunpowder and a bottle of water.

In the same spirit, indemnities were fixed. For the loss of a right arm a brother was recompensed with six hundred piasters or six slaves. A left arm or a right leg was valued at five hundred piasters. A finger or a toe was worth one slave. The hauling down of the flag on a hostile ship was rewarded with fifty piasters, and there were such innumerable minor bounties as the five-piaster reward for the throwing of a hand grenade over the walls of a besieged fort.

There was little variety in the general strategy of a raid. There was a privateer to be boarded; a town to be descended on; a garrison to be put to the sword; churches to be plundered; cellars to be emptied; girls to be ravished; old men to be tortured till they divulged the hiding places of their neighbors' gold; a final ransom to be levied; then, with the holds full, a sailing back to the taverns of Cayon.

Thus it went on, month after month, with every township, every harbor as frightened of this "scourge of the West Indies" as they had been of *El Draqui* a century before.

Among the recruits to this strange brotherhood was a type of adventurer to whom reference has not yet been made, the bondman, the indented man, the *engagé*. He was a free man of white skin with no record of crime who signed on for three years' service in return for his passage out, his board and keep and clothing. He was in a very difficult position. The planter was resolved to make all the possible profit out of him, well aware that the margin of profit was very small. For the first months of his apprenticeship an *engagé* would be of little use. He would be learning his job and getting acclimatized to new conditions. He was of less value than a slave, so that a slave's health and welfare were of greater concern to the planter; a lifetime's service was set in the balance against three years'. In the early years these bondmen had been useful as house servants, and when tobacco was the chief crop in St. Kitts they had worked on the plantations. But when sugar supplanted tobacco their value dropped; they were unequal to the hard work of the canefields. Colbert tried to encourage the sailing of indentured servants; he wanted to maintain the proportion of white to black. Prescient here, as in so much else, he visualized the necessity of a buffer state, loyal to the crown, between the white oligarchy and the slaves, but economic necessity was too strong. Imported Negroes alone were useful in the canefields, and in 1674, on the insistence of the planters, the importation of white "indented labor" was forbidden in the French islands. But at the time when the Brethren of the Coast were gathering in Tortuga, the grievances of the indented man were deep and bitter. He had been brought out under false pretenses. His position was worse than that of a slave. In British colonies, an escaped bondman who was recaptured had branded on his forehead the letters FT—Fugitive Traitor. Their recruitment by the merchants of Dieppe, Le Havre, St. Malo, Brest and La Rochelle was in fact parallel in spirit to the slave trade of the Guinea coast; and in the same way that the African traders forced into the slavers those who had been sold into captivity, so did the merchants find their cargo among the destitute penniless men, unemployed servants, peasants weary of hard conditions, artisans who saw no hope of becoming masters, women who could not find a husband. The women were assured that when they did find a husband they would be released from their engagement; the men were promised a property on the expiry of their service. The terms of contract stipulated the standard of clothes, food, lodging and pay that would be provided. In the early days, when there had been an immediate need for artisans and qualified agriculturists, the system had not worked badly, but the rapacity of the colonists, the low value that was then set on human life, and the impossibility of control soon set it in decline.

The rules for the indented man were very strict. He began to work a quarter of an hour after sunrise; he stayed at his work until a quarter of an hour after sunset. He had two hours off for lunch. He could not leave his billet without his master's permission. Captains of ships could not take him on board. He could not work for another master. He had no remedy against ill-treatment. His cabin was put near the slave quarters. Sometimes he had to share his cabin with a slave. He was dressed poorly. He was thrashed, as the slaves were. It is not surprising that many of them escaped, that some of these fugitives joined the Brethren of the Coast. Among them was a Dutchman, John Alexander Esquemeling, who sailed from Le Havre in May 1666 as a servant of the West India Company of France, and to whom we are indebted for most of our knowledge of this wild fraternity.

Esquemeling sailed, as was the custom of the time, under a convoy, guarded by a man-of-war with twenty-seven guns and a crew of 250. Two of the conducted ships were bound for Senegal, five for the Lesser Antilles, Martinique and her dependencies; his own ship was due at Tortuga. She arrived without the loss of a single man, but there his good fortune ended. The Company of the West Indies was in such grievous financial straits that it had recalled its factors, instructing them to sell at whatever price they could raise such property as they possessed. Esquemeling, as a servant of the company, was regarded as one of its assets, and he found himself sold to the "most cruel tyrant and perfidious man that was ever born of woman," who was then governor, or rather lieutenant general, of that island. "This man treated me," he wrote, "with all the hard usages imaginable, even with that of hunger, with which I thought I should have perished inevitably, withal he was willing to let me buy my freedom and liberty but not under the rate of three hundred pieces of eight, I not being master of one at that time in the whole world. At last, through the manifold miseries I endured, as also affliction of mind, I was thrown into a dangerous fit of sickness. This misfortune, being added to the rest of my calamities, was the cause of my happiness.

For my wicked master, seeing my condition, began to fear lest he should lose his monies with my life. Hereupon he sold me to a surgeon for the price of seventy pieces of eight. Being in the hands of this second master, I began soon after to recover my health through the good usage I received from him, as being much more humane and civil than that of my first patron. He gave me both clothes and very good food and after I had served him but one year he offered me my liberty, with only this condition, that I should pay him one hundred pieces of eight when I was in a capacity of wealth to do so."

We do not know whether he ever did repay this debt, but he took the most effective steps to enable himself to do so; he enrolled with the Brethren of the Coast. He was, he said, received "with common consent both of the superior and vulgar sort." He was the more welcome because his second master was a surgeon, and he had received from him not only kindness, but elementary instruction in medicine that would be highly valuable to a group of pirates. It was in this capacity that he was of particular use to Henry Morgan, the most famous of all pirates, who eventually became a legitimate administrator and, as governor of Jamaica, was knighted by Charles II.

Morgan was the son of a Welsh farmer; his father was not a poor man, but the life of the fields held no attraction for him. As a boy he accepted the lure of the Spanish Main and signed on as a bondman in Barbados. On the voyage out, as the youngest sailor, he was, in order to start the week well, flogged every Monday morning at the mast. Barbados is a small island, for the most part flat; its climate is dry and healthy, so dry that at this time it had no waterpower and its headmills were worked by horses. Its soil is very fertile. It is admirably suited for the sugar crop. It is today the most densely populated territory in the world. No flag other than that of Britain has flown from its mastheads. It was protected so effectively by the trade wind that no French fleet from Martinique or Guadeloupe was ever able to launch an attack against it. Its loyalty to the British crown is constant. After the execution of Charles I, it refused to acknowledge the commonwealth, and declared Charles II King. It has produced some of the world's greatest cricketers.

Morgan served seven years in Barbados, then, on having earned his freedom, crossed to Jamaica, which had been captured by Cromwell from the Spaniards.

The capture of Jamaica was one of the corollaries to the Civil War. During the reigns of James I and Charles I, relatively cordial relations had been maintained with Madrid, but Cromwell, an intolerant Protestant, saw Spain, as Drake had done, as the eternal enemy. When the Spanish ambassador discussed with him the possibility of a treaty, Cromwell told him that the first step to a treaty must be free trading in the New World and the freedom of British sailors from the Inquisition. The ambassador replied that to ask a liberty from the Inquisition and free sailing in the West Indies was to ask his master's two eyes, and that nothing could be done on those points. In accordance with the practice of former times, Cromwell decided on appropriate action. He realized the importance of the Caribbean, and sent two of his admirals, Penn and Venables, to capture Hispaniola; they failed, but captured instead Jamaica, which the Spaniards had occupied very lightly.

Of the colonists there, Bryan Edwards was to write: "They possessed nothing of the elegancies of life nor were they acquainted even with many of those gratifications which, in civilized states, are considered necessary to the comfort and conveniency of it. They were neither polished by social intercourse nor improved by education, but passed their days in gloomy languor, enfeebled by sloth and depressed by poverty. Having at the same time but little or no connection with Europe, nor the means of sending their children thither for education, they had been for many years in a state of progressive degeneracy and would probably, in a short time, have expiated the guilt of their ancestors by falling victims themselves to the vengeance of their slaves."

They had nothing to offer the few ships that stopped at their ports but provisions, cocoa, hog's lard and hides, in return for manufactured European articles.

Bryan Edwards had the typical English distrust of Spain, yet he had nothing but reprobation for the ruthless conditions of surrender that Venables inflicted on the Spanish settlers. They were ordered to hand over their slaves and property and leave the island. They pleaded that they had been born there, that they had neither relations, friends nor country elsewhere, declaring that they would rather perish in the woods than beg their bread on a foreign soil. But their prayers were in vain, and many of them sought shelter in Cuba, the first substantial immigration thither.

In addition to their ill-treatment of the Spaniards, Penn and Venables foolishly devastated the provision grounds and killed the cattle, leaving themselves very little to eat. On their return to England they were imprisoned for their failure in Hispaniola, but Jamaica was to prove more lastingly valuable to England than Hispaniola was to Spain and France.

Cromwell also realized the use of the colonies as an alternative to the cost of maintaining undesirable nationals in prison. He sent to Barbados after the Battle of Worcester a large number of Scottish prisoners who, degenerating into a colony of poor whites, were later to be known as Redlegs. He also sent a number of Irish to Montserrat, and the shamrock is still on the flag that flies from its Government House. A little later he ordered the Scottish government to apprehend all vagrants for transportation. In Grenada today there is a curious little colony of near-whites, many of them flaunting Scottish surnames.

When Henry Morgan reached Jamaica, the island was in the early days of its colonization, and its capital, Port Royal, which was later engulfed in an earthquake, was the most lawless city in the Antilles. It was here that the buccaneers brought their plunder, which they sold for a tenth of its value, and it was in its taverns that they spent the proceeds on rum and wenches. The extent of its lawlessness may be gauged from the fact that a gibbet stood in its public square which anyone with an appearance of authority could use. It was appropriate that the English section of the Tortuga buccaneers should begin to drift here during the 1660s, and it was from here that Esquemeling set sail with Henry Morgan on his raid on Porto Bello.

This was one of the great pirate's most famous actions. Porto Bello was very different from the half-built city of which Baskerville had made a funeral pyre for Francis Drake. It was judged to be the strongest fort in the West Indies, and its entry was guarded by two castles. There was a permanent garrison of three hundred men, and four hundred families were in residence. The climate was unhealthy, so that the big merchants lived in Panama, but their warehouses were in Porto Bello, and its fair, when the Spanish galleons were assembled, lasted forty days. It offered high rewards to enterprise, and Morgan decided to outflank it, anchoring down the coast and proceeding up the river by canoe.

He had with him as a guide an Englishman who had once been imprisoned there. He sent a patrol of four men to capture the sentry at the first post. They succeeded in their task, and Morgan instructed his prisoner to lead him under the walls of the castle. When he arrived and had his men deployed, Morgan told the sentry to charge the commander of the castle to surrender instantly, under pain of massacre. The commander refused, opened fire and alarmed the city.

Morgan fulfilled his promise. He stormed the citadel, herded the survivors of the action into a single room, set alight the powder, of which there was a considerable store in the cellar, and blew its occupants into the air. The pirates then turned upon the city, whose panic-stricken inhabitants threw their jewels and silverware into wells and cisterns, while the governor withdrew to the surviving castle and set it in a state of siege.

The battle was waged with the fiercest desperation from first light until the tropical sun was high. Morgan had started the action with only four hundred men, and he began to doubt whether his forces were strong enough to carry the assault. He attempted to burn the gates with fireballs, but the Spaniards on the walls poured down on them stones, pots of powder and other inflammable material. The defenders, indeed, seemed likely to carry the day, but Morgan had a last card to play. Earlier in the action he had sacked a monastery and taken prisoner a number of monks and nuns. He now had constructed a dozen ladders so broad that five men could ascend them simultaneously. These ladders he ordered to be put in place by the monks and nuns, believing that the governor would not fire upon ecclesiastics. He underestimated the resolution of the governor, who possibly argued to himself that, the souls of the religious being safe, it did not matter what happened to their bodies. The nuns and monks screamed to him to surrender the castle and thus save their lives, but he was adamant and ordered his men to fire upon them as sternly as though they were buccaneers. Possibly his men were less ruthless than he was and wavered in their duty. At any rate, the ladders were fixed, though at the cost of many holy lives, and the pirates mounted them and swept into the castle.

The governor refused to surrender. He would rather, he said, die as a valiant soldier than be hanged as a coward. But the garrison had had enough. Once again the prisoners were herded together, with the men and women separated. The wounded were put in a single room, "to the intent," so Esquemeling said, "that their complaints might be the cure of their own diseases, for no other was afforded."

This done, the pirates, as was their wont, delivered themselves to such an orgy that had fifty resolute men been available the city could have been easily recaptured. But Panama was many miles away.

Next day Morgan and his men set about the task of plunder. This involved, as was customary, the torturing of those of the prisoners who appeared to be the richest, until they revealed the hiding places of their wealth. Several died upon the rack, but the accumulation of wealth proceeded smoothly. In the meantime, news of the disaster reached Panama, and the President prepared himself to exact reprisals.

Morgan, with his ships near at hand, felt no concern, although his manpower had been weakened by the unhealthiness of the climate and the strain of a sustained orgy. He loaded his ships with food and plunder, then he told the prisoners that unless they produced what he considered an adequate ransom he would burn their city and blow their remaining castles into the air. He considered two thousand pieces of eight an adequate ransom, and he advised them to send two emissaries to Panama to collect it. The President of Panama was now ready to attempt an assault. He advanced on Porto Bello. He expected that the pirates would fly at his approach, but Morgan knew that the Panamanians would have to pass through a narrow passage. He set his best men to guard it, and it was the President who retired.

There then ensued a courtly exchange of notes. If Captain Morgan did not retire immediately, said the President, he could expect no quarter. Morgan replied that unless he received the contribution money the castles and the prisoners they contained would fly sky-high. The President prudently decided that Porto Bello could settle its own affairs. Let them pay the ransom for the territory they had so ill defended. Morgan received his two thousand pieces of eight.

The President, in the manner which the laws of chivalry prescribed, expressed to Morgan his admiration of his enemy's achievement and asked if he might receive a sample of the kind of weapon with which so great a city had been taken. The messenger was received with great civility, and returned to Panama with a pistol and a few small bullets of lead, Captain Morgan desiring him "to accept that slender pattern of the arms wherewith he had taken Porto Bello and keep them for a twelvemonth," after which time he promised to come to Panama and fetch them away. The President of Panama returned the pistol and bullets, thanking him for the loan of them. At the same time he sent a gold chain with the message that he did not desire that Morgan "should give himself the labor of coming to Panama as he had done to Porto Bello, for he did certify to him that he should not speed so well here as he had done there."

The superficial courtesies were thus maintained as they had been with Drake a century before, and in a quiet harbor in Cuba, Morgan checked his spoil. It amounted to two hundred and fifty thousand pieces of eight in addition to a large quantity of goods.

That was in 1668, and the high days of piracy were about to

reach their twilight. The sovereigns of Europe were sufficiently committed to the profits of Caribbean trade to realize that it was in the interests of them all to curtail the activities of the buccaneers. But two mighty raids were yet to be accomplished, the assault on Maracaibo and the burning of Panama. Of this final exploit, Esquemeling was to write: "The history thereof I now begin to relate as being so very remarkable in all its circumstances that peradventure nothing more deserving memory may occur to be read by future ages." And indeed, though the world has been distracted by wars for three hundred years since then, it is to be doubted if any of them has produced a campaign more remarkable for cruelty and courage.

Morgan was at this time supposed to be operating under official authority. Spain and Britain were at peace, and Charles II was about to sign a treaty which outlawed buccaneering, but the treaty had not yet been signed and Morgan was able to persuade the governor of Jamaica—he himself was at that time deputy governor—that the safety of the colony depended on the reduction of Spanish power; there were, moreover, a number of persons in Jamaica to whom Morgan's men owed money, and who were ready to assist the launching of an expedition that might reimburse them. Morgan therefore sent out a recruiting summons to as many of his old comrades in arms as were still capable of bearing them, to a rendezvous in Hispaniola, and in late October he set sail for Rio de la Hacha.

Here he had the good fortune to find a large ship that had come from Cartagena to unload maize, a useful cargo for him. As usual, he found the town empty, but he captured a party of Spaniards and by torture extracted from them the necessary information about the hiding places of the city's wealth. He was now joined by a further series of recruits, so that his fleet numbered thirty-seven ships, which were manned by two thousand men besides mariners and boys. His flagship was mounted with twenty-two great guns and six small ones; the other larger ships had twenty, eighteen and sixteen guns apiece; even the smallest had as many as four. They were well stocked "with ammunition, fireballs and other inventions of powder." This was a formidable armada, as large as that with which Drake and Hawkins had sailed upon their final voyage.

As was the way of the buccaneers, Morgan now drew up his articles of association. He divided his fleet into two squadrons, placing a vice admiral over each, and appointing divers officers. To each of these he gave letters patent "to act all manner of hostility against the Spanish nation and take of them what ships they could, either abroad at sea or in the harbors, in like manner as if they were open and declared enemies of his master, the King of England."

He claimed for himself a hundredth part of all that was taken. Each captain should take the share of eight men, in addition to his own share. The surgeon, in addition to his pay, should have two hundred pieces of eight for his medicine chest. Every carpenter should draw, above his salary, one hundred pieces of eight.

Morgan and his captains then had to decide the first object of their attack—Cartagena, Panama or Vera Cruz. Their choice fell on Panama because it was believed to be the richest; but because of its distance from the Atlantic and their own ignorance of the approaches they decided to capture first the island of St. Catherine, where they were likely to find some outlaws who would act as guides.

St. Catherine was a penal settlement, to which were sent all the malefactors of the Spanish West Indies. It was a well-watered island, containing a great many pigeons. It conducted no commerce because its inhabitants were too idle to raise the tobacco which would have produced substantial profits; they were content to plant just enough fruit for their own subsistence. The island was, however, powerfully defended; the pirates' first attack was beaten off, and Morgan's men had to spend the night in the open fields under a streaming tropic rain. They wore nothing but breeches and a shirt; they had neither shoes nor stockings; they had brought no rations; their powder and their guns were wet; it was the rainy season. Morgan decided on a bluff. He tied the colors of truce to a canoe and sent a message warning the governor that if, within the day, he did not deliver himself and his men into the invaders' hands, they would be slaughtered without mercy. The canoe brought back the answer that "the governor desired two hours' time to deliberate with his officers in a full council, which being past he would give his positive answer to the message."

Within two hours the answer had arrived. It contained an ingenious variation on the customary proposition—His Excellency was prepared to surrender against such overwhelming forces, provided that Captain Morgan would be pleased to use a certain stratagem of war for the "better saving of his own credit and the reputation of his officers both abroad and at home," which should be as follows: that Captain Morgan should bring his troops at night to the bridge that joined the lesser island to the greater one, and there attack the fort of St. Jerome; that at the same time all the ships of his fleet should draw near the castle of Santa Teresa and attack it by sea, landing in the meanwhile near the battery called St. Matthew some further troops who should intercept the governor as he was endeavoring to pass to St. Jerome's fort, take him prisoner and force him to lead the English into the castle, under the fraud of their being his own troops. In the meantime, the two sides should fire at each other continuously, either into the air or with blank cartridges.

Morgan accepted these conditions willingly; there was an exchange of hostages, the sham battle was enacted, and without a single casualty or reprisal the pirates took possession of the island. They hunted and cooked and banqueted, while their leader set about finding the outlaws who would guide him to Panama.

The approach to Panama was guarded by the castle of Chagres, and Morgan deputed one of his captains to subdue it, with a force of four hundred men. It was a bitterly contested action; and the day was turned by an accident typical of but unique in the history of this kind of battle. After a number of reverses, the pirates were attempting to reduce the palisades with fireballs, when one of them was shot through the body with an arrow; he pulled it out, wrapped a piece of cotton round it, and in a gesture of bravado put it into his musket and fired it back into the castle. The cotton was kindled by the powder; it landed in a roof thatched with palm leaves; it set the roof alight; the fire spread and reached a load of powder. The explosion caused considerable damage and alarmed the Spaniards, who did not recognize the cause of the disaster. Their resolution wavered and the pirates did not let the opportunity slip.

The pirates' casualties were heavy, but after a day and a half's fighting only thirty defenders remained out of 314. From these thirty prisoners, the pirates learned that the governor of Panama had been already warned from Cartagena that the English were equipping a fleet to attack him, and that this information had been confirmed by a refugee from Rio de la Hacha. It was believed that the governor had lined the Chagres River with ambushes and was waiting in the open fields of Panama with thirty-six hundred men.

In face of this information, Morgan set out himself with twelve hundred men, five boats laden with artillery, and thirty-two canoes. His march on Panama is a major achievement in the annals of war. For eight days he and his men starved; proposing to live off the land, they took scarcely any provisions with them, but the Spaniards followed a scorched earth policy. Every now and then Morgan would find the traces of an ambuscade, but the leather provision bags would be empty; crumbs alone would be strewn upon the ground. The pirates were driven to eat the leather. They sliced it in strips, beat it between stones, rubbed it in intervals of dipping it in the river. They scraped off the hair, roasted it over a fire, cut it into small morsels and consumed it with the aid of water. Once they found two sacks of meal, some bananas and two jars of wine. Morgan divided it among those whose need seemed greatest. The weakest he allowed to travel by canoe. The others had to march. On the sixth day they found a barn filled with maize, on which they gorged themselves. In the distance they kept seeing Indians, who fled at their approach. On the seventh day they saw smoke rising from the chimneys of a village; they hurried forward—surely fire meant food. But the flames were part of the Spaniards' scorched earth policy. There was nothing left except a leather cask full of bread and fifteen jars of Peruvian wine. The men slacked their thirst and hunger, but to their consternation within an hour they were violently sick; at first they thought they had been poisoned, but later they realized that the wine had mixed badly with the trash, grass, bark and leather they had been consuming. After a day's rest they resumed their march.

They had now reached the last point to which canoes could be brought—a small village where the Spaniards stored their merchandise on their trips across the isthmus. Like all the other villages, it had been abandoned. Morgan sent back all his canoes but one, because he could not afford to leave a large company of men for their defense, and sent two hundred men ahead to reconnoiter the road. The paths were very narrow and he feared ambushes. His fears were justified; a rain of arrows descended on the advance party from a high and rocky mountain, but the pirates pushed on into the shelter of a wood, where they engaged in a skirmish with a group of Indians. They eventually routed the Indians, but they failed to capture any prisoners, which was their primary objective.

It was now the eighth day of the march, and heavy rain was falling. They had still had no real food since they left the boats. On the ninth morning they reached a mountain ridge from which they could see the Pacific. A ship and six small boats were sailing northward, presumably from Panama. Below them stretched a valley, well stocked with cattle. Their hunger was at an end. They could scarcely wait for the gobbets of meat to be roasted; they devoured them like cannibals, the blood running from their beards onto their chests. Their confidence was restored, and that night, when they saw the steeples of Panama, they threw their hats into the air, blew their trumpets and beat their drums as though the city were already theirs for plundering.

On the following morning, Morgan set out his forces and marched

toward the city with his drums and trumpets sounding. The Spaniards had expected him to attack by the main highway and had constructed elaborate defenses. But on the advice of one of his guides
Morgan advanced through the woods, by a difficult road which the
Dutch surgeon described as "irksome." The Spaniards had, therefore, to leave their batteries and prepared positions. Even so, it was
with a formidable force that the pirates found themselves opposed:
two squadrons, four regiments of foot and a vast herd of wild bulls
which a party of Indians would stampede at the psychological moment. But the pirates were used to being outnumbered. They must
conquer or die who have no retreat, and they had the same advantage
that the longbowmen had at Creçy. The ground was soggy and un-
even; the cavalry could not maneuver freely; the advance party of two
hundred buccaneers went down upon one knee and fired volley after
volley with unhurried accuracy; the stampeded bulls were terrified by
the noise and turned on the defenders. Within two hours the cavalry
had been wiped out, the infantry had fled in despair and the pirates
were engaged on their familiar task of massacring the survivors.

Morgan spared, however, a captain whom he could interrogate and
from whom he learned the strength of the opposition that awaited
him. It was a body of troops that would have intimidated most commanders. Four hundred horsemen; twenty-four companies of foot,
each of a hundred men, sixty of whom were Indians; a herd of two
thousand wild bulls. In addition to this, trenches had been dug, batteries emplaced, and at the main entry to the city was a fort mounted
with eight great guns and manned by fifty men. This was a considerable body of troops, and Morgan's own casualties had been
heavy. But six hundred Spaniards lay dead upon the field; the spirits
of his men were high. Morgan once again attacked from an unexpected quarter, after an outflanking march through difficult terrain.
Within three hours the city was in his hands.

The capture of Panama was a notable feat of arms; the sacking of
it during the next three weeks was one of the most brutal, ruthless,
and in the last analysis pointless episodes in the Caribbean's blood-
stained history. Panama was the richest and most beautiful city in
the New World. Its houses were built of cedar, and sumptuously
adorned with tapestries and paintings. It contained eight monasteries,
a cathedral and several churches. The altars were richly hung. Affluent merchants are said to have owned two thousand houses, while
small tradesmen and artisans owned another five thousand. The
Genoese had a large mansion from which they conducted their bank-

ing and mercantile business. All this Morgan destroyed. For no good reasons that have ever been given, he sent small groups of men into various sections of the city to start conflagrations. He then camped outside the city and watched it burn.

For twenty-four hours the fire raged; then Morgan returned to plunder the city. For the first day he managed to restrain his men by warning them that the wine was poisoned; he needed them to be in a fit condition to withstand a counterattack. But absolute control could not be maintained, and it was through his men's drunkenness that the galleon escaped in which had been stored all the King's plate and much of the gold and jewelry of the richest merchants; yet in spite of this loss the plunder was very great. Morgan also captured a number of valuable vessels and their cargoes. His men were indiscriminate in their cruelty; no torture was too bestial if it might lead to the discovery of a cache of jewels. Finally, Morgan set out on his return journey with 167 mules laden with gold, silver and jewelry, and with six hundred prisoners, men, women, children and slaves, whom he proposed to take with him to Jamaica unless amply ransomed. The prisoners marched in the middle, and their sentries prodded them in the back with muskets to make them march faster. They were kept short of food and water so that they would be the more anxious to raise their ransoms. When the women besought him to let them return to their families in Panama, he reminded them that he had not come to hear lamentations but to extract money.

At a town called Cruz, on the Chagres River, he halted for three days. He gave his prisoners three days' grace in which to bring in their ransoms; otherwise they would be transported to Jamaica. A certain number failed to produce their ransoms and he continued his march to Chagres, where the divisions of the spoil were made.

According to Esquemeling, Morgan at this point behaved with great niggardliness toward his men, giving them no more than two hundred pieces of eight apiece, a reward with which they were highly discontented. But Morgan was not the man to listen to complaints of that kind at the end of a voyage, when he had no longer any use for his men's services. Without saying good-bye to them, he set sail for Jamaica in his own flagship with his plunder aboard, leaving his late companions to their own devices, to find their own way home as best they could.

Esquemeling was one of those who were left behind "in such a miserable condition as might serve for a lively representation of what rewards attend wickedness at the latter end of life, whence we ought to have learned how to regulate and amend our action for the future," and no doubt this desertion is partly explanatory of the highly unfavorable impression that is given of Morgan in his memoirs. Morgan was indeed so dissatisfied with the portrait of himself that he sued Esquemeling for libel in the London courts and received two hundred pounds in damages.

Posterity, however, is not ungrateful. The account of the journey that Esquemeling made along the coast of Costa Rica is one of the most entertaining in his book. He spent a little while at the port of Bocas del Toro, which was well stocked with tortoises and where the Indians had never been subjugated, had made good friends and traded with the pirates and had offered asylum to a number of escaped Negro slaves. He then reached Cabo Gracias a Dios, where also cordial relations with the pirates were maintained, and where it was the custom for the pirates to purchase wives for the length of their stay with a knife, an old axe, a woodbill or a hatchet. It was a small community of some fifteen hundred inhabitants who lived together in amity, without any fixed laws, living off fish and fruit and brewing a kind of wine out of wild bananas, which they kneaded between their hands with hot water and often put in large calabashes with cold water, where in a week or so it would ferment. His stay here must have been a refreshing pause after the ardors of the Panamanian campaign, and he returned to Jamaica with his hold well stocked with provisions.

His was the first ship home out of Morgan's fleet, and he found his captain busy with plans to transport a group of colonists to the island of St. Catherine and fortify it as a base for pirates. But the days of piracy were on the wane. The sovereigns of Europe were agreeing to pool their differences. Louis XIV of France was on excellent terms with his English cousin, Charles II, who in a secret treaty had promised to restore the Catholic creed when the time seemed appropriate. Louis XIV was planning to place a Bourbon on the throne of Spain. The high stakes of diplomacy were soon to make Flanders once again the cockpit of the greater nations, and all this was to be very costly. It was necessary to make the Caribbean a source of profit. The Pope had recognized the right of Britain to own possessions in the New World, and the King of Spain had conceded certain rights in the Caribbean.

Within a few days of Morgan's return from Panama, a man-of-war arrived from England, recalling the governor to London so that he could give an account of his behavior and the license that he had accorded to privateers to interfere with the property and subjects of the King of Spain. The man-of-war brought with it a new governor, who had strict instructions to see that no ship sailing from a Jamaican port molested the comfort and prosperity of Spanish subjects. Within a few weeks, Morgan himself had been recalled to London to answer for his conduct. He was tried, but he comported himself with such efficiency and dignity that not only was he acquitted, but commissioned in the Royal Navy, and eventually installed and knighted as the governor of Jamaica. The great days of piracy were clearly ending when the scourge of Panama dispensed justice from King's House; his French colleagues decided that they would be wise to retire to Tortuga.

But in Tortuga, too, the days of piracy were numbered. The western section of Hispaniola was now completely in French hands, and the French governor-general had moved his residence thither from Tortuga. The current governor was a reformed buccaneer called d'Ogeron. For twenty years he had been trafficking in these waters. Since all Tortuga could not have ruled d'Ogeron, there was a chance that he might rule Tortuga. He was Colbert's choice when the trade of the Antilles was handed over to the Occidental Company. It was a sound choice. D'Ogeron was practical, hard and middle-aged. He knew the material with which he had to deal. The buccaneers were ready to trust him as far as they were ready to trust anyone. They were French, nine-tenths of them. They were prepared to admit the suzerainty of the King of France. But they had fought for Tortuga before anyone in Paris had realized that it existed. They had made favorable trading treaties. Without the Dutch they would have starved. They were not going to have anyone in Paris telling them that they could not trade with the Dutch.

D'Ogeron realized this; he also realized that it was no use explaining this to Colbert. In faraway Paris the elegant minister would shrug his brocaded shoulders and repeat his instructions to the French marine that any Dutch vessel trading with French possessions was to be treated as contraband. It was no use arguing with Paris. He had to find another solution. He found a typically Latin one. The buccaneers needed to be domesticated. In only one way could you domesticate a Frenchman. Women, that was what he needed. "I will fetch chains from France for the fettering of these rascals," was the way he put it. He did not ask that the women should be beautiful, virtuous or well-bred. He merely asked that they should be capable of childbearing and unscathed of pox.

D'Ogeron got his women, fifty of them, shipped with a cargo of claret from Bordeaux. When he saw them his heart sank. They were the gleanings of the sorriest stock in Paris. They had been little enough to look at when they started. Now, after six weeks on a two-hundred-ton trader, for the first fortnight of which they had been profoundly sick; during the last month of which they had itched with scurvy; during the last fortnight of which they had been sunburned so that the skin on their cheeks and noses had begun to peel; during no period of which they had attended to their personal cleanliness; after six weeks of discomfort, of dirt, of unwholesome food, they looked, in their tawdry, draggled finery, infinitely less appetizing than the erect, firm-breasted Negresses who had gathered on the quay to watch the unloading of this unusual cargo. They were women and they were white. But that was the most that one could say for them. D'Ogeron was not the man to make the worst of a bad job, however. He did his best to cleanse and decorate his cargo; then he sent messages to Tortuga.

Five hundred or so of the buccaneers came over. In a mute, suspicious group they stood, glaring at the nervous, simpering but hard-eyed, hard-mouthed group that had gathered on the veranda of the governor's house.

"My friends," said d'Ogeron, "with great courage and with the cherishing kindness that distinguishes their sex from ours, these gracious ladies, having heard in their country, which is your country too, of your hard and lonely lot, were moved with compassion, and have come across these many miles to share and make sweet that loneliness for you. As you see, there are fifty here. Each has consented to take unto her from among your number a husband whom she will obey and honor. It is fitting that the choice should be made not by her but for her, and by you. So, as there are more of you than there are of them, we have agreed that those of you who wish shall draw lots among yourselves as to the right and precedence of choice. I am confident, as a consolation for those who will be disappointed in the fall of the lots, that the example of these brave ladies will not be overlooked in France and that in a few months others will have come to follow them."

And he looked blandly and encouragingly at the half-circle of surly, bearded faces.

They did not need encouragement. They were five hundred and

there were only fifty women, but they were comrades in arms. They had not quarreled in the past over the division of their booty; they were not going to quarrel now. They drew lots, and there on the veranda of d'Ogeron's bungalow, the fortunate fifty swore each in his turn the marriage oath of the buccaneer, the oath that from history's dawn has been sworn by the outlaws, the Bohemians of life, to one another.

"I take thee," each cried, "without knowing or caring to know who thou art. If anybody from whence thou comest would have had thee, thou wouldst not have come in quest of me. But no matter. I do not desire thee to give me an account of thy past conduct, because I have no right to be offended at it at the time when thou wast at liberty to live either ill or well according to thine own pleasure, and because I shall have no reason to be ashamed of anything thou wast guilty of when thou didst not belong to me. Give me only thy word for the future. I acquit thee of the past." Then with a heavy clatter he smote the palm of his hand against the band of his musket, brandishing it above his head. "This will revenge me," he cried, "of thy breach of faith. If thou shouldst prove false this will surely be true to my aim." The Homeric days of the buccaneers were over.

Smuggling was to continue, as was inevitable when the life of the planters was to be harassed by navigation acts, when central governments were to place the interests of the colonists as secondary to their own, when the need for manufactured goods was paramount and such goods could be obtained more cheaply from privateers. For many years the Caribbean was to be the hunting ground of illicit traders. There were to be notable figures like Captain Kidd and Edward Teach, whose castle, "Bluebeard's," is now a fashionable hotel in St. Thomas, and who was wont on occasions at the dinner table to discharge his pistols at his guests, on the grounds that if he did not shoot some of them sometimes they would forget who he was. But these men were smugglers rather than pirates, and they acted without the connivance of their governors. The era that had begun with Hawkins' first journey, with its cargo of slaves, had ended; a new era had begun.

CHAPTER V

Black Ivory

Europe had by now realized what a treasure had been discovered for it by Christopher Columbus and what a treasure had been abandoned for the sake of the gold and silver mines of Mexico and Peru. The Caribee Islands, as they were originally called, lie for the most part in the semitropical zone; they are cooled by the trade winds that blow from the northeast. The early Spanish colonists divided them into two groups. They called the northern islands the Windward Islands, and the eastern the Leeward Islands. They were also known as the Antilles, after Antilla, the mythical continent that was supposed to exist east of the Azores, the northern islands being called the Greater and the southern group the Lesser.

The ships bound for the West Indies made the island of Désirade. The trade wind always blew from the east, so that all the islands to the north and west of Désirade lay to the leeward, and all the islands of the east or south lay to the windward. Several of the islands are flat, Barbados, Anguilla, Aruba and Curaçao; Antigua, though it has a hilly section and a forest area, is mainly flat. But for the most part the islands are mountainous. The mountains attract the rain; in the majority of islands the rainless day is as rare as the sunless day; deep valleys run between the mountains and usually over one valley or another a rainbow will be curving. Some valleys are little more than gorges, but others run broad and fertile. Most products except the vine and certain berries flourished there, but it soon became apparent that sugar was the most profitable crop.

Originally cultivated in India, with the juice granulated by evaporation, sugar, although mentioned by Lucan in an incident in Pompey's Eastern campaign, was not introduced into Europe till the Crusades. It was then regarded as a luxury and used medicinally. It flourished in Rhodes and Malta, thence it reached Sicily. The Spaniards transported it to the Azores, Madeira and the Canaries. Columbus took it to Hispaniola on his second voyage. But it is Labat's view that it is indigenous to the Caribbean, since it was found in Guadeloupe in 1625, an island which the Spaniards had never colonized.

Its demand, through the popularity of tea and coffee, coincided with the colonization of the Caribbean. In 1665 the West Indian planters learned how to whiten sugar. In 1700 England consumed ten thousand tons, in 1800, one hundred fifty thousand tons, and in 1880 over a million tons. The need for it in Europe and in North America was keen; the pleasures of tea and coffee had been recently discovered. In London, coffeehouses had become the meeting place of politicians and intellectuals. Charles II's bride, Catherine of Braganza, had introduced a taste for tea. Until recently, honey had been used for sweetening. Sugar had also the agreeable by-product of rum. Sugar was an easy crop to raise. You planted the canes; they grew; you cut them down; you pushed them between grinders; the wind worked the sails of the mills, and there were your sugar and your rum. The only thing you required was a strong and obedient labor force, and that luckily existed in large quantities on the Guinea coast. In no other way, with the knowledge that existed at that time, could the canefields have been worked.

Within the next century the slave trade was to develop into a major industry. The speed and extent of its development may be estimated by its dimensions at the outbreak of the French Revolution. There were then forty European "factories" on the Guinea coast. Fifteen were Dutch, fourteen British, four Portuguese, four Danish and three French. The British shipped annually forty thousand slaves, the French twenty thousand, the Portuguese ten thousand, the Dutch four thousand and the Danes three thousand. This was an annual total of seventy-seven thousand. Not all these slaves went to the West Indies; as early as 1620 the tobacco planters of Virginia had purchased a consignment from a Dutch trader, and by the time of the War of Independence there were two hundred thousand slaves in the States. Spain never entered the slave trade, partially because Pope Alexander VI's bill of demarcation forbade her acquiring territory in West Africa, partially because she did not officially approve of the trade, partially because her need of slaves was less, since her colonies were not sugar islands, and she had Indian labor available in Central and South America, partially because, at the time when the slave trade was beginning, Portugal was part of Spain. Portugal was then established on the Guinea coast, and slaves for the Spanish colonies could be carried in Portuguese bottoms. When Portugal recovered her independence, Spain gave to other countries a contract, an *assiento*, to supply her colonies with 4,800 slaves a year. The contract went first to the Dutch, then to the French, finally, after the Treaty of Utrecht in 1713, to Britain, a contract which resulted twenty-six years later in the War of Jenkins' Ear.

The development of this trade was swift. At the start, England's African trade—which included a great deal of other merchandise—was in the hands of exclusive companies, but William and Mary, in the first year of their reign, 1689, opened it to all subjects of the crown, though the African Company continued to flourish and received periodic parliamentary grants. Between 1680 and 1700, some 140,000 slaves were exported by the African Company, and rather more than as many again by independent traders. Between 1700 and 1786, 610,000 slaves were shipped to Jamaica alone. The British trade was operated mainly from Liverpool, but London, Bristol and Lancaster were also involved; over 190 British ships were engaged in the trade, and they had accommodation for 47,146 slaves. But it is not possible to compute the exact extent of the trade because so much of it was in private hands.

From a distance of three hundred years, it is impossible to regard this trade without disgust, and within a few years of its inception enlightened persons had begun to protest against it; but there are certain things to be remembered, the main one being that we cannot judge a distant century in terms of our own. We have to think back imaginatively. Slavery had been accepted from the dawn of time; prisoners of war became slaves; serfdom had only been ended in enlightened countries; Christians captured by the Moors were put to work in galleys; slavery flourished in the Arab world well into the nineteenth century, and was one of the problems of the League of Nations. In Africa, slavery was an institution. It was easy for the slave traders, and for the shareholders in the slave trade, to argue that they were merely transporting men from one condition of slavery to another; they could, moreover, console themselves with the belief that Africans transported to the West Indies would be offered an opportunity of conversion to the faith. The soul was then considered more important than the body, the life in the world hereafter more important than the life in this. To the men and women of that day, life itself was not held to be as important a thing as it is in this. It was a transitory commodity, to be ended in sudden violence or prolonged in pain. Medical science had not learned how to alleviate the final agonies. Who would not have preferred Raleigh's death to

Philip II's? A basic callousness, founded upon a deep central recognition of what ultimately mattered, colored all the thinking of that day; for a brief period it was possible for civilized men to justify the slave trade.

Moreover, events moved so quickly that only the men on the spot knew what was happening. A letter took a long time to cross the Atlantic; there were no roving reporters, no Pathé News, no newspapers as we understand them. Louis XIV in Versailles and Charles II in Whitehall could not visualize the activities in which their subjects were engaged; they knew that there was a boom in sugar; the more sugar that was produced, the better. The canefields needed a labor force, and where else could that labor force be found? Europeans could not withstand heavy manual work under a tropic sun. Charles II regarded the colonies as his personal property and formed a King's Council to deal with them, a council which became later the Colonial Office, and he had a special coin—the guinea—stamped in honor of the slave trade. Louis XIV drew up a series of regulations called *le code noir* for the regulation of the estates, which was humane in spirit, but he did little to see that his orders were obeyed. A monarch who could accept with equanimity the squalid and miserable conditions under which his own peasantry was existing on a starvation level under northern skies was unlikely to worry about the conditions under which transported Africans were faring in the sun. They were warm, weren't they, and surely they must be well-fed or they would not be able to work on the plantations. That was the invariable argument; a peasant cherished the horses on which the prosperity of his land depended. A slave was worth several horses; the planter would protect his property. And the argument was valid, up to a point.

It is still possible to see along the Guinea coast remains of those factories; the huts and palisades have gone, but several of the forts remain, squat and low like Martello towers. The managers of these factories would conduct their bargaining with the local chiefs, occasionally with a local king. The chief and the king would require their commission on the deal, in addition to the direct fee per head. From time immemorial these kings and chiefs had indulged in raids to provide themselves with slaves and plunder. The frequency and fierceness of these raids now increased its tempo. The pattern which Hawkins had set in Sierra Leone was followed on all sides. Wars were conducted for no other reason than to provide the foreign slavers with human cargo. Raids were conducted far into the interior, and the

victims were brought to the coast by river or by canoe, chained together so that they should not escape; the marches from the interior
lasted, sometimes, as long as a month; on these occasions the slaves
were made to carry heavy loads so that they should be too exhausted
to escape. Some of them had been—they and their parents before
them—slaves longer than they could remember. They were docile and
abject, but others were proud and independent warriors who would
cherish forever, they and their heirs, resentment in their hearts. Of
stock such as this were to be bred later men like Toussaint l'Ouverture, Dessalines, Henri Christophe, and the father of Alexandre
Dumas, Napoleon's Black General.

On the coast, the manacled slaves were submitted to the most
acute examination before they were accepted by the slaver's captain.
The joints, limbs, teeth, tongue, eyes, toes of each separate slave were
closely scrutinized. Occasionally one of the slaves would be told to
step aside. The traders were experts at doctoring a sorry creature with
lemon juice and powder till he looked like a Hercules. But the experienced captain could tell from the pulse, the feel of the skin, the
yellow whites of the eyes and the swollen tongue that within thirty-
six hours the air of health would have shown itself to be fictitious.
The rejected slaves were killed, and outside the big factories dead
bodies would float in and out with every tide, the women face down-
ward, the men upon their backs.

The selected slaves were moved into a separate barracoon. For
the most part they accepted their fate with equanimity. They recognized no particular change in their condition. They roared with long
laughs when the ship's barber soaplessly shaved their heads and chins
and cut their toe and finger nails. They entered with a lively zest
into the pleasures of a banquet provided for them before their em-
barkation. With the sounds of the African jungle for the last time in
their ears, they drank and ate and sang and danced. The next morning, tired-eyed and heavy-headed, they were embarked, to be stripped
as they stepped aboard of such shreds of clothing as remained to
them. They carried nothing with them to the world that ultimately
they were to possess except the heart and faith of Africa.

Such was the procedure in the big factories, but there were also a
number of independent traders who would drift down the coast in
search of a river unguarded by any of the companies owning a monopoly of the trade; their holds would be full of cheap cotton goods
and trinkets. They would hang a string or two of beads round a chief's
neck, produce a beaker full of rum and urge him to start a local war

on their behalf, or set fire to a village and capture the inhabitants as they fled to save themselves. Occasionally they would get a small consignment from the manager of one of the regular factories, whose barracoons were overfull owing to a delay in the return of one of his company's ships and who was finding difficulty in nourishing his cargo; sometimes a spy would bring them word of a chance cargo on its way down from the hills and, after hours of waiting, they would intercept at a river's mouth a canoe rowed by dark warriors, with a score of captives lying bound with bamboo withes in the bilge.

The Caribbean planters were always glad to get an illegal cargo; the prices would be easier and the quality was likely to be as sound; very often it was sounder because the difficulty of conducting surreptitious operations encouraged the privateers to sail before their holds were full; through absence of overcrowding, the cargo arrived in good condition.

The journey across the Atlantic was known as "the middle passage," and a great deal has been written about its horrors, particularly by the abolitionists at the end of the eighteenth century. Charts were printed showing how closely the slaves were packed together in the holds. Statisticians have computed that 12½ percent of the slaves died during the voyage, but it must be remembered that the rate of mortality on the high seas was at that time very high, and that the sailors of the Royal Navy traveled in conditions of pitiful squalor. Gillespie, a surgeon to the naval hospital in Martinique during the British occupation, wrote in 1798 a pertinent pamphlet of advice to the commanders and officers of His Majesty's fleet serving in the West Indies, on the preservation of their seamen's health. He referred to the unwholesome air, the overcrowding, the dampness through overwetting of the decks, the dejection of mind that came both from overwork and underwork. Ardent fever, he said, killed off great numbers, and it must be remembered that the argument about the planters' treatment of their slaves on the plantations holds good for "the middle passage"; it was in the captain's interest to bring as much of his cargo as possible safe and sound to the marketplaces of Jamaica, Barbados, Martinique, Hispaniola and Guadeloupe.

For the captain and his crew, "the middle passage" was a grim period too. The slaves, when they discovered the conditions to which they had been brought, proved intractable. Those who were destined for the far corners of the hold had to be driven there with whips. Only the whip could temper them. The shaking and quivering of the ship tore at the manacles upon their legs and arms, ripping the flesh, gangrening the wounds. Suicide was general. They would swallow the vinegar with which they were told to rinse their mouths. They would throttle themselves to death. When the precaution of chaining their wrists as well as their ankles was taken, they would contrive ingeniously to inflict death upon themselves by pressing their throats against the back of the head of their nearest comrade. Usually they were allowed on deck during the mornings. But sometimes one of the slaves availed himself of this liberty to leap overboard, dragging with him by his manacled limbs a couple of his fellows; it would be then decided that this privilege must be denied them. They were allowed on deck only during such time as was necessary to scrub out the holds. Every morning they were brought on deck to be sluiced down with buckets of salt water, the men first and then the women. The stench of a slaver carried for miles across the water.

The passage would last from six weeks to two months. They would be frail and sickly objects when eventually they were landed at Port Royal or Cap Français and stood drawn up, completely naked, to be prodded, overhauled, to have their muscles pinched and their teeth examined by their prospective owners. They would be weak with scurvy and bad food. But so delighted would they be to think that their journey was at an end that as soon as they realized that the planters who had rowed out from shore to meet them were not a tribe of cannibals eager to devour them, they would do everything in their power to endear themselves to their prospective purchasers. They would chatter incessantly as the inspection was being made. And should one of their number be refused for some blemish or other, they would roar with laughter at his discomfiture.

The planters would bring down with them to the sale a couple of Negroes to interrogate the newly arrived cargo. On the shoulder of those who had been selected would be set the silver stamp of the plantation; they would then be issued such scanty clothing as was considered necessary—a hat, a shirt, a pair of trousers—and taken to the plantation to recover.

Of those that survived the journey, five percent would die during their stay in the harbors, where they were exposed for the first time to the fevers of the port. Lady Nugent, before she had been many days in Jamaica, was writing of "this deceitful, dreadful climate." Then there was the "seasoning up" process; the Africans were strong but they were exposed to maladies against which they were not immune. It was held that only half the slaves who were shipped from Africa lived to be effective laborers in the islands.

Of the life that they lived there it is possible to get a picture from the many casual accounts that have been left to us, by the writings of Bryan Edwards and "Monk" Lewis, by the charming eighteenth-century engravings that recreate the pastoral characteristics of the life, by the patient industry of a number of French historians, and also by the architectural survivals that may be still seen in so many of the islands.

Wars and hurricanes and fires have destroyed a great deal. Saint-Pierre, that loveliest of cities, has been laid low by a volcano, but there remain the forts guarding every harbor, the cannon still mounted upon the battlements. There are the red brick warehouses at Grenada, the estate houses of Barbados, the old Danish castle of St. Thomas, the broken windmills in Antigua and St. Croix, the terraces of Pétionville above Port-au-Prince, the ruins of the old factories, the aqueducts in Grenada, the sulphur baths in St. Lucia where Louis XVI's soldiers eased their rheumatism, the caldrons where the cocoa seeds were trodden. It is not impossible to recreate the patrician life of the landowners and the mercenary struggle of the small businessmen who carried on as ship's chandlers, as artisans, as architects, but it is less easy to recreate the life of the transported Africans. They have left no record. We know how they lived, but we do not know how they thought and felt.

Bryan Edwards, writing of them at the end of the eighteenth century, said that "though born in various and widely separated countries it is not easy to discriminate their peculiar manners and native properties. The familiar and uniform system of life to which they are all reduced; the few opportunities and the little encouragement that are given them for mental improvement, are circumstances that necessarily induce a predominant and prevailing cast of character and disposition. 'The day,' says Homer, 'which makes a man a slave takes away half his worth,' and in fact he loses every impulse to action except that of fear. Nevertheless, there are among several of the African nations some striking and predominant features that cannot easily be overlooked by a person residing in any of the sugar plantations."

Most of the tribes to the north and east of Sierra Leone were Mohammedans, and Edwards had a servant who could write in Arabic. The Mandingoes, he said, thought themselves superior to other Africans because their hair, though bushy and crimped, was not woolly but soft and silky to the touch, and they had not the thick lips and flat noses of the more southern Negroes. But the dif-

ference lay less in their appearance than in their character. They were
not fitted for hard labor. They were, he complained, prone to theft.
He found the Gold Coast Negroes tough, ferocious, hardworking.
Very often slaves in their own country, they were known as Koromantyns. On the whole, the people of Whidah a Fida (Papaws) were
the most satisfactory; they were not so ferocious as the Koromantyns
nor as timid and despondent as the Eboes. They were industrious,
adroit agriculturists; they dreaded pain and were afraid of death.

The Eboes came from the Bight of Benin, an extent of coast
three hundred English leagues in length. They were yellowish in color
and their eyes appeared to be suffused with bile even when they
were in perfect health. "Their faces looked like that of a baboon."
The great objection to the Eboes, according to Edwards, was "their
continued timidity and despondency of mind, which are so great as
to occasion them very frequently to seek in a voluntary death a refuge from their own melancholy reflections. . . . Mild though these
people seem, however, they were cannibals at home."

Edwards found the Negroes from Angola and the Congo better
fitted for domestic service than for field labor. They could be trained
into excellent mechanics and were less dishonest than other Africans.

He noted that there was a great fellowship between fellow countrymen who traveled in the same ship. The term "shipmate" had a
special significance. Their amatory relations were, he said, "temporary connections which they form without ceremony and dissolve
without reluctance. When age begins to mitigate the ardor and
lessen the fickleness of youth, many of them form attachments which,
strengthened by habit and endeared by the consciousness of mutual
interdependence, produce a union for life. It is not uncommon to behold a venerable couple of this stamp who, tottering under the load
of years, contribute to each other's comfort with a cheerful assiduity
which is at once amiable and affecting. The aged are well looked
after on a plantation."

They were, he said, very loquacious, as fond of delivering set
speeches as professional orators, and it required a considerable share
of patience to hear them to the end. Yet they could be concise. Once
a slave went to sleep while awaiting his master's writing of a letter.
It was hard to rouse him. The servant shouted to him, "You no hear
Massa call you?" He replied, "Sleep hab no master."

Every attempt was made to keep groups of friends separate. It was
easier to break a slave's links with the past when he and his fellows in

the cane fields did not have a common tongue, when they could learn the white man's language and start a new life in the white and Christian tradition. In consequence, most of the islands, particularly the French islands, have built up a patois consisting of European words mingled with African. No Englishman listening today to four long-shore Barbadians chattering together would be able to understand what they were saying, nor could a Frenchman understand the gossip of Martinique fishermen. One of the jobs of the planter was to see that the slaves forgot as soon as was possible that they were African.

The handbooks which were given to young planters at the end of the eighteenth century stress the differences between the various tribes in character and appearance; in view of this and the fact that each colonizing power had its own factories along the Guinea coast and that the navigation acts of each country forbade its colonies to trade with ships of another country, one would have imagined that there would be marked differences between the native populations of the various islands, that a Martinique man would be as different from a Jamaican as a Chinese man from a Japanese. But this is not the case. It is easier for an Englishman to recognize differences between his own compatriots than between one kind of Frenchman and another, and it is not difficult for an Englishman to detect the difference in accent between a Barbadian, a Jamaican and a Trinidadian; but the difference would seem to be the result of climate and of the kinds of Europeans with which the original slaves had been brought in contact. Barbados has never been colonized by any except Britons. There were Spaniards in Jamaica for 150 years before Cromwell captured it; Trinidad was Spanish for three hundred years. Trinidad had been neglected by the Spaniards and was underpopulated. The slave trade was abolished in the year that the British captured it, so that it was impossible to develop its resources with African labor. The British therefore introduced "indented labor" from India. Intermarriage between Spanish, Indian, African and British stock has given the Trinidadian a special air. The great variety of feature between the completely Negroid inhabitants of the various islands can be, however, explained by the different parts of Africa, the different tribes, from which their ancestors had come.

The women of Martinique have always been famous for their elegance, and it has been suggested that their beauty is due to the fact that the plantations of Martinique were populated by Africans from a special area, but there is no proof of this. The difference between one island and another is not the outcome of the different tribes from which they have been populated, but from the differences in the masters, the national characters of their masters, and the variety of masters to whom they were subjected. For, with the exception of Barbados, every island changed hands at least once during the two centuries of conflict that lay between Elizabeth's death and the battle of Waterloo; the present condition of the islands has indeed largely been determined by what happened to them during the Napoleonic Wars, when a number of islands, in particular Hispaniola, Guadeloupe, St. Lucia and Grenada, were exposed to the full force of revolutionary ardor.

Every attempt was made to break down the slaves' links with Africa, and in time the slaves learned their masters' language. They accepted the profession of their masters' faith, but deep in their hearts they cherished the dark gods of Africa. Their loyalty to their witch doctors never weakened; it is indeed still active, and no one who has lived in the islands has questioned the validity of their magic.

Labat includes in the records of his travels three examples of what is known generally as Obeah; firstly there is the instance of a voyage by sea that was so delayed and hindered that the ship appeared to be nailed to the sea, although the winds were favorable. The captain and his officers were desperate; they could find no remedy because they did not know the cause. There was soon a shortage of food and water; the Negroes began to die, and in order to save the survivors a number were thrown into the sea. Some of the sufferers as they were dying complained that there was a sorceress on board who had threatened to eat their hearts, causing them to perish with great pain. The captain ordered an autopsy and indeed discovered that their hearts and livers were as dry and empty as punctured balloons.

The captain therefore had the accused woman roped to a cannon and fiercely flogged in the hope of extracting a confession, but she did not appear to feel the blows. The ship's surgeon, feeling that the intendant was not striking hard enough, took a rope himself and belabored her with all his might. This flogging had no more effect than the previous one; the woman assured him that she had felt no pain whatsoever, but that since the surgeon had wished to hurt her, which he had no right to do, she would make him repent of his brutality and announced that she would eat his heart. Two days later the surgeon died in great agony; his heart was found to be as dry as a sheet of parchment.

The captain was desperate; he could have had the woman strangled or flung into the sea, but he was afraid that she might have accomplices who would take their revenge on him and on his crew. So he decided to be gentle with her and promised her anything she wanted if she would cease these practices. A bargain was struck and it was agreed that if she and three of her friends were put ashore, the ship could continue on its way. As her signature upon the document she offered him a sample of her powers. She asked the captain if he had any fruit or anything else that it would be pleasurable for her to eat. Yes, he said, he had some watermelons. "Show them to me," she said. They were brought on deck. "I will not touch them," she said. "I will not go near them, but rest assured that within twenty-four hours I shall have eaten them." He accepted the bet and locked the melons in a chest, putting the key in his own pocket because he could not trust the crew.

Next morning she asked him where the melons were; he brought the chest on deck and opened it. To his delight he saw that the melons were whole, but his delight was brief. When he picked up a melon to show it to her, it collapsed between his hands; only the skin remained. She had won her bet. He returned to land to water and victual the ship. He set her and her three friends ashore and the ship was able to continue its voyage without hindrance.

Père Labat was the witness of two other examples of sorcery. One of the monks in Guadeloupe had a nine-year-old Negro boy who had not yet been baptized. One day this boy heard the monks complaining of a lack of rain. He asked if they would like a heavy downfall or a light shower. He would procure for them whichever they preferred. Their curiosity overcoming their sense of what was right, they asked for a light shower for their garden. The boy then set out on the ground three oranges. He knelt before each orange with a reverence which surprised the monks. He then took three branches from an orange tree and, having bowed before them, placed them on the oranges. Once again he performed his genuflections, speaking with great reverence some words which the monks could not understand. He then stood up, one of the orange twigs in his hand, and gazed at the horizon in all directions, till at last he saw, far away but very clear, a minute cloud. He stretched the twig toward it and immediately a light rain began to fall. The shower lasted an hour and fell only on the garden. The boy then buried the oranges and branches. He said he had been taught how to do this by two fellow slaves during "the middle passage."

The other story is macabre. A Negress had been afflicted for some time by an illness that no doctor could cure. Labat, convinced that she was being poisoned, brought her back to his house and gave instructions that she was not to be given any food that had not been prepared by the doctor himself.

One night Labat learned that a Negro who practiced medicine was in her hut. He went down and looked through the latticework of the walls. The sick woman was stretched on a mat. A clay monkey was on a chair; the quack doctor knelt before it in prayer. He then put some powder in a calabash, lit it, and incense rose before the idol. After numerous genuflections, he demanded of the idol whether or not the invalid would survive. Labat heard the question, but not the answer. The invalid, however, appeared to do so, because she and the two or three other slaves who were with her began to shout and wail. Labat pushed open the door; he was accompanied by his overseer and several witnesses. He ordered them to seize the witch doctor and those of the spectators who did not work on his estate. He picked up the monkey, the incense and the calabash, and asked the invalid why she was crying. She replied that the devil had spoken out of the mouth of the clay monkey, telling her that she would die in four days' time. The spectators confirmed this.

Angrily Labat insisted that the witch doctor was a ventriloquist who could disguise and throw his voice. "If the devil had really been here," he cried, "would he not have warned you that I was outside the door?" He had the witch doctor tied up and proceeded to thrash him personally, three hundred strokes from his shoulders to his knees. The witch doctor screamed like a man who was lost to hope. The spectators begged for mercy for him, but Labat told them that sorcerers could not feel pain and that he was only crying out of mockery. He then put the monkey on a chair in front of the sorcerer. "If he is the devil," said Labat, "tell him to rescue you from my hands."

The sorcerer did nothing, so Labat went on beating him. The spectators were terrified; they were convinced that the sorcerer would kill Père Labat. To assure them that he feared neither witch doctor nor devil, the priest broke the idol and the calabash and had the whole paraphernalia set alight and the ashes scattered in the river. He then ordered that a mixture of pepper and small lemons should be rubbed into the Negro's back. This would cause him acute pain, but it would prevent gangrene from setting up in the sores. He sent the sorcerer back to his own plantation with a report on what had happened. The owner thanked Labat for having been at so many pains and thrashed the Negro. Labat was confident that he had set a

good example to the slaves, but to his annoyance the invalid did die
on the fourth day.

No one who has lived in the islands has ever questioned the power
of the witch doctors. To this day the planter has realized that he must
accommodate himself to these dark mysteries.

In addition to Obeah, the slaves brought with them a form of
snake worship that was known as voodoo. This was a religion, and
the voodoo man stood as high socially above the Obeah man as a
priest does above a doctor. Voodoo ceremonies were ruthlessly re-
pressed on the plantations, but they survived into the nineteenth
century. In Haiti they are practiced still.

Père Labat arrived in the islands in 1694, and his memoirs are the
most valuable document we possess about the early colonial days. He
was a warmhearted man, intelligent and educated, attached to the
pleasures of the table, tolerant, accepting the *status quo,* in the certain knowledge that in paradise a peace not of this earth awaited the
unfortunate in this. When he arrived at Martinique a crowd of Negroes rowed out to welcome him. "Many," he wrote, "bore the marks
of stripes upon their backs. This excited the pity of those among us
who were not accustomed to seeing this sort of thing."

Père Labat, during the twelve years that he spent in the islands,
visited not only the French islands but Barbados and Jamaica. He
accepted what he saw and he approved of what he saw. It was a stage
in the progress of mankind. From these islands wealth would come to
France. The owner of a plantation was a useful citizen and, viewed
by the standards of the day, the life to which the slaves were introduced was little harder than that which the peasants of Ireland
and Scotland were enduring across the water, while the climate was
infinitely preferable.

The slave quarters were set a quarter of a mile from the main mill,
and downwind for the master's comfort. The cabins were arranged in
regularly spaced rows round a large square garden. They were simple,
palm-thatched erections, made of handposts driven deep into the
ground and interlaced with plaster and with wattles. They were a
man's length long, and high enough to allow a tall man to walk erect.
That was the cabin for a couple living together in what passed for
marriage. The men outnumbered the women by two to one; no
woman lived alone. A connubial couple would have little furniture.
Their bedstead was a platform of boards; the bed was a mat covered

with a blanket. They had a table and a stool or two, with such pots and pans as their simple cookery demanded. There was wood in plenty for the fire within doors at night without which no Negro could sleep at peace.

Probably through the village would run a stream clustered with fruit trees, the plantain, the avocado pear, the orange. It looked pretty and picturesque.

Life followed a simple enough routine. Shortly before sunrise there would be the blowing of a conch shell. At the roll call the slaves would gather with their bills and breakfasts. While the men and the stronger of the women worked in the fields, the cooks would prepare the breakfast. It would be a savory but strange-looking hash composed of plantains, yams, eddoes, calalu, okra, seasoned with salt and cayenne pepper. On chill and foggy mornings there would usually be a number of absentees. During the three quarters of an hour's interval for breakfast, the backs of the delinquents would be basted by the driver's whip. At noon there would be another interval for food. Many, preferring to eat their main meal at night, lay out in the shade during the two hours of heavy heat, and slept.

It was in the afternoon that the most strenuous work was done. Refreshed with rest and food, their muscles loosened by the sun, the slaves would work almost heartily among the canes, with the sound of singing as frequent as the crack of the driver's whip.

They accepted the blows that fell on them as they accepted the other details of their life. Torture held no mysteries for them. In Africa they had seen the slaughtering of their fellows; the yelling sacrifice of the virgin; they had eaten in their religious feasts the flesh of the young child. They expected to be beaten when they arrived late at roll call, when they were lazy in the fields, when they made blunders in their work. And should they be aggressive and unruly, should they be rebellious toward their employers, worse still, should they escape into the hills, they expected to receive heavy punishment.

And indeed heavy punishments were served out to them, brutal and licentious punishments, by overseers who had no personal interest in the plantation's welfare, to whom a slave's health was not his capital; by planters bored, cruel, dissipated, their nerves frayed by heat and fever, who had no better employment for their imagination than the devising of refined tortures for refractory slaves. There was the driver's whip and the weight of chains; chains cunningly set in an iron collar round the neck from which a short chain to the ankle held the foot into the small of the back, so that the slave could only hobble, with his chained leg numb and agonized. There was the iron cage studded with spikes that fitted close to neck and foot, so that the pain in one limb could be relieved only by shifting it to the other. There were those and there were other tortures. There was the burying of the slave up to the neck in earth, the covering of the head and face with sugar, so that the flies and mosquitoes would slowly sting him to a frenzy. There was the coating of the naked slave with sugar and the pouring over him of ladle after ladle of living ants.

Sullenly but patiently the slaves bore these punishments. There were times when the nostalgia for Africa grew intolerable. Then in groups or alone they would go apart and hang themselves, believing that when they were dead the dark gods of Africa would carry their bodies back to the high green jungles. There were times when their hatred for their masters grew so great that in order to do them damage they would kill themselves, knowing that their death would be a loss of money. They sought death in the most casual and sometimes the most ingenious manners, contriving at times to throttle themselves with their own tongues while their masters were in the act of thrashing them. They learned how to acquire dropsy by eating earth. Occasionally they revolted, setting upon one of their overseers and tearing him to pieces, indifferent to the punishment that they knew awaited them, provided they could be avenged upon a particular tyrant. The reprisals taken on such an insurrection would be pitiless. A favorite punishment was to hang one of them in a cage and leave him to die of rage and hunger. This was called "putting a man out to dry."

But for the most part they endured their subjection patiently. Freedom was a foreign country to them. They had their amusements. There were Sundays when, from all parts of the country, in their finest clothes, they would go down to the market, laden with fruits and vegetables and poultry, to barter their provisions for salted beef and pork and the bright cotton and ornaments with which they loved to deck themselves.

It was to Sunday that, during the hard hours of labor in the canefields, they would count the hours. For many that day would be simply so many hours of rest, when men and women would sit silent before their doors, the men smoking their pipes, the women catching and subsequently eating the lice off their children's heads. But for the younger ones Sunday was a day of life and laughter, when they could walk through the bright streets of the town, gazing with envying wonderment at the gaudy half-castes with their gay madras handkerchiefs knotted in their hair; their fine linen blouses, low-cut and trimmed with lace upon their bosoms, with flowers fastened at the breast, their necks hung with coral necklaces, and from the ears heavy gold earrings hanging. Back in the village, their eyes tired with the new bright sights, they would dance in the cool evening.

A couple of Negroes seated on their haunches would beat with their wrists and fingers on a taut stretched drum. The dancers would stand facing each other in two long lines. One of them would improvise a song with a refrain to be echoed by the circle of spectators. Their arms raised sideways as though they were playing castanets, their shoulders motionless, they would sway between their knees and navel, in a circular rhythm now fast, now slow. Sometimes they would break the slow rhythm with leaps into the air, with screams, with rushings together and a beating of their thighs. Occasionally they would throw their arms about each other, and spin round and round. Then once again they would break away, to stand opposite each other, swaying to the music's beat.

For hours they would dance, the tafia warm in their veins, their senses subjugated by the music, till they had ceased to be themselves, till they had become a pulse in that music's rhythm, a vehicle through which forces moved. They would dance and dance and dance, their senses reeling, their blood afire, maddened by the music and the dance, till suddenly one of the women could endure the strain no longer. With a wild cry she would break through the circle of spectators and run for the dark shadows. There would be the sound of overtaking footsteps at her back, the sound of hard breathing at her side. There would be the check suddenly of firm hands upon her shoulders and through her reeling senses an ecstasy that made every bone in her body seem to melt.

It is possible indeed that the women were happier in the West Indies than they had been at home. In many African tribes, when a chief died, his wives and slaves were sacrificed at his funeral. One plantation woman stated that on that account she preferred Jamaica. She was a little ashamed of this preference. It was a symptom of degeneracy. "Massa, since I come to white man's country, I love life too much."

When a child was born, the mother would present it proudly to her master on his next visit to the village. "Fine nigger chile to work for Massa." He would play with the other children in the garden. Later, when strength came to him, he was employed, under the care of an old woman, in the collecting of green meal for the pigs, and in the weeding of the garden. He looked forward to the day when he would be strong enough to work in the cane fields, to clear, hole and plant the ground, and in crop time cut the cane, feed the mills and attend to the manufacture of the sugar.

The month of the sugar crop was a happy period, as happy as the harvest time in the vineyards of Bordeaux and Burgundy. Even the most meager of the Negroes looked healthy when once the mills were set in action, so constantly were they indulged with the green tops of the cane and the skimmings from the boiling-house. Pigs and poultry fattened upon the refuse. Though everyone was working hard every-one was happy. There was an atmosphere through the whole planta-tion of health, plenty and busy cheerfulness. This atmosphere was enjoyed equally by the master. He could forget his ill-humor, his impatience, his loneliness, his nostalgia for the country of his birth as he stood by the mills, watching the canes squeezed and pressed be-tween the rollers, till the last drop of juice was wrung from them. With his eyes aglow he would watch the juice run down the lead-lined gutter to the boiling-house, to the great copper clarifiers, to seethe under the heat of the fire a degree or two short of boiling point, till there rose blistering to the surface the white scum, through which the pure, almost transparent liquid would be drawn into the grand copper.

For hours he would stand in the heated room watching the liquor boil, while Negroes swept the rising foam with scummers till the seething residue took on the fine richness of Madeira coloring. When the froth rose in large clean bubbles he would chuckle to himself, knowing that the brew was good, and he would watch the Negroes test the liquid, to decide the hour when it was fit for striking. They would take up with their thumbs a small portion of the hot liquid, drawing it, as the heat diminished, into a thread with their fore-fingers. Then, when the thread snapped and shrank from the thumb to the suspended finger, they would judge by its length whether the order to strike could be bawled out.

Later, in the curing house, he would watch avidly the thick molas-ses drip slowly through the spongy plantain stalk into the tank be-low; soon this golden drained juice would ferment and mellow into the magic potion that for the West Indian planter could cure all griefs and heighten every happiness.

It was a patriarchal way of life, one which had in those early years, in terms of the general living conditions of the day, a great deal to

commend it, and Père Labat can only have been delighted at the
prospect of these heathen creatures being converted to the Christian
faith. In one of his chapters he instructs how newly arrived slaves
should be treated; after explaining how they should be massaged to
render their muscles supple, he suggests that they should be put
under the charge of an experienced slave who will give them information about the kind of life awaiting them, but that they should not
be allowed to eat with these seniors nor sleep in the same room, because these seniors are Christians while they are not; this will make
them appreciate that Christians belong to a higher class of mortal.

Père Labat wrote of the slaves with warmth, with affection and with
understanding. His account of them is so fresh in spirit, so contemporary in approach that it is difficult to realize that it was written two
and a half centuries ago. He recognizes that their religion is often only
skin-deep; they enjoy going to church; they enjoy singing hymns; they
enjoy the ritual of baptism; but he suspects that if they returned to
their own countries they would return to their old faiths. How, he
wondered, with their warm, volatile, sensual natures, could they
easily appreciate a religion based on justice, mortification, humility,
continence, refusal of pleasure, love of one's enemies and distrust of
riches. He recognizes that they are idolatrous, that they are given to
sorcery and the use of poisons. He had no illusions about the purity of
"the noble savage," but he did not love him any the less on that account. He was disconcerted by the lasciviousness of their dances, in
particular the calinda, but he liked to see them happy and hoped that
the introduction of the French minuet would prove popular. It did
not. He disapproved of their lighthearted acceptance of the delights
of venery, yet he could recount with a chuckle an incident when
he ordered the whipping of a group of very young people—the eldest
was only nine—whom he discovered anticipating the privileges of
the married state. The course of discipline had just begun, under the
administrations of the cook, when one of the older Negroes intervened. He wished, he said, to present an argument in their defense.
Père Labat ordered the cook to stop. "Well, and what is it?" he
inquired.

"Did you not send one of your men to the cooper to learn how
to make casks?"

"Certainly, I did."

"Has he brought you any casks yet?"

Père Labat explained that the making of casks required an apprenticeship, that in time the man would learn how to make good casks.

The old Negro laughed. Why did he not apply the same principle to these urchins? Did not the good father want them to marry one day and produce children? They could not produce children unless they had learned how to when they were young, any more than your man can become a cooper and make good casks without serving an apprenticeship. Look at the case of this friend of his beside him; he had no children because he had not learned to make them when he was young. Père Labat was unable to argue him out of his belief that all skills needed to be acquired.

The Negro characteristics that Père Labat detected at the end of the seventeenth century are more applicable than one would expect to the peasants of today. They respect their family, and they respect the old. They respect their masters when their masters deserve respect. They are extremely eloquent when they have a favor to ask or an accusation to repulse. And so, Père Labat adjures his reader, you must listen to them carefully, and to the end, if you want to be liked by them. They will, he says, enumerate at length their good qualities, their industry, their assiduity in your service, the number of their children; then they will enumerate the kindnesses you have shown them, and express the depth of their gratitude for them. Finally, they will produce their request; and, says Labat, if the request is reasonable, as it usually is, they should be granted it at once. If it cannot be granted, the reasons for the refusal should be given, and they should be sent away with some small token; that is the way to earn their loyalty. When they quarrel among themselves, he advises, listen patiently. Let each party have its say. The cause of trouble is ordinarily trivial. The dispute can usually be healed with a glass of brandy.

He accepts the necessity for firm treatment. But he insists on one point: if you have to flog a man, flog him on the spot. If you are going to pardon him, do that also on the spot. Don't threaten him, don't keep him in suspense. If you do, he will brood and may escape into the bush and join the Maroons. Maroons, groups of escaped slaves living in the bush, were to be found in every island. The best way, he counsels, of preventing them from trying to escape is to give them something of their own which they can value—a garden, poultry, pigs; something they will be afraid to lose.

He remarks on their love of gambling; they play dice with shells; some of them, through watching their masters, have learned how to play cards. This he deplores; they will gamble away their possessions. He regards gambling, dancing and alcohol as their great temptations. He recommends early marriages to curb their warm-blooded natures. They are, he states, nimble thieves, and he regrets that closer observance is not taken of an excellent law that forbids the unauthorized purchase of an article from a Negro. They are great teases, he insists; they are quick to recognize idiosyncrasies, particularly in their masters, which they can ridicule. When the master has a fault, he earns a nickname. Père Labat learned their language so that he could detect their raillery. They are loyal to each other and expert at hiding Maroons who visit them. Small though their cabins are, they are able to build double rooms which defeat inspection. They are equally adroit at concealing their thefts. He is highly amused at the astonishment, the injured innocence they display when their misdemeanor has been discovered. The expression on their face, the tone in their voice, make it hard to believe that they are lying. When they are confronted with those who know their tricks, their final ruse is to attribute the whole unfortunate business to the devil's handiwork. As the devil is not there to pay for his misdeeds, then, the good priest explains, the slave must act as a replacement.

He speaks of their vanity, of their trick of attempting to prove less intelligent than they really are; of their vindictiveness when their pride has been hurt. The seventh chapter of the fourth volume of Père Labat's memoirs might have been written yesterday. If he could return to the Antilles today he would find much to surprise him, but he would feel himself at home and he would be delighted that his old friends, for whose comfort, spiritual and physical, he sincerely strove, had achieved not only their own independence but also a way of life personal to and characteristic of themselves.

Labat had the good fortune to travel in a period of relative international good will. He was once through mistake captured by the Spaniards, and was amused at their surprise at his being so good a Catholic. The ship on one of his trips had two cannon but only one cannonball, which could not be used in action because it was needed to crush mustard for that favorite delicacy, roasted pig (*cochon boucanné*), a dish that was always served at picnics when everyone pretended to be a buccaneer; where there were no plates, spoons, forks, tablecloths; where a pig replaced the wild boar of d'Ogeron's day. One must drink frequently, he said. "The law compels it, the sauces invite one; few err in this respect."

Labat appreciated the Creole cuisine. He spoke of the fricasseed iguana with high approbation, comparing the whiteness of its flesh and the delicacy of its flavor with that of chicken. He describes the hunting of the animal. "We were attended," he said, "by a Negro who carried a long rod, at one end of which was a piece of whipcord with a running knot. After beating the bushes for some time, he discovered our game basking in the sun on the dry limb of a tree. Hereupon he began whistling with all his might, to which the iguana was wonderfully attentive, stretching out his neck and turning his head as if to enjoy it more fully. The Negro now approached, still whistling, and advancing his rod gently, began tickling with it the sides and throat of the iguana, who seemed mightily pleased with the operation, for he turned on his back and stretched himself out like a cat before a fire, and at length fairly fell asleep; the Negro then dexterously slipped the noose over his head and with a jerk brought it to the ground, and good sport it afforded to see the creature swell like a turkey-cock to find itself entrapped. We caught others in the same way and kept one of them alive seven or eight days, but it grieved me to the heart to find that it thereby lost much delicious fat."

The Indians of Cuba were equally adroit in the catching of wild fowl. They would throw calabashes into the ponds which the birds frequented. These calabashes would float upon the water and the birds would become accustomed to them, and would even perch on them. The hunter would then put a calabash on his own head, having first pierced eyeholes in it and a hole to breathe through, so that he could creep into the water, either swimming or walking where the stream was shallow, with his head above the surface. When he at last got among the fowl he would seize one by the feet, drag it under the surface, fasten it to his girdle and proceed to load himself with as many as he could carry away without creating the least alarm or disturbance among the rest.

Greatly though he relished the pleasures of the table, Labat deplored extreme indulgence, which he considered an English weakness. In Barbados, he said approvingly of General Codrington that he was far more sober than were most of his nation as a rule.

Labat suffered from yellow sickness, *le mal de Siam*, and he was bitten by a snake, the *fer-de-lance*, which for many years was such a pest in Martinique and St. Lucia that the mongoose was introduced to exterminate it. Later the mongoose became a pest itself.

He visited Barbados, and his description of his visit to an island that was likely to prove hostile at any moment, as it had so often in the past, is a proof of his own broad-mindedness. He was able to see many merits in the English way of life. He was impressed by the good manners of the English officials and the excellence of the French they spoke. He was also impressed by the prosperity of the island: the large, clean streets of Bridgetown, the strong, well-built houses with glass windows, the shops and stores that contained goods from every quarter of the globe; there were goldsmiths, jewelers, clockmakers. He attributes this general air of opulence to the trade that Barbados could carry on with the American colonies. He had been told that the climate was unhealthy, but he could detect no sign of this in the complexions of the colonists, particularly in those of the women. Children ran about like ants. He was impressed too with the rich furnishing of the houses. The plantations were, he noticed, smaller than the ones in the French islands, because, he assumed, the island being smaller had to accommodate a large number of inhabitants, and land was scarce and expensive, but the houses were even larger and better built than those in the town—an English trait, though he did not recognize it as such, the Englishman setting chief store by his "country seat," while the Frenchman devotes himself to his "hôtel" in Paris, Lyons or Bordeaux. These plantation houses were approached by broad avenues lined with tamarinds and orange trees. The good taste of the planters was as remarkable as their riches. There was so much silverware that he thought the French marine would be better employed plundering this island than attempting to intercept the galleons of the Spanish treasure fleet. He regrets that a plan to capture the island was abandoned because its commander felt that his first duty was to search for treasure. But patience, the good father says; what has been deferred is not necessarily lost.

He took as close an inventory of the defenses and resources of the island as if he had been preparing an intelligence summary for the authorities in Martinique. Perhaps he was. He attended a military parade. The troops were well armed and well turned out, with drums and bugles. The officers wore tight-fitting scarlet jackets, heavily braided with gold, and white-plumed helmets—a most inappropriate uniform for the climate; the aristocrats served in the cavalry, and the minor artisans and shopkeepers in the infantry. It appeared to Labat that the infantry were little more than servants for the cavalry. He estimated that some five thousand men were under arms, but he did not consider that this would be a very formidable force

in time of crisis, as a great number of the infantry were bondmen
and Irishmen shipped out against their will for periods of five to seven
years under harsh masters who, at the expiry of their sentence, usually
found some excuse for prolonging their durance. These men would
probably welcome an invader, as would the slaves. Labat considered
that Barbados would be an easy prey; French troops under the tuition
of Vauban were masters of siege operations, but here there would
be no need of their expertise because Barbados had neither a fortified
city nor a citadel. The vulnerability of Barbados was never, however,
to be tested. It did not need fortifications, since it had the protection
of the trade wind. When the French in Martinique in 1781 planned
an attack upon Barbados, they had to abandon the attempt, and sailed
for St. Kitts instead.

It is usual for the nationals of a colonizing power to consider that
the natives of other powers' colonies receive worse treatment than
their own. Labat was no exception. He did not consider that the
Barbadians treated their slaves well, underfeeding them but allowing them a free day on Saturdays, when they could work in their
own gardens for their own profit. A slave was treated less well
than a horse, partly, Labat considered, because slaves were much
cheaper in Barbados than they were in Martinique, the Barbadians
having more opportunities of benefiting from the privateers. He
points out that the English clergy gave them no instruction and did
not baptize them, that they were treated like beasts, that they were
allowed as many wives as they liked, whom they could change at
will, provided they produced plenty of children, worked hard and
kept in health. Their masters overworked them, thrashing them on
the least excuse. Whether they were worked harder in the British islands is debatable. But they certainly worked hard. Lady Nugent,
writing of Jamaica in 1800, said that during the sugar harvest the
slaves worked for twelve hours a day over a boiling caldron; and that
they so often fell asleep and got their hands caught in the mills that
a man was kept standing by with a hatchet so as to release the
slave by cutting off his arm.

In Labat's opinion, slave revolts were more frequent in the English
islands than in the French; he attributes this to the fact that the
French slaves received religious instruction and the English ones did
not. It is probably true that there was less religious instruction in the
English than in the French and Spanish islands. There is no indication that the English had any but business reasons or excuses for
the slave trade, whereas the French and Spaniards did believe that

they were conferring a benefit upon the Africans by offering them the opportunity of salvation. Yet the savage outbreaks of violence in Hispaniola and Guadeloupe a century later make one wonder whether the French planters were any more humane than the English, or whether the French slaves had been softened by their change of faith. In St. Kitts, Labat asked the English ministers why they did not baptize their slaves. The ministers replied that they considered it wrong to keep a Christian soul in slavery. Labat retorted that it was surely worse to deny to a human being the opportunity of salvation. Many of the planters were opposed to Christianity for the slaves because it would give the various tribes a sense of unity. In their opinion, there was no greater security than a diversity of language.

Père Labat comments on the drunkenness and brutality of the English overseers, but he recognizes the need for summary treatment of revolt. A recent rising in Martinique had been put down with what could be described as a massacre. Such action he admits is cruel, but he reminds his reader that the white man is outnumbered by ten to one and he has sometimes to pass the bounds of moderation in order to inspire fear, lest he himself should be the victim. Père Labat was an excellent and broad-minded man, but he never condemns the institution of slavery or the trade itself.

CHAPTER VI

Rich as a Creole

In 1702 the peace of Europe was disturbed by the war of the Spanish succession. It lasted for eleven years. It was a curious war to have been fought within a hundred years of Philip II's death. A Bourbon prince, the grandson of Louis XIV, was sitting on the throne of Spain, Louis was proudly announcing that there were no longer any Pyrenees, and the other kings of Europe were uniting in a grand alliance to prevent the complete subjugation of Spain by France. It has been described as a war with limited aims, waged by monarchs with mercenary forces, in their personal, dynastic interests. As far as England and Holland were concerned, it was waged to curtail Louis XIV's ambitions.

Labat was in Guadeloupe when war broke out. That was in May. The news reached the English islands in July, but the French did not learn of it until the capture of their ships by English corsairs warned them of trouble in the air. That kind of thing was likely to happen in the Caribbean. Eighty years later Rodney was to sack St. Eustatius when the Dutch believed themselves to be at peace, and in 1667 the French government was so dilatory in warning their colony in St. Kitts that its governor had been killed in action before the news of war had reached the island.

Labat's accounts of the steps taken at Guadeloupe to alert the populace is typical of what a war was like at that time, in that area. A muster was taken of all the inhabitants capable of bearing arms, and an inventory of all the available military supplies. A store of manioc was requisitioned, to be lodged in the fort and to be renewed every three months. Manioc, peas and potatoes were to be planted in high areas and in valleys distant from the sea; a team of patrols and coast guards was enrolled. The inhabitants of remote districts were instructed to take their families into the hills. Alarm posts were established. Inhabitants were told where to muster in case of crisis.

It was all very much what happened in England in the summer of 1940. And as the inhabitants of England were a quarter of a century later to remember that time in terms of their personal peradventures, Labat was in the main concerned with an earthquake that shook Martinique and a whitlow that afflicted his left hand. His doctor wished to operate, but Labat preferred to experiment with a local remedy that he had not yet tried. He took an egg that had just been laid and broke it with a piece of clean wood shaped like a spatula, since it was essential that iron should not touch it. The white of the egg was separated from the yolk; twice as much salt as would be needed for the eating of an egg was then mixed with the yolk. This was spread on a feather and wrapped round the finger; a compress was put on top which was strapped on firmly but not tightly. After two days Labat found that the whitlow had dissolved into a small hole in the flesh through which the pus had flowed. A little oil was applied to soften and close the wound and the good father's discomfort was at an end.

The war followed its course desultorily, as far as the West Indies were concerned. The British took over the French section of St. Kitts, the French raided St. Kitts, Nevis and Montserrat. Although one of the main aims of the Grand Alliance had been to prevent Louis XIV from gaining control of Spain's colonial interests, the monarchs involved were more concerned with the European than the colonial battlefields, believing that they could settle the Caribbean issue in Flanders; and indeed Marlborough's succession of victories —Blenheim, Ramillies, Oudenarde, Malplaquet—did effectively contain Louis within his frontiers. It was a humiliating war for France. The only benefit that she derived was the beaver catch of Hudson Bay, which established her supremacy in the hat trade. But that was not an immediate advantage. Spain too fared badly. Gibraltar was captured by the British, and at the Treaty of Utrecht in 1713 she surrendered her Italian and her French possessions. But in terms of her eventual interests, she was better off without a stake in Flanders, and with a Bourbon on her throne, her finances were in the hands of French advisers. The internal customhouses were put down; Castile was no longer the administrative center of the country; the American trade was centered in Cádiz. States once independent lost local privileges, and though there were separatist agitations in Aragon, Catalonia and Valencia which had to be reduced by armed campaigns, a unification of the country started. A genuine measure of prosperity returned to the Spanish people; the population rose, public works were undertaken, industry and shipping increased, the power of the Inquisition was reduced, and the country as a whole began to shake off the sloth which had settled on it during the seventeenth century. And all the time the treasure fleets were sailing from Panama.

When the Treaty of Utrecht was signed, it may well have seemed that the development of the West Indies had reached a decisive stage. Spain's monopoly had been broken, and Spain had accepted her limited position as owner of the treasure fleets, with stout bastions in Cuba and Puerto Rico. The buccaneers were a common black-market enemy. France was established between Guadeloupe and Grenada; she had originally owned St. Croix, and a small but prosperous colony had taken root there, but it was too close to the Danish island of St. Thomas and was trading with it in defiance of Colbert's *pacte coloniale*; orders were consequently issued to the colonists to move to Hispaniola, where there was a need of colonists, and they established themselves at Léogane. The British owned what are now known as the Leeward Islands—St. Kitts, Nevis, Antigua, Montserrat —along with Jamaica and Barbados. The Danes held St. Thomas. Labat considered St. Thomas the most prosperous of all the islands because Denmark was never involved in wars, and it was one of the first points of call for ships bound westward on the northeast trade. Her warehouses were invaluable for privateers. The Dutch, who were more interested in the East Indies than the West, and whose concern in the area was less agricultural than mercantile, owned Curaçao, Saba and St. Eustatius.

The Caribs, who had proved so truculent to the Spanish settlers in Guadeloupe, had been for the most part reduced or domesticated. In Dominica, where today their last settlement remains, they capitulated peacefully. In Grenada they put up a desperate resistance. They signed a treaty with the French but made no attempt to keep it. Forming themselves into small squads, they ambushed and killed every Frenchman whom they found traveling alone; finally a troop of three hundred Frenchmen was sent to deal with them. After a series of savage battles a remnant of forty men were surrounded on a mountain; rather than surrender they jumped to their destruction. The rock is named today Carib's Leap, and the village beside it, Sotairs, an anglicizing of the French *Sauteurs*. Fighting continued until the last Carib had been slain. In St. Lucia and St. Vincent the Caribs were more successful, but the area as a whole was engaged in a brisk and broadening economy.

Conditions were in fact sufficiently stable for white women to accompany their husbands to the Caribbean and for marriages to be contracted by young persons of good family. A new word was coined, "Creole," meaning native to the colonies. It bore no relation to the color of the skin; in terms of human beings it meant "born in the islands." You could have a black, white or mulatto Creole. In the same way you could have Creole cooking—dishes prepared out of local ingredients—and Creole dresses—costumes that were appropriate to the climate. Men and women were being born in the West Indies, were growing up and being educated there; families who thought of Barbados, Martinique and Cuba as their homes were creating a civilization of their own.

In each case that civilization was an echo, a reflection, an amplification of the home country. Colonies bear the same resemblances to their mother country that children do to their parents. Cuba and Puerto Rico were Spanish, just as Martinique was French and Barbados English. Cuba reproduced the life of the Hidalgos of Seville and Andalusia; the sugar planters of Barbados lived on their estates as did titled Englishmen in their country seats; the French tried to reproduce in Fort Royal and Cap Français the life of Versailles and Fontainebleau.

The extent of these differences was to have an effect upon the course of history. England in the eighteenth century was Whig and Protestant, with a German-speaking King who "did not like boetry and did not like bainting." Squire Western in *Tom Jones* is the prototype of the eighteenth-century English gentleman; they were hard-hunting, hard-drinking men consuming their daily bottle of port; and port at that time was very different from the noble and mellowed wine that today graces our dinner table. It was a fierce mixture of rough wine and raw spirit. They were heavy trenchermen with florid complexions and persistent gout. They lived in the Caribbean as they lived in Shropshire.

In France, on the other hand, under Louis XV, the worst punishment that could befall a nobleman was expulsion from Versailles to an exile on his own estate, and in St. Domingue and Martinique the French planters labored in the sun so that they could return with full pockets to a holiday at home. Paris, Paris, Paris. That was their constant dream. They relieved their loneliness and boredom, as their cousins did in France, with gallantry. The British, fettered by a Puritan conscience, though not addicted to excessive chastity, concentrated upon sport. In Jamaica, as in Wiltshire, they rated the pleasures of the table more highly than the pleasures of the bed.

Père Labat was deeply impressed by the comfort of the Barbadians' plantation houses. He would not, fifty years later, have found a parallel situation in Jamaica, both because it was colonized more recently and because the climate was less clement. The Jamaican was more concerned than the Barbadian with making a quick profit and getting back to England. He did not spend as much money upon his home. Lady Nugent referred to the contrast between the general plenty and magnificence of their tables and the meanness of their houses and apartments, it being no uncommon thing to find, at the country habitations of the planters, a splendid sideboard loaded with plate and vintage wines, a table covered with the finest damask and a dinner of perhaps sixteen or twenty courses, and all this in a hovel not superior to an English barn. A stranger could not fail also to observe a strange incongruity and inconsistency between the great number of Negro domestics and their appearance and apparel, the butler, and he but seldom, being the only attendant who was allowed the luxury of shoes and stockings. All the others, and there was usually one to each guest, waited at table in barefooted majesty, some of them perhaps half naked.

Yet the Jamaican as much as the Barbadian tried to take root in the country of his adoption and to reproduce the customs of the shires. Labat, by no means an abstemious man, commented both on the heavy drinking and the copious meals of the British colonists. Lady Nugent, a century later, was shocked by their gluttony. "I don't wonder now at the fever that people suffer from here," she wrote in her diary. "Such eating and drinking I never saw. Such loads of all sorts of high, rich and seasoned things and really gallons of wine and mixed liquors. They eat a late breakfast as if they had never eaten before. It is as astonishing as it is disgusting." She described as typical a dinner that started with black-crab pepper pot. The pepper pot consisted of a capon "stewed down," a ham also stewed to a jelly, six dozen land crabs with their eggs and fat, flavored with onions, okra, sweet herbs and such vegetables as were in season, the whole well-stewed. This was the prelude to further courses of turtle, mutton, beef, turkey, goose, duck, chickens, capons, ham, tongues, crab patties. The meal was rounded off with various sweets and fruits.

Such a regime was not conducive to a life of gallantry, and though Lady Nugent was continually deploring the moral lapses of the young Jamaicans, the British way of life did not lead, to anything like the extent that the French way did, to the creation of an important half-white class. Jamaica and Barbados were reproducing the atmosphere of *Tom Jones*, Martinique and St. Domingue that of *Les Liaisons Dangereuses*. In Jamaica most of the young unmarried planters had native housekeepers who spoke of them as their husbands, but these were established relationships, and Monk Lewis considered that mulatto girls would not accept such relationships unless they could think of themselves as morganatic wives. In St. Domingue, on the other hand, the dusky mistress was as accepted a feature of Creole as of Parisian life, and the children of these unions had a status in the French islands that they did not have in the British. Their fathers sent them back to the Sorbonne for their education, and Paris took kindly to the type. It was an exciting novelty. These young men were handsome, dashing, lively; they had money to spend. Why should not Paris welcome them? Paris could afford to welcome them. Paris had not a color problem. The Parisians, indeed, preferred them to the Creole planters who annoyed them with their ostentation and thoughtless extravagance. There was no equivalent to this class in London.

These differences in national characteristics were to have important consequences later.

Throughout the eighteenth century the Caribbean was a boom area, and the phrase "rich as a Creole" was in familiar use in London and in Paris. Yet the life of the planter was very far from easy. At the moment of writing—the 1960s—the West Indies are the most favored playground in the world. The most popular period for tourists is from December 15 to April 15. But this is only because the climate in northern latitudes is then at its worst. From the Caribbean point of view one month is very like another. There is officially a dry and a wet season, but a Rip Van Winkle suddenly marooned there could only recognize the season from the shrubs and trees that were in flower. The only poor period is in the early autumn when there is danger of a hurricane. These come, when they do, between late August and late September. As the jingle has it:

> June too soon,
> July stand by,
> August you must
> Remember September,
> October all over.

The hurricanes blow at a speed of 150 miles an hour, and most islands have been visited by them at some time or another. They inflict great damage, destroying houses and uprooting trees. The gaps between their visitations are considerable, and it is the custom every year nowadays, when the hurricane season approaches, for the prudent family to ensure that their shutters and locks are firm, and that there is a store of food and blankets in case of trouble. But otherwise there is little difference between June and January. One day is like another; too like another. There is no variety. When Lady Nugent arrived in Jamaica in 1800 as the wife of its governor, she remarked to Lord Balcarres that it was a very fine day. His Lordship replied, "I assure you that you will be tired of saying this before many days are over."

To the contemporary tourist, as to Christopher Columbus, the West Indies seem an earthly paradise, but the lack of variety in the climate has a deleterious and debilitating effect upon the northern settler. Moreover, in the eighteenth century, the incidence of fever was very great. Lady Nugent's diary is full of references to residents and members of her husband's staff who suddenly fall sick and die. She was soon writing of "this dreadful, this deceitful climate."

The planter had a great deal to contend with besides the climate. The sugar islands were mainly in the hands of the French and British, and each group of settlers had their separate problems. The French and English managed their estates on a different method. The English planter had an agent in London with whom he placed his orders and he sent home sugar on his own account. The French merchants resident in France sent out cargoes at their own risk, which were sold for them by agents in the islands or by captains of the ships; the proceeds were invested in West Indian produce. To a far greater extent, therefore, the English planter had a stake in the colony, and from the start the system of absentee ownership was more firmly established in the French islands.

The French planter was harassed by the restrictions of the *pacte coloniale*, but the administrative difficulties of the English planters were in their own way just as great. Bryan Edwards, who at the moment of his death in 1793 had nearly finished a history of the British West Indies, is our most reliable informant on those difficulties. He himself was a typical example of a Jamaican planter; he was born in Wiltshire, in Westbury, in 1743. His father inherited a small estate which yielded him about £100 a year. Without any experience, he tried to supplement this income by trading in malt and corn; he was not successful, and when he died in 1756 his widow and six children found themselves in distressed circumstances. Luckily this widow had two rich brothers in Jamaica; one of them undertook the education of

Bryan, who was the eldest son, and sent him to a French boarding school in Bristol. He spent three years at this school, acquiring there a knowledge of French and a love of literature. When he was sixteen, his younger uncle returned to England, established himself in London in a style worthy of a rich Creole, and soon had a seat in Parliament. Nephew and uncle did not, however, get on well together, and Bryan was dispatched to Jamaica, where his education was continued.

He was to write, in describing the planter's life, "There seems universally a promptitude for pleasure. This has been ascribed, perhaps justly, to the levity of the atmosphere. To the same cause is commonly imputed the propensity observable in most of the West Indians to indulge extravagant ideas of their riches, to view their circumstances through a magnifying medium and to feast their fancies on what another year will effect. This anticipation of imaginary wealth is so prevalent as to become justly ridiculous; yet I am inclined to think that it is a propensity that exists independent of the climate and atmosphere and that it arises principally from the peculiar situation of the West Indian planters as landholders. Not having, like the proprietors of landed estates in Great Britain, frequent opportunities of letting their plantations to substantial tenants, they are for the most part compelled to become practical farmers on their own lands, of which the returns are in the highest degree fluctuating and uncertain. Under these circumstances a West Indian property is a species of lottery. As such it gives birth to a spirit of adventure and enterprise and awakens extravagant hopes and expectations—too frequently terminating in perplexity and disappointment.

"The business of sugar planting is a sort of adventure in which the man that engages must engage deeply. There is very seldom the possibility of retreat; a British country gentleman who is content to jog on without risk on the modest profits of his own moderate farm will be startled to hear that it requires a capital of no less than thirty thousand pounds to embark in this employment with a fair prospect of advantage. To elucidate this position, it must be understood that the annual contingencies of a small or moderate plantation are very nearly equal to those of an estate of three times the magnitude. . . . In speaking of capital, I mean either money or a solid, well-established credit; for there is this essential difference attending loans obtained on landed estates in Great Britain and those which are advanced on the credit of West Indian plantations. An English mortgage is a marketable commodity while a West Indian mortgage is not. In England if a mortgagee calls for his money other persons are ready to advance it; now this seldom happens in regard to property in the West Indies. The credit obtained by the sugar planter is commonly given by men in trade, on the prospect of speedy returns and considerable advantage, but as men in trade seldom find it convenient to place their money out of their reach for any length of time the credit which they give is ofttimes suddenly withdrawn and the ill-fated planter compelled, on this account, to sell his property at much less than half its first cost. The credit therefore must not only be extensive but permanent."

Every colonist complained about the trade restrictions that were imposed on him. At the very start of the colonial period Sir Thomas Warner had written: "Through the restraint on tobacco, the poor planters are debarred from Free Trade and unable to furnish themselves with necessities, much less to buy ammunition," while the Barbadians were later to complain: "If our island is an integral part of the British Commonwealth, we have a right to that trade with foreign nations that is enjoyed by Britain." They objected to having to buy in Britain goods produced abroad. The citizens of Rome, though they lived in the remotest parts of the world, were still Roman citizens to all extents. "But we poor citizens of England, as soon as our backs are turned, and we are gone a spit and a stride, are presently reputed aliens and used accordingly."

The planters' political situation also was anomalous. The governor was a go-between. He was the King's representative, working under the privy council, but he was also part of the colonial legislature. The legislature of Jamaica, for instance, was composed of the governor, of a council nominated by the crown consisting of twelve gentlemen, and a house of assembly containing forty-three members who were elected by the freeholders. The qualification required in the elector was a freehold of ten pounds a year in the parish where the election was made, and in the representative a landed freehold of three hundred pounds per annum in any part of the island, or a personal estate of three thousand pounds. The assembly copied, as nearly as local circumstances permitted, the legislature of Great Britain, all their bills having the force of laws as soon as the governor's assent was obtained. The most important of these laws dealt with regulations of local policy, to which the laws of England were not applicable, such as the slave system; on which, and other cases, the English laws were silent. The colonial legislation made such provision as the exigencies of the colony were supposed to require. But the crown retained the right of veto.

"Rich as a Creole" had its obverse side, and Edwards is the planter's advocate with this special pleading. "Seeing," he argues, "that a capital is wanted which few men can command and considering withal that the returns are in general but small, and at best uncertain, how has it happened that the sugar islands have been so rapidly settled and many a great estate purchased in the mother country from the profits that have accrued from their cultivation? It is to be wished that those who make such enquiry should note on the other hand how many unhappy persons have been totally and irretrievably ruined by adventuring in the cultivation of these islands, without possessing any adequate means to support them in such great undertakings. On the failure of some of these unfortunate men, vast estates have indeed been raised by persons who have had money at command; men there are who, reflecting on the advantages to be derived from this circumstance, behold a sugar planter struggling in distress with the same emotions that are felt by the Cornish peasants in contemplating a shipwreck on the coast, who hasten with equal rapaciousness to participate in the spoil. Like them too, they sometimes hold out false lights to lead the unwary adventurer to destruction; more especially if he has anything considerable of his own to set out with.

"Money is advanced and encouragement given, to a certain point, but a skilful practitioner well knows where to stop; he very well knows what very large sums must be expended in the purchase of the freehold, and in the first operations of clearing and planting the lands and erecting the buildings, before any return can be made. One third of the money thus expended he has perhaps furnished, but the time soon arrives when a further advance is requisite to give life and activity to the system by the addition of the Negroes and the stock. This is the moment for oppression, aided by the letter of the law and the process of office, to reap a golden harvest. If the property answers expectation and the lands promise great returns, the sagacious creditor, instead of giving further aid or leaving his too confident debtor to make the best of his way by his own exertions, pleads a sudden and unexpected emergency and insists on immediate repayment of the sum already lent. The law on this occasion is far from being chargeable with delay, and avarice is inexorable. A sale is hurried on and no bidders appear but the creditor himself. Ready money is re-

quired in payment and everyone sees that a further sum will be wanting to make the estate productive. Few therefore have the means who
even have the wish efficaciously to assist the victim. Thus the creditor
gets the estate at his own price, usually for his first advance, while
the miserable debtor has reason to thank his stars if, consoling himself with only the loss of his own original capital and his labor for
a series of years, he escapes a prison for life." Piracy, in fact, under a
different banner, was still afloat in the Caribbean.

Richard Pares in *A West India Fortune*—a book of exceptionally
alert erudition, the result of long and acute research—has told the
story of an English west country family whose prosperity was based
on a West Indian adventure. Pinney is one of the best-known and
respected family names in Dorset. In 1685 Azariah Pinney, a refugee
from the Monmouth Rebellion, landed in Nevis with £15 in his
pocket. He died in 1719. His son survived him by only a few
months, but his grandson's plantations were to be valued at £20,000,
and his great grandson John Pinney, when he retired to settle in
England in 1783, was worth £70,000. For another thirty years, John
Pinney, an absentee owner, acted as a merchant and a factor in Bristol. In September 1817, a few years before his death, he distributed
his wealth among his children. The paper value of his assets was estimated at £267,000 and the moneys that were owed him in debts and
mortgages raised the score to £340,000.

This clearly is one of those West Indian fortunes that justified the
label "rich as a Creole," but Richard Pares' narrative explains to what
extent John Pinney was exceptional, in his prudence, caution, temperance and meticulous regard for detail. He made substantial profits
as a planter, and as a factor he drew a 2½ percent commission on
the consignments of sugar that he handled, but the great part of his
wealth came from the interest on his loans to planters. Most of his
friends were in debt and he was very careful how he invested his
money. He never, for instance, loaned money to planters who had
colored heirs. "Judgment," says Pares, "rather than activity, was the
factor's contribution to the sugar market."

Bryan Edwards' contemporary estimate of the situation is amply
endorsed by Pares' twentieth-century researches. Pares points out that
so heavily were the estates in debt in the 1830s that only a small
proportion of the £20,000,000 compensation that the British government paid to the planters, when slavery was abolished, reached the
planters' pockets. Most of it went to the mortgagors. Of the £145,000

that was paid to Nevis, £32,500 went to the Pinney estate in England, and Pinney was only one of the mortgagors in Nevis.

Merchants and financiers made money much faster out of the sugar estates than the planters did.

Another constant problem for all the settlers in the Caribbean was the long-distance control exercised over them by the home government—British, Spanish, French and Dutch. It was very difficult for the home government to obtain exact information from and about the colonies. It was easy to make a mistake in their administration. And since a letter could not receive an answer for many weeks, it took a long time to rectify a mistake once it had been made. The history of Antigua during the first decade of the eighteenth century provides a pertinent example of these conditions.

In 1704 a Mr. Park, while serving as an officer in Flanders, had the good luck to attract the notice of the Duke of Marlborough, whom he served as an aide-de-camp and by whom he was sent to England to announce to the Queen the victory of Ramillies. The Queen rewarded him with a purse of a thousand guineas and her picture richly set in diamonds. In the following year, when the government of the Leeward Islands became vacant, Mr. Park was offered the appointment.

A less judicious choice could not have been made. Mr. Park, a native of Virginia, was a man of singularly dissolute behavior. Having married a rich American woman, he possessed himself of her wealth and deserted her. With this money he came to England and obtained a seat in Parliament. Exceptional bribery having been proved against him, he was dismissed from the House. A friend whose wife he had seduced having opened proceedings against him, he escaped, as other men have done, by accepting his sovereign's service in a foreign field. Here, as has been already told, fortune smiled on him.

He arrived in Antigua in July 1706, and was warmly welcomed by the community, who believed that his connection with America would prove profitable to their commerce; they added a thousand pounds a year to his income to relieve him of the expense of house rent. But their delight in him was of short duration. Having seduced the wife of a Mr. Chester, the most considerable merchant in the country and the factor to the Royal African Company, and fearing that the injured husband might attempt revenge, he decided to protect himself "by adding the crime of murder to the misdemeanour of adultery." Chester had recently by accident killed a man. The governor brought him to trial for his life, having first taken the precaution of raising a common soldier to the office of provost marshal, directing "his creature" to impound a jury of persons who would bring in Chester guilty. The evidence was, however, so overwhelmingly in the defendant's favor that even a pressed jury was compelled to acquit him.

Mr. Park then got the bit between his teeth. He ordered the Codrington family to prove before himself and his council their title to the island of Barbuda, of which they had held unchallenged possession for thirty years; an act which made every proprietor in the island wonder whether he himself held any other security for his own possessions than the governor's forbearance.

Park insisted that the provost marshal should always summon juries of his own selection; he changed the mode of electing members to the assembly so that he would be able to exclude persons he did not like, and when he failed even by these means to procure a subservient assembly, he refused to summon it, even when the French threatened an invasion. He raided Mr. Chester's house, arrested a number of the men he found there, on the grounds that they were concerting measures against himself, and kept them in the common jail without bail or trial.

The community in their indignation sent an agent to England to complain against him, but, unable to endure the delay that was inevitable in such a case, they had resort to violence. Several attempts were made upon His Excellency's life, through one of which Park was seriously wounded. His behavior now became more arrogant and unrestrained. At last instructions came from the crown, ordering him to resign his command to the lieutenant governor and return to England by the first convenient opportunity; at the same time commissioners were appointed to listen to evidence on the spot. The Antiguans gave way to transports of delight not dissimilar to those which they were to exhibit two and a half centuries later when Lord Baldwin returned to the island confirmed in office. Their exuberance provoked the governor beyond the frontiers of sanity. He announced that he had no intention of leaving the country, although a ship was about to sail for Europe, and issued a proclamation dissolving the assembly. The assembly, however, refused to be dissolved, asserting that, since Mr. Park had been recalled by his sovereign, his continuance in the government was usurpation and tyranny, and that it was their duty to protect the peace and safety of the island.

The governor retorted by surrounding the assembly house with troops. But the representatives had been warned; they escaped and summoned the inhabitants from all parts of the island to gather, armed, to protect their rights and representatives. They intended no ill to the governor, they asserted. They were concerned only with his removal from the island.

A body of five hundred colonists marched upon Government House, which Park had converted into a garrison to be defended by every regular soldier at his command. At this point Park lost his nerve, and when it was too late attempted a concession. He sent by his provost marshal a promise that he would meet the assembly and consent to whatever laws they might think fit to pass; moreover, he offered to dismiss his soldiers, provided six of the principal inhabitants would remain with him as hostages for the safety of his person.

The speaker of the assembly and one of the members of the council offered themselves as hostages, but the crowd was not prepared to prevaricate; delay might prove fatal to their cause. In two divisions they marched upon Government House. For a couple of hours there was a fierce exchange of fire, then the assailants burst through the palisades. The governor, at the last, showed courage. With his own hand he shot dead one of the chief men in the assembly, but a bullet brought him to his knees. His attendants, seeing him fall, threw down their arms and the enraged populace seized the prostrate governor and, tearing him to pieces, "scattered the street," so the record has it, "with his reeking limbs."

It was an episode without parallel in British colonial history, and the people of England heard of it with astonishment and indignation, looking upon it "as an act of rebellion against the crown." But when the British government had investigated the matter, they were so satisfied of Park's misconduct that they issued a general pardon to all who were concerned in his death; two of the principal actors in the drama were later promoted to seats in the council.

The episode is important because it shows how easily an unsuitable man could be appointed to an important post, how difficult it was for the victims of this appointment to obtain redress, and to what lengths of savagery a mob can go under a tropic sun. It must be remembered that the mob in question was composed of white men, and it was a white man who was dismembered.

There was another phrase, too, that was familiar to Europeans: "beautiful as a Creole." The exotic conditions of the tropics were breeding a special type of woman, pale and languid, with small hands and feet, with luminous long-lashed eyes, with indolent and graceful movements, and the slow singsong voice which had been acquired from a colored nurse. It was from this type of beauty that was to spring Josephine de Beauharnais.

Bryan Edwards, with appropriate Anglican reserve, was temperate in his encomia, but he was far from unimpressed. He spoke of "the even tenor of their lives and of their habitual temperance and self-denial. . . . Except the exercise of dancing, in which they excel, they have no amusement or avocation to impel them to much exertion of either mind or body. Those midnight assemblies and gambling conventions, wherein health, fortune and beauty are so frequently sacrificed in the cities of Europe, are here happily unknown. In their diet the Creole women are, I think, abstemious even to a fault. Simple water or lemonade is the strongest beverage in which they indulge; and a vegetable meal at noon, seasoned with cayenne pepper, constitutes their principal repast. The effect of this mode of life, in a hot and oppressive atmosphere, is a lax fiber and a complexion in which the lily predominates over the rose. To the stranger newly arrived, the ladies appear as just risen from the bed of sickness. Their voice is soft and spiritless and every step betrays languor and lassitude; they lack that glow of health in the countenance, that delicious crimson which in colder countries enlivens the coarsest set of features and renders a beautiful one irresistible. . . . In one of the principal features of beauty, however, few ladies surpass the Creoles, for they have, in general, the finest eyes in the world, large, languishing, expressive, sometimes beaming with animation and sometimes melting with tenderness." In Bryan Edwards' opinion, no women on earth made better wives or better mothers. The Creole ladies were also noted for their white teeth, which they polished with juice of a withe called the chewstick; it was strong, bitter and a powerful detergent. The withe was cut into small pieces and used as a toothbrush.

The beauty of Creole women did not, however, do more than meagerly diminish the loneliness of the planter's life. Creole women might be exquisite, but there were deplorably few of them.

From the very beginning, indeed, the lack of white women had been a problem in the islands, and Colbert's insistence on the need for *engagées* was due to a recognition of the inevitable consequences of this lack. In the early days it was possible for French officers and officials to get leave on the grounds that they were returning to France to find a wife. Anxious to restrict illicit unions between planters and their slaves, Colbert issued a number of discriminatory measures. The father of a mulatto child was fined two thousand pounds of sugar if the mother of the child was the master's slave; in addition to this fine, the Negress and the child were confiscated and sold for the benefit of the hospital.

This ordinance Labat heartily approved, though he regretted that it led to an even graver offense—the practice of abortion. Very often a master who saw himself likely to be convicted of paternity promised the Negress her release if she would deny his guilt. At one time it was the custom for masters to free their mulatto sons when they reached the age of twenty-four, the argument being that the youth by his work from the age of sixteen had repaid his father for the expense of his upbringing. But when the French islands passed under the direct rule of the throne, this law was changed and it was ruled that the child of a slave was a slave no matter who the father was. Labat only met two instances of a white man marrying a black woman, and nowhere does he approve of such marriages. When a young white girl seduced a black man and became pregnant, his advice was rationalistic. Send the slave to St. Domingue, where he could be sold, and the girl to Grenada, where she could have the child in secret. It could be adopted and she could pretend on her return that she had been on a holiday.

In Labat's time the problem of the half-colored and quarter-colored population was not as acute as it was to become in the course of the eighteenth century. Although colonization in the islands by the French and British was eighty years old, stability had been existing there for barely the length of a generation, and only recently had the scene been crowded by the large half-colored class which was to present so very acute a temptation to the young emigrant.

European men have not generally considered the purebred African woman physically attractive. Her features are coarse, her hair short and crinkly, the nose squashed back against the cheeks, the lips large and protuberant. For such a woman a European man was unlikely to form a strong and permanent attraction. On the other hand, the mixture of African and European blood produced a highly attractive female, for whom it was most natural for a young man to form a strong attachment. The prevalence of such attachments became the problem of the eighteenth century, particularly in the French islands, where the establishment of a mistress was a national institution. In St. Domingue, even married planters kept colored women, whose children they displayed proudly as their own, brought up in the same nursery as their legitimate offspring and made allowance for in their wills. The wives submitted to the system on the excuse that the black mistress was invaluable as a spy, and that there was no other sure means of knowing what the slaves were planning. For bachelors it was the invariable custom. To be the mistress of a white planter was the goal of a colored girl's ambition. It was, among other things, her only avenue to freedom. For it was by no means rare for a man to free his mistress and have her children educated. Such a relationship was indeed the chief distraction in his life.

Except during crop time, the work on a plantation was unvaried and uninteresting. Cane grew itself. There was little for the planter to do except to ride round his estate and supervise the discipline of the slaves, the digging of the ditches, the weeding of the fields. When crop time came, there was, in contrast, a wave of such intense concentration in the heat of the factories that he soon longed for the quiet boredom of the planting season.

The best picture of that life is to be found in Matthew Lewis' *Journal of a West Indian Planter*, which was published after his death in 1817, and was highly praised by Coleridge. Lewis was a remarkable man. Born in 1775, he did not inherit his West Indian estate until 1812, and was not able to visit it until after the Napoleonic Wars, when the slave trade had been abolished, though the slaves had not yet been freed. His early years were devoted to the pleasures of Bohemian society; he was the friend of Byron and Shelley, and he frequented Madame de Staël's salon. At the age of twenty, when he was an attaché at the British Embassy at the Hague, he wrote a lurid novel called *Ambrosia, or The Monk*, and was nearly prosecuted for its indecency. Byron said it "ought to have been written by Tiberius at Capri. . . ." He dismissed it as "the philtred ideas of a jaded voluptuary; they have no nature, all the sour cream of cantharides. . . . It is to me inconceivable that they could have been composed by a man of only twenty." Yet it sold prodigiously and earned its author the nickname "Monk."

Lewis exasperated his friends. "Short-sighted and loquacious," Byron found him, "pestilently prolix," and he wished that "he would but talk half and reduce his visits to an hour." Yet Byron was fond of him:

I would give many a sugar cane
Matt Lewis were alive again.

Lewis was clearly a generous, warmhearted man. He knew Wilberforce and was anxious to improve the conditions of the slaves, though
he was not in favor of their emancipation, and considered that *The
African Reporter*—the organ of the abolitionists—presented a highly
biased picture of plantation life. He recognized the dangers of the
absentee system, with an attorney managing the estate, a salaried
lawyer supervising the planting and in charge of labor, with white sub-
ordinates, known as bookkeepers, who were nursing their own interests, not those of the proprietor or his slaves, and he inserted a clause
in his own will to the effect that his heirs would forfeit their rights
to his Jamaican estates unless they spent three months every third
year there. He disapproved of flogging, and such a humanitarian was
he that other planters accused him of spoiling his Negroes and spreading dissatisfaction. But in spite of his genuine affection for his slaves,
he had no illusions about them. He knew that they were indiscriminate poisoners, that they grew arsenic beans in their gardens, although
the beans were of no use for food or ornament, and that they fermented the juice of the cassava root until it produced a worm which
they hid under their thumbnail until an opportunity occurred to
drop it in the victim's drink. He knew that they were subject to the
orders of their Obeah men.

He was exasperated by their idleness, stupidity and secretiveness.
"There is no folly and imprudence like unto Negro folly and imprudence." The slaves often went lame, because a small fly, the chica,
would work its way into their feet and lay its eggs. They were provided with small knives to extract the eggs, but as there was no
pain until the sore had formed they were too lazy to use them. Frequent foot inspections had to be ordered. The slaves were constantly
reporting sick, to avoid work, yet when they were ill they concealed
the nature of their illness. It was thus very difficult to diagnose the
nature of the complaint. A woman, for instance, who had allowed
her baby to slip out of her arms, vigorously denied that the child
had had a fall, although another woman insisted that she had. After
the closing of the slave trade, there was a shortage of labor in the
cane fields, and the planters tried to replace Negroes with machinery
and cattle, but the Negroes distrusted these innovations; they broke
the plows and starved the cattle. Lewis soon realized that a little
flogging was necessary.

He presents the planter's life as an endless succession of irritations and complaints. His patience needs to be inexhaustible, and all the time his nerves are exposed to the strain of an exhausting climate. Lewis himself caught fever during his second visit, and died on the voyage home.

"Rich as a Creole" indeed, but it is not surprising that many planters dreamed of the day when they could retire and live in Europe on the revenue of their estates.

CHAPTER VII

The War of Jenkins' Ear

The Treaty of Utrecht kept Europe out of war for twenty-six years. It ended when a Spanish commander, after rummaging a British ship for contraband without success, tortured her captain, a Welshman called Jenkins, and cut off one of his ears, telling him to take it home to his king and master. This Jenkins did, preserving it in a bottle which he displayed to the House of Commons. One of the members asked him what he thought or expected when he was in the hands of such a barbarian. "I recommended my soul to God," he said, "and my cause to my country."

History records that those members who were averse to war "hung low their heads and sneaked out of the chamber," and the popular outcry was so great that the Prime Minister, Sir Robert Walpole, who had assumed power after the financial crisis of the South Sea Bubble, shrugged his shoulders. He was convinced that his country's interests could be best served by peace. In his opinion, bribery was a cheaper activity than war. But there were certain concatenations of circumstance against which common sense could not prevail. He remarked as the joybells rang, "They are ringing their bells now; they'll be wringing their hands soon."

Jenkins' ear was, in fact, only the final straw in a long series of disagreements whose complete story has been told at length and with much wit by Richard Pares in *War and Trade in the West Indies*.

The origin of the dispute went back seventy years to the treaties of 1667 and 1670, which were phrased with such face-saving vagueness that it was impossible to tell what had been agreed. The clause, "This present treaty shall in no way derogate from any pre-eminence, right or seigniory which either the one of the other allies have in the seas, straits and fresh waters of America, and they shall have and retain the same in as full and ample a manner as of right they ought to belong to them," referred to Spain's claims that all America belonged to her, but did not include Britain's acceptance of this claim. A later clause asserted that "it is always to be understood that the freedom of navigation ought by no manner of means to be interrupted, when there is nothing committed contrary to the true sense and meaning of these articles." This presumably meant that Spain realized that Britain had certain claims, without recognizing what they were or their validity. Many years later a British ambassador in Madrid was to say of this treaty that it consisted of "reciprocal propositions made between an English and a Spanish minister, corrective of each other, without bringing the point to so precise a conclusion as might effectually and at all times and in all dispositions of the two crowns toward one another, prevent the evil it was intended to remove."

But at the time, the British ministers who arranged the treaty were content in the knowledge that something had been achieved by Spain's recognition that British ships were actually allowed in the Caribbean. And certainly the treaty of 1670, which, had it been signed a little earlier, would have stopped Henry Morgan's raid on Panama, did end the power of the buccaneers.

The Treaty of Utrecht held better promise; a long and bitter war was over. Louis XIV's reign could only have a few weeks to last; though a Frenchman sat upon the throne of Spain, the two kingdoms were separate. France, England and Holland no longer appeared in the Caribbean as filibusters bleeding the Spanish empire white. Each country had a stake in the area; they had solid settlements, as opposed to bases for smuggling, with which they were conducting legitimate trade. And Britain had been granted the *assiento*, the monopoly of the slave trade to the Spanish colonies, the right to open factories in the Spanish Main and to send every year a ship of five hundred tons to the fair in Porto Bello. Surely now the European nations could settle down to cultivate their own private gardens.

But the tradition of lawlessness in the Caribbean died hard. Buccaneers could not become respectable citizens overnight, particularly when the Spanish governors were prepared to approve their raids, provided they themselves had their percentage of the booty. The Spanish definition of contraband was responsible for innumerable disputes. The Spaniards tended to regard as contraband goods that not only had been, but that might have been, exported from Spain, and on these grounds they claimed the right to interfere with ships plying between two British colonies. Under this interpretation of the law, a cargo that had been landed in Jamaica and was then being reshipped to Boston could be confiscated. Once a Spanish product, always a

Spanish product, although Spanish products could have been acquired legitimately by the annual *assiento* ship, or surreptitiously through the practice of certain Spanish governors of obtaining the necessities for their parishes by sending to British colonies the merchandise they could exchange for them. Spanish coin was regarded as contraband wherever it might be found, although it was the recognized currency in the French Antilles.

Dyewood in particular presented a problem. It came from the Bahamas, and the Spaniards claimed the Bahamas as their own, although they had never settled them. An even more pressing issue concerned the logwood trade. Logwood was of great value to the English woolen manufacturers for dyeing purposes. Some logwood grew in Jamaica and was occasionally shipped to England, but most of the English logwood came from the Spanish provinces of Honduras and Campeche. In these areas definite British settlements had been founded. It was a hard life that was led there by these pioneers; while they were at work they were up to their knees in swamp; but there is a certain type of man who can tolerate any existence, provided he is independent and his leisure can be relieved by heavy drinking and native women. The Spanish themselves had no wish to make use of the land, but they resented the presence of the English, whom they were continually attempting to evict; the English maintained that they had a right there under a vague clause in the treaties of 1667 and 1670. The question of effective occupation was one of the most vexed in Anglo-Spanish relations, the Spaniards regarding as illegal any settlement in the New World that they had not expressly licensed. The logwood controversy was still an irritant on the eve of the Anglo-Spanish War in 1762, and was a contributory cause of it.

Illegal confiscation led to constant lawsuits. The most fervent admirers of the Spaniards will hesitate to number alacrity among their qualities, and the machinery by which claims for depredations were adjusted would have been slow even if it had been handled by a twentieth-century American. If an English captain felt that he had been ill-used, he was expected to apply for redress in the Spanish courts, but knowing how long such an action would take and how expensive it would prove, he preferred to approach his own government. If the British ambassador could be persuaded to take up his case, the Spanish authorities would at first retort that the captain must have acknowledged his own guilt because he had not complained through the proper channels. When that objection had been overcome, the Spanish authorities would explain that they had not yet received their own governor's report; they must hear both sides of the case. The law's delays were indefinitely prolonged, and even when it was accepted that the plaintiff had a legitimate complaint and the ship and cargo were ordered to be returned, the case was far from finished.

An order to restore the ship and cargo would be given and the claimant would be provided with a royal letter, a *cédula*. The restitution had, however, to be made at the spot where the action had taken place. This necessitated a costly voyage, from which the prudent claimant would endeavor to recoup himself by taking out a cargo of merchandise. Often this was his sole reward. The governor would question the *cédula's* authenticity and send a protest home. The ship and the cargo had probably been sold, and it would be impossible to recover the proceeds which had been dispersed in a hundred directions. In vain would the claimants protest that the money should be paid in Spain, since the *guarda costas* were acting under the King of Spain's directions. Many sea captains felt that it was easier to obtain redress in the way that Henry Morgan favored.

Nor did the Spaniards lack causes of complaint. The South Sea Company, which held the rights in the *assiento*, made no attempt to keep to their agreement. Their single ship was followed into harbor by a flock of frigates, from which the ship was reloaded overnight. Far more than five hundred tons were brought into Porto Bello, and there is little doubt that the single ship used its privileged position for smuggling. It is surprising that the declared profits of the company were so small; it can only be assumed that the profits found their way into the pockets of the chief shareholders by concealed channels, particularly in view of the fact that a quarter of the stock was held by the King of Spain himself.

> Nobody's morals were overnice
> When Walpole talked of "a man and his price."

And this was a very curious transaction. The Spanish King never seems to have received any return for his investment. The sum of £95,000 keeps cropping up in all the discussions; it was owed by Spain to Britain in return for the depredations of certain *guarda costas*; the obligation was partially admitted, and there was a point when George II suggested that the £60,000 owed him by the South Sea Company should be set against it. It is a confused story. It is probably simpler and not wholly inaccurate to say that the issue of the war of 1739 was concerned with the right of search, and the final occasion of it was the presentation of Jenkins' ear to the House of Commons.

The War of Jenkins' Ear began in 1739. A year later Frederick II of Prussia, who had ascended the throne a few weeks earlier, established a national precedent by invading Silesia without a declaration of war; the War of Jenkins' Ear became the war of the Austrian succession. It lasted till 1748, and most of Europe became involved; the fortunes of war swayed from one side to another; each side had victories to celebrate, but at the end nobody had much to show for it except Frederick, who set out with a limited territorial aim, the acquisition of Silesia, and the glorification of himself. By the treaty of Aix-la-Chapelle he was recognized as one of the most important monarchs of his day, and his army had more than held its own against Europe's most seasoned troops.

In the Caribbean it was a minor war, if indeed it could be called a war at all. No possessions changed hands. British and French troops never got to grips there; the campaigns between the Spanish and British fleets were languid and ineffective, and the British at the end of the war inflicted so decisive a defeat upon the French in the Atlantic—in spite of the great skill and gallantry displayed by their admiral against heavy odds—that the French did not make any further major attempt at sea.

From such Caribbean campaigns as there were, however, the language of the English-speaking people was to receive two additions. It has often happened that a man will give his name to a certain type of action. Boycott is the readiest example. But it may be questioned whether there is another example of one man providing the vocabulary with two different words. In 1739 the British fleet made an unsuccessful attack upon Havana. Its admiral had under his command 3,600 colonial troops, one of whose junior lieutenants was called Frederick Washington. Though the attack failed, the young lieutenant was so impressed by the skill and courage of his admiral that he asked his brother George, who was building a country house in Virginia, to name it after this admiral—whose name was Vernon.

Vernon was popular with his men. He wore a weatherworn cloak made out of grogram, and was nicknamed affectionately "Old Grog." The admiral insisted that his men, as a precaution against scurvy, should drink rum and water. This beverage was nicknamed "grog." Many hundreds of tourists visit Mount Vernon every day; and in a thousand bars, in winter, a hot grog will be ordered as a precaution against the cold. But scarcely a soul remembers the victor of Porto Bello.

From the colonial aspect, the most significant incident in the war was the capture by the British of the French-Canadian fortress of Louisburg, which until then had been regarded as little more than a sneakhole for privateers. At the end of the war it was returned readily to France. But British strategists had recognized its value, and its capture in the Seven Years' War was an important step in the conquest of Canada.

In the treaty of Aix-la-Chapelle, a first attempt was made to fix the status of the four islands which were later to be known as the neutral islands, Tobago, St. Lucia, Dominica and St. Vincent. The situation in these islands was confused by the persistent and effective opposition of the Caribs. St. Vincent and Dominica were supposed to belong to the Caribs, but in Dominica the French had bought a large section of the island from them. St. Lucia, as Tobago, had been occupied by the English and the French, but ownership had never been established, and in St. Lucia the Caribs were more powerful than either party. There were more French there than British, and half of those British were actually Irish.

These islands as a whole were settled by small communities who disliked government and laws, and, in the case of St. Lucia, by Frenchmen who found a lack of opportunity in Martinique. In addition to the usual minor crops, they produced hardwood timber, which was extremely important to the French sugar planters, who could not get the kind of wood they wanted from America. These islands were also useful in providing ground provisions. The French used them as an *entrepôt* for slaves from Barbados.

The islands had also a strategic value. Tobago lay to the windward of Barbados and could interfere with the American and British trade. St. Vincent and Dominica were of value to France since they could protect her communications between Martinique, Guadeloupe and Grenada; but it was St. Lucia that was of the greatest value. It had a superb harbor and lay slightly to the windward of Martinique. It was from here that Rodney in 1782 was to develop the campaign that ended in the Battle of the Saints. He said afterward that it was the key island strategically in the Windward group.

At Aix-la-Chapelle, Dominica and Tobago were returned to France, and St. Lucia was declared a neutral island, as was St. Vincent, where the Caribs had proved even more bellicose than in Grenada. They not only beat off the first French settlers, but provided a refuge for escaped Negroes, mainly from Barbados, who intermarried with them and bred a race known as Black Caribs that routed quite a large French expeditionary force. In fact, they never were subdued. In the Seven Years' War, St. Vincent was captured by the British, but the Caribs refused to admit their sovereignty; after ten years' fighting, a peace was arranged and the Caribs were given a reserve in the north part of the island. Trouble began again during the American War of Independence, when the island was captured by the French. It was restored to Britain at the peace conference, but the Caribs had come to regard the French as allies against their resented guests. With the assistance of the French, they rose again, and there was long and bitter fighting. Eventually the residue of this fierce race was transplanted to Honduras.

The neutral islands presented a number of awkward problems. But on one principle the French and British were agreed. Each side was afraid that there might be a glut of sugar, so that neither side really wanted the islands colonized, yet neither wanted them occupied by the other. At Aix-la-Chapelle they agreed to evacuate St. Lucia and St. Vincent, but it was not so easy to put the process into operation. The French were quite happy as they were. The islands were largely French; they could very easily be occupied when occasion required. It was the British, not they, who kept asking when the evacuation was going to begin. In the end, the choice and chance of battle closed the argument.

Europe was to know little peace as long as Frederick II sat on the throne of Prussia, and the war of the Austrian succession was soon followed by the Seven Years' War (1756–1763). This was a very different business. During the eight years that had passed since the treaty of Aix-la-Chapelle, the rise of Prussian power had been so swift and formidable that a coalition to limit it was formed by France, Russia, Sweden, Saxony and Austria. Britain was Prussia's chief ally. Spain eventually came in on the side of France. It was one of the most successful wars ever fought by either Prussia or Britain, and at the end of it both had acquired a great deal of plunder. Prussia won four major battles and in spite of the opposition kept her frontiers intact. Britain played a very minor role in the European campaigns, but laid the foundation of her empire. She captured Canada, broke the French influence in India, asserting her own there, and established her dominance in the Caribbean.

As in the case of the War of Jenkins' Ear, a local war had broken out in the New World a year before Frederick's invasion of Saxony started the European conflict. The French had been acting aggressively toward the British possessions in North America, and a British squadron was sent in retaliation to intercept a convoy of French ships that was carrying troops and stores to Quebec. The commission was successfully executed; two French line-of-battle ships, fitted out as transports, were captured, along with a large number of unprotected merchant ships, so that before the Prussian invasion the English prisons were crowded with French sailors.

For the French it was a disastrous war. The French economy was in a crippled state, and the British government, under the vigorous leadership of the elder Pitt, concentrated on the distant areas where France was weakest. Let Frederick carry on his continental campaigns; Britain would help him with money and mercenaries. She had more to gain overseas.

The Squadron, cooperating with Clive in the conquest of Bengal, was strengthened. Within a short time the British navy was in complete command of the Bay of Bengal and the coast of Malabar. In North America, the lessons of the war of the Austrian succession were remembered. Louisburg was recaptured and served as a base for the capture of Quebec. Further south, though an attack on Martinique was beaten off, Dominica and Guadeloupe were captured. So complete indeed was the destruction of the French marine that Britain was able to capture the island of Belle-Ile off the French coast, which she used as a base for blockading operations and found highly profitable in the eventual bargaining at the peace conference.

This collapse of the French navy and mercantile marine had one curious result: it drove the mercantile marine to seek a livelihood on the high seas with its privateers, thus reviving the old traditions of the filibusters of Tortuga. They were exceedingly successful. It has been estimated that a tenth of Britain's merchant fleet was captured, but this loss was more than compensated by the ruin of France's commercial rivalry. Britain's commercial predominance dates from that war.

In 1761 Spain was rash enough to enter the war, in recognition of what it called "a family compact" with France. A British assault was immediately launched against Havana. The Morro Castle was one of the strongest citadels in the New World. It put up a sturdy resistance. Yellow fever and dysentery laid low three quarters of the expeditionary force, ten thousand strong, that had been landed, but the castle eventually fell. Cuba was returned to Spain at the subsequent peace treaty, but its brief occupancy by the British was of great importance to it. During those twelve months, the island was granted a number of trading concessions, some of which it managed to retain when Spain resumed her ownership, but even more important was the discovery by the English of the delights of Havana tobacco. From that time on, British appreciation of a good cigar was a most valuable factor in the island's annual budget. In return for her honoring of the "family compact," Spain received at the peace conference the city of New Orleans. As Britain acquired Florida—which, though it then geographically reached the Mississippi, consisted only of the port of Fort Augustine—France was left without a single possession on the North American continent.

In the same campaign in which Havana fell, Martinique was at last captured; St. Lucia, St. Vincent and Grenada had already fallen into British hands, and St. Domingue was France's only remaining possession in the New World.

From 1739, war was intermittent in the Caribbean, but war there in the eighteenth century was very different from the total war of the twentieth century. Each island consisted of a large agricultural area and a town or two towns protected by artillery and forts. An island could not be captured till the forts had fallen, but a raid on an island could do a great deal of damage. In 1706 the French sacked Nevis and St. Kitts. St. Kitts recovered quickly because of the especial fertility of its soil, but Nevis, from which over three thousand slaves were taken, was a backward island for many years; so was Montserrat, which was attacked in 1712. An important semiabsentee Jamaican landowner was to write to a friend in 1745: "I think as you do that the conquest of the island is out of the question, but if you and I are ruined it is the same thing to us." To damage an enemy's island in wartime could be as useful as to capture it, and up to the Seven Years' War the nations had fought not to capture islands but to destroy property.

The defense of an island depended on its militia; regular troops were usually only resident in wartime. The militia was ordinarily small and contained a disproportionate amount of officers. The recruitment of Negroes was avoided, except in extremities. Planters, with justice, distrusted the loyalty of their slaves, who would often take advantage of a battle to escape into the hills, while invaders were reluctant to encourage slaves to revolt against their masters, even though their masters might be enemies. Their own turn might come later. In 1740, the governor of St. Domingue, the Marquis de Larange, debated this problem when he was planning with the Spaniards the invasion of Jamaica. He had learned that the British intended to arm their slaves; he did not think that they would make very formidable soldiers, and he believed that he could effectively impair their efficiency by proclaiming that any slave found in arms should suffer the penalty of death, while those who surrendered themselves and their arms should receive their liberty. He did not feel, however, that "the laws of war and religion" would permit him to follow the advise of a predecessor who had been prepared to offer liberty to any slave who arrived bearing the head of his master, and he was disturbed when he learned that the Spaniards in Cuba had imported a number of muskets with which to arm the Jamaican Maroons. He did not consider that a "very Catholic way of destroying the English." Moreover, if the plan succeeded, "surely an island occupied by more than a hundred thousand Negroes would be a very disagreeable neighbor; it would provide for our own slaves a safe asylum from which we should never get them back."

Jamaica was indeed to find itself in precisely the same position in regard to Haiti sixty-five years later. Though France might be at war with Britain, the two countries still had common interests. Larange, when he heard that the Negroes in Jamaica had rebelled, hoped that they would be subdued.

The judicious employment of slaves was a major problem in the West Indian wars, and each island adopted different measures. It was generally agreed that they could be used as unarmed pioneers and fatiguemen. Mulattoes and freed Negroes were in a different position. They had a stake in the colony and their loyalty could be relied upon. They were, however, reluctant to enlist, because they were afraid that if they were taken prisoner they would be sold as slaves.

Home governments were not anxious to maintain permanent garrisons in the West Indies. They were expensive and the climate was bad. Indeed, when wars broke out, commanders were instructed to capture islands quickly, before their troops were incapacitated by fever and rum. Home governments considered that the islands should defend themselves with their own militia, and that when regular troops were stationed there the colonists should make up the difference between the rates of living at home and abroad. This was a logical demand since the cost of living was very high, the colonists concentrating on the profitable sugar crop and having to import provisions. The electoral assemblies were, however, loth to accept this responsibility. West Indian stations were not popular with the military.

The navy was in a different position. In peacetime as well as war it was as necessary for the French and British as it was for the Spaniards to protect their own shipping and interrupt illegal dealings with their colonies. The Dutch were in a different position. Curaçao and St. Eustatius had no agricultural possibilities; they were simply *entrepôts*, bases for trade, mainly of a devious nature, retaining their neutrality whenever the European situation permitted them. The Danes were in a similar position. They did not acquire St. Croix till the middle of the century, when they developed its potentialities as a sugar island. St. Thomas was mountainous and arid, but it lay in the direct line of the trade winds, a convenient landfall for westbound ships. As a neutral port it was of great use to both the Greater and Lesser Antilles. The Danes and the Dutch tried to stand apart from the main drama of the Caribbean as it was waged by the Spanish, the British and the French.

For the belligerent nations, the problem of survival was both simplified and complicated by the fact that, owing to the prevalence of the trade wind and of the Gulf Stream, there were only three exits from the Caribbean; the Florida Channel and the Windward and Mona passages.

British ships to and from Jamaica had the most difficult passage. Before they reached the West Indies they would strike their latitude and then sail downwind; this course carried them along the south coasts of Puerto Rico and Santo Domingo, where Spanish *guarda costas* might intercept them. They had two alternatives for return, and both were difficult. The Windward Passage between Cuba and St. Domingue was the nearest, but it was not easy to round the eastern tip of Jamaica against the wind. The journey could take a week. The passage was narrow, and to avoid being driven into the Bight of Léogane, between the two prongs of St. Domingue, they had to keep close to the Cuban coast, where the land winds were helpful. But they were perilously near Santiago, that smugglers' haven. If, on the other hand, they chose the Gulf Channel, they had to follow the coast of Cuba, keeping close to it at the western extremity by Cape Antonio to avoid a contrary current that very often ran from the Gulf of Mexico into the Caribbean. There were often calms off Havana, and a ship hovering there was an easy prey.

The ships of the Lesser Antilles were in an easier position. Their only danger on the way out was a cruising privateer, and on the journey home, through the wide passage, the ships' only danger was from a privateer from Puerto Rico. The American ships had the most difficult voyages because they had to reach Jamaica by the Windward Passage. They were exposed both ways to the maximum of danger. The French had the easiest journeys. They could sail straight across the Atlantic to Martinique; they were never at war with Spain, and their return journey through the Mona Passage was unlikely to be hindered. In peacetime the ships for St. Domingue had a direct entrance and exit route to Cap Français in the north; though in wartime Cap Français was blockaded by the ships of the Jamaica station.

In those days seamen had not learned how to measure longitude. It was easy for them to miss an island; they therefore set themselves on the latitude of the island that they wished to reach. The French ships made the latitude of Martinique; the English the latitude of Barbados or Antigua. North American vessels also made for Barbados; they found it, as the most windward island, the best starting point for their adventure. This method of navigation simplified the task both of the protecting warships and the privateers.

The French and British navies worked on different systems. The French employed squadrons which they sent out when the hurricane season had ended and recalled to the Mediterranean when it was about to start. The British maintained two permanent stations, one in Jamaica, the other in the Leeward Islands. Each method had its advantages. The French could do two tours of duty, a summer one in Europe and a winter one in the tropics, while the British ships were immobilized during the hurricane months. On the other hand, it was difficult for the French to meet a sudden emergency, as happened when the British attacked Guadeloupe in 1759, though it has to be remembered that help might have come from Martinique if its governor, the Marquis de Beauharnais—Josephine's future father-in-law—had not at that time been exclusively engrossed in the charms of Josephine's aunt. Moreover, the defenses of Guadeloupe had been consistently neglected. There were too many small garrisons. There were not enough mobile men in the hills. And the governor had bought from St. Eustatius a number of muskets, of which three quarters exploded at the first shot. They had not been intended for action, but for barter on the Guinea coast. That is the kind of incident that makes it difficult not to regard much of West Indian history in terms of a Palais Royale farce.

The French system of defense had much to recommend it. But on the whole the British system was more practical. The campaigning season was limited to the summer months, and ships could not carry more than seven months' provisions aboard; very often the French ships carried less because their officers filled their holds with merchandise which they sold to the planters. The French were unable to obtain provisions from their colonies because the planters concentrated upon the sugar crop. The English, on the other hand, could revictual their ships with produce from their American colonies. It cannot be too often repeated that geography had decreed the interdependence of America and the West Indies.

Jamaica was to the leeward of Antigua; it was difficult for Jamaica to help the Leewards, but it was easy for the Leewards to help Jamaica, particularly as the attacking ships would be observed in the Leewards. It was Rodney's view that Jamaica was safe as long as there was a strong force in the Leewards. The British ships in the West Indian stations were able to be of service, during the hurricane season, in North America, where many of the great ports and rivers were frozen during the winter; they could occasionally act as convoys between New England and the West Indies.

One great advantage of the French method was that the French ships came out in excellent condition, whereas there was not enough equipment in the West Indies to keep the British ships in perfect trim. Even so, after a battle the British were able to repair their ships more quickly than the French could, English Harbour and Port Royal being better equipped as dockyards than Cap Français and Fort Royal. But perhaps the chief advantage of the British system was that for certain months it had command of the sea.

In wartime—and after 1739 that was more often than not—the British station squadrons fulfilled three main functions and one subsidiary one; they attacked the enemy, defended their own island, and gave convoy service; on occasion they assisted military operations. The ships from Europe brought out the necessities for plantation life and took back the sugar, coffee, indigo, cotton and cocoa by whose sale the plantations were financed. The French relied more than the British on provisions sent from the home country because the British could draw supplies from their American colonies. The only indispensable cargoes that the British received from Europe were the salt beef, butter and candles that came from Ireland.

Flour and bread came from America. Many difficulties accompanied this trade. The independent New Englanders did not like to confine themselves to convoy; they were small dealers who went to the best market; very often that market was French. If they were intercepted they would explain that they had gone into harbor with a leak and that they had paid for repair services with their cargo. There were also the slavers from the west coast of Africa, some of which carried their rum and molasses northward to New England; others went straight back to Europe.

The merchants on both sides were more interested in having their own cargoes protected than those of the enemy attacked. Everyone put his own interests first, and governments recognized that trade had to continue, and that peace would follow war. The economists preached the theory of "channels of trade." "A trade once lost cannot be easily retrieved. The currents of trade, like those of waters, make themselves channels out of which they are afterwards as hard to be diverted as rivers that have worn themselves deep within their banks."

Some trade had to be continued. Insurance, for instance. It would be disastrous if French merchantmen placed their insurance in Amsterdam instead of London, so that the ridiculous situation arose of British men-of-war sinking ships whose loss would be reimbursed by Lloyd's. Irish beef was another case in point. The French at the start of each war talked glibly about obtaining beef from Jutland and mutton from Iceland, and such talk had a diplomatic value in Copenhagen, but the meat that came from the Baltic was badly packed; the French would have been undernourished had they not received supplies from Ireland. An embargo was placed on Irish beef, but cargoes continued to arrive.

Considerable weight was attached to the theory of "dependence," of making a customer rely on your services. It was at one time suggested that the French islands might be supplied with American produce from a free port in Dominica; then, if need arose, the trade could be discontinued and the French starved into submission.

There was another line of argument—was a trade harmful or beneficial? Trade was held to be a battle in which one side was the gainer, the other the loser; and the English believed that while their trade with Spain was beneficial, their trade with France was disadvantageous. In the case of Spain, badly needed cash came into the national exchequer in return for manufactured articles, while, in the case of France, money went out in return for luxuries. A high-court judge contended, in a case concerning the activities of a British ship which was trading with the enemy, that "to send to an enemy things that tend to the gratification of their luxury and wantonness is said to be lawful, for such supplies contribute to render them weak and effeminate and from this reason whatever debilitates the enemy may be deemed lawful. . . ."

The law was therefore concerned with discovering which kinds of trade were harmful to the enemy and which were not. Right through the Seven Years' War, tobacco was allowed free passage into France, while the French merchants, afraid that because of the British blockade their colonists would lose their taste for French luxuries, gave special permits to neutral traders. At one point the colonists were forced to eat clams and cassava—slave food. This frightened the French merchants. The colonists must not be allowed to abandon an opulent way of life.

Spain opened a free port at Monte Cristi, on the north coast of Santo Domingo, from which the British operated under a flag of truce. It was irritating to the Americans to find that, while their trade with the French islands was prohibited, the British and West Indians traded briskly with the Spaniards. It seemed to the American colonists that the burdens of patriotism imposed by the British were borne chiefly by the Irish and themselves. In wartime, Monte Cristi, St. Eustatius and, to a lesser degree, the Danish islands of St. Thomas and St. Croix, flourished abundantly, particularly St. Eustatius. Their warehouses were stacked with American goods, which were dispatched in small cargoes to the French islands. It was easy for an Irishman to acquire Dutch nationality and thus give a spurious legality to his transactions. Monte Cristi was of great value to the Americans who wished to trade with Cap Français.

On the whole, the English colonies were far less affected than the French in terms of trade in wartime. But figures are often puzzling. It is not easy to find an explanation of the fact that though fewer English ships sailed to Africa during the war of 1739, more Negroes were imported into Jamaica. Every lobby, and there were innumerable lobbies, considered its own interests. Everyone concerned with the war was unashamedly a profiteer; each person was convinced that the more money he earned, the more he would be fulfilling his duty to his country. It would seem to have occurred to no one that during a war soldiers and sailors are being killed and that in their interests it is desirable to bring a war to the speediest conclusion.

In 1763, once again the great powers gathered, this time in Paris, to settle their disputes. In Europe, Frederick II was in a position to dictate terms; in colonial matters Britain was. Britain had indeed regarded the war as a means to establishing her empire. She saw war as an extension of commerce, and from the attitude that she adopted at the peace table may be gauged the importance that she attached to her West Indian possessions. She retained Dominica and St. Vincent, restored Grenada and St. Lucia to France, and Cuba to Spain in return for Florida. She then had to decide whether she would keep Canada or restore it to France in exchange for Martinique and Guadeloupe. This was the most significant issue at stake. It had been assumed in 1759 when she captured it that Britain would retain Guadeloupe. A great deal of money was invested there. Pointe-à-Pitre was developed and slaves were introduced in large numbers, to the irritation of the Jamaican planters, who were short of slaves. In 1762, at the very end of operations, Rodney captured Martinique and stated that it was of immense strategic importance and should, if possible, be retained at the peace treaty. There is no clearer indication of the importance at that time of the sugar islands than Britain's doubt as to whether Canada was as important as Guadeloupe and Martinique.

It is impossible to assess the exact value of a colony to a mother country. There are so many invisible exports and imports, and the value of the various currencies has changed so much that the actual figures usually have little contemporary significance. But the value of the West Indies to Britain may be gauged from these figures of 1788. The capital employed was estimated at seventy million pounds. Britain exported to the West Indies 3.8 millions; imported and exported, with profit coming to England, 7.2 millions; the duties to the government were 1.8 millions. One hundred and fifty thousand tons of shipping were employed. East Indian trade was about half that.

In the opinion of French historians, Guadeloupe was at the time of the French Revolution the richest island not only in the French group but in the whole area of the Lesser Antilles; its exports, first of sugar, then of coffee, cotton and cocoa, were greater than those of Martinique and St. Lucia; exports worth twenty-seven million francs against imports valued at fifteen million francs showed an immense balance of trade in the island's favor. Some historians argue that this prosperity was illusory, because so many landowners lived abroad, dissipating the profits that should have been plowed back into their estates, and leaving themselves without the balances of credit that they would need to meet emergencies. In addition, the extravagance of these planters in London and in Paris drove the estates into debt. But that, surely, is a criticism not of the island itself but of its administration. An island with such a considerable credit balance of trade cannot be anything but a highly valuable possession. Britain was, moreover, better placed to make such an island pay because of her ownership of the thirteen colonies in North America. The American colonies needed the products of the sugar islands and the sugar islands needed the products of North America; an excellent triangle of trade could be maintained between New England, the Guinea coast and the Caribbean. Canada was not yet rich enough to participate in this trade by converting the triangle into a quadrilateral. Canada had been of little use to France, and Guadeloupe had never been as prosperous as it has been during its four years under British ownership.

Under French ownership, Guadeloupe's hands had been tied by its inability to buy the slaves and manufactured goods it needed. Guadeloupe had always had to play second fiddle to Martinique. All its produce was shipped to Europe via Martinique, labeled as Martinique rum, sugar, coffee. Martinique's prestige stood higher. A distinction was made between *les messieurs* (the gentlemen) *de la Martinique* and *les bonnes gens* (the good folk) *de la Guadeloupe*. The only advantage to Guadeloupe of this social inferiority was that, in war, Martinique was generally attacked first. Otherwise Guadeloupe suffered. Because the governor of the islands was resident in Martinique, prizes were taken thither, so that the other islands could not recoup their losses. All arms-makers were in Martinique. All the shipping was there. Martinique was the *entrepôt*. Guadeloupe had a great deal to gain by being annexed by Britain. It was what lawyers call "a pretty point."

Colbert's *pacte coloniale* was only sound economy if the home government was in a position to supply the islands' needs. St. Domingue developed more quickly than Martinique and Guadeloupe because in its early years it was less restricted by orders from Paris. It is not surprising that the British ministers should have wondered whether Canada, if it had been of so little use to France, was going to be of much use to Britain.

One English lobby was wholly in favor of annexing Guadeloupe. The slave traders were delighted at the prospect of an enlarged market; but the West Indian lobby did not really decide in favor of annexation till Martinique was included in the deal. The price of sugar

had dropped after the capture of Guadeloupe, and it was likely to fall
still further if Martinique sugar as well were to be put upon the market. There was also the problem of slaves. The planters found it hard
enough as it was to manage their estates with the supply they had.
There had been a definite shortage when Guadeloupe was being so
improvidently supplied. If England was going to take over Guadeloupe and Martinique, then the African territory must be enlarged.
During the war England had captured Senegal; she should retain
possession of it. There were some who favored a scorched earth policy;
retaining the French islands but destroying the crops so that there
should not be a glut of sugar. In the end, however, the West Indian
lobby was in favor of annexation. During the two last wars, no invasion had landed upon an English colony, but there was no reason
why one should not. Martinique and Guadeloupe were uncomfortably
close as neighbors. Might not Barbados, Antigua and St. Kitts suffer
the same fate as the French islands; had not Nevis, Montserrat and
St. Kitts been devastated in the war of the Spanish succession? Many
of the planters had borrowed money in England to insure their properties. The premiums and the rates of interest depended on the
public's faith in their security. "The planters," Rodney wrote to Lord
Lyttleton, "are divided between avarice and fear; they think that if
Martinique is retained, they will be obliged to lower the price of their
sugar. On the other hand, if it is given up, they fear that in the case
of another war, the French will overrun their plantations before they
can receive succour from Europe which, as I said before, may easily
happen; the example of this war has taught them a lesson which I
fancy they will never forget."

To the West Indians, fear in the end proved stronger than avarice.
And, in addition to the pleadings of the West Indian lobby, there
were quite a number of cogent reasons why England would be as
well-off without Canada. The war had been started because of the
threat which France and her Indian allies had presented to the New
England colonies, and the North American colonists had always demanded the expulsion of the French from Canada; yet would it be
altogether wise to rob the northern colonies of the threat that had
kept them loyal? Might not the North American colonies grow too
big and powerful? A large army would be required to protect Canada,
whereas the sugar islands could be defended by the navy. There was
the question of trade. Already the North American traders could not
find a large enough market for their goods in the British West Indies
and had to sell them, surreptitiously, to the French. The trade of

Canada was negligible—except for the fisheries. Guadeloupe could produce a larger revenue. Who was going to pay for the war that had
been waged on the colonists' behalf? It was easier to raise revenue
from the sugar islands.

The northern colonies were admittedly a better market for English goods than a sugar island. Free and white colonists bought more
than slaves. But where did the eventual profit of all this trade return?
The Americans made small profits and invested those profits in their
own land; they had no intention of returning to England. The West
Indian planter, on the other hand, always thought of "going home";
very often he invested his profits in Britain. The argument seemed
in favor of retaining Guadeloupe rather than Canada; and yet it was
Canada that was kept.

The difficulty lay in this; if Guadeloupe was to be kept then Martinique must too, and Pitt and Bute, who conducted the negotiations,
did not believe that there could be peace with France if a settled
colony was taken over. Martinique was truly French, in a way that
Guadeloupe was not, and the French wanted it back. It was a good
bargaining point. Let France keep her two main islands, let Britain
have her share of the neutral ones, Grenada, Tobago, St. Vincent
and Dominica, and in addition let Britain keep not only Canada but
the whole continent of North America as far as the north bank of the
Mississippi. France would lose very few subjects and not much face;
England might have acquired a number of new islands which were
unprotected, but those islands offered scope for English enterprise,
and the North American colonies had now an impregnable frontier.
Bute, who completed the negotiations, was as prepared as Pitt to
sacrifice the West Indian interest to the American. "Conquer in the
islands and annex on the continent" was a pretty packaged deal; it
left only one question unanswered: Who was going to pay for the
war? That question was to cause very soon a great deal of trouble.

Among the many arguments adducing in favor of retaining Guadeloupe, the one that carried, it seems, least weight was doubt as to the
wisdom of freeing the thirteen colonies from the necessity of keeping
on good terms with the King of England and his ministers. Until
then Britain had provided protection for the colonies against the Indians and the French. The French held the view that if a colonizing
power discovered a river it owned all that lay along that river until it
reached the sea. It had assumed those rights in regard to the Mississippi, and had indicated that the time might come when it would

assert the same rights toward the Hudson. The French were a constant menace, and when the royal governors and justices of the peace appointed by the crown passed the boundaries of what the colonists considered equitable, as they frequently did, the colonists had to admit that, anyhow, the British were a bulwark against their enemies. After the Treaty of Paris, however, there was no longer a French menace, and two years later a last desperate combination of the Indian tribes was crushed so decisively that the New Englanders could feel that they had no more to dread from them, and that they could present with unfettered hands their complaints against their English rulers.

They had a number of complaints. The British as colonists present a record little less vulnerable than that of the French and Spanish, though a Briton is entitled to consider that his compatriots have shown in their colonial transactions a good deal of common sense, have been prepared to ignore the danger of creating precedents in view of an immediate necessity; have, through an inborn indolence, a love of privacy, a wish to "avoid unpleasantness," a belief that problems if left alone will solve themselves, a readiness to call a revolution the Reform Bill of 1832; have been always prepared to accept a compromise, to do whatever seemed immediately needed to maintain the status quo. This tendency may every now and again have led to unfortunate results, as it appeared to do in 1938 at Munich, although there is no proof that a sudden rush to arms would have been in the final analysis any less unfortunate. It is never easy to deal with a madman; far less with a country dominated by a madman. By and large this tendency to compromise has not worked out too badly in the handling and dismemberment of what was once the British Empire; a bond remains between Britain and most of the countries that she once administered.

In the eighteenth century, Britain no less than France and Spain considered that colonies existed for the benefit of the home country. Most of her kings regarded the colonies as private property, to be administered in their own best interests. The colonists were, in fact, their tenants. The New England shipowners and farmers and the cotton and tobacco merchants in Virginia had as many counts of complaint as the sugar barons of Martinique and Guadeloupe. The stages of the quarrel that led to the War of Independence lie outside the scope of this narrative, except insofar as the quarrel was brought to a head by the retention of Canada and the restitution of Guadeloupe, and for the fact that one of the chief causes of dispute was a direct outcome of West Indian commerce: a dispute that should never have been permitted, since the prosperity of the British West Indian Islands was so largely due to their trade with the North American colonies.

In the early 1770s, the West Indians were importing annually from the colonies three quarters of a million pounds' worth of goods, lumber, fish, flour, grain, and the wood for their sugar barrels. The ships involved could make two or three journeys in one year. In return, the islands supplied the colonies with sugar, rum, molasses and coffee, to the value annually of four hundred thousand pounds, leaving a balance in favor of the Americans which was commonly paid in dollars or bills of exchange, enabling them to reduce their debts to British merchants. The American colonies, besides affording an inexhaustible source of supply, were also a sure market for the disposal of the planters' surplus production, the whole importation of rum into Great Britain and Ireland being little more than half the quantity consumed in America. From whatever angle the trade is considered, Great Britain will be seen to have received substantial benefits from it. The sugar planters, being cheaply supplied with horses, provisions and lumber, were enabled to adopt a system of management useful not only to themselves but to the mother country. Much of the land in the West Indies which otherwise must have been applied to the cultivation of provisions for the maintenance of their Negroes and the raising of cattle was appropriated to the cultivation of sugar. By this means the quantity of sugar and rum were greatly increased, and the British revenues, navigation and general commerce were augmented. On the other hand, the American colonies, which were indebted to Great Britain to an extent that their tobacco, indigo, rice and naval stores were insufficient to discharge, were able to make good their deficiencies through their circuitous trade with the West Indies, foreign as well as British. The result was as advantageous to Britain as if the sugar planters instead of the Americans had been the purchasers. But Whitehall did not appreciate this. It made blunder after blunder.

In the 1720s the *pacte coloniale* had been slightly modified for the benefit of the French colonies; they had an excess of molasses and they needed the poorer kind of fish that could be best supplied by the New England fishermen; the French were allowed to take nothing but fish in return for the molasses, some of which served domestic uses, the remainder being distilled into rum, a large part of which was shipped to Africa for the slave trade. New England's prosperity was largely dependent on their fishing trade along the coast and the Newfoundland banks. They could sell their best fish in Europe, but for their poorer fish they had no market other than the French Antilles. The trade was profitable to everyone. It necessitated the building and maintenance of many ships, it found a use for New England lumber and employment for a great number of sailors and shipwrights, yet in 1733 the British government, in an attempt to protect its sugar planters in the West Indies, decided to compel the New England merchants to buy all their molasses from the British islands; to this end, therefore, it levied such a heavy tax upon the sugar and molasses imported from the French islands that the trade could not be continued.

The Barbadian planters approved the Molasses Act because there was a temporary slump in sugar. They could not produce sugar as cheaply as the French could, so there was no longer a profitable re-export sale for their sugar on the continent. They were anxious to keep the price of sugar high in the protected home market, and they thought that by producing less sugar for Britain and more rum and molasses for the American market, they could keep their mills busy and the price of sugar high, and, indeed, by the start of the war of Jenkins' Ear in 1739, the price of sugar had been stabilized in Britain by protective methods. The Molasses Act itself, however, was a short-sighted measure because the British islands did not want the kind of fish the French did, any more than the English wanted the "penitential cod" for which the Cornish fishermen found such a profitable demand in Portugal. If the act had been enforced, the New Englanders would have lost a market for their cheaper kind of fish; they would have been short of molasses and rum, their lumber trade would have been injured, a number of shipyards would have been forced to close. It was estimated that five thousand sailors would have been out of work, the annual loss to New England would have exceeded a quarter of a million pounds, and the eventual loss to Britain would have been considerable, since the New Englanders were her best customers for farming tools, crockery, furniture, clothing, wines and luxuries. The government of the time had the good sense to recognize its error and did not enforce the act. It remained, however, on the register, and after the Seven Years' War, when Britain was heavily taxed and needed some assistance from the colonies in whose interests, so it was maintained, the war had been conducted, it was decided to enforce the Molasses Act; either the prohibitory duty was to be paid or the cargoes of molasses would be seized.

The general indignation was so great that even without further provocation the New England colonies might have been driven to arms, but further provocation was to be provided by the Stamp Act, a levy made on the entire American people by the British Parliament, a body in which they were not represented. In essence it was neither a tyrannical nor a foolish tax; it seemed just to the British Parliament that the colonies should make some contribution to the costs of the war and the defense of the frontier, and George Grenville, the British Prime Minister, was a reasonable man. He would not, he told Benjamin Franklin, insist upon the Act if the Americans could devise a better method. As no satisfactory alternative was offered, the Act was passed. The British government had failed to realize that a principle was at stake. Taxation was being levied without representation. The power of taxation should not be vested in any body other than the colonial assemblies.

History took its course; the Stamp Act was repealed, with a bad grace, the British Parliament claiming that it had a right to levy such taxes if it chose. In England itself there was clamor for parliamentary reform, and George III became resolved to teach these tiresome reformers a lesson. Grenville was followed by Lord North, and Boston Harbor was soon black with discarded tea. The New Englanders were as independent as any human beings could be, and they no longer had the French and the Indians on their frontier. The Virginians, many of whom were Stuart at heart, had no love of the Hanoverians. For four disastrous years George III was his own Prime Minister. And Paul Revere galloped from Lexington.

Three thousand miles away in Paris, Louis XVI and his ministers watched the course of the war with satisfaction. His country's finances were in a desperate state and the humiliations of the Seven Years' War smarted. It was pleasant that Britain should be having difficulties of her own. It was desirable that she and her colonies should exhaust themselves. France herself, in her enfeebled state, was not prepared to commit herself to the test and expense of war, but the American envoy to Paris, though not publicly recognized, was shown sympathy and assistance, and his mission was granted an unofficial agent. Benjamin Franklin's arrival in Paris increased the popularity of the revolutionaries. Lafayette, at his own cost, fitted out a ship which he put, under his own command, at their service.

The situation was changed by the defeat and capture of Burgoyne's army. The news of it was received with delight, but at the same time with apprehension. The French ambassador in London reported that George III's power had been considerably weakened by this reverse, that North was about to change his policy, repealing the tea duty and the immediately subsequent acts that had so exasperated the colonists, and admitting the principles of colonial independence. "Parliament," so the new act was to read, "will not impose any duty, taxes or assessment whatever . . . in North America and the West Indies, except only such duties as it may be expedient to impose for the regulation of commerce, the net produce of such duties to be always paid and applied for the use of the colony in which the same shall be levied." Commissioners were being sent to America with powers that were practically unlimited, to resolve the colonies' complaints. The traditional British spirit of compromise seemed to be in full operation; the colonies were to be granted everything they wanted. The Declaration of Independence could be conveniently forgotten; the *status quo* could be resumed.

That did not suit the French book at all. If Britain, realizing that she could not subjugate her colonies, made peace with them on terms that left them within the Empire, Britain's strength would be only momentarily impaired. Clearly she must not be allowed to resume her old ascendancy. Now surely was the moment to revenge the defeats that had been inflicted during the Seven Years' War. Then France's hands had been tied by her campaigns in Europe, but now she could throw all her forces against her traditional enemy. Strike while the foe is weak. She promptly recognized the independence of the United States, and declared war on Britain.

From that moment the whole spirit of the war changed, as far as Britain was concerned. From the beginning, a powerful minority had opposed the war; now was the time, that party argued, to make peace with America and concentrate the country's forces against France. If the colonies were granted full independence they might be prepared to dissolve their pact with France. One man alone, the Earl of Chatham, could have carried through such delicate negotiations. He had opposed George III's policy from the start, and Congress trusted him. The public clamored for Chatham, but King George was adamant. "No advantage to the country, no personal danger to myself," he said, "can ever make me address myself to Lord Chatham or to any other branch of the opposition." He might have been forced to yield, but Chatham's health broke down and Lord North remained in office. Spain declared war on Britain; and the British commissioners returned with nothing accomplished. The war followed its course.

That course lies mainly outside the scope of this narrative. It continued for four more years; there was an ebb and flow of fortunes, with the tide running mainly for the colonists, until finally Cornwallis found himself trapped at Yorktown. Washington and Lafayette held the heights, and the French fleet was in the Chesapeake.

It may well be surprising that such a fleet should be there. Eighteen years earlier, the British were dominant at sea; they had swept the Caribbean clear. How had it come about that French ships were able to maneuver with such impunity and so disastrously for British interests? It is one of the examples of the important part played by the West Indies in the large affairs of Europe.

Rodney was then the chief British admiral. He was one of the greatest seamen in English history, but he was not a wholly admirable person. He was ruthless, brutal, selfish, and he was overconcerned with the claims of prize money. He was sixty years old when the war began, and his health was weakened by many years of foreign service; it was he who in the Seven Years' War had captured Martinique, St. Lucia and Grenada. When peace was signed, he received the thanks of both houses of Parliament. In the interval between the wars he was commander in chief of the Jamaican station. As soon as France and Spain allied themselves with the rebel colonists, he was sent back to the West Indies as commander in chief of the Leewards, with instructions to relieve Gibraltar on the way there. After capturing a Spanish convoy off Cape Finisterre, he routed a week later a large Spanish fleet off St. Vincent.

In the meantime, England was having trouble with the Dutch. The English coast was being frequently raided by American captains, of whom Paul Donce was the most famous. Donce held a regular commission in the American navy, but the British did not recognize the legality of Congress and rated him a pirate. When he took his prizes into a Dutch port, the British requested the Dutch to hand him over as though he were a criminal. The Dutch were neutrals and behaved as neutrals, allowing Donce to remain in port ten days and depart unmolested. This incensed the British, who decided to make it an excuse for declaring war on Holland.

The chief object of this war was, from the British view, the capture of St. Eustatius. High and green, a few miles north of St. Kitts, it is an island that is little visited today; it has nothing to attract

the tourist or the trader. Its area of eight square miles supports a
population of two thousand; it conducts a desultory trade in cattle,
yams and sweet potatoes. Yet the traveler who sails past it in a
schooner will see on the leeward side, along the beaches, the ruins of
the great warehouses that made it in the eighteenth century one of
the chief *entrepôts* of the Caribbean. It became particularly important after 1763; British trade was then prohibited between the French
and Spanish islands, so that the trade passed into the hands of the
Danes and Dutch; St. Eustatius vied with St. Thomas for the international trade of the area. In times of war its prosperity soared, and
the British were well aware it was maintaining an extensive trade between Holland and the United States. St. Eustatius was, in fact, the
first port to salute the American flag, an action that was observed in
St. Kitts. The British were convinced that by stopping its trade a
powerful blow would be leveled at the rebels' economy. Rodney was
ordered to capture it.

He found it unarmed and unprepared; its governor did not even
know that he was at war. Rodney's sacking of the defenseless island
was ruthlessly complete. He confiscated four million pounds' worth
of booty, destroyed the warehouses, and treated the inhabitants without consideration. He moreover kept the Dutch flag flying from its
towers, so that foreign vessels might seek refuge there unawares. The
island never recovered its prosperity.

It was at this point that Rodney's rapacity proved fatal to Britain's
interests. De Grasse was in mid-Atlantic, with a powerful fleet. It
should have been possible for Rodney to intercept him. But Rodney
was too occupied with plundering. Instead of throwing his full forces
against the French, he sent Hood south with a command of nine
ships only. Hood was incapable of offering effective opposition, and
de Grasse anchored in Fort Royal. Had Rodney been less rapacious,
had Martinique been retained by the British at the Peace of Paris,
Yorktown could not have been relieved. But Rodney was rapacious,
Martinique was in French hands, and Cornwallis had no alternative
to surrender. That was in October 1781, and Lord North strode back
and forth across his London office, wringing his hands. "Oh, God,"
he cried, "it is all over."

It was all over as far as the thirteen colonies were concerned; they
had achieved their independence and become the United States. But
in the warm waters of the Caribbean much had yet to be resolved.
The British forces—apart from the Hessians, who liked fighting anyhow, and, as long as they were well fed, did not mind whether they

were bayoneting "Froggies" or "Dom Yonkees"—had had no particular stomach for a war against men of their own flesh and blood, with whose grievances they had a considerable amount of sympathy. But when France and Spain were allied against them their spirits rose; they were glad to be back in the familiar seas, coasting from one palm-fringed island to another, waiting to pounce on an improvident convoy, to outflank a fort, to plunder an unguarded city. This was the kind of war that Britons knew and liked, and they flung themselves into it with full hearts.

At the start it had not fared well for them. Their forces were divided and extended. During the Seven Years' War Britain had kept France occupied by financing Prussia, and had concentrated upon colonial expeditions. In the War of American Independence, Britain was occupied in the north, and France was free to maneuver in the Caribbean. She captured Dominica and St. Vincent and prepared an expedition against Barbados, but the winds were contrary and instead she turned against St. Kitts. Each side was picking up what it could. Britain had captured St. Lucia, and it was to prove of immense value. Spain had captured Minorca and had laid siege to Gibraltar. The focus of French and Spanish strategy was a joint assault upon Jamaica. St. Kitts seemed an essential hinge in that campaign, and early in January 1782, de Grasse's victorious fleet of twenty-nine ships of The Line drew up in front of Brimstone Hill, the large high mountain that has been described as "the Gibraltar of the West Indies." It had been described as equally impregnable, but it was then in no condition to resist an army of eight thousand French troops under the trusted and competent Marquis de Bouillé.

St. Kitts lay only seven miles southeast of St. Eustatius. Most of its merchants had had some of their goods confiscated by Rodney, and many of them were in sympathy with the North American colonists. They were not prepared to inconvenience themselves by going into action on behalf of a tyrannical home government. They were prepared to welcome liberation for themselves and, refusing to put Brimstone Hill into a proper condition of defense, they left at its foot eight brass sixteen-pounders with six thousand shot and two fifteen-inch brass mortars with fifteen hundred shell, which the French were to find highly useful when they began their siege. The governor of the island had less than a thousand men at his command, of whom nearly half were local militiamen. A prolonged resistance was impossible.

At this point Rodney reappears upon the scene. Although he had been acting under orders when he captured St. Eustatius, his conduct there occasioned an immediate outcry in London, since a great deal of his booty belonged to British merchants. Burke demanded in Parliament that a committee should inquire into the affair. Rodney was recalled to England; he had to justify himself before Parliament and he found himself involved in extensive and costly litigation. It might well have seemed that his career was at an end, but England's position was too desperate for that to be allowed to happen; with France and Spain gathering for the kill, England's greatest admiral could not be allowed to loiter in Whitehall corridors. He was over sixty and his health was shattered, but once again he was ordered back to the Caribbean. Lord Sandwich said to him, "The fate of this empire is in your hands, and I have no wish that it should be in those of any other."

The news of his imminent return became known in the islands, and desperate though the position might be at St. Kitts, it was important that the defense of Brimstone Hill should be maintained as long as possible. To strengthen that defense, Hood was in the area with a fleet of twenty-two ships, and on January 24 he sailed round Nevis Point and made for the capital, Basseterre, in whose open roadway de Grasse was anchored. The action that ensued does not figure prominently in either French or British history, yet Admiral Mahan in his *Influence of Sea Power upon History* has described it as being in "the very first rank of naval battles," and, by delaying de Grasse's timetable, as having prepared the situation that culminated in "The Battle of the Saints."

De Grasse's ships were arranged somewhat irregularly, and Hood had hoped to attack them at their anchorage, as Nelson did sixteen years later at Aboukir; but he was prevented from doing so by a collision between two of his ships, and de Grasse had time to weigh anchor and draw out to sea. Hood, taking advantage of the northeast trade wind, held close to the island of Nevis, forcing de Grasse to leeward. During the afternoon, night, and following morning, Hood kept to windward, so that at noon, rapidly forming his line on the starboard tack and heading north for Basseterre, he was able to seize the anchorage that de Grasse had left, cutting the French fleet off from their shore base. De Grasse recognized his plan too late.

The battle lasted for thirty hours. Hood shortened sail and "brought his unmolested van, his center, and heavily pressed and outnumbered rear" to anchor. The Frenchmen filed past on their way southward, firing as they went. During the night, Hood rearranged his

line in a triangle; his first ship was so close to the shoals round Salt
Pond that nothing could get to windward of her; his own ship, the
Barsteur, stood at the apex. "Springs" were put out, enabling every
ship to swing round and deliver two broadsides to the enemy's one.
De Grasse delivered his first attack early in the morning, the whole
French line passing before the British. At three o'clock in the afternoon he attacked again. When night fell, his flagship, the *Ville de
Paris*, had received over eighty shots in her hull; all his ships were
damaged. He had lost over a thousand men against Hood's seventy-
three killed and 244 wounded. He decided not to attack again, but
to leave the siege of Brimstone Hill to de Bouillé's troops.

Here the situation had become desperate, but Hood was still in a
position to provide diversions. He had taken on board at Antigua a
force of six hundred men and the sixty-ninth regiment. These he
landed at Frigate Bay, where they captured and then fortified a battery position. The curious situation had thus arisen of de Bouillé, who
was besieging Brimstone Hill, having his rear menaced by a handful of
men who were protected by Hood's squadron. Hood, in his turn, was
kept in check by de Grasse's fleet, which now numbered thirty-three
ships, and all the time Rodney was drawing closer. Could Brimstone
Hill hold out? Another week might have sufficed, but the defenders
could not know that. The fire from the hill grew weaker every day,
and the advancing line grew closer. The sixty-ninth regiment was re-
embarked. On the evening of the twelfth the northern flank of the
defense was breached. At midnight the governor decided to surrender. Twenty hours later, Hood summoned his captains on board the
Barsteur; he ordered them to cut their cables at eleven o'clock that
night, slip away to leeward, and wait there for Rodney.

Rodney landed at Barbados on February 19. The campaign of the
next sixty days was to send him home to honor, to a barony and an
annual pension of £2,000, all calumny forgotten; it was one of the
greatest campaigns, not only in British naval history, but in the history of naval strategy. It initiated the tactic of "breaking the line"
that was to be exploited later so effectively by Nelson.

When Rodney arrived upon the scene, the Comte de Grasse, his
spirits high after his victories at Yorktown and St. Kitts, was at
Fort Royal in Martinique with a fleet of thirty-three ships. He was
planning to join the Spanish fleet in Havana and attack Jamaica. St.
Lucia was at this time in British hands, and Rodney anchored in
Gros Islet Bay. In front of the bay is a low, humped piece of land
that is called Pigeon Island. On this island he placed his sentinels

to watch for the first movement of the French fleet. Time passed slowly, and the courtly traditions of eighteenth-century warfare were observed. Late in March, de Grasse received a rich convoy of supply ships. He decided to give a ball, which he invited English officers to attend under a flag of truce. Rodney was prevented by his gout from accepting the invitation, but several of his officers went, and the commanders exchanged gifts, French liqueurs and sweetmeats against English ale and cheese.

It was now early April; the rainy season was nearly over; the tulip and flamboyant trees were in flower; in the hills the pale pink of the *immortelle* protected the immature cocoa plants, and the sun shone brightly fifty miles away on the mountains of Martinique. Across that narrow channel de Grasse and Rodney watched and waited; de Grasse to slip northward to his waiting ally; Rodney to intercept him. Everything depended on the wind. The trade wind was at its strongest between February and March, at its weakest in the hurricane season between August and September. The breezes now were light and variable. At last, on April 8, Rodney's frigates reported that the French had sailed, and Rodney started in pursuit.

De Grasse's object was to sail through the channel between Dominica and Guadeloupe and thence catch the trade wind to Havana. He was hampered by the number of troops and stores that he was transporting to the siege. Rodney was traveling light and anxious to force a battle. On April 9, eight British ships which had got ahead of the remainder encountered and were attacked by fifteen French ships off the leeward coast of Dominica. They were at a disadvantage, but de Grasse did not press home his attack. He was concerned with getting through the channel, and during the night of the eleventh he did manage to get most of his ships through; there was, however, a collision between two of his ships, one of which was badly damaged. When this ship was spotted and pursued by the British van, de Grasse decided to recall his ships, and at eight o'clock in the morning the first shots were fired in the action which the French call "The Battle of Dominica" and the British "The Battle of the Saints," after the small rocky islets in the channel. Rodney had thirty-five sail of the line and de Grasse had thirty-three, but the British advantage in numbers was more than counterbalanced by the greater size and superior qualities of the French ships.

The battle opened in the traditional and classic manner, with the two fleets in line of battle slowly passing each other, the British sailing to the north, the French to the south. By ten o'clock the first of the British ships had passed the last of the French. Then the caprice of weather intervened. The northern extremities of the fleets were in an easterly breeze when suddenly a land breeze blew up from the south. In the confusion that followed, a large gap appeared in the French line, immediately in front of Rodney's flagship, *Formidable*. This was the decisive moment. The captain of the fleet, Sir Charles Douglas, excitedly called Rodney's attention to it. "Look there, sir. Let's steer through it." Rodney hesitated. That was not the traditional manner of fighting a sea battle. The manual of instructions laid down that an admiral should preserve unchanged the order in which an action started; but Whitehall was far away. Rodney gave the order, and *Formidable* and the six ships immediately following steered through the gap. The technique of "breaking the line" had been evolved. It is not certain whether the credit for this innovation should go to Rodney or Sir Charles Douglas, but since it was Rodney who would have been held to account if the attack had failed, its success must surely be allowed to him.

By the early afternoon its success was manifest. In the confusion and the smoke, the British rear guard sailed through the French ships, not realizing that they had done so till they were past the enemy. Those British ships that were not beyond the French went to the east of them. The French were broken into three bodies and disorganized. The Comte de Grasse, in his flagship, *Ville de Paris*, was cut off from his van and rear with five other ships. Rodney concentrated upon and eventually captured them. He was thus enabled to boast, "Within two little years I have taken four admirals, two Spanish, one Dutch, and now a French one."

Two of the escaping French ships were captured a week later in the Mona Passage, but a great many of Rodney's men felt that the victory could have been exploited a great deal further had the fleeing Frenchmen been pursued more hotly and Rodney been less interested in the prize money that would be his personal share. Be that as it may, his was a notable victory against odds; it saved Jamaica, it restored British and lowered French prestige in the Caribbean; it was the kind of victory that has led to the saying, "England loses every battle except the last."

From one point of view, the war ended in a complete defeat for Britain. She lost everything for which she went to war; no surrender could have been more unconditional; yet in regard to her larger interests, she ended the war on good terms with herself. France had gained nothing from the war except the spectacle of her old foe's abasement. She had further depleted her exchequer; she had not won or regained a foot of soil in the New World. Spain had acquired New Orleans and Minorca, but had not recovered Gibraltar, and her prestige as a naval power had been further diminished by the defeat which Rodney had administered to her off St. Vincent. Britain could, in fact, view the situation of her chief rivals with some complacence, and thanks to The Battle of the Saints she was, in spite of the capitulation at Yorktown, still mistress of the seas.

CHAPTER VIII

The Lull Before the Storm

The war was ended, peace was signed, and "the fortunate islands" could return to their lucrative pursuits. A few minor problems were still unsettled. One of these concerned the resumption of commercial relations between the West Indies and the United States. Wars in those days were not "total," in the sense that they are now, and private citizens and subjects often tended to regard them as a nuisance with which they were only casually concerned. Byron made his grand tour of Europe and the Levant during the Napoleonic era. During the War of American Independence Louis XVI ordered that Cook's vessel was to be respected. It is not apparent from her novels that Jane Austen was aware that she was living through a momentous period. This was particularly true of men engaged in commerce. For a long while friendly relations had existed between the merchants and brokers of New England and the planters and ship chandlers of the British West Indies. They were men of the same stock, united now and again by ties of blood; they could scarcely think of themselves as enemies; their overlords might have quarreled, but that did not concern them. They must wait till "the silly thing blew over." When it did, they would pick up the threads and resume their old relations. When peace was signed, the West Indians and the New England merchants very naturally thought, "Now we can go back to where we started."

They were disconcerted to find that there were differences; the first difference being that the New England merchants were no longer British subjects but foreigners, and though they were no longer exposed to stamp and molasses acts, they were exposed to navigation acts, and the harbors of Kingston, Bridgetown and St. John's no longer flew the same flag as they. They were, however, practical persons, and they had acquired from their ancestors a due regard for compromise. It was wiser not to raise certain issues, not to ask certain questions.

Their vessels had originally been registered as British; let them therefore continue to fly the Union Jack when they were in British waters. But since their owners were now American subjects, let the ships be also registered in Boston, Baltimore and Maine. Let the ships have dual nationality. That way the thing could be had both ways. It was an arrangement that suited everyone, except the officers of His Majesty's Customs and Excise. On that score there was a loss of revenue, and Whitehall felt that action should be taken.

With this end partially in view, the Lords of the Admiralty appointed to its Leeward Islands West Indian station, four years after the cessation of hostilities, a twenty-six-year-old naval officer of somewhat unusual character, slightly odd in appearance, with a great power to arouse affection and an inner glow indicative of fire. Prince William, Duke of Clarence, who was later to be King William IV, had met him three years earlier and has left the following description of him. "He appeared," wrote the Prince, "to be the merest boy of a captain I ever beheld, and his dress was worthy of attention. He had on a full-laced uniform; his lank unpowdered hair was tied in a stiff Hessian tail of an extraordinary length; the old-fashioned flaps of his waistcoat added to the general quaintness of his figure and produced an appearance which particularly attracted my notice, for I had never seen anything like it before, nor could I imagine who he was or what he came about. My doubts were, however, removed when Lord Hood introduced me to him. There was something irresistibly pleasing in his address and conversation and an enthusiasm when speaking on professional subjects, that showed he was no common being."

This exceptional officer was Horatio Nelson. He had already had experience of the West Indies; he had been sent there by his uncle as a boy in a merchant vessel, and he had been posted there directly after he had passed his examinations as a lieutenant. He had not seen a great deal of active service, but he had impressed his superiors with his potentiality, and when the American War was over and the establishment was considerably reduced, he was not relegated to unemployment. He, no doubt, thought himself lucky when he was given command of the frigate *Boreas*, with Antigua as his base.

Antigua is one of the most charming and friendly of the West Indian islands. It has not the majestic grandeur of the mountainous Martinique, Grenada and Dominica. It is an island of low, rounded hills, set with squat stone windmills and red brick plantation houses, with cane stalks swaying in the wind, and a succession of white-sanded beaches. Its capital, St. John's, lies behind an open roadstead;

the harbor where the *Boreas* was anchored was on the other side of the island and has recently, by the energies of a former governor, Sir Kenneth Blackburne, been restored so successfully that it looks very much as it did in Nelson's day. On the hill above it stands a charming eighteenth-century bungalow that was once the residence of the future William IV and is known now as Clarence House. It was protected by the battlements of Shirley Heights.

Nelson was stationed here three years. It should have been one of the happiest periods of his service, but it was the dreariest. He was a highly conscientious officer, and the seriousness with which he accepted his responsibilities may be gauged from his first public act, his refusal to recognize as his superior a half-pay officer who was acting as commissioner of the dockyard at Antigua.

It was Nelson's first command. He was a very ambitious man. He had spoken already to his friends of "the radiant orb" which urged him "onward to renown." He was not prepared to compromise with what he held to be his duty, and he was shocked at the amount of corruption that was operative in the Antigua dockyard, with American vessels sailing in and out as though they were still British. He strictly enforced the navigation acts. His actions were invariably correct, but even the Admiralty considered him at times overpunctilious, and he soon found himself involved in lawsuits that, even though they were defended by the government, were to be the cause of irritation to him for many years. The inhabitants of the island were naturally incensed; they refused to call on him or invite him to their houses. It was an exceedingly lonely time for him, and he was in a state of mind and heart to welcome the mildest friendliness. He found that friendliness in another island.

His parish of the Leewards included St. Kitts, Nevis, Anguilla and Montserrat. Nevis is a very different island from Antigua. Its central mountain is so high that it is usually encircled by a cone of cloud, hence its name, a corruption of the Spanish *nives*, snow. During the first half of the twentieth century the tide of its good fortune ebbed, but in the first half of the nineteenth century its hot springs made it a fashionable resort, and the ruins of large plantation houses in the bush testify today to the extent of its former prominence. In Nevis, Nelson met the widow of a doctor, Frances Nisbet. She had a small son, with whom it amused Nelson to romp on all fours under the drawing-room table. His kindness to the small boy touched her heart. She was three years younger than Nelson. She was not uncomely. Nelson had no illusions about himself; he had already been involved in two tempestuous love affairs, in Quebec and Paris. He was well aware that the emotion he felt for Frances Nisbet bore no relation to the high ardors he had survived and to which, at his age, he must surely expect successors. But he was in a mood to appreciate the attractions of domesticity, and in his twenty-ninth year he was married in the parish church of the county of Charlestown, Nevis.

History, so Gibbon said, would have been different had Cleopatra's nose been shorter. History might have been different if Nelson, when he landed at Naples, had had in England a wife for whom he felt a quarter of the devotion that he was to feel for Emma Hamilton, or if he had had no wife at all. If Nelson had not quarreled with the Antiguans he would not presumably have married a woman with whom he was not in love. There were many repercussions to that enforcement of the navigation acts in the Leeward Islands.

On the surface, life in the Caribbean was moving smoothly and pleasantly during those months which now, in the perspective of history, can be seen as the climax of an era. The land was fertile, Europe needed sugar, and on the African coast there was an inexhaustible stock of human machinery to supply that need. But below the surface there was a mounting tension.

In an earlier chapter it was said that the difference in national characteristics between the French and English was to have important consequences later. The nature of those consequences had now become apparent. The French islands were as prosperous as, if not more prosperous than the British ones, yet there was an unhappy atmosphere in their cities, particularly in those of St. Domingue.

St. Domingue had always been in a different position than Martinique and Guadeloupe. It had lain beyond the fighting of the Seven Years' War and the American War of Independence. The *pacte coloniale* had been less rigorously applied. Special concessions had been permitted in its early days. It had obtained slaves more easily, by contraband from Jamaica. Prosperity had come to it quickly. It had a population of 480,000 blacks, 24,000 mulattoes and 30,000 whites. Like the seeds sown on stony ground, it had no deep roots; it was susceptible to each wind of change. And not only was France on the brink of bankruptcy, she had a sickness in her soul. England had settled her issue over the divine right of kings; France still had hers to fight. There was an air of insecurity. In St. Domingue, the rich planters were too concerned about their return to Paris to worry about the conditions under which they lived. They did not bother to furnish their houses suitably. They had no homelife. According to contemporary reports, the towns of St. Domingue were full of inns and travelers, but the streets of the Cap were infected by the stagnant waters of the streams that cut across them. The town was badly paved. Port-au-Prince was a conglomeration of five or six hundred cabins, one-storied, arranged in terraces, in an area that could accommodate twenty thousand houses. If it rained in the night, you could not walk in the streets next morning; they had become long, broad rivers of mud with ditches at the side and bullfrogs croaking in them. Of the Cap, Moreau de St. Mery said, "There are few towns with so few police. The streets are cesspools, into which one throws any filth one likes." The citizens of Port-au-Prince were beseeched to keep their dogs shut up at night. They were so numerous that, attracted by the smells and dirt, their barking prevented anyone from sleeping.

There was the appearance of gaiety; there were clubs in the cities, in particular the *Cercle des Philadelphus* at the Cap. There were Masonic lodges, which caused considerable concern to the Creole wives, who imagined that they were houses of assignation; there were public baths open to both sexes. There were gaming houses, there were theaters, and the mulattresses displayed their charms, "without prejudice and without religion," in their classical costume, wearing with grace and skill the glittering scarves that adorned their heads. Six to eight inches high, drawn tightly round the base of the skull, twisted in front into the form of a fan, worn low over the forehead almost to the eyebrows, and pinned onto the hair, each scarf was decorated with brooches and jewels. The mulattress regarded it as sacred, and you could not offend her worse than by deranging it. Her blouse was made of the finest cambric, bordered with lace, which veiled rather than covered her bosom. It was embellished with flowers. The arms were bare below the elbows. The skirt was voluminous. Often they carried parasols. They walked slowly, swaying their hips. They usually held a piece of wood in their mouths with which they brushed their teeth.

The balls given by these "ladies of the town" to their male acquaintances were the chief social events of the community. Men went there in the certainty that they would enjoy themselves. Elsewhere it was very different. When a reception was organized by someone who could claim to be a member of society, questions were asked: "Who would be there? Whom would one meet?" There were a thousand considerations that might combine to make a failure of the party. The society of Cap Français and Port-au-Prince was very mixed. There were fresh arrivals every day; many of them were adventurers, many were fugitives from justice and their families, who had changed their names. The social life of the island was on its guard against such suspect riffraff. In a country where fortunes were made overnight, where money was the sole valid visa on a passport, one could not know who one's associates really were.

No one trusted anyone. The social structure was based upon mistrust. This was true of all the islands, but particularly of the French. The white planters were outnumbered by ten to one. Every month brought its fresh cargo of slaves to keep alight the spirit of rebellion and resentment. The laborers in the cane fields and the storerooms might have been able to accept their condition of servitude if they were not being constantly reminded of the freedom they had lost. The children of slaves, who had known no other kind of existence, might well have grown accustomed to it. It was not such a bad life at all; they were fed and clothed and housed; their old age was protected, their children cherished. Could the Irish peasants claim as much? But they were never allowed to settle down when every month new voices spoke to them of Africa. The planters were on their guard. They were outnumbered. They had to keep the blacks in subjection. They could not allow the black man to consider himself the equal of the white; nor could they allow the black man to consider himself the equal of a quarter-caste.

The British classified people of color as samboes, mulattoes, quadroons and mestizos; a sambo being the offspring of a black woman by a mulatto man, a mulatto of a black woman by a white man, a quadroon of a mulatto woman by a white man, a mestizo of a quadroon woman by a white man; the offspring of a mestizo by a white man being white by law. The Spaniards, from whom these appellations were borrowed, were more discriminatory, and they called the offspring of a mestizo by a white man a quinteron, and only the offspring of a white man and a quinteron was considered free of colored blood. But the French indulged in far more elaborate definitions. Moreau de St. Mery drew up a table showing the various proportions of mixed blood that could exist; a man with seven fifteenths of white blood was inferior to the man who was half and half. The strict regard of these distinctions was essential if the submissiveness of the slaves was to be maintained.

Residents of the West Indies have always resented the European indifference to the fact of color. In 1778 Robert Browning's grandfather married a Creole from St. Kitts. There is little doubt that she was partly African. Her son, the poet's father, was so dark that when he went to St. Kitts as a small boy, to visit his relatives, he was ordered to sit on the side of the church that was reserved for mulattoes. Browning himself had, as a young man, such an olive complexion that a nephew in Paris mistook him for an Italian. No one in England seems to have worried over this. But Dr. Barrett's fortune came from sugar estates in Jamaica. This may well provide a partial explanation of his refusal to accept Browning as a son-in-law.

By the middle of the eighteenth century, the French planters had become not only indignant but alarmed at the warmth of the welcome that was being given in Paris to the young mulattoes who were being sent to the Sorbonne to study. How could these pampered officials, seated in their comfortable offices, served by an obedient staff, with an army to maintain order in the streets, appreciate what life was like under this burning sun, with this seething, rebellious labor force that could only be restrained by whips and chains?

Well, thought the planters, we have the remedy in our hands. When these popinjays came home, they would be taught their place; they would have no vote, no civic rights; they would not be represented in the island's government; they could not sit in assemblies; they were not allowed to give evidence in a court of law when it was a white man's word they were disputing. It did not matter how rich they were if they had one drop of black blood in their veins. Some parents, indeed, wondered whether it was fair to bring their sons back to the colonies after they had breathed the free air of Europe.

The mulattoes resented their treatment, but they accepted the situation, partially. They accepted Moreau de St. Mery's list of distinctions; they considered themselves to be superior to the blacks, just as they considered their fathers to be superior to themselves; but they could not tolerate the insolence of the "poor whites," the *petits blancs*, men who would not be endured by their friends in Paris; in Cap Français, when a poor white was walking on the pavement they had to step down into the gutter. If they struck a white man they might have their hand cut off. Who were these wretched grandchildren of bondmen and prisoners, to give themselves such airs? Yet they themselves had no redress. They would be sitting in a tavern, laughing and chattering together. A white man would walk in, and constraint would fall upon the group. They could no longer be natural together. They would be conscious of the white man. Although he would take no notice of them, all their conversation would be

turned toward him. Everything they said or did would be for effect.
If they had a girl with them he might beckon her across. She would
meekly rise. A mulattress would prefer the sorriest white to the most
distinguished quadroon.

A mixed society was growing up in the West Indies. Each section
of that mixed society had its own grievance, particularly in the French
West Indies. The aristocrats, the sugar barons, had their disputes with
the central government, as throughout the world and throughout history colonists have quarreled with the home governments who have
considered that the colonists existed solely for their own benefit, and
have refused to recognize the special difficulties of each individual
colony. The French colonies in general were continually complaining
about the inelasticity of Colbert's *pacte coloniale*, of the rigidity with
which it was interpreted. They were not only handicapped but throt-
tled by France's refusal to allow them to make purchases from any
but French merchants. They were short of slaves. Guadeloupe had
never been so well off as she was during the Seven Years' War, when
for four years, 1759–1763, she was in British hands. The British,
when they returned Guadeloupe to France, took away with them all
the slaves that the French could not afford to buy.

France had immense financial difficulties of her own; her ministers were irritated that her colonists could not appreciate those difficulties. The colonists must wait in patience. Foreign fleets must not
be allowed to profit by France's weakness. So the argument ran; an
endless reiteration of complaints and politely evasive answers. The
financial insecurity of France, which was to lead to the revolution,
exacerbated and accentuated the difficulties of the French planters.
France was worried by the number of sugar factories that were being
built in the islands; they would interfere with the sugar factories in
France. Paris tried to limit the number of factories in the islands; she
urged the landowners to plant less sugar and concentrate on the secondary crops, indigo, cocoa, ginger, cotton. There was bitter opposition to these ordinances. The various currency restrictions were exas-
perating. The colonial money issued from France was no use in
France. Spanish money became legal, with the franc as an ancillary.
Small proprietors could no longer afford to manage their sugar estates
and were driven to farming land in the mountains. Guadeloupe was
also long resentful at being treated as a colony of Martinique that
could not trade directly with France. The British, during their brief
occupancy, established the port of Pointe-à-Pitre, but after the Treaty
of Paris in 1763, the port was abandoned until the protests of the

planters became uncomfortably insistent. There was among the sugar barons a feeling of loyalty for the crown, but little for the ministers of the crown. In spite of their wealth, they were discontented.

The least discontented section of the community was the group for which poor whites is a misnomer; there is no precise English equivalent for *petits blancs*. They were the descendants of the bondmen, they were the artisans, shopkeepers, minor landowners, who had been sent out with government assistance, most of whom had improved their situation and were living more comfortably than they would have done in Europe; they also had a feeling of superiority through the authority they could exert over a subject race. One of the attractions of colonial life for the European is the sense of importance he acquires through being white. He has the status of a *pukka sahib*. He may have felt envious of his superiors; but if he had had an envious nature, he would have been more envious in the country of his birth. He could feel secure about his future; a white man was looked after in the tropics, and he had every opportunity of improving himself. He had probably done so, to some extent, already. The *petits blancs* might be the most disliked section of the community, looked down on by the *grands blancs*, despised and resented by the freed mulattoes, hated by the slaves; yet they were in themselves the most contented section; as they were too poor, for the most part, to own more than a few domestic slaves, they were spared the constant anxiety of the big landowners against a slaves' revolt.

The most discontented class was that of the freed mulatto; he felt that everybody's hand was against him. He was an object of official distrust and disapproval. Each country drew up different regulations concerning the liberation of a slave, and those regulations were changed to meet changing day-to-day conditions. At the start it seemed logical that a man should be able to dispose of his own property, but French lawyers argued that a slave was part of a man's patrimony and therefore was subject to the royal will. The central governments were glad to approve certain kinds of liberation; freedom could be awarded to a slave who had shown courage in a crisis, at an invasion, who captured an enemy, who reported a plot against authority or the nature of an unknown poison. Poisoning was very widespread; arsenic was the main ingredient. Female jealousy was one of the main reasons for poisoning. Sometimes slaves would poison their comrades, so as to reduce the value of a property and prevent a master from starting projects that would entail too much work for them. Nurses in a hospital would poison soldiers to save themselves the trouble of looking after them. Poisons were given in small doses. In pillows and mattresses would be put herbs whose fumes would gradually destroy their user. The lockjaw which afflicted so many children was believed to be the result of poisoning.

Authority often felt that it was pitted against a world of maniacs; the men who had proved their loyalty to the regime deserved reward, but the uncontrolled liberation of mistresses and illegitimate children would soon create a class that would threaten the stability of the regime.

The government was also afraid that haphazard liberation would create a parasitic class of "rogues and vagabonds." The regulations controlling the freeing of slaves became so strict that planters were driven to divers devices to circumvent them. French planters would go to British islands, organize a bogus sale and return with someone whom they described as a freed slave; but though these laws were passed, it was impossible to control the free unions which produced the steady flow of mulattoes and mulattresses, most of whom became free at an early adult age. The river of brown blood grew deeper, broader, stronger. Authority was aware of the problem it presented, but saw no means of stemming it, and as a background to these three groups, the sugar barons, the poor whites and the freed men and women of color or mixed blood, was the growling, anonymous labor force, surly, impatient, ready for revenge; whose grievances were kept alive by angry compatriots who had been torn only a few weeks back from the freedom of their homes.

The planters had other causes for concern. After the surrender at Yorktown, the French and Spanish governments could congratulate themselves on having contributed so substantially to Britain's loss of face, but they had established precedents that were later to cost them dear. They had encouraged ideas that were to prove injurious to their own constitutions. A people had risen against a king and had prevailed. The American Revolution was very different from a revolt of nobles in which one king had replaced another. In this, a republic had been proclaimed. Phrases like "the rights of man" had been given a new significance by the Declaration of Independence. Men had begun to question the principles under which their lives had previously been ordered. The horizons of men's minds had been enlarged by the writings of Voltaire and Rousseau. It was a period of doubt, yet at the same time it was a period of hope. There was a belief that man's lot might be bettered, that "life, liberty and the pursuit of happiness" was a realizable objective; certain truths had at last become self-evident, and among the principles that had been accepted unquestioningly for centuries, and that were now for the first time under examination, was the right of man to keep a fellow man in bondage except in punishment for crime. Was there any justification for the slave trade?

The first signs of doubt had come from the country that had accepted the necessity for the trade with the greatest readiness. The Spanish had never felt happy about it. The French had consoled themselves with the belief that they were giving to the heathen the opportunity of redemption, but the English, as the Danes and Dutch, had accepted the need for human machinery in the cane fields. Yet it was from Englishmen that the first effective protests against the slave trade came. As early as 1727, the Quakers had declared that it was a practice "not commendable or allowed"; thirty-four years later, they excluded from membership of their society all who should be found concerned with it; in 1783 they formed an association "for the relief and liberation of the Negro slaves in the West Indies and for the discouragement of the slave trade on the coast of Africa." The Quakers in Pennsylvania had taken similar action a little earlier. But Quakers might have been expected to promulgate such a point of view, and public opinion would not be heavily influenced by their opinion, deep though the respect might be in which their way of life was held. In other more influential quarters objections were now being raised.

The legal status of slavery had been first raised in England in 1729, when the attorney general and the solicitor general then in office ruled that a slave did not become free by landing in the United Kingdom, and that he might be forced by his master to return to the plantations. This decision was questioned by other jurists, and in 1772 Lord Mansfield decided in the name of the whole bench that as soon as a slave set his foot on the soil of the British Isles he became free. This was a most important ruling, and four years later David Hartley, whose father had written *Observations on Man*, moved in the House of Commons that "the slave trade was contrary to the laws of God and the rights of man." The motion failed, as first motions usually do, but the subject had been aired at last. The world had been forced to realize that there was a problem.

Liberal ideas were in the open. Dr. Johnson had a Negro servant before whom he would give as a toast "a speedy rebellion to the Negroes in Jamaica and success to them." The vice-chancellor of

Cambridge University proposed in 1785, as a subject for a Latin essay, a dissertation on the subject. The prize was won by Thomas Clarkson, who translated his essay into English and published it in an enlarged form under the title *Essay on the Slavery and Commerce of the Human Species*. A year later a committee was formed for the abolition of the slave trade. The driving force behind these reformers was definitely Christian ethics. Public feeling became so strong and so many petitions were presented to Parliament that in 1788 a committee of the Privy Council was appointed by the crown to inquire into the conditions of the slave trade, and Pitt moved that the House of Commons should consider the matter during the next session. He appointed William Wilberforce as the protagonist of the debate.

The name of William Wilberforce is the one that occurs first in connection with the antislavery campaign, and Wilberforce was an unusual man. Born in Yorkshire in the city of Hull, he came of a long line of Yorkshiremen, his family having held the manor of Wilberfoss in the East Riding from the reign of Henry II into the middle of the eighteenth century. He inherited from his mother an acute brain and a weak physical constitution. As a young schoolboy his tutors were impressed both by his idleness and his powers of elocution. Later, at what would be called now a public school, his taste for social pleasures interfered with his advancement as a scholar; yet, even so, he managed to pass into St. John's College, Cambridge. Much later, in retrospect, he said that "he could not look back without unfeigned regret on the opportunities that he had wasted." Luckily, however, he was always at his best in the examination room; and he was extremely popular, both because of his personal charm and his generosity. He was a lavish host. So popular was he, indeed, that at the age of twenty-one he was elected to represent his native town in the House of Commons, where he promptly found his way into the most profligate political set in London. It was there that he met Pitt, and an acquaintanceship that had begun at Cambridge ripened into a close friendship. His eloquence was of the greatest value to his friend when Pitt was opposed by the majority of the Commons.

A year later, Wilberforce went to Nice—which was not then a part of France—with a former schoolmaster who converted him to an Evangelical Christianity. It was a case of "the reformed rake," and within a few weeks Wilberforce was busying himself with the establishment of a society for the reformation of the church; at the same time he met Thomas Clarkson and decided that the curtailment and eventual stopping of the slave trade was a cause worth his espousal. Pitt strongly recommended Wilberforce to throw himself into this particular campaign.

As a first step, in 1788 an act was passed restricting, according to the size of its tonnage, the number of slaves that any one ship might carry. By this time the conditions of the "middle passage" had, in fact, been considerably improved. Between November 1789 and July 1791, thirty-eight ships transported to Montego Bay 9,993 slaves. Of these, 746 died during the voyage. This is a loss of 7½ percent. But of those 746 deaths, 328 occurred in four ships, all of them from the Bight of Benin; it is therefore reasonable to assume that the slaves had brought a disease aboard. The loss of slaves in harbor had by now been reduced to ¾ percent. In 1792 Sir William Young visited a slaver in Barbados, which in three trips had lost only eight seamen and one slave. He reported that there were a number of children on board who had no relations and had presumably been stolen or sold into slavery by their parents. The height below decks was six feet, and there were no shelves or double tiers.

The rules for the treatment of the slaves in the British islands had also become more lenient. Ten slaves were entitled to one acre between them for their private use. They were not to be given more than ten lashes, unless the owner was present, and even in his presence floggings were limited to thirty-nine lashes. Iron collars round the neck were forbidden. Slaves were allowed one free day a fortnight, apart from public holidays and Sundays. Their hours of work were limited to the hours between 5 A.M. and 7 P.M., and there had to be a half hour for breakfast and two hours for a midday dinner. To encourage childbearing, the mothers of six children did not have to work.

Strenuous efforts were being made to maintain the system, but even now a slave could not give evidence against a white man in a court of law. Death was the penalty for striking at a white man. There could be no assemblies. Funerals must take place by day. Obeah men were punished by death or transportation. There were many regulations against slaves owning horses.

In the following May, Wilberforce again presented to the House the case for abolition; the planters had a strong lobby in Westminster and the discussion was deferred; before it could be reopened the Bastille had fallen, and Europe was on the brink of a quarter of a century of war.

That quarter of a century is the most important in the history of the West Indies, and the present condition of each individual island has been determined by the extent to which it was affected during it.

CHAPTER IX

After the Bastille

Louis XVI summoned the States General in the spring of 1789, and within four years France was at war with Britain. Except for a few months between 1801 and 1803, the state of war was to be continued until the Battle of Waterloo. Louis XVI was executed in January 1793, and the forty-five months between the convocation of the States General and his death are as crowded as any in French history, one plot succeeding another, one act of treason following another. The oath of the tennis court was followed by the night of August 4. One group of royalists intrigued against another. There were the Fouillants, there were the Girondists. There was Marat; there was Robespierre; there was war on the Belgian frontier; there were the Prussians at Verdun; there was Louis attempting to escape to Austria. If it was a confused story to the Chanceries of Europe, it was a still more confused story to the planters and officials of the French Antilles. They had no idea what was happening.

In France there had been a movement equivalent to, but very different from, Wilberforce's society in London. The English movement had been entirely instigated by British Christians, but in France the movement was largely inspired by mulattoes from St. Domingue, a class for which there was no equivalent in England. It was at their instigation that in 1788 the *Société des Amis des Noirs* was formed. It proposed to abolish not only the slave trade but slavery itself. It numbered among its members the Duc de la Rochefoucauld, Abbé Gregoire, Brissot, Lafayette. Mirabeau was not a member, but a warm sympathizer. These men were not inspired, as Wilberforce's followers had been, by Christian feeling, but by the general feeling of humanity on which the revolutionary movement was based.

The States General opened its proceedings with a philosophical declaration of the rights of man and of the citizen, based on Rousseau's social contract. The various ideas that it expressed have come

to be accepted as axioms—law by general consent, the sovereign right
of the nation, the equality and dignity of man; that all men born
upon French soil were free. It was presented as the philosophical
base on which the assembly would found the new constitution.

The news of its promulgation reached Port-au-Prince through the
mouths of sailors. It caused an immediate and intense excitement.
The *petits blancs* were exuberant. There were to be no rich, there
were to be no poor. The land would no longer be the property of the
few. There would be an end to the arrogance and insolence of the
planters. All men would share equally in the soil's abundance. The
mulattoes welcomed with equal fervor this end of tyranny. A man
was to be judged by his intrinsic quality and not by birth. "Liberty,
Equality, Fraternity" was to be the watchword of the New World.
Into the sluggish minds of the black slaves the idea filtered slowly
that soon they would be able to knock off work. Each party saw the
dawn of liberty in a different light. The *petits blancs* saw themselves
as the equal of the aristocrats, but did not picture the mulattoes as
being equal to themelves. The mulattoes took freedom to mean a
state of equality that did not include full-black Africans. To the slaves
it was a question of working or not working. The stage was set, half
for melodrama, half for harlequinade.

It was a tangled play.

History, watching from the stalls, with the perspective of a century
and a half, can tell how scene followed upon scene. But the actual
actors in the drama, hurried breathlessly from the wings, with their
lines half learned, unaware of the role that they are playing; rushed
back to the dressing room at the very instant they have begun to feel
themselves at home upon the stage, then hurried back again, ignorant
of what has been happening in their absence; the actors themselves
know little of the play. They can only guess how great is their part
in it, whether they are the play itself or merely the attendants who
prepare an entrance, who divert the audience while the main characters are resting.

In Paris there was a government that changed its mind only less
often than it changed its leaders; that sent out commissioners, then
recalled them; that imprisoned colonial representatives as traitors;
that one month passed an act abolishing slavery and the next repealed
it. *Les Amis des Noirs* were demanding that white and brown and
black should be placed on a basis of equality. There was the Club
Massiac, composed largely of absentee planters, asserting that only
on the old color basis could the allegiance of the colonies be main-

tained; there was Robespierre thundering back that it was better to
lose a colony than a principle. In London there were Clarkson and
Wilberforce financing a mulatto insurrection. In St. Domingue there
were the planters terrified at the thought that everything they had
believed in was to be taken from them—the constitution, the King of
France, the tradition of colonial rule, the bar of color. There were
the revolutionary bureaucrats sent out from France, distrustful of
everyone who sympathized with the old regime. There were the
petits blancs, crafty and worthless, with nothing to lose, trusting
that any commotion could be turned to their advantage. There were
the mulattoes, uncertain with whom to side. There were the slaves,
ignorant, misinformed and ready to revolt. It was a tangled play.

One name out of that chaotic period has left its mark on history.
A number of mulatto delegates had come from St. Domingue to press
their claims. One of these was a young mulatto called Vincent Ogé.
His mother had a plantation near Cap Français. His father had been
dead some while. His mother supported him. He had visited New
England and been made a lieutenant colonel in the army of one of
the German electors through the influence of *Les Amis des Noirs*.
He was disgusted on his arrival in Paris to learn that the assembly had
denied that its assertion of liberty and equality applied to the colonies.
He returned promptly to St. Domingue and informed the governor
in a letter that if the wrongs of the mulattoes were not redressed he
would have to resort to arms.

It was a stupid little revolt; or rather, it seemed stupid because it
was ineffectual. His small band of followers was routed, and he fled
for safety to the Spanish section of the island. The Spaniards handed
him over to the French. He was tried, found guilty and broken on
the wheel.

This sentence, in view of the general standard of the times, brutal
though it was, does not astonish us. Ogé was a traitor; the country
was in an inflammable condition; an example was needed. Far worse
things happened in England during Elizabeth's reign. Ogé's death,
however, caused in Paris a violent reaction against the planters; a
tragedy on his death was performed on the public stage, and Abbé
Gregoire succeeded in getting passed by the assembly a motion that
"the people of colour, resident in the French colonies, born of free
parents, were entitled to as of right and should be allowed the enjoyment of all the privileges of French citizens and among those of
being eligible to seats both in the parochial and colonial assemblies."

Ogé is venerated today as the first of the martyrs. But it was a short-lived victory; as soon as a rebellion broke out in St. Domingue, the French assembly rescinded its own law, and chaos followed. There was pillage, there was slaughter. The blacks marched into battle with the impaled body of a dead child as their standard. Houses were burned, sugar mills gutted; young women raped and disemboweled. White men were placed between planks and sawn in half. If a man was considered too tall his ankles were lopped away. If too short he was lengthened by a dislocation of his joints. Within two months, 2,000 whites were massacred, 180 sugar and 900 coffee plantations destroyed, and 1,200 Christian families were destitute. The revolt was put down with appropriate reprisals—10,000 slaves were killed, 400 executed. But the spirit of revolt was in the land.

A commissioner came out from France, resolved to break the power of the planters. They were aristocrats in his opinion. He fancied that it was through the blacks that his interests could best be served. "It is with the real inhabitants of the country, the Africans," he wrote back to Paris, "that we will save for France the possession of St. Domingue." The planters, in their desperation, offered their allegiance to the British.

When the wind is high, the lowest branches of a tree may touch the highest. In France, private soldiers were rising within a year's space to the rank of general. In St. Domingue it was by a released slave, a little old coachman called Toussaint l'Ouverture, that the invading armies of Spain and England were flung upon the coast in chaos; that the Spanish section of the island was annexed for France; that after ten years of civil war the island was restored to industry; that the Negroes, though technically free, were sent back to the fields to work under a system more rigorous than the old regime had known; that the white planters were encouraged to return to the management of their estates.

Situations not too dissimilar were being created in the other French islands. In Martinique, at the beginning of the French Revolution there was an outbreak of the slaves that considerably strengthened in London the arguments of the planter lobby and delayed the discussion of Wilberforce's proposals for several sessions; it was suppressed, but the island remained in a highly disturbed condition. In 1792, when Britain was still at peace with France, Sir William Young, an Englishman with estates in the West Indies, paused at Martinique on a trip between Barbados and St. Vincent. "All was calm," he wrote, "but it was such a calm as generally precedes a hurricane.

The free mulattoes and *gens de couleur,* who are twice as numerous as the white inhabitants, are awaiting the results of the ascendant parties in old France. . . . The whites generally are friends of the old government. . . . Commerce has lost its activity. Credit has gone. There is money in plenty, but no trade. There were only nine small ships in the harbour, . . . trade being virtually extinguished there, but the embers of what it has been glimmer in the shops; the jewellers and silversmiths are as brilliant as any in London."

On the outbreak of war between France and Britain in February 1793, the British government, in pursuance of its habitual policy, decided to recapture all of the West Indian islands which had been restored to France in 1763 and 1782. An attack on Tobago having been successful, and one on Martinique repulsed, a substantial expedition was commissioned to capture the entire French heritage in the eastern Caribbean. At the last moment the authorities in Whitehall reduced the size of the expedition because the intelligence department had been informed that the French colonists were so incensed against the Republican government in Paris that a British force would be most welcome, and that "a body of 800 regular troops would be more than sufficient to overcome all possible resistance." This information was, in fact, correct. Martinique was captured with seventy-one men killed and 193 wounded; St. Lucia was captured within fourteen hours of landing, and Guadeloupe, which was reputed to have a garrison of nearly six thousand men, cost the British only seventeen deaths and fifty walking wounded. Until this point, Whitehall's estimate of her general's requirements had been fully justified. But Whitehall had failed to realize that the mosquitoes of the mangrove swamps were more lethal than the bayonets of the French grenadiers. Sickness became a pestilence to which the British governor, General Dundas, succumbed. And at this point there appeared upon the scene one of the most remarkable of the men who have spread terror through the Caribbean.

Of less than medium height, with a corpulent torso that he encased in clothes that were too tight for it, with thick, stocky legs and a plebeian, sensual mouth, pitted by smallpox, abrupt in manner, jerky, with a Southern accent, Victor Hugues rarely looked anyone in the face, but when he did, his small gray eyes inspired either terror or repulsion. Born in Marseilles in 1752 in a small bakery shop, he ran away to sea when young and settled in St. Domingue; conducting a surreptitious trade with Havana, shipping thither silk from Lyons by North American ships that had brought flour to the Antilles, he was in a prosperous situation when the revolution started, and he was made a member of the local assembly. His brother, however, was murdered by the slaves, and he lost all his money. But he did not lose his faith in the new ideas, and on his return to Paris addressed to the security authorities a denunciation of the Spaniards who had assisted emigrants and priests in St. Domingue.

His letter ended, "If twenty years as a colonial, if local knowledge of foreign colonies and the continent of America, after twelve years of travel there and in the Spanish possessions, if this knowledge, citizen minister, can be of any use to the Republic, dispose of my fortune and my life. They are my country's." And when the revolutionary tribunals were set up, the minister, remembering the patriot who had returned from many travels with an eloquent denunciation, made him a public prosecutor and appointed him to Brest. In one respect, Hugues was admirably fitted for the post. He had imposed on himself the first discipline required for the office of a leader of men. He had no friends.

His first victim was a mulatto, symbolically offered to placate the spirit of his brother, and he threw himself into his task with fanatical devotion. The commissioners were highly impressed. In their report they wrote, "At the fall of each head, patriotic songs and cries of *Vive le tribunal* paid a fitting tribute to the members who composed it. We take this opportunity of expressing our approval of Victor Hugues, an excellent Jacobin whose civic sense is distinguished in a high degree." Hugues' skill and energy were rewarded with the governorship of Guadeloupe.

Just as the terror was about to end in France, he sailed late in April in 1794 to establish it in the Antilles. His expedition consisted of two frigates, a brig and five troop transports. His force of fifteen hundred men was composed of a company of artillery, two of infantry, and a battalion of Pyrennean rifles. But that was not all he carried; he had on board a printing press, which he considered as important an instrument of war as a battery of cannon, and he had three hundred posters printed of the Decree of the 16th Pluvios of the year 2, abolishing slavery. "All men domiciled in our colonies are declared to be French citizens without distinction of race and with an absolute equality of rights."

No chaplains had joined his expedition. Columbus had had crosses painted on his sails, "a symbol," so Hugues said, "of the servitude about to be imposed." Instead of a cross, he carried a guillotine; he installed it, shrouded, in the bows, gaunt as a figure in a theorem, reduced to one horizontal and one vertical plane. As he approached land, he tore off the tarpaulin sheet, and the sunlight glittered on its steel blade.

No one in France had known for certain what had been happening in the Caribbean. Hugues found on his arrival that the island was held by the British with four thousand well-trained men, and with the population on their side. Hugues was under no obligation to attempt a forlorn hope. His orders read, "If it is impossible to disembark, go to the U.S.A., and return to France." To that he countered, "We set sail for Guadeloupe. We must not let ourselves be hindered because these vile satellites of despotism got there first. Let us land."

He was heavily outnumbered, but he was resolute, intrepid and astute. He appreciated the situation speedily. His troops were fresh, but they would not be able for long to resist the debilitating August weather. He had learned that in the British camp more than half of the men were on the sick list; that there were not available enough men to guard the batteries; that the neighboring islands had been drained of troops and that a body of French Royalists had been persuaded to perform military duties. Hugues, therefore, decided to arm as many blacks and mulattoes as he could muster. They were inured to the climate; they had nothing to lose; they flocked to his standard readily and he soon dragooned them into a standard of discipline adequate to the launching of an assault.

Strategically the British commander had selected his site soundly, on a commanding piece of ground flanked on one side by the sea and on the other by an impassable morass. About a mile to the rear was a narrow pass, the only approach to the camp, while in front was the River Sallé, on whose opposite bank stood the town of Point-à-Pitre. The British commander had, however, left out of his reckoning the evil exhalations of bad air that hovered above the swamp. Within a short time, several of his companies could not produce a single man fit for duty, and one whole regiment could not raise a corporal and three men to stand on guard at night. Hugues gloated and waited, then attacked. He loaded a large number of his troops into small vessels, which on a dark night eluded the British men-of-war. He drove in the outposts, thus cutting the communication between the British garrison and its shipping. His first attacks were beaten back with heavy losses, but he had an indefinite and expendable supply of reserves; the British grew shorter of supplies; finally they had no alternative to capitulation.

The terms which Hugues was prepared to accept on behalf of the

British were generous enough, but he refused to allow the French Royalists to be treated as British subjects. He would not listen to the arguments put forward by the general's representative. He walked back and forth, his hands clasped behind his back. He had said his last word. "Tell your general that I'll capture your camp tomorrow and have him guillotined." The most he would concede was the sending away of twenty-five Royalist officers in a covered boat. The remainder, three hundred of them, were surrendered.

At this time the ruthlessness of Victor Hugues' character was not properly appreciated by his enemies. To them he was a courageous and resourceful leader of troops, and the British commander no doubt imagined that the French Royalists would be treated as honorable captives, in terms of the traditions of civilized warfare. Subsequent events disabused him on that score.

The guillotine was set up on the field of battle, and in the space of an hour, fifty of the prisoners were beheaded. Hugues then grew impatient. At this rate his troops would be kept unprofitably occupied for five more hours. He therefore ordered that the remainder be fettered together and lined up on the edge of the trenches that they had recently defended. His irregular and half-trained troops were then instructed to fire at them. The first volley by unskilled soldiers killed some, wounded others and left many untouched. But the weight of the dead pulling on the chains dragged the dying as well as the unwounded into the trenches, into which the earth was immediately thrown. Hugues, having shown the world what it could expect of him, had the body of General Dundas dug up from its grave and thrown into the river, and he had bayoneted a number of British soldiers who were recovering in the hospital from wounds and sickness.

Hugues was now ready to proceed to the full rigors of the "terror." In Paris he had been a friend of Robespierre; he prided himself on his nickname, "the Robespierre of the Isles." The pupil's little finger should be thicker than his master's loins. He ordered the destruction of the church that had stood on the *Morne du Governement*, stigmatizing it as a symbol of idolatry. The priests in hiding were instructed to take an oath of loyalty to the constitution. The *Morne* was renamed *de la Victoire*. He established a series of traveling tribunals to bring to justice all those who had opposed the revolution. He coined the phrase, *assermenté*, for anyone who had taken an oath of allegiance either to Louis XVI or George III. *As-tu prêté serment à l'imbécile George?* he would demand. "The state," he would announce, "rewards the denunciator." In Brest he had had the guillotine placed near enough to the prison for its inmates to hear its action. He followed the same practice here. At the start it was mounted in the marketplace, but as the surface was unpaved, the blood did not run away but formed a red mud round the scaffold. Earth was flung over it, but the putrefying blood broke its crust, and flies swarmed round it to such an extent that the marketplace was deserted.

This did not suit Hugues at all. He wanted his executions to be public and applauded. He had the guillotine moved to the *Place de la Victoire*, near a river into which the blood could drain. The loyalists met their death in Pointe-à-Pitre as bravely as had their friends in Paris. Each morning there was a roll call of the victims. One of them who had a cold laughingly remarked that a better day could not have been chosen. "I'll gladly be rid of my head." They sang hymns as they waited at the scaffold. The volume of sound diminished till there was only one voice left, then silence.

So that the whole island should learn its lesson, he had the guillotine sent on tour from village to village, pausing at taverns on the way, where the executioner was bribed to give exhibitions of how the mechanism worked: a large bass drum was carried round in the cart to give the occasion an air of festival.

Hugues interpreted his commission to involve the transference of all authority into his own hands. He curtailed the power of the army. He described the military as salaried republicans devoted to the safety of the state, whose authority did not extend outside their camp. He suppressed legality, killed the judges, and became himself the accuser, the jury and the judge. He forbade private commerce and became himself the trader. It was state socialism, with himself the state.

The slaves were free, but it is doubtful if they could appreciate the difference between their previous and their present position. Those who would not work were threatened with death. "The republic," he said, "in recognizing the rights you have inherited from nature did not absolve you of the need to suppport yourself. No pity will be given the man who does not work. He will be treated as a traitor."

The work was as strictly regimented as it had been on the old plantations. At 5:30 each morning a bell would summon citizens and citizenesses to a meeting place appointed by the overseer. At 5:45 the chief intoned a couplet of the revolutionary hymn ending, "Long live the Republic." The roll would be read and the citizens would start off for work, singing with that "simple and lively gaiety that characterizes a good child of *La Patrie*." The overseer would then make a tour of the houses and see who was not at work. Every tenth day he sent in a report.

At eight o'clock, breakfast was taken on the grass, in the manner of the Parisian *sansculottes*. Work was resumed at 8:30 and continued until 11:30. There was an interval of two and a half hours, then a bell announced the end of the siesta. A roll call was taken and work continued until nightfall. During the harvest season they would work longer hours, "as good republicans." Punishments were strict and they received no real pay. Distinctions of color were retained; there were white, colored, and black citizens. In the army, a black citizen could not rise above the rank of captain, and was never placed in a high administrative post.

In the meantime, the situation in Paris was changing rapidly. Within a few days of the destruction of the church on the *Morne de la Victoire*, a French ship arrived with newspapers announcing that religion was once again permitted: men without Gods were now designated as "abandoned monsters." A little later the events of the 9th Thermidor and the fall of Robespierre were general knowledge.

France had ceased to be a convention and had become the *Directoire*, "delivered," in its own words, "from the yoke of those vile men who in the name of liberty sullied the name of France by their blood-stained brigandage." But correspondence between France and Guadeloupe was intermittent; Marat was still being deified in Pointe-à-Pitre when his body was rotting in a ditch, and Hugues was in the habit of interpreting such orders as he received in the light of his own convenience; a constitution that might be fine for France could, he argued, be impossible in the colonies. Its implementation would result in the destruction of the colonies. But he was a practical man; he recognized that the wind had changed, and he could console himself with the knowledge that, as far as Guadeloupe was concerned, he had carried out Robespierre's instructions thoroughly. In 1790, Basse-Terre had 9,371 inhabitants, of whom 1,640 were white. Five years later there were 5,223 inhabitants, and of the 1,092 whites only 225 were male. Though he might have had qualms as to what might be the fate of "the Robespierre of the Isles," he continued to behave as though he enjoyed the privileges of an independent emperor.

As soon as he got the plantations back to work, he felt himself free to enlarge the area of his parish. To Dominica, Martinique, St. Lucia, Grenada, St. Eustatius and St. Martin, he sent revolutionary missionaries to explain the happenings in St. Domingue and to encourage a rising against the English. "Spare no Englishmen," he ordered. In Martinique his missionaries were captured and shot, but he roused the Caribs of St. Vincent to attack the English, and he prepared the ground for his invasions of the other islands.

Grenada in particular seemed to offer opportunities for his prose-lytizing zeal. For years the island had been shaken with disputes be-tween the French and English. When England took possession of it in 1763, the French were allowed complete religious freedom, a privi-lege that was not accorded to the English, who bitterly resented the superior position of their fellow colonists; this resentment was exac-erbated during the War of American Independence, when the French recovered the island and they themselves were subjected to innumer-able hardships. The French had acted unwisely, for there was at this period no security of tenure in the Caribbean. Within four years the English had recovered the island and taken their revenge, confiscat-ing all church lands from the French and depriving them of their political rights.

Once again the dispossessed party bided its time, and the French planters naturally learned with delight of Victor Hugues' success in Guadeloupe. They besought his aid and he was quick to give it. He laid his plans carefully. He chose as his leader a French planter with colored blood, called Julien Fédon. We know nothing of Fédon out-side of the events of the next few months, except that he was as ruth-less and brutal as Hugues himself. The plot was worked out in secret, and arms were smuggled to the conspirators. Two attacks were launched, one against a small town on the windward coast, called La Baye, the other against Gouyave. At La Baye the English residents were slaughtered—men, women and children—and the rebels fled with their booty to the hills. At Gouyave the residents were captured, carried to Fédon's camp and put into stocks. Among the prisoners was the governor. Fédon gave him the alternatives of death or sur-render of the island. The governor refused to surrender, but took the precaution of warning the acting governor that it had been threat-ened that if the camp was attacked by British troops, the prisoners would be shot.

The acting governor, just as the British general in Guadeloupe, did not believe that such a barbarity would be committed. But Fédon was a worthy disciple of Hugues. As soon as the assault was launched, the massacre of the prisoners started. Forty-eight were shot, and the attack was beaten off.

For a year the rebels were in control; and the crops and houses of every resident who did not share their views were burned. When at last the British returned in force, there remained very few of their compatriots to welcome them. The retribution that followed their return was thorough. Fédon himself escaped, though there is no record of his survival. It was believed that he was drowned in a canoe on his way to Trinidad. But nearly all the other leaders were captured; a number of them were shot and the rest deported to British Honduras.

Those fifteen months of civil war were to have a lasting effect upon Grenada. So few of the older planter families remained that it was not difficult to set up later a system of peasant proprietorship.

In the meantime, Hugues had a number of other irons in the fire. Trade in the Caribbean had been disorganized by the revolution, the war with Britain, and the confused political situation in St. Domingue, and it occurred to Hugues that this might be an opportune moment to imitate and emulate the seventeenth-century buccaneers. He organized, therefore, a fleet of corsairs to prey upon foreign shipping. He employed small ships which were easy to maneuver, which could hide in secluded bays, make quick getaways, and which provided more awkward targets than larger, slower ships. They were especially effective against the British, whose gunners followed a different tactic from the French, firing not at the masts but at the timbers of the hulls, their aim being steadier as the mouths of their cannon descended with the waves.

St. Bartholomew, which was owned by Sweden from 1784 to 1877, proved a useful neutral base, from which his corsairs operated so successfully that during Hugues' period of power nearly six hundred ships were sacked. The harbor of Pointe-à-Pitre was filled with shipping, and sheds had to be built on the edge of the mangrove plantations that fringed the town. Pointe-à-Pitre became the richest town in the West Indies; once there had been a lack of currency, but now there were French louis, British guineas and Portuguese moidores.

Wild scenes attended the unloading of each cargo; and the people of the town adopted a curious comic-opera uniform—bare feet or shoeless stockings, braided dress coats, shirts trimmed with fur and ribbons at the collar, felt hats with brims half turned down, decorated with feathers dyed with the colors of the republic. Hugues ceased to read the newspapers and put on weight. He was more interested in commerce than the constitution, and the guillotine worked only one day in five. He regularly sent back to France a generous proportion of his plunder.

In this he showed sound common sense. The committee in Paris had learned of his massacres with concern. Yet his achievements on behalf of the republic were so considerable that in January 1796, it confirmed him in his role as an agent with full powers for eighteen months. Two months later he married a young Creole, and the extent to which he found his office profitable may be gauged from the fact that though he had arrived in the island penniless, he was able to make her a marriage settlement of one hundred thousand livres. He would have been able to make her a larger settlement if he had not been such an insatiable gambler, for not only had he control of the island's commerce and had benefited from the confiscations of Royalist property, but he was a considerable shareholder in the piratical activities of the corsairs. He should have been an extremely wealthy man, but night after night he sat at the tables, losing with complete indifference the moneys that he had filched from his victims.

His fortunes might have prospered indefinitely had not *hubris* undermined his power. Incensed at the freedom with which the United States were selling arms and ammunitions to the British, in his opinion a base attempt to drive France and the Revolution out of the Caribbean, he urged the Refectory to declare war on the United States. The Refectory refusing, he increased the tempo of his raids on American shipping to such an extent that in July 1798, the U.S.A. declared war on France within American waters. It was called the Brigand's War.

The outbreak of this war, which does not appear to have been announced in Guadeloupe, turned Paris against Hugues, and a replacement was sent out with instructions to dismantle the guillotine, the only one, it is believed, that ever crossed the Atlantic. Hugues, one of the most bloodthirsty of the Jacobins, was in private life a fond father and a tender spouse, and since his wife was pregnant, he refused to leave the island. He was, however, tricked on board a homebound ship and made a prisoner. From the bows of the ship he hurled imprecations at his successor.

His reluctance to leave the island, apart from his concern about his wife's condition, is easily understandable. Most of the executives of the terror met a sudden and violent end, and Hugues must have had considerable doubts as to the reception that he would receive in Paris. To his surprise, however, he found himself still in official favor, and he was shortly posted to the governorship of Cayenne.

The news of his appointment caused consternation to the inhabitants of that obscure little colony, but Hugues was as adaptable as the vicar of Bray. Once again he traveled with a printing press, but this time its posters were assurances to the public that there would be no repetition of the sanguinary incidents that had been unfortunately necessary in Guadeloupe, and he installed in the bows of the ship, instead of a guillotine, a company of musicians, equipped with the latest songs from Paris, marches by Gossec, and country-dances for the fife and clarionet. He himself was decked in a quasi-military uniform, braided and embroidered, surmounted by a plumed helmet.

Cayenne, which had escaped the ferocities both of war and the Revolution, had provided a refuge for many exiles from less lucky islands, though it had been nicknamed "the dry guillotine," since so many of these exiles died of fever. Hugues' regime was paternalistic. He opened roads and irrigated fields. Paris was now at peace with the holy see. Monks and nuns returned and church bells chimed. Then, by the law of the 30th Floreal of the year 10, slavery was reinstated. Hugues shrugged. He was a politician; if the restoration of slavery was a political necessity, there was nothing he could do about it. He proceeded to restore slavery in Cayenne, as vigorously and ruthlessly as he had liquidated it in Guadeloupe.

He summoned the owners of nearby haciendas and the leaders of the militia to a secret meeting, and explained his plans. At dusk, the gates of the town were closed and the farms occupied by troops. At eight o'clock a gun was fired, and several hundred Negroes were herded into a small clearing. Hugues climbed onto a barrel, unrolled the parchment of the law, and by the light of torches sonorously delivered it. The former free citizens were informed that next day their former masters would be calling for them, to conduct them back to their old hutments.

A turbulent period followed. Many of the Negroes escaped in the darkness, hid in the hills, and poisoned the fish streams with mullion seed. There was a succession of grim atrocities. The freed men of color were refused permission to return to France in fear lest their excessive number might transmit to European blood the same dark tinge that had spread through Spain after the Moorish invasion. In the guerrilla warfare that ensued, what was known as the Egyptian disease struck the island and affected Hugues' eyesight. But order was eventually established.

The European war followed its course. The Dutch joined forces with Britain against the French and captured Cayenne. Hugues was tried in Paris by court-martial, but was acquitted with honor. Little is known about his final years. He had been a baker, trader, Mason, Anti-Mason, Jacobin, military hero, rebel, prisoner, agent of the directory, agent of the consulate; he was now absolved by the men who had killed the man who made him, and he remained in France. He had links with Fouché. He was in Paris when Napoleon's regime collapsed. In 1814 an old comrade saw in the Palais Royale the fierce little dictator who once strode up and down his study in Guadeloupe, his hands behind his back, a cigar in his mouth, shouting, "Spare no Englishman," soberly attired and wearing an enormous white cockade. "Once," his friend said, "you executed anyone wearing that." Hugues shrugged. "What would you? The Bourbons are our legitimate rulers."

He died in the early 1820s, but the date and place of his death are uncertain. Some say he died in France, but according to the Spanish novelist, Alejo Carpentier, who made extensive researches for his novel, *Explosion in a Cathedral*, the gossip of Guadeloupe insists that he returned to his property in Guiana, where he died, slowly, painfully, and blind.

The present condition of the West Indian islands has been determined by what did or did not happen to them during this quarter century of war. Certain islands were scarcely affected, Barbados and the northern Leewards—Antigua, St. Kitts, Nevis and Montserrat —owing their immunity to the direction of the northeast trade winds. It was difficult to attack against it. But St. Lucia, Grenada and Guadeloupe felt the full impact of the Revolution; Martinique was captured twice and was a British island for fifteen years. This was to have a profound effect on her future history. Her landowners were not dispossessed, as those of Guadeloupe were. They could not return to France, so they lived on their estates in affluent isolation, nothing being done to interfere with the maintenance of the French way of life.

One of Britain's great merits as a colonizing power has been her willingness to allow a defeated people to continue to conduct its affairs in exactly the same manner as it had before. The English have transported for themselves the life of the shires to Malaya, India and the Antilles, with their sport and clubs, their prejudices and their shibboleths, ignoring the customs of their neighbors, leaving well enough alone when that seemed practical and peaceful. In Canada Britain has maintained the French language, the French laws, the Catholic religion. Quebec today is not only bilingual; it is a French rather than a British city. During the Napoleonic Wars Britain captured Mauritius and the Seychelles Islands. The French way of life was maintained so uninterruptedly that not only were the *grands blancs* of the Seychelles considered more French than the French, but in the summer of 1940 they wondered whether they did not owe allegiance to Pétain's government in Vichy rather than Churchill's government in London.

In Martinique, during Napoleon's revolutionary wars, though the Union Jack flew from the turrets of Saint-Pierre and Fort Royal, the big planters and the little whites continued to lead exactly the same life that they had when de Grasse sailed northward to the Dominica Channel. For the slaves the regime was unchanged. The resolutions that were passed and then rescinded in Paris had no effect on them. They continued to plant sugarcane, then cut it, feed it into the mills and scrape the thick scum from the boiling vats; they danced in the evenings and sang songs, cultivated their own gardens on their day of leisure; attended the white man's services on Sunday but worshiped the dark gods of Africa in their hearts, and dreamed of freedom and revenge, wondering what truth there was in the stories that reached them from Guadeloupe. It was not unnatural that Napoleon, in the pause allowed him in 1801 by the Treaty of Amiens, took Martinique as the model for his new colonial enterprise.

Fifteen years later in St. Helena, Napoleon was to describe this enterprise as the biggest mistake of his life, but it had a great deal to commend it. He had recently acquired New Orleans from the Spanish. He was at peace with Europe. He had sixty thousand troops that he would be glad to see out of France. If he were to reassert his authority in Guadeloupe and St. Domingue he could form a colonial empire, moving in a circle from Martinique up the Mississippi, that would make France self-supporting and invulnerable. The situations in Guadeloupe and St. Domingue were not dissimilar. In each case, contact with France had been largely severed by the difficulties of wartime communication. In each case there had been sanguinary massacres; in each case order of a kind had been restored, with the sugar mills turning and a certain number of white planters enjoying the fruits of their estates; in each case a black general was in command —in St. Domingue, Toussaint l'Ouverture; in Guadeloupe, Pelage. It was reasonable for Napoleon to assume that without the distraction of a war in Europe he should be able, with his armies that had conquered Europe, to restore completely the authority of Paris, and had he succeeded he need never have developed his continental plans for Europe; he need never have launched his campaign across the Russian snows. He might have deferred his ambitions for the imperial laurels. Later he would have been faced, he or his successors, with a different set of problems. The United States would not have tolerated a European empire stretching along its western boundry and curtailing its own expansion. Sooner or later there must have been a war between France and the United States. So many things would have happened differently if Napoleon's colonial enterprise had succeeded. It is one of the big ifs of history, and the enterprise so nearly did succeed.

It had been carefully thought out, with that simplicity which is so often the secret of success. Two expeditions were dispatched side by side across the Atlantic, the one to Guadeloupe, the other to St. Domingue. They carried similar instructions. The black leaders were to be cajoled, flattered, confirmed in their ranks; then, when the French army and French rule had been established, the black leaders were to be returned to France, as prisoners if they had been obstinate, to serve in the French army had they been obedient. To Guadeloupe he sent Richepanse, to St. Domingue his brother-in-law, Leclerc, "a fellow almost damned in a fair wife."

The expedition to Guadeloupe succeeded admirably. It was far from being easy sailing for Richepanse. There was fighting, there were misunderstandings; a fort with three hundred men in it was blown sky-high, but within a few days there was no resistance except for a few groups in the hills; Pelage was on his way back to France to serve in Napoleon's army and to die in Spain. Slavery was restored, though the word "slave" was not used. Only whites could be French citizens. The word "proprietor" was substituted for the word "master"; "correctional discipline" for "the whip." A weekly wage was replaced by food, clothes and medical attention. Proprietors were reinstated. Colored men and Negroes without a card of freedom had to return to their old properties. Chains and dungeons punished those who attempted to escape. All was, in fact, very much as it had been twenty years before, except that a great many white planters had been killed, with their heirs preferring to remain in Paris. Within a few months the island had been recaptured by the British, and a period of uncontentious prosperity began.

It was all to turn out very differently in St. Domingue. Up to a point the plan succeeded well enough. Leclerc had been instructed to treat the black generals as Richepanse had. Toussaint was the equivalent for Pelage, and within a few weeks Toussaint had been tricked on board and sent back to France in chains. Toussaint is one of the great names in history. He was to inspire a sonnet by Wordsworth, a tragedy by Lamartine and a novel by Harriet Martineau. He was the son of an African chief; he had no white blood in his veins; he had been born on an estate in St. Domingue. He had been trusted as a slave; he had been promoted early from the cane fields to be his master's coachman. As far as a slave's life can be congenial, his had been. He had not been ill-treated; he had had a comfortable house. He had felt loyalty for his master, and when the revolution broke out he had not only helped him to escape but sent after him to the United States a cargo of cotton and sugar. He had been born with a power to rule; he was a natural leader; as a general he outmaneuvered the Spanish and the British, and as an administrator he restored order in the island. He was not disloyal to France. It was his intention that the island should enjoy something akin to dominion status, acknowledging the suzerainty and commercial monopoly of France. He was not a bloodthirsty revolutionary, and if Napoleon's schemes had prospered in St. Domingue, Toussaint might be no more than a footnote in history. The spotlight has fallen on him because he was captured through treachery, and died in prison without trial, and because the subsequent history of the island is so dramatic, with a drama that is still tangible today. He is famous, in fact, as a forerunner, as the man who prepared the road for Dessalines and Henri Christophe; he is famous because of them rather than of himself, and it was through Leclerc's tactless handling of Dessalines and Henri Christophe that the campaign miscarried.

When Leclerc arrived, Toussaint l'Ouverture was in Port-au-Prince, and it was here that Leclerc lured him into captivity. But Henri Christophe was at Cap Français, as general of the north. And it was in his handling of Christophe that Leclerc was most at fault. Though the island was technically at peace and work was proceeding on the estates, there were brigands in the hills, and three separate forces were under arms; Leclerc might at one bold blow have taken Cap Français or he might by skillful diplomacy have outwitted the black generals. He delayed assault, however, and sent as an ambassador Lebrun, an ignorant, ill-bred popinjay who later, on a diplomatic visit to Jamaica, was so outrageous in his behavior as to merit a reprimand from Nugent. It is hard to understand why Leclerc chose him as an aide-de-camp. Possibly Lebrun was handsome; possibly he was Pauline's choice.

Christophe could have been won over. As it was, distrustful and offended by Lebrun's tactlessness, he burned Cap Français and fled into the hills. By the time that he and the other generals had surrendered into the acceptance of commissions as French generals, Leclerc had lost half his men.

Even so, for the moment it looked as though the French had won. Toussaint had been shipped to France. Christophe and Dessalines were generals in the French army; according to Napoleon's plan, they, too, should have been sent back. But fighting once begun is hard to stop; the hills were filled with untamed brigands. Leclerc could not risk the loss of his troops in guerilla warfare. Bandits had to be set against bandits. Christophe and Dessalines were the only men that he could trust. He had to keep them on. "A little while," he thought, "a little longer. When the last brigand has been captured; then will I send Dessalines back to France."

But the dice were loaded against Leclerc. Long before the last brigand had been brought in, yellow fever, decimating his men, had broken out along the coast, and before the epidemic was at an end the news had come from Guadeloupe that slavery had been reestablished there.

It was the news from Guadeloupe that decided the St. Domingue expedition, by uniting with a common dread not only the black but the mulatto forces. Until then the black forces of St. Domingue had consisted of three armies: the mulattoes of the south, the center under Dessalines, the north under Christophe. There had been no true combination. The generals had fought and acted independently of each other. Christophe had indeed made a separate peace with Leclerc. The news that slavery was reestablished in Guadeloupe, with the certainty that it was the plan of the French to restore slavery in St. Domingue, united the black forces. Christophe and Dessalines went back into the hills, and with them Pétion, the mulatto general who had been Dessalines' chief opponent in the early war.

For the next three years Dessalines' and St. Domingue's become one story.

Today Dessalines is Haiti's hero. Streets and cigarettes are christened after him. His tomb is in the Champ de l'Indépendence. His statue faces the Chapel of Cap Haitien. In Port-au-Prince it brandishes a sword in face of the green-roofed houses and the dim outline of Gonâve. The visitor in Port-au-Prince will gaze wonderingly at that statue. He will scan the aristocratic, thin-lipped, straight-nosed face below the cockaded hat, and he will ask himself where in those bloodless features the signs of savagery are concealed. He may well ask himself. It was never for ungentle Dessalines that that mask was cut.

It was ordered by a Central American president who was cast out of office before the statue could be delivered. His fall coincided with the arrival in Paris of a delegation from Haiti to commission a statue of Dessalines to celebrate the centenary of Haitian independence. As there was a statue going cheap, they took it. That was the way they did things in Haiti then. And, indeed, they might well have found a statue less symbolic of the tiger. As you sit at twilight on the veranda of the El Dorado, the outline of the cockaded hat and the thin curve of the brandished sword is dark and ominous against the scarlet sunset. They are the last things you see as the swift dusk settles on the Champ de Mars.

Today Dessalines' many brutalities are forgiven and forgotten. There was much to forget and to forgive. In Haiti's bloodstained story he is the most ruthless figure. He was a great fighter and he loved fighting. As long as he was fighting he did not much mind whom he fought. As long as he was killing he did not much mind whom he killed. In the intervals there were women. But women were a sideshow.

It is impossible to detect in his behavior a consistent policy. During the two years of Toussaint's pacific administration he drove his Negroes to work at the sword's point. During his war with Leclerc he butchered, because they were white, every Frenchman whose property lay across his line of retreat. As a general in Leclerc's army he was known as the butcher of the Negroes, and slaughtered with the liveliest ferocity a hundred blacks because a few French officers had been assaulted. The war he waged with the French when the news of French treachery in Guadeloupe was known is the bloodiest in history. Terrible things happened during those weeks when Leclerc, his body faint and his eyes bright with fever, wrote dispatch after desperate dispatch to France, and Pauline dangled her pretty toes over the palace wall, her eyes fixed broodingly on the green mangroves and the lilac outline of the hills, her ears avid for the caressing words of the young aide-de-camp beside her. Darker things were to happen after Leclerc had sunk to death, after Pauline had sailed away to a less ill-starred marriage, and the fierce Rochambeau was left in charge of the French army. On neither side was any quarter given; no refinement of torture was left unpracticed. Rochambeau imported bloodhounds from Cuba. He prepared black dummies, their stomachs stuffed with food, with which he trained the bloodhounds to make always for the bellies of the blacks. The disemboweling of prisoners was the favorite Sunday afternoon amusement of the Creoles at Cap

Français. Lady Nugent's journal, in the intervals of deploring the moral lapses of the young Jamaicans, makes wistful reference to the atrocities that were being staged four hundred miles away, while her husband was complacently informing Lord Hobart that the French would be unable to hold out—which was to the good, he thought. "We shall have nothing to fear from the blacks," he wrote, "provided we resume our former commercial intercourse, thereby preventing them from raising a marine. There are still chiefs of Toussaint's school. We should only have to play the same game as before between Toussaint and Rigaud to succeed as well in neutralising the power of the brigands."

A few months later, England and France were again at war. With the outbreak of war, Rochambeau's last hope had gone. He could get no reinforcements. He could get no supplies. The blacks were attacking him by land, the English were blockading him by sea. He made peace with Dessalines and, with the honors of war, delivered himself into English hands.

It is from this moment that Dessalines appears in his full stature. Over a distance of a century and a half one reads now with a brooding wonderment the story of the next two years. Say what you will of him, Dessalines was on the heroic scale. He was of the lineage of Tamburlaine. Though his speeches and proclamations were doubtless prepared by another hand, the voice of a conqueror rings through them. Each phrase is like the roll of musketry. There is the heroic gesture, a reckless arrogance of hate, in his tearing of the white from the tricolor and making the colors of his country red and blue; in his rechristening of St. Domingue; in his wiping away of the last semblance of white rule in the new name, Haiti. He let Rochambeau go on Rochambeau's own terms. He signed the papers that they brought him. He promised immunity to the white Creoles. They could go or stay as it pleased them. They would be safe, he promised. Why should he not promise if it served his purpose? A good many promises had been made in the last twenty years. Had any of them been kept? With Rochambeau safely imprisoned in Jamaica, he would decide what it was best for him to do.

He decided quickly. The French had scarcely sailed before he was thundering out his hatred of those that stayed, before he had issued orders that none of those who remained should be allowed to leave. As the weeks passed, his intention grew more clear. Edward Colbert, the English representative, was writing back to Nugent that he had little hope for their safety and that Dessalines was counting his own

departure as the signal for commencing the work of death. He had
wanted to intercede for them with Dessalines, but "as their destruction," he wrote, "was not openly avowed by him, I was apprehensive
that I might accelerate what I was anxious to avoid." He reports
Dessalines' visit to the south. "In his present progress through the
southern and western parts of the island he is accompanied by between three and four hundred followers, the greatest part of whom
have the appearance of being extremely well qualified for every species
of rapine and mischief."

Colbert had prophesied correctly. Within a week of his return to
Jamaica the process of slaughter had begun. Dessalines knew that as
long as there was a Frenchman left in Haiti his position would be
insecure. The total extermination of the French that he had planned
was a task that he could entrust to no one else. From the south,
through Jeremie and Aux Cayes, he marched north to Port-au-Prince.

"Dessalines arrived here on Friday afternoon," records a letter
found among Nugent's correspondence. "Turned loose four hundred
to five hundred bloodthirsty villains on the poor defenceless inhabitants. He gave a general order for a general massacre (strangers ex-
cepted).[1] I had five in my house. It gave me great pain to be unable
to save a single one of them. They were all informed against by
black wenches. . . . The murderers are chosen by Dessalines. They
accompany him from the south to the north. What havoc when they
arrive at the Cap. The poor victims were slaughtered in the streets,
in the square, on the seaside, stripped naked and carried out of the
gates of Leogane and St. Joseph and thrown in heaps. A few days, I
fear, will breed a pestilence. . . . Had you seen with what avidity
these wretches flew at a white man you would have been astonished."

A few days later he was at the Cap. The massacre was carefully
stage-managed. Guards were placed outside the house of every English and American. It was the French only who were to be killed. For
a day and a night the narrow, cobble-paved streets echoed with groans
and cries. Then, suddenly, Dessalines grew weary. It was a waste of
time breaking into houses, searching cupboards, dragging people from
under beds. He announced that he would give safety to all whites,
provided that they came into the square to testify their allegiance to
him. One by one the terrified creatures crept from their lairs into the
open. Dessalines waited patiently beside his soldiers till the square

---

[1] In the original letter amusingly misspelled "accepted."

was full. Then he tapped upon his snuffbox. It was the signal for his men to shoot.

Next day he issued the challenge of his own defence:

Quel est ce vil Haitien si peu digne de sa régénération qui ne croit pas avoir accompli les décrets de l'Eternel en exterminant ces tigres attérés de sang. S'il en est un, qu'il s'éloigne la nature indigne de reprendre de notre sein, qu'il aille cacher sa honte loin de ces lieux, l'air qu'on y respire ne fait point pour ces organes grossiers, c'est l'air pur de la liberté auguste et triomphante. . . .[2]

In the constitution of Haiti was drafted the proud clause: *Jamais aucun colon ni Européen ne mettra le pied sur cette en titre de maître ou de propriétaire.*[3]

But there was nothing to be feared any longer from Napoleon. He had cut his losses, disposing of New Orleans in the Louisiana Purchase. "This," he said, "confirms forever the power of the United States. I have given England a maritime rival who sooner or later will humble her pride."

Four hundred miles away across the windward passage, Nugent, in his yellow-colored residence in Spanish Town, addressed Dessalines, whom he described to Hobart as the brigand chief, as "Your Excellency," and in the weary well-bred indifference of official English explained the terms on which Jamaica would be ready to trade with Haiti. Nugent had no doubt of what would happen. With a tired smile he listened to the accounts that came to him of Dessalines' extravagance, of the splendor and corruption of the court, of the troops encouraged to supplement by plunder a daily ration of a herring and a half loaf. Dessalines might declare himself an emperor, but the country was on the edge of bankruptcy. Dessalines might assert that Haiti, brown and black, consisted of one brotherhood. He might offer his sister to Pétion in marriage. But no declaration would convince the mulatto that he was not the superior of the Negro. No declaration would persuade the Negro to trust another Negro. The Negro could be ruled, on occasion he could rule. But he was incapable of cooperation, of rule by cabinet. When the news of Dessalines' murder was brought to Nugent—a murder, if not actually insti-

[2] "Is there any Haitian so vile, so unworthy of his regeneration as to doubt that the orders of the Almighty have been fulfilled in the extermination of these tigers gorged with blood? If there is such a one let him hide his shame far from here. The air we breathe, the pure air of triumphant liberty, was not made for his gross lungs."

[3] "Never shall any colonist or European set foot here as a master or landowner."

gated, at least approved by Christophe—he was not surprised. He was not surprised six months later when history repeated itself; when the conflict of Rigaud and Toussaint, the conflict of brown and black that was to be the main issue in Haitian history for the next hundred years, had been resumed between Pétion and Christophe.

Christophe was Dessalines' second-in-command. With terror he had watched the gradual disintegration of the country under Dessalines, the disorganization of the troops, the emptying of the treasury, the abandoned plantations. What would happen, he asked himself, when the French returned? Once the invaders had been flung back. But Leclerc had advanced on a country prosperous and prepared by Toussaint's rule. What chance would a disorganized and impoverished country stand against Napoleon? Haiti must be made powerful and rich, proud of itself, respected by other nations. Dessalines stood in the way of Haiti.

Thus Christophe argued. He had no doubt of what was needed. He had no doubt of his own power to realize those needs. When, after Dessalines' death, representatives of the various departments had met to draw up new constitutions, he was so sure that that convention would place him with unlimited powers at its head that he did not trouble to attend the meeting. He remained at the Cap with the quick-brained little mulatto who was to be raised to the dignity of rank under the title Pompey Baron de Vastey, planning the details of his campaign. He was the only man in Haiti who could save Haiti; he knew that.

He had counted, however, without two things. One was his own unpopularity; a year earlier Leclerc had written home that Christophe was so hated by the blacks that there was nothing to be feared from him. On that he had not counted, nor on Pétion.

Pétion was one of the few with intellect in Haiti. He was the son of a French artist and a mulattress. He was almost white; he had spent much of his time in Paris. He had served in the French army and had studied in the military schools. He was mild and sweet-natured, with a poetic mind. He brought with him to the convention one firm resolution: that he had not driven out the French tyranny to authorize another tyranny, and a black tyranny, in its place.

Patiently, tactfully, diplomatically, he argued clause by clause the constitution that was to defend the Haitians' liberty and limit the power of their ruler. It was no easy task. Sometimes as he looked round at that black semicircle of surly, stupid faces, a feeling of discouragement came over him, a feeling of doubt. "This is not really what I meant," he thought. It was something quite other than this that he had planned. What was it that he had planned? He had forgotten. It was so long ago. When one was young one saw life in clear issues. Afterward things grew confused. You fought for people with whom you were only three parts in sympathy against people to whom with a quarter of yourself you still belonged. You could never enter wholeheartedly into any quarrel. There was always a part of you left outside. Just as in life he had never anywhere been quite himself. Not here in St. Domingue, where his father had been ashamed of him; nor in Paris, where they had pretended to ignore his coloring. Not even in Paris among the young officers with whom he had joked and drunk, with the woman he had loved. Always between himself and them there had been the veil of difference, this quartering of savage blood. Never anywhere had he been quite himself. That was the thing that he had dreamed of, that was the thing he had fought for, a condition of society with which man could be in tune, in which he could be himself. It was for that that he was arguing now in this hot room, to these ignorant savages. It was this he dreamed of—a Utopia, where man could be off his guard.

But even as he argued, his faith weakened in the thing he argued for. They were not educated yet to democracy, these Negroes. Christophe would never accept these limitations to his power. Later, Christophe's indignant repudiation of the constitution came as no surprise to him. It was with no surprise that he learned of Christophe's angry mustering of men, of his forced march over the hills into the long, sun-parched, arid plain that stretches from Ennery to Saint-Marc.

Without surprise, but wearily, Pétion heard the news. Wearily and halfheartedly he gathered together the remnants of the army, marched out with it to the plain, to be flung back, wrecked and scattered; himself escaping with his life, and in the disguise of a peasant woman, upon the outskirts of Port-au-Prince. A few hours more and Christophe would be in the capital. Pétion, for one last effort, gathered his strength together; with the hatred of the brown for the black, with the hatred of brain for force, with the hatred of breeding for unsponsored vigor, he mobilized his troops, marched out with them into the plain and, employing fully for the last time all that France and his father's blood had taught him, he broke and dismembered Christophe's untutored powers; broke them, scattered them; then let them go.

His generals turned to him with amazement. What, was he about
to let the tyrant free? Now, when he had him in his power, when the
whole of Haiti was his for the plundering! Pétion shrugged his shoulders. That irresolution, that mulatto's doubting of himself that stood
always between him and real greatness, mingled a little, possibly, with
the poet's indifference, the poet's sense of all things' ultimate futility,
made him stay his hand.

Let Christophe, he said, go north beyond the mountains; the south
was safe.

So Christophe went north to crown himself a king, and Pétion, in
Port-au-Prince, drew up a constitution; a republican constitution with
himself as president, and in Spanish Town, four hundred miles away,
the governor of Jamaica smiled.

It was less easy than Pétion had imagined. He needed money to
strengthen his frontier against Christophe, to prepare his defense
against the French. And Rigaud had come back from France. There
was a year of civil war to empty the exchequer, an exchequer that it
was impossible to fill unless the people worked. They would not
work if they were not driven. He lacked the heart to drive them. In
his way he loved them as they loved him; the simple people who
laughed so readily, who would forgive you anything provided you
could make them laugh. But to be loved was not enough when you
were beset by enemies.

Pétion grew despondent. The doubting of himself—the mulatto's
doubting of himself—and the mulatto's contempt and hatred of the
black, mingled with the mulatto's envy of the white, returned to
him, making it easy for him to shrug his shoulders, to let things
drift. Why worry? Why fight for a liberty that its possessors could not
use? Let the blacks go back to savagery. Why try to inoculate them
with a sense of mission?

There was a sneer on his lips as he listened to the tales of Christophe that his spies brought to him. So Christophe was making a
great man of himself up there! He had a splendid court and many
palaces and counts and dukes and barons. He had a gold currency.
And English admirals called on him. Professors came out from England to establish schools. The country was rich and that meant that
the people of the country were enslaved. He smiled when they told
him of the palace of Sans Souci. The Negro's love of vanity, he
called it. They told him of the citadel above Milhot, of how the
people of the plains struggled to carry bronze cannon up the slope.

How when the slaves paused, panting at their load, Christophe would line them up and shoot every tenth man, with the remark, "You were too many. No doubt now you are fewer you will find it easier." Of how to prove his authority he would give his troops on the citadel the order to advance and watch file after file crash over the wall to death.

Pétion sneered at Christophe. What else could you expect from an illiterate nigger? How long did they imagine it would last? Tyranny had its own medicine.

He sneered, too, at the citadel. What was it, he asked, but an expression, as was all else that Christophe staged up there, of the Negro's inordinate self-pride? What was the use of it, after all? It would be the easiest thing in the world to surround it, to starve it out. And as for all that gold stored there in its recesses, of what use would that be there? What could it buy but ransoms? Bullion was not wealth. One day he would take his troops up there to show what it was worth.

He never did.

Pétion was never to see the citadel, never to see the sun strike yellow on its curved prow from the road to Milhot. But with the mind's clearer eye, the poet's eye, he saw it, and seeing it foresaw how that proud ship would outlive the purpose it was built for, the imperial idea that it enthroned; how it would stand, derelict through the decades, to outlive ultimately even the quarrel, so eternal-seeming, of brown and black.

Today those pages of John Vandercook's in *Black Majesty* that describe all that Christophe achieved within his brief fourteen years of power read like a fairy tale. You cannot believe that the book is history, that one man, and at that a Negro, could in so short a time have done so much. You have to go to the Cap itself to realize that.

Milhot, from Cap Haitien, is a half hour's drive. It is a bad road through a green and lovely wilderness. You can scarcely believe that this bumpy track was once an even carriage drive, that these untended fields were orderly with care, that the crumbling stone gateways, half buried in the hedge, opened on carefully kept lawns, on verandaed houses, on aqueducts and sugar mills. Along the road passes an unending stream of women carrying, some of them on their heads, some of them on donkeys, bags of charcoal and sticks of sugarcane to market. They move slowly. The sun is hot. There is no hurry.

Milhot was once a pretty suburb of Cap Français. It is now a collection of squat, white-plastered houses, the majority of them with cone-shaped corrugated iron roofs; looking down on them from the hills they seem like the bell tents of a military encampment. Nothing remains of the old Milhot except the ruins of Christophe's palace, and of that only the facade and the terraces are left. Goats and lizards drowse under the trees where the King delivered judgment. The underground passage to La Ferrière is blocked. The outhouse walls are creeper-covered.

Christophe's carriage drive to the citadel is little more than a mountain path. It is a hard two and a half hours' climb by mule or pony. You pass little along the way: a thatch-roofed hut or two from whose doors natives will run out in the hope of selling you bananas, a gendarme returning from the citadel to duty, a Negro collecting coconuts. For a hundred years that road had been abandoned. The natives were frightened of the citadel. It was a symbol of tyranny. They could not be prevailed upon to go there. As the road mounts you have a feeling of nature returned into possession of its own. The lizards are larger and greener that dart across the road, the butterflies brighter and more numerous, the birds that dip into a richer foliage are wider-winged. For ninety minutes you climb in silence. Then, suddenly, at a bend of the road, you see high above you the citadel's red-rusted prow.

Words cannot describe the citadel. In photographs it would look like any other ruin. A cinematograph, worked from a circling airplane, would give no more than an impression of it. To appreciate its meaning you have to come to it as they that built it did, with the hot sun upon you, with your back damp against your shirt, with the fatigue of riding in your knees, with the infinitely varied landscape before your eyes, with the innumerable jungle sounds in your ears, and in your nostrils the innumerable jungle scents. Then you can walk along the grass-grown courtyards, the galleries with their guns that will never fire, the battlements through whose windows trees are sprouting; then you can realize the prodigious effort that the citadel's building cost; you realize that nothing that has been said of it has been an exaggeration, that it is the most remarkable monument in the modern world.

CHAPTER X

Trafalgar

With Rochambeau's surrender, Napoleon recognized that his plans for a colonial empire had foundered. He was a man to cut his losses. New Orleans was now no use to him. He negotiated the Louisiana Purchase, and concentrated upon creating a self-sufficient European fortress behind which he could disregard his rivals, very much as Hitler was to do a century and a half later. He was only to be concerned once again with the Caribbean, and then indirectly, in the campaign that was to lead to the battle of Trafalgar. As Hitler was to do, he decided that an invasion of England was the essential prelude to the establishment of Europe as a fortress. For twenty-six months, from May 1803, when the Treaty of Amiens proved itself to have been no more than an uneasy truce during which the English ladies of fashion were enabled to see how far they had been outstripped by their Parisian counterparts, Napoleon maintained at Boulogne an army of 130,000 men, which he hoped to throw on the coast between Dover and Hastings. To transport this army he amassed a flotilla of over two thousand flat-bottomed vessels, built to be rowed, of shallow draught, so that they could take the ground without suffering damage. An immense sum of money was spent on the assembly and equipment of this flotilla. He had at first believed that during a calm it could cross the Channel, but he soon recognized that it was very unlikely that any calm would last long enough for the transportation of so many vessels. He must therefore create sufficient concentration of his fleet in the Channel to give him a temporary command of its waters.

This was not an easy project. He had squadrons at Brest, at Toulon and Cádiz. He had ships at L'Orient, Rochefort and El Ferrol, but all these ships were watched by British blockading squadrons. Napoleon's problem was how to get these ships together before the British fleet could combine against them.

He decided that the French vessels must slip out of harbor and sail for the Caribbean; the English would give chase; his ships would elude their pursuers and join forces in the Channel before the English could return. Villeneuve was the officer chosen for this operation. The plan was to be modified by Britain's declaration of war on Spain, since Napoleon could now enlist the Spanish navy. Britain was in the meantime provided with useful information by a French Royalist who was employed in Dresden as a Russian diplomatic agent.

Nelson was at this time blockading Toulon, where Villeneuve was in command. Villeneuve was one of those unlucky men who appear at the start of their lives to be fate-favored mortals but on whom, it is later recognized, fortune has smiled too soon. Born in Provence in 1763, he entered the French navy as one of the corps of "noble officers" (*Garde du Pavillon*). Most of his comrades were massacred or driven into exile during the terror, but he had good looks and southern charm; and he convinced the Jacobins of the sincerity of his revolutionary sentiments. There was a lack of trained officers and he was promoted quickly. He was a captain at the age of thirty, a rear admiral at thirty-three. In the Battle of the Nile his ship was one of the few that escaped unscathed. He was severely criticized by his superiors on this account, but Napoleon took his side, maintaining that the only reproach he had to make of Villeneuve was that he did not retreat sooner, since the position taken by the French commander had been broken and surrounded. In St. Helena, Napoleon was to retract this commendation. The defeat of the Nile, he said, was largely due to "the bad conduct of Admiral Villeneuve." But that change of opinion was probably due to subsequent events. He had not yet lost faith in his admiral's ability. And here was Villeneuve's supreme chance.

Villeneuve did not welcome it. He was not ready for such high responsibility. He felt that the operation could only succeed through a remarkable combination of good luck and skill. He lingered in Paris, till Napoleon rapped his knuckles with a curt command. New Year's Day, 1805, found him in Toulon, at the age of forty-two, with the fate of two empires in his hands. The giant's robe hung loosely on his shoulders.

Nelson had no such qualms. His policy was to lure Villeneuve into the open by not staying too near the port. For some time a cat-and-mouse game proceeded. Then, at last, in late March, Villeneuve managed to slip out of Toulon, eluding Nelson's scrutiny. The winds were friendly, and he reached Cádiz, where he strengthened his fleet of eleven ships with one French and six Spanish ships. He then sailed for the West Indies, reaching Martinique, which was then still French, on May 14. His instructions were clear: to wait in Martinique till he was joined by ships from Brest and Rochefort; if they had not arrived by July 5 he was to sail for El Ferrol, pick up the French and Spanish ships and make for the Channel. With the consequent command of the seas, Napoleon's flotilla could attempt the crossing from Boulogne.

The drama of the next few weeks has the intensity and speed of a motion picture. On June 8, Villeneuve learned in Martinique that Nelson, in his pursuit, had arrived four days earlier in Barbados, having been delayed by contrary winds in the Mediterranean. Villeneuve had little faith either in his own ships or the seamanship of his Spanish allies. Convinced that an action in the West Indies would ruin the Emperor's plans for concentrating in the Channel, he decided to return right away to El Ferrol. Nelson, receiving false information, believed that Villeneuve was planning to attack the British islands, and began a frantic search for him; he went south as far as Trinidad; he watered in Antigua and was there for a brief twenty hours; no letter of his is extant to record with what emotions he saw, after an interval of twenty years, the ocher-brown barracks of the dockyard, the low hills guarding it, and the veranda of Clarence House, where he had spent so many lonely months, months whose loneliness had driven him to the dreary experiment in domesticity that was so opposed to his volatile, tempestuous nature. He watered his ships and was away, with the high cloud-covered cone of Nevis to his starboard. Not till June 13 did he learn the truth, or rather half the truth. He knew that Villeneuve was on his way back to Europe, but he had not been informed of Napoleon's master plan; he believed that Villeneuve was bound for Toulon, so he himself made for Gibraltar, but sent a brig home with dispatches, and on the nineteenth this brig sighted the French fleet heading for the Bay of Biscay.

The French plan was now apparent. The brig hurried back to England and the Admiralty took action; a fleet was sent to intercept the French outside El Ferrol. On July 25, on a day of fog, the British and French fleets met, thirty-five leagues northwest of Finisterre. The action was confused. Two Spanish ships were captured, but the British admiral, who was outnumbered, was irresolute and withdrew to Brest. Now was Villeneuve's chance. His ships were in poor condition, their crews exhausted by the double trip across the Atlantic and

their recent battle, but he was at last able to join the fleet at El
Ferrol; had he pushed forward up the Channel he would have given
Napoleon that two days' command of its waters that the army wait-
ing at Boulogne required.

On the very day when the action took place off Finisterre, Nelson
reached Gibraltar. He could not have intervened. For over two years
Napoleon had been waiting for this moment. But Villeneuve did not
know how dispersed were his adversaries' forces. He only knew how
inefficient his own fleet was. He had no faith in the Spaniards. He believed that a large British fleet was awaiting him in the Channel. He
held that his first duty lay to his own fleet, even if its safety ruined
his emperor's plan. Instead of pushing northward, he sailed south for
Cádiz. Napoleon, when the news reached him, broke up his camp
at Boulogne and marched into Germany. He knew that he had missed
his moment.

For Villeneuve, two months later, came the grim sequel to his long
voyage to Martinique. For a month he waited in Cádiz with a fleet
of thirty-four ships and with the British watching him. In mid-Sep-
tember, on the fourteenth, Napoleon issued orders that he was to set
sail at the first opportunity and make for Naples. If on the way he
encountered an inferior British fleet he was to attack it. In his estimate of numerical superiority, two Spanish ships were to be reckoned
as the equivalent of one French. On the next day Napoleon decided
that Villeneuve's "excessive pusillanimity" rendered a change of
command essential, and he sent a replacement, Admiral Rosily. Villeneuve did not receive Napoleon's orders till September 28. On that
very day Nelson arrived in supreme command of the operations. Villeneuve by now knew that Rosily was on his way, but he did not
know that he himself was to be superseded. On October 5 Villeneuve
held a council of war. His officers agreed with him that their ships
were in no condition to meet the British; at the same time Napoleon's orders gave him no alternative. The council admitted that a
sortie must be made. At the moment, however, a strong wind was
blowing from the west. Only in an east wind could a cumbersome
fleet be maneuvered out of Cádiz.

On the fourteenth, the wind fell; but Villeneuve lingered. He
seemed to be waiting for some intervention of providence, and on
October 18 providence played its card. Villeneuve learned that Rosily
was at Madrid and on his way to supersede him. Villeneuve might
be overcautious as a warrior, but he had his pride. He was not going
to wait for his dismissal. On the following morning, although once

again the wind was westerly, he took advantage of a light land breeze from the east and sailed out to meet destruction at Trafalgar.

Eighteen of his ships were captured; only eleven found their way back to Cádiz, where a fragment of the French squadron under Rosily remained until 1808, when it was forced to surrender to the Spaniards. Villeneuve himself was captured. He was taken back to England, but he was soon released. He returned to France, his spirit broken, to die in April, by his own hand, in an inn at Rennes.

The battle of Trafalgar not only freed Britain from the danger of invasion, but it removed the Caribbean from the arena of operations. Napoleon continued to build line-of-battle ships, but he never again sent a fleet to sea; his ships filled the role of privateers, harassing British trade and forcing Britain to maintain exhausting and expensive blockades. The role of the British fleet, as it was in the 1914–1918 war, was to provide convoy service, to protect commerce and to transport troops on colonial expeditions. West Indian products became of immense value to Britain now that she was cut off from European markets. One by one the West Indian colonies of France and Spain fell into British hands: Trinidad, Martinique, St. Lucia and Guadeloupe. Holland and Denmark were also involved in the war. Curaçao was captured. The Swedish island of St. Bartholomew alone retained neutrality; the graveyards of St. Croix and the Episcopalian church at Frederiksted testify to British residence.

Before this happened, one remarkable action in the early months of the war has attached a footnote to the history of the period. The tourist today, looking northward from St. Lucia, will see on the horizon a small high rock. It is a part of Martinique. It rises sheer out of the water, six hundred feet high. It is about a mile in circumference. It can be reached only from one point on the leeward side, when there is no surf. It is uninhabited. But once, for eighteen months, it bore in the books of the British Admiralty the designation H.M.S.

When war broke out again in 1803 between France and Britain, Sir Samuel Hood, who was in charge of the ships stationed in St. Lucia, realized toward the end of the year that the French ships bound for Fort Royal eluded him by sailing through the channel between this rock and Pointe du Diamante on the mainland of Martinique. Hood decided that he must try to bring fire to bear upon this channel. He therefore brought one of his ships alongside it, attached a hawser to the top of the rock, and contrived to have five guns hauled up on it. The naval chronicles of the day described the sailors who performed this operation, "hanging like clusters," looking "like mice hauling a little sausage." Under the command of Lieutenant James Wilkie Maurice, this curious fortress was maintained by 120 men and boys, with ammunition, provisions and water for months, and was registered at the Admiralty as a sloop, His Majesty's Ship *Diamond Rock*.

For eighteen months the guns of this fortress swept the channel, until she was forced to surrender for want of powder to a French squadron, dispatched by Villeneuve, of two 74s, a frigate, a corvette, a schooner and eleven gunboats. In the final action she inflicted seventy casualties upon her besiegers and sank three gunboats. It is an episode without parallel in naval history.

CHAPTER XI

Twilight in the Antilles

In the summer of 1815 the crowned heads of Europe assembled at Vienna to install order in the chaos that had been created by Napoleon's imperialism, and in the case of the Caribbean colonies there was much the same shuffling of cards that there had been at Paris in 1763 and at Versailles in 1782. The Virgin Islands went back to Denmark, Holland got Curaçao, Saba, Aruba and St. Eustatius; Martinique and Guadeloupe were restored to France; Grenada, St. Vincent, St. Lucia and Dominica were retained by Britain. The signatories made pious declarations of their devotion to peace, assuring one another that at last, thanks to the grace of God, they had arrived at a final settlement, but it is doubtful whether any of the distinguished diplomats believed, in their secret thoughts, that they were doing anything more than sign a truce. And, indeed, within a very few years cracks were showing in the fabric.

In respect of the Caribbean, however, the Treaty of Vienna was to prove a "final settlement." The islands were not to change hands again, except in two major and one minor instance. Cuba and Puerto Rico, at the end of the century, severed their connection with Spain to become independent, and in 1917 Denmark sold her share of the Virgin Islands—St. Thomas, St. John and St. Croix—to the United States, while St. Bartholomew, which had become a liability to Sweden, was transferred to France. Otherwise the *status quo* has been maintained for a century and a half.

It was through an unexpected intervention that this happened. For Spain the Napoleonic period was a distracted and disastrous interlude. She found herself fighting first on one side, then on another, not really of her choice and never to her advantage. During the American War of Independence and afterward, she had felt that her one chance of recovering her colonial and naval ascendancy at the expense of Britain was through the "family compact" with France. But there could hardly be a "family compact" with France when Louis XVI was a victim of the terror, and soon she was engaged in a war with France that cost her the eastern part of Santo Domingo.

For the next few years she shifted miserably and ineffectively from one side to the other. She reallied herself with France, but her defeat in the battle of St. Vincent only seems slight in comparison with her defeat at Trafalgar. Her servility to France increased, and she ceded Louisiana to Napoleon. Her servility indeed seemed to him so complete that he imagined that he could place his brother Joseph upon her throne. But there he failed to reckon with the pride, the dignity and the intense national feeling of the Spaniard. Soon British bayonets in the peninsula were helping to rescue her from foreign domination.

While this was happening in Europe, her colonies in Central and South America were one by one breaking from Spanish domination. There was no War of Independence as there had been between Britain and the thirteen colonies. The system just ceased to work, and the Spanish Empire dissolved, with states now independent managing their own affairs, a fact which constituted a considerable problem when Napoleon was at St. Helena, for Spain herself had not acknowledged their independence. Her former colonies might be trading freely with France and Britain, but technically this commerce was, under her colonial laws, illegal, and pirates under the Spanish flag were preying on it without there being any possibility of redress from the Spanish government. In the meantime, the chaos of that government was so complete that the European governments were deciding to give France a free hand in Spain. This appeared to give Britain the opportunity that she needed to acquire fresh power in the Caribbean, and when it appeared certain that there would be an invasion of Spain with the cooperation of Russia, the British Prime Minister, Canning, warned the French government that Britain would not accept the subjugation of the Spanish colonies by foreign force. There was a moment of uncertainty, when it seemed possible that the Caribbean would become once again a cockpit. But a solution came from an unexpected quarter; the President of the United States, delivering himself of a message that came to be known as the Monroe Doctrine, asserted that his country would not tolerate any interference by a foreign power in the affairs of the American continent.

He had little legal right to deliver such a pronouncement, and it is doubtful if he had at his command sufficient power to enforce his doctrine, but he made Europe pause, and before Europe was in a position to question its validity, the United States did possess enough power to protect a doctrine that had become an essential part of her policy. Russia and France held their hand, and in the British House of Commons George Canning was "saving face" with the announcement that he had called "a new world into existence to redress the balance of the old."

That was in 1823; eighteen months later, in return for a recompense of 150 million francs, France recognized the independence of Haiti; the eastern part of the island dissolved its links with Spain and the area, in terms of national allegiance, settled into the pattern it was to maintain until the end of the century.

It has been already said that the social structure of each island has been determined by its experiences or lack of experiences during the Napoleonic Wars. The French and Spanish islands, because of their closer involvement in the war and because of their defeat in it, suffered the greatest change. St. Domingue was lost to France forever, so were St. Lucia, Dominica and Grenada. Spain lost Trinidad and the eastern section of Santo Domingo. She retained Cuba and Puerto Rico. They were no longer of the same value to her, since she had lost Mexico and Peru and therefore no longer needed bastions to protect her treasure fleets, but the taste for Havana tobacco which had been acquired by the English during those few months of occupancy was to bring the islands considerable prosperity during the nineteenth century. Cuban sugar was to find a big market in the United States, and Cuban rum, which is lighter in body and texture than Jamaican and Barbadian rum, was found to have a distinctive and agreeable flavor which later was to become the basis of a number of pleasant cocktails, in particular the Daiquiri.

Spain's share of the New World was now limited to these two islands. For the eastern section of Santo Domingo there was to begin a long and confused period of divided rule which is not yet ended. Sometimes it was linked to Haiti, sometimes it was not. Throughout the nineteenth century it remained Spanish-speaking and Spanish in tone and manner.

Trinidad, under Spanish rule, had been a neglected dependency. Up to 1783 a single vessel belonging to a Dutch house in St. Eustatius, making two or three trips a year, was sufficient for its entire trade. In that year, however, a Grenadian, a M. de St. Laurent, strongly advised Madrid to develop its potentialities. A little was done, but even so, it had a population of only seven thousand when

the British captured it. Its development presented a considerable
problem to the British because, with the slave trade ended, it was
difficult to find a labor force to work on its estates. Resource was
eventually had to indented East Indian labor, an equivalent of the
old *engagé* system. The imported East Indians worked on a five-
year contract, and many decided to stay on when it expired. They
were made grants of land, some of which were to prove highly profitable, as they lay on land that contained oil; the development of the
Trinidad oil fields at the end of the century laid the basis of a number
of fortunes among Indian families. There was also a considerable Chinese immigration. Trinidad's society is international in a sense that
no other island's is, and when in the 1950s the project was formed
of creating a federation of the British West Indian islands, Trinidad was chosen as its capital. The project, however, was not imple-
mented.

East Indian labor was also introduced into St. Vincent, whose
Carib population had been deported to British Honduras and in
which, because of the ferocity of the Caribs, colonization had been
slow and slight. But here most of the Indians returned to their own
country when their contracts had expired; the visitor there today will
see few signs of East Indian features, the long straight black hair,
thé straight noses and thin lips, the small hands and feet. It is probably because of its late development that the family atmosphere in
St. Vincent is so strong, and the planter class so white. St. Vincent
is a very charming little island; it never raised sugar to the extent that
the other islands did, its main products being arrowroot and sea island cotton. It has suffered grievously from the volcanic explosions
of Soufrière.

The situation in Grenada and St. Lucia was highly different. Both
felt the full force of the Revolution. Almost the entire original planter
class in Grenada was exterminated. The survivors were absentee landlords who had no wish to return to homes that were homes no longer,
and many of the actual owners of land were the heirs of revolutionary
victims; they had no emotional stake in the country. St. Lucia was
less affected because it was under British occupation longer and
Hugues' occupancy was short-lived, but a great many of the planters
perished. There did remain, however, a very definite number of white-
skinned planters. Its family links with Martinique were close, and
cousins came across to take over estates that had been abandoned.
The atmosphere of the island is still markedly French; the peasants
speak a French patois; the island is predominantly Roman Catholic,

the names of the leading families are French—de Vaux, Castenet, Michellet. Barnard is one of the few English names. In Grenada also, the peasants speak a French patois, but the island is only half Roman Catholic, and fewer of the surnames of the leading families are French. It may be inferred that under British ownership there was less the resumption of an old regime than the organization of a new. Castries, the capital of St. Lucia, has been gutted by fire so often that there are few remaining signs of its eighteenth-century past. But Grenada, in spite of its exposure to the terror, is architecturally one of the least damaged of the islands. The harbor of St. George's, with its red-brick, red-tiled warehouses and Georgian houses, is one of the loveliest in the area. Sir William Young in 1790 described St. George's as "a handsome town, built chiefly of brick, consisting of many good houses. It is divided by a ridge, which running into the sea forms on one side a *carénage* and on the other the bay. There is the bay town where there is a handsome square and market place and the *carénage* town where the chief mercantile houses are situated, the ships lying land-locked and in deep water close to the wharf. On the ridge just above the road of communication between the towns stands the church, and on the promontory or buffhead of the ridge stands a large old fort. It is built of freestone, is very substantial if not scientifically constructed and contains an entire regiment. Another regiment is quartered in the new barracks on Richmond Hill."

It does not look so very different now, and in 1956 when the Twentieth Century-Fox Film Corporation decided to film a novel called *Island in the Sun*, which had achieved a certain measure of popularity, a group of photographers were sent down to take stills of the various islands. When the producer, Mr. Darryl Zanuck, saw those of Grenada, he said, "This is the place," and most of the film was shot there.

It might have been expected that Dominica, lying as it does between Martinique and Guadeloupe, would have been deeply affected by the Revolution, but Dominica has been always an exception. It is one of the loveliest of the islands, but also the unluckiest; nothing has ever quite gone right for it. Ceded to Britain in 1763, its start as a British colony was inauspicious. A number of estates were sold to Englishmen, but none of this purchase money was used to benefit the economy of the island; it went instead into the coffers of Queen Charlotte's dowry. The island was too mountainous to make the cultivation of sugar profitable, except on the windward coast, and owing to the number of its rivers there was no road across or round the island; transportation to the leeward coast had to be made by ship. It is a very rainy island. The soil is fertile and its fruit is exquisite, particularly the lime. But owing to the lack of roads it had to be "headed" to the coast. The rains were continually washing away such roads and bridges as there were. Trade was not made easier by the existence of a Carib colony on the windward coast.

Dominica has not profited from British ownership. Before the American War of Independence it served illegally as an *entrepôt*, French and Spaniards acquiring slaves and manufactured goods in return for bullion and commodities, while Americans sent down timber and livestock in return for rum and molasses. This trade collapsed when the war began.

Its sympathies were with the French; even in its neutral period it had had a number of French settlers. Its priests were appointed by their superiors in Martinique.

When France joined the side of the rebel colonies, the French inhabitants entered the fort under the guise of friendship, made the sentries drunk, and spiked the cannon. The island did not gain from the take-over, its cattle being destroyed to feed French troops, a fate that was to be repeated during the Second World War. Her only trade at this time was with St. Eustatius, in Dutch bottoms. This trade ceased as a result of Rodney's action. While St. Lucia was flourishing as a British possession, Dominica's propinquity to Guadeloupe made commerce difficult for her during the first half of the Napoleonic period, and during the second half, when the Caribbean had become of minor strategic importance, she was overlooked.

Perhaps that has been her problem always. Stationed between two islands of great importance, she has belonged to neither. She should have been French; as it is, she has never known where she belonged, not even as a British island. When the British Lesser Antilles were divided between the Leewards and the Windwards, Dominica was first of all classified as one of the Leewards, with Antigua, St. Kitts, Nevis and Montserrat. But later, in the 1940s, she requested to be included in the Windward group, with their mountainous islands and French background. But even then she felt separate and apart. She was the hinge between the Leewards and Windwards, but she belonged to neither. Financially she has always been a liability, and yet she has appealed to the imagination in a way that larger and more prominent islands have never done. She has "the fatal gift of beauty." She has attracted artists, intellectuals, eccentrics, misfits generally; a phrase has indeed grown up in the islands, "typical Dominica." Her mountains are too high for her size; they attract the rain and there is not enough territory to absorb the rain. That is the explanation that is given usually, but there is more to it than that.

To the north of Dominica is Guadeloupe, to the south Martinique. They are sister islands with different histories and different physical conformation—Martinique is mountainous throughout, traversed by fertile valleys, Guadeloupe is in fact two islands, one mountainous, the other flat. In 1815 they returned to their allegiance to their mother country in very different moods. Guadeloupe had been subject to the terror and the rule of slaves; nearly all of the planters who had been resident when Victor Hugues set up his guillotine had perished by it. The survivors were absentee proprietors who, like those in Grenada, had no wish to return after twenty years to a country that was completely different. They were content to sell out or to have their estates managed by agents. In a very short time the island had passed into the hands of limited companies based on Paris and Bordeaux. It was a prosperous island but it had no landed aristocracy.

Martinique, on the other hand, had had its landed families cushioned by the British occupation. Sitting in the hills, managing their estates, they had dreamed of their return to Paris, but when they did return they were disappointed. It was no longer the Paris of their youth. Their old friends were dead or impoverished. The court of Louis XVIII was vulgar, the *nouveaux riches* were ostentatious. The young who had listened to their parents' stories about the wonders of Versailles were disappointed. The climate was bleak; life was more pleasant on the other side of the Atlantic, and so they returned to their estates and the administration of the island stayed in the hands of the six leading families. They grew richer every year; the wealth of the island was not wasted on absentee landowners and spent in Paris. They intermarried, they were as exclusive as the most proper Bostonians, they entertained each other at large Sunday luncheons; the Rhum St. James and the Rhum Negrita were honored wherever rum was drunk, and under the shadow of Mont Pelé the city of Saint-Pierre waxed in charm and beauty, in culture and graciousness of living.

Certain islands had suffered little change; the British Leewards had been protected by the trade winds, so had Barbados. Jamaica too had been immune. She was out of reach of Victor Hugues; the Spanish in Cuba were too weak to trouble her; and St. Domingue had enough problems of her own. Jamaica was only affected by the war because she was, in early days, a base of operations against St. Domingue,

and during the period of Leclerc's ill-starred campaign she provided
a retreat for his officers. Lady Nugent's journal deals largely with
the period of truce, but when war is finally resumed between France
and Britain, the temper of her diary does not change. She is concerned as much as ever with parties, outbreaks of fever and the
moral lapses of the young British planters and officials. Life went on
very much as it had before; and when the news of Waterloo reached
the Caribbean there was a confident assumption on the part of landowners and administrators alike that commerce could now be resumed pleasantly and profitably without the inconveniences of war,
that the nineteenth century would repeat the eighteenth century only
with a general amelioration of amenities. Hardly anyone seems to
have realized that the bell had tolled for the sugar islands and the
phrase "rich as a Creole" was soon to be extinct.

The abolition of the slave trade was the first nail in the coffin. It
was a slow process. The French Revolution had broken out at the
very moment when Wilberforce and his followers were beginning to
influence public thought. Many liberal-minded persons were affected
by the excesses in the French colonies; and the planters found ready
support for their argument that slavery and the slave trade were essential to the prosperity of the sugar islands. The first bill that was
introduced into the British Parliament to prevent the further importation of slaves into the British West Indies was defeated by a
majority of two to one, but the first step had been taken. The issue
was hotly argued; the planters had powerful support, and bills that
were passed in the House of Commons were thrown out by the House
of Lords. A great many meetings were addressed and a great many
pamphlets printed; these pamphlets are not reliable as witnesses to
the conditions that existed at this time in the plantations. The abolitionists were as prejudiced as the antiabolitionists, and many of the
late eighteenth-century and early nineteenth-century books on the
West Indies that are found in colonial libraries should be read with
reservations.

The abolition first of the slave trade, then of slavery itself, provides
one of the few completely disinterested chapters in the history of
mankind. Slavery is in itself a crime, and the organization of the
slave trade is one of the major crimes committed by the Christian
peoples of Europe, yet it cannot be repeated too often that the right
of the conqueror to enslave those whom he has defeated had been
accepted from earliest times. John Hawkins never thought he was a

criminal when he bought slaves on the Guinea coast. The abolition of the slave trade, on the other hand, was an act of sheer benevolence, of public-spirited, Christian fellow feeling. It was in everybody's interest that the slave trade should continue and the institution of slavery be maintained. Its abolition was a very costly operation for the countries concerned, and eventually it destroyed the prosperity of the sugar islands.

To Denmark lies the honor of being the first country to abolish the trade. In 1792 she issued a royal mandate that after 1802 the traffic should cease in the Danish colonies; in 1794 the United States of America forbade their subjects to engage in the trade to foreign countries, and a little later prohibited the importation of slaves into their own territories. Britain, by its bill of 1807, forbidding the landing of any slave in the colonies after March 1808, felt that the problem had been solved, but she soon found that she had only opened the door for the privateers. The profits in an illegal slave trade were soon so enormous that the traders estimated that if one voyage in three was successful, the operation would show a profit; and if the trade was regarded as a dealing in contraband rather than a felony, the traders were well content to pay their fine and hope to escape detection next time. Three years later a bill was passed, declaring that the trade was a felony, punishable by transportation. Up to a point this tactic was successful, but only up to a point.

In the meantime, other nations were working on parallel tracks. The subject was discussed at the first Congress of Vienna, before the Hundred Days, and it was accepted in principle that the trade should be abolished as soon as possible, but each nation was left free to make her own arrangements. France and Britain agreed that no foreigner should introduce slaves into the French colonies and that the French themselves should cease the trade after 1819. This gap was allowed because the French still cherished the hope that they would recover Haiti, for which a new supply of slaves would be required, the abolition of slavery itself being still a subject that no country was prepared to face.

Negotiations were conducted between the various countries, Britain paying £300,000 to the Portuguese and £400,000 to the Spaniards in compensation for their losses through the ending of the trade. The Dutch and Swedes abandoned their share in the traffic, and in 1831 Britain and France agreed on a mutual right of search on certain seas. Officially the slave trade was at an end, but the fact of slavery remained.

Indeed, in many ways, the period between the abolition of the slave trade and the emancipation of the slaves was for the slaves themselves the worst period of all. There was now a definite lack of slaves, and because there was no chance of acquiring more slaves by legitimate means, the planters grossly overworked the slaves they had. Since the end of the nineteenth century, the population of the West Indian islands has risen at a rate that has alarmed sociologists, but during the eighteenth century the population was less than static. In Jamaica in 1690 there were 40,000 slaves; between then and 1820 800,000 were imported, yet there were only 340,000 slaves on the island. This was due partly to the inequality in the numbers of the sexes, a third as many females being transported annually; firstly because polygamy existed in Africa, secondly because men were more likely to commit civil offenses than women and consequently there were more male prisoners, thirdly because women became unfit for the slave market at an earlier age.

In Jamaica in 1789 there were thirty thousand more males than females. But the dropping population on the plantations was also caused by the conditions of plantation life not being conducive to the building of homes and the raising of families.

The sugar barons were, in fact, faced with a serious problem; those who took a short view solved it by overworking their slaves. It was estimated that the slave population in the islands was reduced by one eighth between 1807 and 1830. The sugar barons also tried to solve their problem by encouraging contraband slave traders. This was the worst period of the slave trade. The abolitionists in their propaganda had presented grisly diagrams of the way in which the slaves were packed close in the holds, but such conditions were Elysian compared with those under which contraband cargo was transported.

The traders, both because of the risks attached to the trade and the rich rewards attending a successful voyage, overcrowded their ships. Moreover, the slaves were not only fettered but weighted, so that if an inspecting vessel hove in sight the hatches could be opened and the illicit cargo shot into the sea. It was estimated that two thirds of the Negroes who were exported were drowned. It was not, moreover, in the interests of the cruisers that watched the Guinea coast to hinder the loading of the slaves. The cruisers shared in the price of the captured slave ship, and the price would be raised if it was captured with a full cargo. It was alleged that a greater number of Negroes was shipped after the abolition of the slave trade than there had been before. It was clear that one remedy alone was possible, the abolition of slavery itself.

Wilberforce and his friends had a long battle before they could convince Parliament of this necessity, and during the 1820s a rain of pamphlets was maintained by the opposing parties. The planters had powerful friends in England; they suspected that they themselves would be ruined by emancipation, but they argued that it was the islands, the trade of the islands and some of the richest possessions of the empire that would be ruined. Chaos would supervene. Look what had happened in Haiti. No white woman would be safe. The Negroes were lazy, incurably lazy unless a whip was being cracked over their shoulders; Negroes were children; they needed the paternal care of the plantation system.

Nor could it be denied that many of their arguments were valid. There was always the example of Haiti. Even the abolitionists were in favor of a gradual system of emancipation. A race that had been enslaved, in some cases for several generations, could not suddenly be confronted with freedom. How would it support itself? Britain had led the way in the antislavery campaign, but in the British colonies the situation was complicated by the existence of colonial assemblies, which had very definite rights as to the ordering of their own affairs, as Britain had found to her cost when she had questioned those rights in the case of the thirteen colonies. She had learned that lesson.

The arguments adopted by some of the antiabolitionists resembled those which in the 1950s opposed disarmament. You cannot start until the others do. The Dutch and the French would have to abandon slavery simultaneously. They also argued that if Europeans did not buy slaves there would be a glut of slaves and the unwanted slaves would be slaughtered.

It was at first believed that a solution might be found by establishing a kind of serfdom for existing slaves, in conjunction with a measure emancipating all the children born after a certain day. But a counterproposal was carried, by which the home government should make to the colonial legislatures certain suggestions for the improvement of the condition of the slaves, which would only be enforced in the case of resistance. Britain was moving, that is to say, in terms of her traditional policy of compromise, her belief that time solves everything, and she presented to the colonial authorities a list of very sensible recommendations.

There was an immediate outcry in Barbados and Jamaica. No type of reactionary is more hidebound than the colonial man of property. What, the government siding with these damned radicals? In Demerara, an attempt was made to conceal from the slaves that an order-in-council was on its way, and the slaves, getting confused about the facts, gained the impression that they were already free, and declined to work. The consequent disturbance was put down with great severity and a missionary was victimized. The ill-treatment of this missionary roused the English public. As Parliament procrastinated, the wave of popular feeling mounted. The power of the West Indian planter lobby had been damaged by the abolition of the rotten boroughs. It had become clear by now that the planters would do nothing unless they were forced. There was only one course—to declare emancipation and leave the islanders to work out the problem for themselves.

That was what was done. A system of apprenticeship was decreed for seven years. The ex-slaves had to work for their masters for three quarters of the day, and they were liable to be flogged if they were idle. Their master had to feed and clothe them. Children under six years of age were freed at once, and they were to be offered religious and moral guidance; a sum of twenty million pounds was voted to the planters in compensation.

That was in 1833, and there were many who considered the postponement of emancipation to be unwise. In Antigua the experiment was made of announcing liberation immediately. So calmly was the news received that the following Christmas was the first in twenty years when martial law had not to be declared to preserve the peace. It was accepted that the probationary period was unnecessary, and emancipation was declared generally in the British islands in 1838.

In the French islands, freedom was announced ten years later, on the fall of Louis Philippe. The Dutch freed their slaves in 1863; the Portuguese announced in 1858 that every slave belonging to a Portuguese subject should be free in twenty years. Most of the former Spanish colonies on the Spanish Main abandoned slavery when they achieved their independence. There remained the two Spanish colonies of Cuba and Puerto Rico, for which a very different destiny was waiting, a destiny whose outcome is still far from clear.

From the beginning, Cuba's history had been different from that of the other islands. Lying well to the north, it was the one island in which it was possible for the white man to carry out manual labor. The Spaniards were able to acclimatize themselves to Cuba in a way that the British and French were unable to do in Barbados and Martinique. That is one of the reasons why its tobacco crop was so suc-

TWILIGHT IN THE ANTILLES 247

cessful. The delicate handling that is required for the rolling of cigars
could scarcely have been performed by slave labor. In consequence,
the Negro population was small in comparison with what it was in
other islands. The census of 1867 gave a population of 1,370,211, of
whom 746,750 were whites, and 605,461 were black or colored; of
these latter, 225,938 were free.

The Spanish slave code which was issued in 1789 was humane, and
it was relatively easy for a black slave to purchase his freedom. At
the same time, owing to the inefficiency of the Spanish authorities,
this code was rarely observed, and slavery continued to exist right
into the middle of the nineteenth century. The following figures are
evidence of that. In 1792 there were 84,000 slaves in Cuba, in 1817
there were 179,000, in 1827 there were 286,000, and in 1843 there
were 436,000. Yet all the time the institution of slavery was disinte-
grating. General abolition was declared in 1880; definitive abolition
in 1886; and in 1893 equality of status between blacks and whites
was announced, but in fact the system had ended earlier. This was
typical of Spain's whole handling of her Caribbean possessions. She
had continued to maintain that she alone had any rights in the area
long after the British and French were settled in the Lesser Antilles,
the Dutch in Curaçao and the Danes in St. Thomas.

By the middle of the century, slavery had ceased to be an issue in
the Caribbean; under the most favorable conditions the second half
of the century must inevitably have been a difficult time for the
sugar barons. Their whole economy had to be constructed on a new
basis, and it was at this very moment of test and trial that an unexpected rival appeared upon the scene—sugar that had been made from
beet.

As early as the middle of the eighteenth century, a German scien-
tist had discovered that sugar was contained in beet and other roots
that could be grown in temperate regions. But no use was made of
his discovery during his lifetime. In 1801, however, a pupil of his
established a beet-sugar factory in Silesia, near Breslau; the results at
first were not very satisfactory, but there was at this time a great
scarcity of sugar, owing to Napoleon's continental system, and the
price of such sugar as there was, was high. A number of factories were
established in France and Germany. With Napoleon's defeat, Germany lost interest in the industry, but the French persisted in it.
By 1830 it was established and by 1840 it was ready to sweep the
market. Protectionist countries stimulated the beet-sugar industry by

bounties on exports, and the production of sugar was pushed far beyond the point at which it would have been profitable without state aid; the price of sugar had to be raised in bounty-paying countries to meet the cost of these bounties. This reduced the consumption of sugar. There was a glut of sugar, and the British markets were flooded with sugar at a price that often fell below the price at which it was produced. The effect on British refineries and on the sugar-producing colonies was so disastrous that by the end of the century the British colonial secretary, Joseph Chamberlain, was asking the treasury to send out a royal commission to the West Indies to discover what effect these foreign sugar bounties were having on their principal industry. In his opinion, the advantages to the British public and to certain British industries of the importation of cheap sugar were ruining some of Britain's colonies. That was a long way off, but the British planters did have cause for alarm when they faced the prospect of competition from bounty-sponsored beet sugar and, in the 1840s, from sugar produced in the Spanish and French colonies by slaves.

The British planters had received twenty million pounds in compensation, and that is a substantial sum of money. Yet they were almost without exception heavily in debt, and very few of them were in a position to plow their money back into their estates and seek for alternative crops. For the most part, they shrugged their shoulders, went back to England, bought themselves country houses, and handed over their estates to agents who swindled them and neglected their interests, while the laborers sat in the sun doing as little as they could, cultivating their own gardens in the hills. They were not used to the idea of working for a wage; they expected to be clothed and fed and housed, work as little as they could conveniently manage, and cultivate their own gardens for their individual needs. The idea of personal ambition in a career was alien to them. That this was likely to happen was denied, very naturally, by the abolitionists, and, indeed, many English manufacturers supported emancipation in the belief that it would help their business. In 1840 a Baptist minister made a tour of the islands and reported enthusiastically on the bettered conditions there. His name was Joseph John Gurney, and he published his reflections in a series of letters addressed to his American friend Henry Clay, under the title A *Winter in the West Indies*. He was a pious gentleman, as may be gathered from his comments on the rum trade.

"The new rum of the West Indies is a tempting but most unhealthy liquor," he said, "and has doubtless caused an unnumbered multitude of untimely deaths. It is a circumstance much to be lamented that the distillery is an almost unvarying appendage to the boiler house, and every two hogsheads of sugar are accompanied by at least one puncheon of rum." He hoped that the example might be followed of an abstemious friend who reconverted his molasses into sugar. He said of St. Thomas that the pursuits of religion were generally forgotten. Merchandise by day and gaiety by night seemed chiefly to engross the attention of the residents. But his enthusiasm for the new conditions was unbounded. He claimed the value of estates had risen in St. Kitts since emancipation. Everyone seemed happy. "They will do an infinity of work for wages," the governor of Antigua told him. "At the lowest computation the land, without a single slave on it, is fully as valuable now as it was, including all the slaves, before emancipation." An estate that once employed two hundred slaves could now be worked by forty. Freed Negroes who before emancipation refused to work in the cane fields were now glad to do so. "The old notion that the Negro is, by constitution, a lazy creature who will do no work at all except by compulsion is now forever exploded," he concluded. "Concubinage, the universal practice of the coloured people, has wholly disappeared from among them. No young woman of colour thinks of forming such connections now."

He believed what he wanted to believe, though he did note regretfully that the Negroes were less willing to go to church in the rain because they now had shoes and stockings which they did not wish to expose to the mud.

Gurney's book is typical of the pro-abolitionist pamphlet. But in fact the prophecies of the reactionary planters were fulfilled. The prosperity of the islands did depend on the maintenance of the slave trade and of slavery. Between Europe and the New World lies the Sargasso Sea, a flat, drab, tideless area filled with seaweed, where, in the schoolboy serials of 1910 in *Chums* and *Boys' Own Paper*, galleons were continually being stranded. And it was into a kind of Sargasso Sea that the West Indies socially, politically and economically drifted during the middle years of the nineteenth century. Nothing particular was happening; the sun shone and the earth was fertile and the laboratories of Europe and North America discovered medicines for the maladies that had afflicted the first settlers; the recession was gradual. First one planter and then another decided to stay on in England. His estates were in debt; he could not understand his agent's figures. Better to sell out now while the market was still good.

The agent was usually a man of color, and when the estate was put upon the market he got either a cut upon the deal or a share in the property, which passed into the hands of a colored family. White men went home; no white immigrants came to take their place. The change was slow and it was more rapid in some islands than in others, but gradually it became apparent that the rule of the white man was less exclusive. Men of color were sitting in legislative assemblies. Men of color were representing the colony at cricket. The color bar was ceasing to be so restrictive. In certain islands like Barbados, the one island from which no other flag has ever flown, whose loyalty to the crown is beyond question, the process was more slow. The island was rich in sugar. The planters loved their island. They wanted to see their grandchildren inherit the land that they had received from their grandparents; they were sound men of affairs and they had been Barbadians for two hundred years. But they were exceptional, and even in Barbados the tide was receding slowly. In the other islands it was receding faster. The modern tourist has only to travel through the countryside of Nevis, Antigua and Jamaica, and examine there in the bush the ruins of former mansions, to recognize how considerable was the prosperity that existed in the days when "rich as a Creole" was in daily use.

CHAPTER XII

Two Scandals

1 THE CASE OF GOVERNOR EYRE

The modern traveler who is familiar with the world of the West Indies often wishes himself back a hundred years so that he could see exactly how things were in the days when twilight was settling on the Antilles. Few accounts remain for him to study. The West Indies had been news while the abolitionists and the antiabolitionists were waging their war of pamphlets; and they were news immediately after emancipation, when the public was wondering which of the two parties had been right; but when nothing particular happened, the public decided that the issue had been settled, and turned to other matters.

In London, after the Reform Bill of 1832, there was no longer a West Indian lobby in the House of Commons to urge the planters' claims, and as regards the British islands, the picture was confused by the fact that in each island the situation was a little different, because the separate islands were often governed on a different system and because in some islands, like Trinidad, there was a great deal of idle land on which the freed slaves could settle, while in islands like Barbados there was not.

The systems of government differed to the extent that some had assemblies and some had not. The colonies like Barbados and Jamaica had assemblies, in the same way that the thirteen colonies had had, and the British government had learned to be chary of infringing the privileges of colonial assemblies. Grenada when it was taken over by the British was granted an assembly, and as a result of that grant, a Grenadian planter was able to protest against a tax levied against him by the home government; a claim that was upheld by Lord Mansfield in the English courts. After that decision, Whitehall prudently protected itself by not granting assemblies to new colonies, like Trinidad. In the islands that had a house of elected representatives, there was constant friction between the governor and his assembly, and it was the imperial government's pious hope that the problem would be settled by the assembly proving itself incompetent and appealing to Britain for a loan. When there is a loan there are strings attached, and it was expected that sooner or later the islands would relegate themselves to the status of crown colonies—as indeed most of them did. But the fact that there was this difference of systems makes it difficult to present a precise composite picture of the situation as it was at that time in the British islands.

The situation was even more confused by the problem of idle land. The idea of working for a wage was alien to the Negro. He expected to be housed, clothed and fed by a master, while he provided himself with the minor luxuries he cherished out of his own labor, on his own plot of land. Emancipation to him meant emancipation not from slavery but from work. To lie in the sun, munching yams and breadfruit, was his idea of freedom. His retort to inducements to industry was, "No tankee, master, me tired now, me want no more money." In islands where there was little idle land he had to continue working or he would starve. In an island like Barbados, which was overpopulated, labor was cheap and plentiful. In Antigua, for instance, a laborer's daily wage was 9d. with cottage and grounds; in Trinidad it was 2s. without cottage and grounds, since both were plentiful. In Jamaica it was 1s.8d. with a cottage. In 1848 it cost 22s.7d. to produce a hundredweight of sugar in Jamaica, in Barbados only 15s.4d. And it was just at this time, when conditions were most difficult for the West Indian planter, who was faced with competition not only from the East Indies and from the newly acquired Mauritius but also from slave-run Cuba, that the home government decided to remove the protective tariffs.

It was a period of great hardship for the British public. Cheap food was essential. Free trade was the obvious answer. A West Indian planter calling at Cuba in 1847 found the streets of Havana illuminated because of the good news from England. Three trains of expensive machinery had just arrived from France. Engineers from America were pouring in, new estates were being formed, and coffee was being abandoned. Sugar was selling in London at 22s.6d. a hundredweight, and on to the Jamaican production cost of 22s.7d. had to be added 7s. to cover freightage and merchants' charges. Jamaica, with its narrow valleys and narrow outlets, could not enter into competition with Cuba's wide harbors and vast plains, with its slave labor and the advantages of American techniques. Cuba was a challenge to every island. When the Louisiana crops were poor, the U.S. bought from Cuba, but when they were good, a glut of surplus Cuban sugar was available for Europe; the Barbadians prayed for rain in Louisiana. The Jamaicans threw up their hands; what was there for them to do? In 1845, two hundred thousand hundredweight of Cuban sugar were shipped to England; in 1864 nearly a million. Jamaica's plight was very real.

In 1859 Anthony Trollope was sent to Jamaica as an official by the post office, to report on the postal services. On his return he published a book entitled *The West Indies and the Spanish Main*. It caused considerable offense, as such books tend to do. Provincial societies are very sensitive to criticism. "We have lived here all our lives," they say. "Who is this man to pronounce a verdict on us on the strength of a three-week visit, during which he saw none of the right people?" To which the author retorts that he has a trained capacity to recognize essentials, that he is justified in trusting first impressions. And certainly, after a hundred years, most of Trollope's prophecies have been justified. They read like self-evident truths. He had no doubt that emancipation was right, but he considered that far too great and far too quick a result was expected from it. Nor had he any doubt that the area would be soon ruled by men of color. Of the white men he writes, "The light of their star is waning, their ascendancy is over; their work, if not done, is on the decline." He exhorts the visitor to "go into the house of assembly and see how large a proportion of their debates is carried on by men of color. . . . They have forced their way up and now loudly protest that they intend to keep it. I think that they will keep it and that on the whole it will be well for us Anglo-Saxons to have created a race capable of living and working in the climate without inconvenience."

He had a proper regard for the condition of the black man, whose labor must be protected, though he recognizes the need for immigration. He is amused, too, by the black man's independence. In his hotel he calls for a bath; the servant who is occupied with the cleaning of a pair of boots ignores the summons. "Hullo, old fellow, what about that bath?" he shouts. The servant turns slowly round. "Who you call fellow? You speak to a gen'leman gen'lemanly and den he fill de bath." Trollope bowed. "James, might I trouble you to leave those boots and see the bath filled for me?" James bowed in return. "Yes, sir, go at once."

Trollope is acutely aware of one of the most obstinate obstacles in the way of a free society. Indians have argued that Britain lost her Indian empire through the snobbery of the memsahib. Trollope diagnoses the same complaint. "The difficulty is with the women. . . . In questions of high society there is always the same stumbling block. All manners of men can get themselves into a room without difficulty and can behave themselves with moderate forbearance when in it. But there are points on which ladies are harder than steel, stiffer than their brocaded silks, more obdurate than whalebone." He repeats a conversation that he had with a planter's wife. " 'My husband,' she said, 'wishes me to meet Mrs. So-and-so, because Mr. So-and-so is a very respectable good sort of man. I have no objection whatever to Mr. So-and-so, but if I begin with him, I know there will be no end.'

" 'Probably not,' I answered. 'When you once begin you will doubtless have to go on.'

" 'Exactly. That is just what I said to my husband. But he never thinks about such things. He is very imprudent. If I ask Mrs. So-and-so, how can I keep out Mrs. Such-a-one? They are both very respectable, no doubt, but what were their grandparents?' "

This sounds a very obvious dialogue, but it was not so obvious a hundred years ago. Trollope was the first man to hit that particular nail upon the head. His final comment is particularly prophetic. "Jamaica is one of the few sores in our large and healthy carcase." Six years later, Jamaica was to provide a dramatic scandal that is still the subject of controversy. The conduct of Governor Eyre in Jamaica in 1865 was as hotly argued as that of General Dyer in Amritsar in 1920.

Whichever side one takes in the dispute, it can scarcely be questioned that Eyre was an unlucky man. As a minor administrator in Australia and New Zealand, he had been a considerable success, and had befriended the aborigines there. He was posted to Jamaica only as a stopgap, because of the ill health of the governor, but through a series of mishaps his relief did not arrive punctually. It had never been intended that he should be permanently promoted, and it was not till he had been an acting governor for two years, from 1862 to 1864, that his posting was confirmed. His enemies have agreed that he was not made out of "gubernatorial timber"; that is as may be, but he certainly inherited an extremely delicate situation, and his difficulties were increased by his insecurity of tenure, both in his own eyes and in those of his officials. The island was deep in debt; there had been a succession of years of drought; the American Civil War was raising the price of breadstuffs and of cotton. In 1853 Britain had loaned Jamaica half a million pounds. The governor was responsible for the taxes out of which the interest on this loan had to be met, but he had to deal with a refractory assembly. It had no nominated members, and public business was managed by forty-seven independent legislators, on whose annual votes the revenue was dependent. The assembly made grants of supply, not to the governor but to itself. It could remit taxes. Out of a population of four hundred and forty thousand, there were less than two thousand voters. Trollope had noted that most of the talking in the assembly was done by men of color, but there were many more white members in it. A system that had worked badly under slavery was working worse under emancipation.

Eyre also inherited from his predecessor a point of dissension that was to be known later as the Tramway scandal; this involved the granting to a government official of a monopoly to run a tramline on a road that was the only thoroughfare for the traffic into Spanish Town of the whole south side of the island. Hundreds of three-mule drays passed down it daily, and now its fairway was to be obstructed by tramlines. There was an indignant outcry, to which Eyre retorted by closing the assembly and sending an inaccurate account of the proceedings to the secretary of state, who, having once backed Eyre, could not easily withdraw his support later. The incident is significant as showing Eyre's high-handed attitude toward constituted authority, his self-righteousness, his trust in his own judgment, and his belief that the end justifies the means.

Eyre was at this time forty-three years old. He has been described as having a petulant streak to his nature. He was also a rabidly stern stickler for decorum, and in Jamaica, of all places, issued a morality proclamation stating that "no one was eligible for a public appointment who was not honest, sober and moral," and that "no one immoral was to be promoted." This provoked a protest from the Duke of Newcastle, who wrote, "I feel sure that you will find it most conducive to the public interests you have at heart, to occupy yourself rather with the substance of acts and proceedings with which you have to deal than with the private characters of the persons who may assail or defend them."

Eyre did, however, by his proclamation win the support of the Baptist missionaries, who were causing considerable concern to the plantocracy by their insistence on the equality of all men, irrespective of color, before the Lord. It was, however, to be a short-lived alliance; indeed, the missionaries were to prove one of his most acute concerns.

The presence of these missionaries was a new phenomenon in the British islands. In the Spanish islands—and in a much lesser degree in the French—the church had been from the start an important civilizing factor, had been one of the two main pillars on which the establishment had been sustained. Isabella had seen to that. It had organized schools, it had influenced the administration and the judiciary. It had maintained the Holy Office. It had been occupied with the spiritual salvation of the slaves. The Church of England had not. The priests who were sent out acted as chaplains to the plantocracy. The available livings offered few attractions. Small pay and a bad climate. The Baptists and the Methodists were able to work in a fresh field. They were shocked at the state in which they found their flock, and the first cause of Eyre's troubles was a letter addressed by a Baptist minister named Underhill to the secretary of state, calling his attention to the pitiable conditions in which the Jamaican peasantry and city laborers were existing. The secretary of state sent this letter to Eyre, with a request for his comments on it. Eyre, to obtain the material on which to base his reply, had copies made of Underhill's letter and sent them to all the magistrates and a number of influential residents and officials. This amounted to a publication of the letter, and its publication at such a time was highly injudicious.

The laboring classes were discontented; they were enduring considerable suffering and they had many grievances, some of them imaginary. They resented, for example, the tax on wheels and horses because the idea of taxation was unfamiliar to them. But many of these grievances were genuine, particularly those that were concerned with idle land. A good deal of territory had been abandoned during the slump. Much of this land, which lay between the estates and the mountains, had been taken over by the crown, partly to prevent the abandonment by the labor force of the estates that were still in operation. The Negroes, who regarded Queen Victoria as their fairy godmother, believed that this land had been given to them. They also suspected that there was in existence a plot to reenslave them; in a sense this was an imaginary grievance, yet there were ideas in the air that made such a suspicion tenable. The plight of the planters was making a number of people in England feel that some coercion was essential. Thomas Carlyle, who appears to have believed in the divine right of the whites to rule the blacks, had published in *Fraser's Magazine* in November 1849 "A discourse on niggers," in which he wrote: "Wherever in British territory there exists a black man, and needful work to the just extent is not got out of him, such a law in default of a better should be brought to bear on such a black man . . . on the whole it ought to be rendered possible, ought it not, for white men to live beside black men and in some just manner to command black men and to produce West Indian fruitfulness by way of them. . . . Not a square inch of soil in these fruitful isles, purchased by British blood, shall any black man hold to grow pumpkins for him, except on terms that are fair to Britain." It is easy to see how such an article, repeated by word of mouth across a distance of four thousand miles, could be construed as a plot to reestablish slavery. Their credulity went so far as to believe that Prince Albert was the instigator of the plot, for which cause God had struck him dead.

Unemployment was mounting; cotton was scarce, bread was dear and abandoned estates were padlocked. The Islanders insisted on their right to petition their fairy godmother. Eyre resented this petition; though he had no illusions about the state of the island—he saw "everywhere deterioration, decadence, decay"—he described the petitioners as "deluded people." It may well be that the letter with which the petition was forwarded prejudiced its contents. At any rate, the reply from the fairy godmother first puzzled, then outraged the Jamaicans. "The Queen," so it read, "desired the petitioners to be told that prosperity depended upon their working for wages, not uncertainly or capriciously but steadily and continuously, at the times when their labour is wanted . . . not from any such schemes as had been suggested to them." This message, headed "The Queen's Advice," was under Eyre's orders reproduced and placarded round the island.

Puzzled and then outraged—but outraged not against Her Majesty but against the governor—they believed that the placard was a forgery, that the Queen's real reply had been suppressed. A highly electric situation had been created, and it can be assumed that the fervor of religious revival was inflamed by the privations of the drought. All over the island what were known as Underhill meetings were held—meetings that Eyre called seditious—to discuss Underhill's complaints that the number of prisoners in the jails had doubled, and that there was very little coin in the country, as well as Underhill's recommendation that there should be an inquiry into the legislation, an encouragement of exports, and that capital could be induced to enter by a lowering of taxes. Of all this turmoil George William Gordon was the mouthpiece.

Gordon was a man of color; he was a landed proprietor, he owned

a newspaper, *The Sentinel,* and he had a seat in the assembly. He was
a magistrate and a Baptist; he was eloquent and bellicose, a type that
is familiar enough today in West Indian politics. His eloquence and
bellicosity were inflamed by his Bible reading. He told his followers
that "the Lord would send them their day of deliverance"—a prophecy that was later interpreted as an instigation to revolt. From the
start he was against authority. Because he objected to the conditions
of the local lockup, he was dismissed from his magistracy by Eyre's
predecessor for "false and unfounded imputations." He was told that
he had usurped the prerogative of the crown. Eyre, regarding him
with particular distrust, opposed his candidature as a churchwarden,
to which Gordon retorted that he "had never seen an animal more
voracious of cruelty and power than the present governor of Jamaica."

The air was tense, and across a few miles of water there was in
Haiti a perpetual warning. The blacks outnumbered the whites by
fifty to one. There was tension in several areas. A popular doctor was
told, "I don't think any black people would harm you, but take my
advice, go away somewhere." And then, in Morant Bay, on October
11, 1865, the powder house exploded.

A royal commission was later to explore the causes of the outbreak, but by then the men who would have been most valuable as
witnesses were dead. On the actual sequence of events there was a
concurrence of agreement. It began outside a courthouse. A woman
had brought a case of assault against a boy. He was fined 4/-, with
costs estimated at 12/6d. There was an outburst of indignation from
the mob. A man who protested was seized by the police; his friends
rescued him and beat up the police; there was a throwing of stones,
the riot act was read, more stones were thrown, the volunteers
opened fire, the mob broke loose, the volunteers were killed, the
courthouse burned; next day there was a kind of war, with a maddened
crowd of rioters chanting their death march:

> Buckra[1] blood we want,
> Buckra blood we'll have,
> Buckra blood we're going for,
> Till there's no more to have.

During a two-days' massacre, twenty-two civilians were killed and
thirty-four wounded.

Eyre acted with vigor, speed and courage. He cordoned off the

[1] White

danger area, proclaimed martial law in it and brought troops and Maroon volunteers into action. Within four days effective resistance had ceased. Up to this point, he had the full support of the court of inquiry, but he continued martial law in the affected area, and the reprisals that he took were as ruthless as they were thorough. The official tally of the executions was 439, 345 of which followed a court-martial, the remainder being summarily shot by government troops. A further 147 were shot after martial law had ceased. There were innumerable floggings, both of men and women, and it was sometimes found that prisoners who were being tried in a court-martial had been already flogged. All the ringleaders, with the exception of those who were already dead, were hanged. Gordon was included among the leaders.

Eyre was resolved to make an example. Just as sixty years later the memory of the Indian mutiny and fear of its repetition goaded General Dyer into issuing the crawling order at Amritsar, so in Jamaica the memory of the massacres in Haiti warned Governor Eyre against any soft-handed treatment. The lives and property of Britons were in danger. He was convinced that the rebellion in Morant Bay was the result of a daring and determined intention to make Jamaica a second Haiti, and he saw in the occasion an excellent opportunity to change the constitution. He persuaded the cowed and rattled assembly to vote its own dissolution and place the fortunes of the island under the direct control of the crown. This was what he had wanted all along. Fate, he felt, had played into his hands. He was the instrument of destiny. He had been sent out as a stopgap, but his name would be remembered and revered as one of the island's greatest governors. He awaited with confident complacency the salvos of congratulatory rhetoric which would greet in London the dispatch that announced his triumph.

It was not till November 16 that the news reached London, and when the dispatch was published in the *Times* there was an outcry of incredulous indignation. It was by the hanging of Gordon that popular opinion was most affronted. Gordon had not been in Morant Bay when the revolt broke out. He had been at Kingston, and when the disturbance began he voluntarily presented himself at the police station, where he was taken into custody. There was no martial law in Kingston, and had he been put on trial there he would have had to be tried, formally, before a judge and jury. Eyre therefore had him taken by boat to Morant Bay to be tried by a court-martial.

This was a flagrant breach of justice, and the British public recognized it as such. They demanded an inquiry. Eyre faced the inquiry with dignity and composure, satisfied that he had carried out his duty. He was convinced that Gordon had inspired the revolt. Fine points of the law had to be waived at a time of crisis. You have to make swift and stern decisions. The French had not been firm enough in Haiti. But a course of action that may appear reasonable when blood-maddened hooligans are chanting "It's buckra blood we want," appears in a very different light under the calm scrutiny of a court of law. The inspectors had nothing but praise for the promptitude and courage with which the governor had acted, and for the skill with which he had localized the disturbance, but they were unable to find any proof of an organized rebellion.

The trouble was that all the chief witnesses were dead. It seemed to the court of inquiry that the whole thing was unpremeditated. There had been admittedly a demonstration outside the courthouse; local resentment had in the first place risen over the leasing out of some land to small occupiers, to whom it was felt injustice had been done. As a result of these first disturbances, a number of warrants had been issued. Feelings were running high. Then the incident of the woman and the boy had started a mob riot. It was the kind of thing that can easily happen in a hot place with a hot-blooded populace that has a sense of grievance. Had any of the leaders of the demonstration been still alive, it might have been shown under cross-examination that the outbreak in Morant Bay had been planned as the spearhead of a general rising, but the leaders were all dead. The only real proof of a plot was that the demonstrators had marched up to the courthouse as though they had been drilled for it. Very few of them were armed with muskets, a few swung cutlasses, but the majority only carried cudgels which a witness described as not being "decent, pleasing sticks such as you would choose to walk with." The procession had been joined by vagrants, and it may well have been that the first stones were thrown by them. When the riot had begun, and the murders had been committed, events had followed a logical course. As well be hanged for a sheep as for a lamb. While they were still at liberty, let them glut their hatred. That was the judges' verdict on the incident in general. In the view of that verdict, the judges could not fail to condemn the measures that Eyre had adopted after all resistance had been broken. His treatment of captives was inhuman; in particular the floggings. By maintaining martial law long after it was necessary, he had given license not only to British troops but to the Maroon volunteers. Martial law was the suspension of all law, and it was recommended that in future colonial governors should be denied the right to declare martial law.

In view also of that verdict no case could stand against Gordon. Eyre's policy had been directed by his belief that Gordon was plotting to turn Jamaica into a second Haiti. Gordon was a friend of the rebel leaders, and in the Morant Bay post office were found addressed to them two pamphlets written by Gordon on *The State of the Island*; and it was Gordon's enemies, the men who had opposed his church-wardenship, who were murdered in the courthouse. He had announced publicly that in a few years' time all the whites would have left the island. But he had been many miles away from Morant Bay when the action took place; he had been illegally transported thither so that he could be tried by court-martial. It transpired during the investigation that prisoners had been flogged until they admitted Gordon's guilt, and that a brigadier had never delivered to Gordon a letter of legal advice that had been sent to him while he was awaiting trial at Morant Bay. There is no doubt that the governor was resolved to rid himself of the turbulent Baptist. It was as much a murder as Banquo's was. He had only one defense—"the man on the spot knows best."

The man on the spot is always in a dangerous position. A situation arises without warning. He has to trust his instinct, and he is judged subsequently by men and women who cannot appreciate the emotional vibrations in the air and the irrational responses of unbalanced human beings. It is hard to judge in a cold climate things that happen in a hot one. Similar situations constantly arose during the period of European domination over colored peoples.

This particular scandal was not, however, to end with the findings of the royal commission and the recall of Governor Eyre. It was to become a *cause célèbre*, on which the final curtain did not fall until July 1872.

During six years of acrimony and argument, in which jury after English jury had to listen to the rival claims of relative responsibility, families were to turn against each other and political parties were to be divided. The outcry following General Dyer's shooting of the Indians at Amritsar fifty years later was shorter and less violent. Ideologies were involved. T. H. Huxley described the case as "at bottom one of the most important constitutional battles in which Englishmen have for many years been engaged," while John Stuart Mill, whose last years it shadowed with failure and disappointment, asserted that "the question was whether the British dependencies and eventually perhaps Great Britain itself were to be under the government of law or of military license."

Timing is the secret of success. An international best seller might well have passed unnoticed had it been published three years later or three earlier. A scandal only becomes a conflagration when a high pile of dry timber awaits ignition, and in 1865, England was in a highly inflammable condition. The country was enjoying a period of unparalleled prosperity. It had not been involved in a major war for half a century; its empire was supplying it with the raw materials that its factories were turning into exportable merchandise. The world needed its coal and steel. But this prosperity was built upon the squalid living conditions of the working classes. And that condition was stirring the conscience and rousing the indignation of the same type of man who, two generations earlier, had protested against the slave trade, with men like Ruskin inveighing against the industrialists who would shorten the lives of their laborers by thirty years a life if they might get needle packets twopence cheaper. The proletariat not only had a grievance but a mouthpiece.

At this time it had no vote. The middle classes had been enfranchised by the Reform Bill of 1832, which was in itself a revolution, and during the rioting the victor of Waterloo had to barricade his windows against the London mob. The proletariat was now demanding equal rights, and the aristocracy, the merchants and the middle classes were exceedingly apprehensive. What would happen to the country, or rather what would happen to them, if the rabble got control? A few years earlier a strike of the Builders' Union for a nine-hour day had been backed by organized labor, and radical members of Parliament were demanding an enlargement of the franchise. During the summer of 1866 the Reform League was sponsoring demonstrations. Artisans in Trafalgar Square were brandishing red flags; the railings of Hyde Park were being stormed; the mob was on the move. It was not surprising that authority should have seen a kinship between the Negroes of Morant Bay and the rioters in London streets. It must, moreover, be remembered that less than ten years earlier the Indian mutiny had been attended by a series of atrocities on white women. Might not Governor Eyre have protected the planters of Jamaica from a similar fate?

On the Eyre issue the country was split in two. During the American Civil War, upper and middle class British opinion had been on the side of the Confederate south, while the British radicals formed an Emancipation Society in London to back the northern cause. This group included John Stuart Mill and Thomas Hughes, the author of *Tom Brown's School-days*. In Lancashire the Union and Emancipation Society of Manchester was even more influential.

A similar situation arose out of the Eyre case. As has been previously explained, much of the trouble in Jamaica had been due to the missionary activities of the nonconformist sect which held its meetings in a side street off the Strand, from which headquarters they became known as the Essex Hall Group. When the news of the massacres in Morant Bay reached London, this group immediately went into action, and under the letter heading of the Jamaica Committee demanded justice. Nineteen members of Parliament were members of this committee, which was headed by John Bright, the leader for reform in the House. Thomas Hughes and John Stuart Mill were two of its most prominent members. It listed no members of the House of Lords, but a great many clergymen, and it was largely due to the energy of this committee that the Royal Commission was sent out to hold its court of inquiry. Many of the members of the committee were satisfied with the findings of the Commission. They felt that their protest had been vindicated; but the more violent wanted more. They demanded retribution and resolved to prosecute Eyre for murder, it being one of the curious features of English law that any subject of the crown may instigate before a magistrate an action against any other. These threats forced a conservative faction to defend the ex-governor.

The timing of the drama contained so fruitful a coincidence that a novelist would have hesitated to include it in his narrative. It was on the very day after the riots in Hyde Park that Eyre embarked at Kingston for his return to England. He was given a proud send-off. The wharves were thronged. A military band played "God Save the Queen." On board he was presented with an address of praise by a committee representing over a thousand of the leading merchants and planters, thanking him for his services to the island. Another address was presented by the bishop and clergy of Kingston. Eighteen months earlier he had been an object of distrust to those very signatories, but his prompt action at the time of the rising had erased, for them, the record of his deficiencies. Flags were dipped in his honor, and at Port-Royal a seventeen-gun salute was fired. It is reported that there were tears in the governor's eyes as he made his final speech.

"I now retire into private life, dismissed from the public service, after nearly a lifetime spent in it, but I have at least the consolation of feeling that there has been nothing in my conduct to merit it, nothing to occasion self-reproach, nothing to regret."

He left with a heavy heart and with considerable apprehension as to the reception that he would receive in England, for he was aware that plans were in preparation to have him tried for murder. He could scarcely have been more surprised at being welcomed at Southampton by a committee of local gentlemen who announced that they wanted to give a dinner in his honor. He had not known when he embarked that twenty-four hours earlier the railings of Hyde Park had been pulled up by an indignant mob. He could not have guessed how the events of that day would make a number of Britons reassess their opinion as to the action of the colonial governor. "The mob" was on the move. And Eyre had become a symbol of the necessity for enforcing order in an unstable world.

The dinner of welcome was held a week later and was to prove symptomatic of the conflicting viewpoints held by Eyre's fellow countrymen. The address which was signed by many hundred worthy citizens of Southampton assured him that by his "firmness and determination, joined to that prompt action which alone makes a man in authority equal to the occasion," he had saved an important colony and protected the lives and properties of loyal colonists. They expressed their regret that he had been "sacrificed to circumstances as many a great man has been before." A hundred diners, who were presented to the guest of honor, included in their number Lord Cardigan, the commander of the light brigade at Balaclava, and the novelist Charles Kingsley, who was at that time Regius Professor of Modern History at Cambridge. The speeches in the ex-governor's honor were warm and vigorous, and at the dinner's end Eyre jubilantly voiced his relief at the public vindication of his conduct.

His relief was to be short-lived, however. Outside the hall where the dinner had been held had gathered a large crowd of local toughs, yelling for that "bloodthirsty tyrant." They surrounded each carriage as it passed, trying to open the doors to see if Eyre was in it. The coachmen lashed their horses, forcing a way through the throng, and there were many injuries. At the same time, in another part of the city, the more sedate section of the opposition was holding a meeting of protest against the dinner. Next day the story of the evening, the speeches of Cardigan and Kingsley, the mob hysteria and the protest meeting at the Victoria Rooms, was headline news throughout the country. Six years were to pass before the issue was finally closed.

The story of those six years has been recently told fully and entertainingly by Bernard Semnel in *The Governor Eyre Controversy*. It was a breathless battle. On one side there was the Jamaica Committee raising funds for the prosecution of Eyre and two of the officers involved in Gordon's trial; on the other was the Eyre Defense Committee raising funds for the ex-governor's defense. And one of the curious features of the controversy was the unexpected sides on which various public figures were aligned. A number of writers entered the arena, as writers invariably do on such occasions, and they would have been expected to take the side of the underprivileged, but this was not so in this case. Eyre numbered among his followers Charles Kingsley, Thomas Carlyle, John Ruskin, Alfred Tennyson and Charles Dickens, while the Jamaica Committee could only offer in retort Thomas Hughes, Charles Darwin, T. H. Huxley, and John Stuart Mill, not one of whom could be classified as a man of letters. It was not surprising to find Carlyle, with his veneration of "the hero," taking the side of the strong man, but Dickens was a democrat, the poor man's friend, the founder of the *Daily News*. He was not, however, a radical. In *Barnaby Rudge* and *A Tale of Two Cities* he had shown his distrust of mob hysteria. He was an admirer of Carlyle; as a family man he was a respecter of law and order. But though he registered his vote against chaos, he took no active share in the committee's work; and the committee was ubiquitously busy.

There were questions and motions in the House, there were letters to the *Times* and to the *Daily News*. Eyre was prosecuted twice, once on a charge of murder and once for high crimes and misdemeanors. On the first occasion the case was heard before a Shropshire bench, with the defense superbly argued by an advocate who was later, as Lord Halsbury, to occupy the woolsack, and the magistrates dismissed the case. On the second occasion the evidence was heard in London before a grand jury whose foreman announced that "twelve honest men and true" were agreed that they could not find sufficient grounds for indicting ex-Governor Eyre. A grand jury in London had earlier dismissed the plea for an indictment against the two officers, Colonel Nelson and Lieutenant Brand, who were most prominently concerned in Gordon's trial, though here the jury ignored the charge that had been given to them by the judge in the course of a six hours' speech —the chief point of issue being the legality of martial law in a British colony.

It was in June 1868 that the second case against Eyre was thrown out of court, but the issue was not finished yet. Eyre's personal position had yet to be established. Since he had been vindicated in two courts of law, was he not entitled to a pension and should not the government pay the expenses of the action in which he had been involved through his service to the government? The Eyre Defense Committee eventually won its point, yet the Jamaica Committee left the field with its head high. In the final debate in the House of Commons, Peter Taylor, who had once been chairman of the Committee, claimed that though they had "failed in all their direct aims and almost been overwhelmed amid a storm of obloquy and misrepresentation, they had fulfilled their mission; they had stamped out a policy. Never again in a British colony, whatever may be the outcome of the contemptible vote tonight, never again in a British colony shall be enacted the policy of ex-Governor Eyre nor the world stand aghast at the atrocities of a Jamaica massacre."

One of the most curious features of the case was the silence maintained by the ex-governor. He retired into private life and survived for thirty years, but never issued any public statement about himself.

2   THE PANAMA CANAL

A few years later the sultry peace of the Caribbean was disturbed by another scandal. For over a century, Americans had been concerned over the narrow isthmus of Panama and the difficulties that it presented to their trade and shipping. That concern was quickened by the gold rush of '49. It was ridiculous that the east and west coasts of the same country should be so far apart. The successful opening of the Suez Canal suggested an obvious solution. Why not a canal across the isthmus? The only problem was—where should it be driven? Through Nicaraguan or through Colombian territory? For a while, two corrupt governments played power politics against each other. At first it appeared that the Nicaraguans would gain the prize, and United States scientists made a preliminary survey. The Colombians had to work fast, clearly, and they leaped at the offer of ten million francs for a concession made by two French engineers, Wyse and Reclus. Louis Buonaparte Wyse was an old man when he made the survey, yet he rode for eleven days across the mountains to reach the appropriate authorities. He returned to Paris with the concession signed. That was in 1878; and in that summer there gathered in Paris a great congress of savants to discuss the feasibility of opening operations.

The idea of the canal fired the imagination of a France humiliated by the defeats of 1870. She still longed for *la gloire*, but not upon the battlefield. She could prove her superiority by intellectual achievements, and was not Lesseps at hand, *le grand Français* in Gambetta's phrase, who had restored to France the prestige that her generals had lost? As president of the Geographical Society, he presented to this international gathering the resolution "that this Congress is of the opinion that a canal on the level between the two oceans is feasible and most desirable in the interests of commerce and shipping, and that in conformity with the indispensable requirements of access and operation, it ought to be cut between the Gulf of Limón—on which is situated the town of Colón—and the Bay of Panama." The resolution was carried by a large majority, the only noes being cast by those who, like Eiffel, preferred locks for this "oceanic Bosphorus." The evidence that most affected the delegates was the survey that had been made by Wyse. That survey may still be seen in Paris. The drawings were exquisitely executed, but it has since been discovered that they were inaccurate. It had also been stated that of the 136 members who attended the congress, only forty-six were engineers or geographers.

When he took his seat as chairman of the congress, Lesseps had no intention of joining the enterprise. He was close upon seventy-five. His life had been a succession of postings here and there. He wanted to settle down with his family in the provinces, but the pressure of opinion was too strong, and he was an adventurer at heart. When his son Charles opposed the plan, he shrugged. "If one asks a general who has just won a first victory whether he wishes to win a second, would he refuse?"

It is hard not to detect a parallel here between Lesseps and Drake. Both believed in the eternal quality of youth. They could not believe they had grown old. The dreams of both were broken in the fever-strewn jungles of the isthmus.

For Lesseps the next years were his most dramatic and most glamorous. He was the figurehead, the defender of his country's honor. Hugo urged him to astonish the world with the great deeds that can be won without a war. He set about raising, personally, the funds which the enterprise required. He refused at first to rely on the government and on professional financiers. He would appeal direct to the small investor. Those who had made Suez should make Panama. He estimated the final cost at a thousand million francs. He asked for four hundred million, but received only thirty million, and the moneys had to be returned to the subscribers. He was forced to turn to the professional financiers, and turning, took his first false step. The racketeers sharpened their knives. Not four hundred, but six hundred million francs were asked for, and an appeal was launched, with the backing not only of the press but of every bank in France. Within three days, twelve hundred million francs had been subscribed. Champagne flowed in abundance and everybody took his cut. Lesseps himself was so delighted with the result that he pledged himself to visit Panama, and in order to disprove the rumor that the climate was fatal to the white man he arranged to take out with him his wife and three of his children. His paper, *The Bulletin*, was established as the propaganda mouthpiece of the company.

Lesseps was received at the isthmus even more jubilantly than he had been in Paris on his return from Suez. Troops were reviewed, windows decorated, the sky was bright with fireworks. On the first of January 1880, the first blow of the pickax was struck by his seven-year-old daughter, Ferdinande, and a bishop blessed the spot where the canal would emerge into the Pacific.

Lesseps foresaw no dangers. If there were such large crowds to welcome him, the climate must be innocuous. Fevers were caused by decay and its effluvia. A proper regard for hygiene should protect the workers during the seven months' rainy season. It was not till the end of the century that medical science was able to recognize and combat the malevolence of the mosquito—Aedes Aegypti.

From the isthmus he sailed northward to the United States. He was welcomed and he was honored, but the financiers held back. They felt that if there was to be a canal it should be theirs. They had no intention of advancing funds to assist foreigners on a project that should have been their own. President Hayes said in a message to Congress, "The policy of this country is to advocate a canal under American control." But Lesseps, who was perhaps unused to diplomatic formulas, referred in *The Bulletin* to "the enthusiastic and unanimous adherence to our cause." He appeared to think that the President's message "had assured the security of the canal."

He returned to Europe in the highest spirits. He was honored everywhere he went, in England, Belgium, Holland, but he received no funds. He did not, however, let this worry him. He was sustained by the euphoria of senility. His propaganda value was immense. Vast sums of money were changing hands, and whenever this happened, a ten or fifteen percent commission slid into receptive pockets, while the claims of publicity demanded that this journalist and that minister should receive his *douceur*. Yet all the time work was actually proceeding. The contractors were urgently prosecuting their immense task of recruiting personnel, assembling the varied types of machinery that were required, and taking what seemed the appropriate precautions for the health and comfort of the staff.

For the West Indians, the enterprise was an unbelievable bonanza. A large proportion of the labor force was recruited in Jamaica. They could hardly credit their good fortune. Half a century ago their parents and grandparents had been slaves. Now they were heading for an El Dorado richer than that which had inflamed the imagination of their captors. "The lure of easy money," so J. A. Froude was to write eight years later, "is drawing thousands of West Indians to the isthmus." The interisland boat on which he traveled was full of them. They went out on a year's contract. A number of them did not survive that year, but the survivors went home with the store of dollars that would buy them a few acres of land and the chance of a secure old age, "if," Froude adds, "there is such a thing as a provident West Indian."

It was for the West Indians the most exhilarating event in their manacled history. In retrospect it is easy to dismiss the whole thing as a racket; a number of worthless men made money shoddily, the Bourse was manipulated, stocks were sent down by a false report that the U.S.A. were invoking the Monroe Doctrine, then they were sent up by a misrepresentation of the President's message to Congress, but work was being done, on the spot, by honest men. R. Coureau wrote in his life of Lesseps published in Paris in 1932, "The hospital has been sited in the healthiest place of the locality. . . . It consists of five separate buildings, lightly constructed in wood, between which air and sunlight can play without restriction. Excellent water is laid on in abundance. The hospital has its own farm, *abattoir* and ice house. Every night the soil is removed and taken down to the sea. The wards are so large and well ventilated, even those occupied by Negro patients suffering from fever, that the most sensitive olfactory nerves cannot perceive the slightest odour. There are private rooms for the company's employees, and you would not find more comfortable accommodation in the most expensive nursing home. There are five experienced and devoted medical officers. The administration and nursing is in the hands of thirty sisters."

But in spite of these precautions, the white assistants were no more immune against yellow fever than Leclerc's troops had been in St. Domingue or Dundas' in Guadeloupe. No one realized that it was by mosquitoes that the fever was spread. The windows were uncovered; there were no mosquito screens; the feet of the beds were stood in water to keep off ants, thus providing breeding grounds for mosquitoes.

When fever first appeared in 1882, the West Indians managed with a loss of only ten percent. They possessed a partial immunity to yellow fever, though not to malaria, and the company in Paris was confident. But the contractors were not. Their best men died; an earthquake was followed by a tidal wave; their machinery was clogged, their rail tracks fouled. They decided to pull out, and no large firm was prepared to act as a successor. But even now Lesseps was not deterred. He remembered how at Suez he had disagreed with the experts, and been proved right. He trusted himself and decided that the company should buy out the contractors' equipment and that he should handle the business himself, not through Paris but through a director in Panama. Financially and administratively this was to prove a disastrous decision.

In the meantime, it was not only West Indian laborers who were flocking to the isthmus in search of spoil. The air was heavy with every type of human vulture; there was gambling, drinking, drabbing; pimps announced their special merchandise with the code designation *Langoustes arrivées*. The whole thing was very like a war, with the *embusqués* flourishing at the base, while the troops shivered in the trenches.

Yet just as in wartime everything seems flourishing at the base and at G.H.Q., with medaled staff officers in polished boots supping in elegant restaurants, and the four-star generals seated in high honor, so did the administrators flourish in the Paris headquarters of the company. Never had Lesseps enjoyed more renown. In April 1883 he was elected to the Academy, and Ernest Renan said of him, "The word religion is not too strong to express the enthusiasm which you engendered. Your work was a kind of gospel of redemption, of grace and pardon. . . . I suppose that, after Lamartine, you are in our century the man most beloved, around whose head have formed the greatest number of legends and of dreams. . . . The nation which knows how to love and to admire is not near death. To those who contend that within the breast of this people nothing beats any more, that they no longer know how to worship, that the experience of so many failures, so many deceptions, has extinguished in them all confidence in what is good and great, to them we will cite you. . . ."

Yet at the very moment that Renan was delivering this oration, the financial situation in the isthmus had become so serious that Lesseps had been forced to ask the government for permission to offer lottery bonds, a request that the government had declined to grant till a fresh survey of the area had been made by a government mission.

The head of the mission had the good sense to delay his departure until the dry season; it became harder to maintain the appearance of success, and yet it was maintained; the government mission reported favorably upon the work in progress. In 1886 Lesseps revisited the isthmus. His staff still had faith in him. He was cheered like a general on the eve of battle. Legend states that he traveled in a flowing robe of gorgeous colors like an Oriental monarch. On his return to France he wrote in *The Bulletin,* "From the first of April 1885 to the 31st of May 1886, when there were fourteen thousand people employed at various points along the route of the canal, there were only 735 deaths, that is to say a mortality of 5¼%. Such a figure is not greater than the mortality usual in public works, and definitely lower than that of the navy over the whole of our colonies, which is 7%."

The shareholders read this report with relief and satisfaction, but even as they were reading it, the rains were falling on the isthmus, mosquitoes were breeding in the stretches of stagnant water that the excavations had created, and once again a plague of yellow fever struck. Its venom was particularly felt by the white workers. In October 1886 the *Washington* disembarked thirty engineers. Within a month thirteen of them were dead. The director of works brought out his wife and children. His wife and the two children died. Twenty-four helpers accompanied the mother superior of the Sisters of Ancona. Twenty-one of them died. The British consul at Panama made a trip into the upper valley with an engineer and a group of twenty-two men. The men were left at the installations. Twenty of them caught the fever and half of them died. The consul invited the engineer to lunch with him next day. He awaited his guest in vain. The engineer was already dead. The plague was so fierce that an enterprising man of business was advertising in the local press that he could supply coffins of any size, with a price range of six to one hundred piasters. The Negroes were, however, for the most part immune to yellow fever, and the work continued. It was on the Negroes, mainly from Jamaica, that the company had to rely. The Indians were poor workers, and the Chinese set up as shopkeepers, market gardeners and laundrymen.

The government committee refused to authorize the issue of lottery bonds until more convincing documents were produced, but Lesseps was undaunted. He flung back his challenge. "Six deputies have by their attitude prevented me from going forward, from marching with you to the conquest by France of the Isthmus of Panama. We shall pass over the obstacle. Together we shall go on to this second victory. We shall issue the necessary 600 million. . . . The dogs bark, the caravan passes."

But the country had ceased to share his faith. The mercurial French temperament had swung from one extreme to another. The issue failed, and again the applicants had their subscriptions returned. In the assembly, a deputy spoke of the enterprise as a national humiliation. The committee met again; this time the voting went the other way; in the meantime, presumably, one of the deputies had been bribed, and the issue of lottery bonds was legalized, to the amount of seven hundred and twenty millions. The Crédit Lyonnais stipulated, however, that the whole of the sum must be subscribed at once. This was very far from being what the company wanted. They only needed enough money to meet current expenses. Lesseps was still convinced that the work could be accomplished, as indeed technically it could. He refused to take account of the fever. The company tried to persuade the Crédit Lyonnais to change its mind, but the bankers refused. Reluctantly the company gave way. The issue was announced. But Lesseps had many enemies. He was distrusted by the left and by the right, and at this crucial moment his adversaries had recourse to an act of treachery for which history provides few parallels. On the morning that the subscription lists were opened, every town in France received a telegram announcing Lesseps' death. Not unnaturally, the issue failed completely.

Lesseps was hopeful still, but the world at large was well aware that failure was imminent. The steamer on which Froude sailed for Jamaica was bound for Panama. He was urged to continue his trip in her to see "the greatest undertaking of our age." But he declined. He dreaded what he would find there; a damp tropical jungle swarming with mosquitoes, snakes, alligators, scorpions, centipedes . . . "half buried in mud the scattered wrecks of costly machinery consumed by rust, sent out under lavish orders and found unfit for the work for which it was intended." He anticipated that he would also find the unburied skeletons of the human machinery that had broken down there; while the port itself would be cluttered with "the speculators, cardsharpers, hallkeepers and the doubtful ladies who carried their charms to this delightful market."

The company still hoped that bankruptcy could be delayed. But Paris was being torn by one of its periodic political crises. Gambetta was getting old; the big bankers were not going to risk their capital to succor a man who had despised them. The directors of the company had no alternative to resignation, and Lesseps sent the final telegram to Panama ordering the work to cease.

The court proceedings that were eventually set in motion make sorry reading. It became abundantly clear that the company had largely failed through the rapacity and dubious dealing of Frenchmen in high office. Deputies had been bribed, journalists had been bribed. Even men such as Georges Clemenceau had to face uncomfortable interrogation. Scapegoats had to be found. The builder of the Eiffel Tower was arrested, so was Lesseps' son, so would Lesseps himself have been, had his health permitted it. There were two trials, one before a court of appeal for fraud, one before a jury for corruption; Parliament also called a committee of inquiry. It was the kind of scandal that is a speciality of French public life. The opposition was resolved to discredit the government that had encouraged Lesseps, to bring down the government by its exposure of corruption. Scapegoats were required. Eiffel and Charles Lesseps both got prison sentences, young Lesseps maintaining his dignity under relentless cross-examination. When it was shown that the company had paid money to a certain minister, the President asserted that that constituted corruption. Lesseps replied that it was extortion. "Where was the violence?" the President demanded. Lesseps answered with a smile, "Is violence necessary when a minister of state makes demands in such conditions?"

The scandal was out of all proportion to the crimes committed, but that is the usual consequence when a democracy feels it has been fooled. Three thousand miles away, the Jamaicans settled down to the cultivation of their gardens. For them it had been a great adventure.

CHAPTER XIII

Froudacity

J.A. Froude, when he watched the last Jamaican adventurers hurrying to the isthmus, was obtaining the material for a book which he published under the title *The English in the West Indies*, or *The Bow of Ulysses*. It was to prove as unpopular among his expatriate compatriots as Trollope's had done. A phrase was coined out of the novelist's visit—"to go a-Trolloping," which meant to hurry from one station to another, delivering snap verdicts on the way. Froude also enriched the local language with the noun "Froudacity," whose meaning is self-evident. Froude's book is out of print and it would not pay a publisher to reprint it, but it is essential reading for any student of the area.

Froude left England late in December 1887 and was home by April. He went from island to island, pausing at some for a few hours, spending a couple of weeks in others, concentrating on Barbados, Trinidad, Jamaica, Dominica, Cuba, very much as the modern tourist does. He was then over sixty; he was the most prominent English historian of his day. He was a man of prominence and influence.

A conservative in politics, he made the trip with a definite objective—to study existing conditions in the British West Indian colonies. He went there with an open mind, as far as any mind can be called open that is defended by rigid principles. He was an imperialist. He believed that the strong should rule the weak with firm paternal solicitude, arguing that certain races were incapable of self-government and that it was Britain's and Europe's destiny to administer the countries of such races. He included under this heading not only Africans and Asians but the Irish. The prospect of home rule for Ireland filled him with alarm. He disapproved of democracy, and distrusted oratory which could sway the ignorant masses as Kleon the tanner's had in Athens. A new creed has risen, he said, which "has its priests and its prophets, its formulae and its articles of belief.

"Whoever will be saved, before all things it is necessary that he hold the Radical faith.

"And the Radical faith is this: all men are equal and the voice of one is as the voice of another.

"And whereas one man is wise and another foolish, and one is upright and another crooked, yet in this suffrage none is greater or less than another. The vote is equal, the dignity co-eternal.

"Truth is one and right is one; yet right is right because the majority so declare it and justice is justice because the majority so declare it.

"And if the majority affirm one thing to-day, that is right; and if the majority affirm the opposite to-morrow, that is right.

"Because the will of the majority is the ground of right and there is no other, etc.

"This is the Radical faith which, except every man keep whole and undefiled, he is a Tory and an enemy of the state and without doubt shall perish everlastingly."

His face was set against "the wind of change." He foresaw disaster in Ireland. He was alarmed by the stories that had reached him about the despondency of the West Indian planters. As a historian he reverenced the Caribbean past. "In those waters the men were formed and trained who drove the Armada from the Channel into wreck and ruin. In those waters, in the centuries which followed, France and England fought for the ocean empire and England won it—won it on the day when her own politicians' hearts had failed them and all the powers of the world had combined to humiliate her, and Rodney shattered the French fleet, saved Gibraltar and avenged Yorktown. . . . For England to allow these colonies to drift away from her because they have no immediate marketable value would be a sign that she had lost the feelings with which great nations always treasure the heroic traditions of their fathers." And it was appropriate that on the day Froude left England the morning papers were occupied with Gladstone's comment on Tennyson's *Locksley Hall*, which had just been published. "Tennyson saw in institutions which were passing away the decay of what in its day had been great and noble, and he saw little rising in the place of them which humanly could be called improvement. To Gladstone on the other hand those revolutionary years had been years of the sweeping off of intolerable abuses and of awakening to higher and truer perceptions of duty." Froude was in accord with the poet, not the politician.

Even in his own day Froude was a reactionary, and it may seem to the contemporary reader that there is nothing to be learned now, nearly eighty years later, from a study of his reactions. But, on the contrary, he has a great deal to tell us. Prejudiced though he may have been, he had an acute, sharp mind. Though he had, as a historian, spent much of his life in libraries, he had mixed in the big world. As a traveler he knew what to look for, and he understood what he was seeing. His book presents the best picture—one could say the only picture—of conditions in the West Indies at the point when the power of the plantocracy was reaching the final stage of its decline and the experiment of representative government was being made, with the first steps to universal suffrage being taken.

It was this experiment that in particular roused Froude's ire. He foresaw the day when each colony would be administered by a black assembly, with the white man elbowed out of power. And he was accurate in his prophecy, up to a point. In the British West Indies today there is scarcely a white man seated as an elected member in a legislative assembly, and if there is racial discrimination it is against the white man, not the black; but where he was inaccurate as a prophet was in his belief that this switch of power must lead to anarchy.

The example of Haiti had strengthened this belief. Sir Spencer St. John's exposure had just appeared, with its account of cannibalism and witchcraft, and Froude told an inquirer that one of the main reasons of his trip was to visit Haiti. Few tourists can have given less time to a major project. He spent an hour ashore at Jacmel before breakfast, the only passenger to make the excursion. He affected to be horrified. When he returned to the ship, he found the passengers impatiently awaiting breakfast, which had been held back on his account, yet "before breakfast could be thought of or any other thing I had to strip and plunge into a bath and wash away the odour of the great Negro Republic of the West which clung to my clothes and skin."

That is ridiculous, yet in his actual description of Jacmel he was objective. He complained of the state of the streets, but as he had looked for nothing better than a Kaffir *kraal*, the degree of civilization was higher than he had expected. "The houses were of white stone and of some pretensions, but ragged and uninviting; paint nowhere and the woodwork of the verandahs mouldy and worm-eaten. . . . It was market day . . . a great open space in front of the cathedral was covered with stalls, with blankets stretched on poles to keep the sun off, where hundreds of Haitian dames were sitting or standing disposing of their wares—piles of salt fish, piles of coloured calicoes, knives, scissors, combs and brushes. Of home produce there were great baskets of loaves, fruit, vegetables and butcher's meat on slabs. . . . Children were running about in thousands, not in the least as if they were in fear of being sacrificed, and babies hung upon their mothers as if natural affection existed in Jacmel as much as in other places." He went into the cathedral; it was airy and cool, mass was being said, and there was a large congregation.

He spent a little longer in Port-au-Prince, but not long enough to take a meal there. He anathematized it as the central ulcer of which Jacmel was the symptom, "a miserable cross-birth of ferocity and philanthropic sentiment." Yet once again his actual description of the town was sufficiently objective. He called it "a Paris of the gutter, with boulevards and *places*, *fiacres* and crimson parasols. The boulevards were littered with the refuse of the houses and were foul as pigsties, and the ladies under their parasols were picking their way along them in Parisian boots and silk dresses. . . . There were shops and stores and streets, men and women in tawdry European costume and officers on horseback with a tatter of lace and gilding." Once again he complained about the smell. Cursory though his visits were to Jacmel and Port-au-Prince, his trained writer's sense enabled him to give a vivid picture of them. He prophesied the inevitability of American intervention.

Right through the West Indies he was oppressed by a sense of departed glory, and Haiti was the apotheosis of his dread. What Haiti was, Jamaica would become. "The palaces of the English planters and merchants fall to decay; their wines and their furniture, their books and their pictures are sold or dispersed. Their existence is a struggle to keep afloat and one by one they go under in the waves."

He yearned to put back the clock. He believed that it could be put back. The Irish were happier under the landlords, the West Indians under the planters. Why could not the English rule here and in Ireland as they did in India and Malaya, since the days of the planters and the landowners were over? " 'But what would you do?' I am asked impatiently. 'You can suggest no remedy and mere fault-finding is foolish and mischievous.'

"I might answer a good many things," he wrote. "Government cannot do everything . . . but there is a difference between governors whose hands are tied with local councils and whose feet are tied by instructions from home, and a governor with a free hand and a wise head left to take his own measures on the spot. I presume that no one can seriously expect that an organised nation can be made out of the blacks when, in spite of your schools and missionaries, seventy per cent of the children now born among them are illegitimate.[1] You can do for the West Indies, I repeat over and over again, what you do for the East; you can establish a firm authoritative government which will protect the blacks in their civil rights and protect the whites in theirs. You cannot alter the climate, it is true, or make the earth more fertile. Already it is as fertile as any in the earth and the climate is admirable for the purposes for which it is needed. But you can restore confidence in the stability of your tenure, you can give courage to the whites who are on the spot, to remain there, and you can tempt capital and enterprise to venture there, which now seek investments elsewhere. By keeping the rule in your own hands you will restore the white population to their legitimate influence; the blacks will again look up to them and respect them as they ought to do."

His arguments throughout were logical. At one point he says, "If you choose to take a race like the Irish or like the Negroes whom you have forced into an unwilling subjection and have not treated when in that condition with perfect justice—if you take such a race, strike the fetters off them and arm them all at once with all the powers and privileges of loyal citizens, you ought not to be surprised if they turn against and rend you. When you are brought in contact with races of men who are not strong enough or brave enough to defend their own independence, and whom your own safety cannot allow to fall under any other power, our right and our duty is to govern such races and to govern them well, or they will have a right in turn to cut our throats. This is our mission." How logical such arguments are, and how unfeasible. Yet even as he marshaled them, he half recognized that there was an alternative solution.

Grenada was one of the first islands that he visited. It represented to him a shocking contrast to Barbados, where there still remained some of the opulence that Labat had described. Labat had said of Grenada that if Barbados had such a harbor as Grenada's it would be without a rival in the world, and Labat had added that if Grenada belonged to the English, who knew how to profit from natural advantages, it would be a rich and powerful colony. How different it was now! "The forts," so Froude wrote, "had been dismantled and

[1] This is a surprising statement, since Froude in an earlier chapter had discussed very temperately the fact that marriage had never been a popular institution among the West Indian peasantry.

deserted; the castle on which we had seen our flag flying was a ruin, the walls were crumbling and in many places had fallen down. One solitary gun was left but that was honey-combed and could be fired only with half a charge to salute with. The harbour is the best in the West Indies. There was not a vessel in it, nor so much as a boat-yard where a spar could be replaced or a broken rivet mended. Once there had been a line of wharves, but the piles had been eaten by worms and the platforms had fallen through. Round us when we landed were unroofed warehouses, weed-choked courtyards, doors gone and window frames fallen in or out. . . . Nature had been allowed by us to resume possession of the island."

He was given by a temporary resident a gloomy account of existing conditions. The few English that remained were selling their estates, and Grenada had become an island of small proprietors; the ideal country, Froude commented, of modern social reformers, the special target of his detestation. He delivered himself of a melancholy jeremiad. What a ridiculous mockery to set up a constitution in such a place! "There are but two alternatives," he repeats, "before not only Grenada but all the English West Indies—either an English administration pure and simple like the East Indian or a falling eventually into a state like that of Haiti, where they eat the babies and no white man owns a yard of land."

And yet, and yet . . .

"It was dark night," he continues, "when we drove back to the port. The houses along the road which had looked so miserable on the outside were now lighted with paraffin lamps. I could see into them and was astonished to see signs of comfort and even signs of taste—armchairs, sofas, sideboards with cut glass upon them, engravings and coloured prints upon the walls. The old state of things is gone, but there is a new state of things which may have a worth of its own." Here, unexpectedly, almost in a footnote, he prophesied what has happened. Grenada is today one of the most prosperous of the small islands; it is also one of the happiest, with the least color consciousness. Perhaps because its decline was so early and so swift, it reached the down point of the curve the first and its recovery was consequently quickest.

CHAPTER XIV

Where Black Rules White

One of Froude's declared objectives was to visit Haiti. Bryan Edwards, writing of the Caribs in the Leeward Islands, made this prophecy: "What they are now," he wrote, "the freed negroes of Ste Domingue will hereafter be; savages in the midst of society, without peace, security, agriculture or property, ignorant of the duties of life and unacquainted with all the soft endearing relations which render it desirable; averse to labour, though frequently perishing of want; suspicious of each other and towards the rest of mankind; revengeful and faithless; remorseless and bloody minded; pretending to be free while groaning beneath the capricious despotism of their chiefs and feeling all the miseries of servitude without the benefit of subordination."

In 1830 Edwards was chastised severely by the *Quarterly Review* for making this prophecy, but within a few years it appeared to have been abundantly fulfilled. Politically, the story of Haiti is one of tyranny and mismanagement. Of the twenty-four presidents who held office between the departure of the French and the landing of American marines in 1915, two were murdered, one committed suicide, two died in office, only two retired into civilian life; the remaining seventeen, with as much of the national treasury as they could lay their hands on, fled to Jamaica. In 1907, when Kingston was heavily mauled by an earthquake, the Haitians generously dispatched a shipload of provisions for the destitute, with a naïve letter saying how happy they were to be able to do something for an island that had shown so much hospitality to those of their own countrymen to whom chance had proved capricious. The object of the majority of presidents was to transfer as much money as they could into a neutral bank while the going was still good. "Graft," wrote an English *chargé d'affaires* in his report to the Colonial Office, "is the chief national pastime of the country."

Much of what was written about Haiti during the nineteenth century has to be accepted with reservations. Haiti figured, to the white planters of Jamaica and Barbados, in much the same way that the Soviet Union did in the 1920s and 1930s to the conservatives of Europe and the United States—as a grim example of what must happen when law and order collapse, and power passes into the hands of the illiterate. Just as the mandarins of Wall Street and Whitehall welcomed and gave credence to every account of how tractors broke down in the Ukraine while the citizens of Moscow shivered ill-clad and ill-fed in the winter winds, so did the legislators of the Antilles propagate every report they could discover of the abject, impoverished condition of the "Black Republic." "This is what has happened there," they said. "The same thing will happen here if we are not careful; if we are not very careful."

And very certainly those planters had a good deal to give them satisfaction. Disorder spreads quickly in countries of easy growth. Houses and roads crumbled. "God had spoilt the roads," said the Haitians. "God would mend them." "When you see a bridge always go round it." So the proverb ran. There was no organized industry. Nearly all the land was in the hands of peasant proprietors. Coffee, which grew wild over the hills, was the chief export. When the wind blew down the pods, the peasants gathered them, put them on their heads or on their donkeys and carried them to a middleman, from whom by various stages of bribery they reached the customs shed. No rich families needed to be supported by the land. All that was asked of the land was that it should provide the peasantry with the modest quota of their daily bread, and furnish a sufficient annual sum in export tax to meet the expenses of government. The land was amply capable of doing that, but it could not finance a succession of revolutions, changing presidents and corrupt officials.

In the early part of the century, Haiti and Santo Domingo were united, but by the middle of the century they had drifted apart; Santo Domingo to develop a casual, comic-opera, Spanish-style republic, where nothing in particular happened and little was achieved, but a certain semblance of civilized prosperity was maintained. Santo Domingo had never enjoyed the high-pressure importance that Haiti had; it had been neglected by the Spaniards, stagnating as Trinidad had done. Very few slaves had been introduced and its industries had been neglected. It had not very far to fall. There was not such an abrupt change of regime and there had been no great measure of discontent. Santo Domingo slid along. In Haiti the atmosphere of comic opera alternated with grisly tragedy.

A moment of high comedy was achieved in the middle of the century when the presidency fell vacant, not through revolution, but by a natural process of death. The claims of two rivals being equally persuasive, their supporters compromised by electing an inconspicuous general, Faustin Soulouque, whom they imagined would prove an obedient servant. To their shocked surprise, however, the general's vanity was more substantial than were his abilities. He was brave, unscrupulous and tenacious, and he stayed in office for twelve years.

Black himself, he ordered a massacre of the mulattoes, converted the country into a kingdom, and declared himself an emperor, Faustin I. The preparations for his coronation lasted thirty months and cost a quarter of a million dollars, a hundred thousand of which were spent on the imperial crown. During the ceremony he created four princes, fifty-nine dukes and a large number of counts, barons and chevaliers. He also established a legion of honor and an imperial order of St. Faustin. Lavish insignia were provided and elaborate regulations for court procedure were drawn up. "I am the state," said the Emperor, "and my will is law."

His reign lasted longer than most of the presidencies, but after eleven years a revolution started in the north, and the Emperor considered it prudent to follow the traditional example and sail for Jamaica. The titles of nobility lapsed into desuetude.

Spencer St. John, who was British Resident in Haiti for six years, between 1861–1867, has left an entertaining account of his experiences. The national army consisted then of six thousand generals, seven thousand regimental officers and six thousand other ranks. There was no discipline. The sentries had chairs to sit upon. Justice was casual. Prisoners had to prove their innocence. Policemen arrested a man by battering him into unconsciousness with a large iron-studded cane called a *cocomacaque*. Ordinarily the Negro, who has a great imitative capacity, and therefore a sense of precedent, makes an excellent lawyer. But in Haiti, judges were appointed for political purposes, and instances would arise in court when, it being a case of one witness' word against another's, the judge would turn with a puzzled look toward the prisoner who was accused of theft with no evidence against him other than the plaintiff's testimony. "But she says she saw you steal her purse—you can't get way from that, you know."

As the money destined for public works passed into private possession, the condition of the towns rapidly deteriorated. There was little sanitation. It was maintained that the harbor of Port-au-Prince could be smelled seven miles out to sea. When a revolution raged, the aspirant to the presidency would order his troops: *Mes enfants, pillez en bon ordre.* ("My children, maintain your discipline while you are plundering.") The men in the country did not dare to come into town for fear of being conscripted into the army. The women who brought their produce into market were robbed by soldiers. The hills were infested by brigands.

Spencer St. John's book was unpopular in Haiti, but not for the reasons that would be immediately supposed. The Haitians did not mind being told that their officials were corrupt, their towns filthy and their army inefficient. But they did object very strongly to being told that they were cannibals, addicted to the practice of black magic, and that recently born children were sacrificed at their masses. There are several references to this in Spencer St. John's book. His revelations come under two headings: "Obeah," which is necromancy, and "voodoo," which is a form of religion. The existence of Obeah in the Antilles has never been questioned, and its cult was more widely spread in Haiti, where the Catholic influence was less. The word "zombie" is found only in Haiti. It refers to the belief that dead men could be raised from their graves, animated by spirits, and employed as laborers. This kind of laborer was described as a zombie, and there was at one time a clause in the Haitian law forbidding the employment of dead men in the fields. The appellation is now given to a vague, purposeless human being who moves in a kind of trance, drained of vitality. The Haitians themselves clearly believed in zombies and in witch doctors, and there was no one to interfere with them in the practice of their craft.

Voodoo is very different, and if it is difficult for a white man to speak of Obeah with authority it is quite impossible for him to speak of voodoo. It has been written of since the first African slaves landed in the New World. Labat spells it "Vaudoux." "The name Vaudoux," Peytraud says, "is applied by the Africans to a supernatural being whom they identify with a grass snake whose wishes are interpreted by a high priest or priestess. The slaves invoke him constantly, begging him to guide their master's spirit. Their services become bacchanalian; inspired by alcohol they tremble, quiver, bite each other, lose all self-control." During these dances they recite the famous refrain of the cult of Vaudoux. "Eh, eh, Bomba, Heu, Heu." They had another refrain which said, "We swear to destroy the whites and all that they possess. Let us die rather than renounce this vow."

It is two and a half centuries since Labat was a witness of the Vaudoux dance, and we have learned little more about it in those two and a half centuries than Labat has to tell us. We know, as he did, that it was a religious dance and that it was more moderate in its effects than the *Danse à don Pèdre*, which produced a kind of epilepsy among the participants and was forbidden on most estates. Before the French Revolution, when the slaves were closely supervised, the rites of Vaudoux can only have been practiced with caution and in secrecy. After the withdrawal of the French, when there was no need for secrecy, any ritual may have been accepted in the dark masses in the hills. We cannot know. We shall never know. But it is interesting that the Haitians themselves should have been so indignant at these revelations and were so anxious to rebut them.

In 1927 a similar effect was achieved by William Seabrook's *The Magic Island*; its references to cannibalism and voodoo festivals were the subject of vehement protests. For a time, writers as a race were most unwelcome, and any visitor arriving with a typewriter was closely watched.

Thirty years earlier, Hesketh Pritchard had a similar experience. "There is one thing common to the whole country," he wrote, "of which every Haitian denies the existence. Vaudoux is the one thing which they declare they have not. They tell you there is no snake worship (I am speaking of the higher classes) within the bounds of the Republic. But when you betray certain knowledge of the subject they admit that though sacrifices and savage dances may take place in other departments, no such things are known in the one in which you at the moment find yourself."

Hesketh Pritchard visited Haiti at the turn of the century, and a book called *Where Black Rules White* was the result. Pritchard's name is little, if at all, known today, though he created the fictional character on which the Douglas Fairbanks *Zorro* and *Son of Zorro* films was built. But he was a man of considerable gifts; he had traveled widely, he was a soldier with much foreign service, he was a first-class cricketer who played as a fast bowler for Hampshire and The Gentlemen. In 1909 he represented the Authors against the Publishers in a one-day match at Lord's. The Publishers objected to the opposition of a player of such quality, but there were few members of the Authors' side so fully entitled to a place on the qualification of literary merit. He was a sound writer, who did his writing before the vogue of sensational journalism, and he is one of the most valuable witnesses that we have to that period of Haitian history.

He wrote at length on Vaudoux. He considered that it was "so inextricably woven in with every side of the Haitian's life, his politics, his religion, his outlook upon the world, his social and family relations, his prejudices and peculiarities, that he cannot be judged apart from it." He considered that the official Roman Catholicism of the island was no more than a thin veneer. At this time the Vaudoux priests were known as papalois, the priestesses as mamalois, a corruption of *Papa le roi* and *Mama le roi*. The priests and priestesses lived mainly in the mountains. The services took place at night and under conditions of pseudosecrecy. A serpent kept in a box was the symbol of the deity. There were dancing, sacrificing, incantations, and at the end wild dancing by the mamaloi; exactly as it was in Labat's day.

Labat, however, does not refer to the sacrificial side of the ceremony, and it may be presumed that this side could only be conducted with the greatest secrecy in plantation days, that it was a clandestine cult only emerging into the open in Haiti when French dominance was removed. It is extremely doubtful whether today it exists anywhere else in the West Indies, and presumably even in Haiti it has "gone underground."

According to Hesketh Pritchard, there were two sects of Vaudoux; one which sacrificed only fruit, white cocks and white goats; the other at which the blood of a black goat was the prelude to the sacrifice of the "goat without horns"—the human child. White was the color of the former ceremony, red of the latter. Pritchard was the witness of a ceremony where the flags and handkerchiefs were red and white; the cocks sacrificed were black and white, which suggested to him that this particular service combined the ritual of the two cults.

Very few white men can have seen a Vaudoux ceremony. Most accounts come, as this present one does, at second or third hand. And it is probable that many of the descriptions of such ceremonies are based on Pritchard's account. He does not say in which town he saw it, though he states that in the south the cult was stronger than in the north and that it was strongest in Jacmel. He was told that he must visit after nightfall one of the poorer sections of the town, and then shortly before midnight he would hear the beating of a drum. He stresses the peculiarities of the drum that summons the faithful to their worship. It was four feet high, made out of some jointed wood like bamboo; it was as wide as a man's trunk. Black goatskin was pegged across the top.

Since the publication of *Where Black Rules White* this style of drum has been made familiar to the western world by jazz orchestras, but it is the special peculiarity of the Vaudoux drum, or rather of the Vaudoux drummer, that while the rhythm can be clearly heard a mile away, near at hand it is indistinct and low. It can thus warn the initiate from a long way off, but it can confuse the uninitiated. Pritchard said that he found it extremely difficult to follow the dull throb of the drum at close quarters. Its muffled and mysterious beat had for him a thrilling quality.

On this particular occasion he followed the sound of the drum through a succession of mean streets. The town was under martial law, and a sentry challenged him, but he bribed his way till he reached the place that his informant had instructed him to seek.

There was a large crowd outside the house, peering through its windows. A large Negro with a *cocomacaque* stood at the door. Pritchard eventually secured admission. He found himself in a dark, shuttered room. A song was being chanted. He could not tell how many people were inside; it was very hot. A candle was lit and the song ceased suddenly. Some two hundred people were crowded into two small rooms; some stood against the walls, others squatted on their haunches. The walls were incongruously decorated with prints from Parisian newspapers and a photograph of the German Emperor. A narrow passage had been left across the unboarded floor. Every glistening face was turned toward the mamaloi.

The singing began again; it was led by a vast, gross creature wearing a voluminous white and purple cotton dress. She held a live cock in her hands. She swayed as she sang; the congregation swayed in time with her. The chant was insistent, monotonous; the drum drove it into the brain like blows. The mamaloi was dancing now between the knees of the worshipers. She was small-faced, snub-nosed, middle-aged. She had a white robe, gold beads and a red sash. More candles were lit. They were set in pots decorated with pink melon flowers; the feast was spread upon the floor; beans, rice, watermelons; bottles of wine and rum. Every so often the mamaloi would sprinkle the feast with water. Each time she did, the pitch of the song rose. Its dirge-like quality persisted. Then, suddenly, it loudened. The steps of the mamaloi grew tigerish; her eyes dilated; she cleared her throat and spat. There was the clink of metal.

The papaloi was a small, dirty old man. He crouched at the side.

The mamaloi seized the cock from the fat leader of the chant. Her dancing grew more frenzied; as she whirled to the insistent, maddening drumming, she laid the cock upon the heads of the worshipers. Her face was contorted. Her dancing grew faster, faster; she straightened her arm; there was a flapping of wings, a snowstorm of feathers, and the cock was headless. Her frenzy mounted. She pressed the neck of the carcass to her mouth. She stopped, motionless. Slowly she withdrew her hand from her stained lips and teeth. Then, screaming, she began to run up and down, till she fell in a trance, the cock still in her hand.

The ceremony was now under way. Six more cocks were sacrificed; fetishes were produced, wooden images, stones and bones; the blood of one of the cocks was set apart in a basin, which the mamaloi took outside and sprinkled over the doors and gates. On her return, with the blood that remained, she made the sign of the cross on the foreheads of the congregation.

Soon the dancing became universal; the noise was deafening; the heat grew heavier. The feasting and revelry would continue, so Pritchard had been informed, for two days more. He had had enough. He did not give himself the chance of seeing whether the program included the sacrifice of "the goat without horns." Many similar descriptions have appeared during the last sixty years, but Hesketh Pritchard's was the first, and it is authentic.

The snake used in these ceremonies was generally the macajuel, a harmless animal like the boa. Pritchard, in a remote part of the country, found a peasant with a snake of this kind. He offered five dollars for it, but his offer was refused.

The power of the papaloi in Haiti was very strong. Not only was he a high priest, but a physician. He was an expert poisoner, but he also had the remedy for the poisons that he administered. The populace was in his power. His influence in the army was great. The Obeah man in the British and the French islands was and is very strong. But he is not nearly as powerful as was the Vaudoux papaloi, because he has not the backing of religion, of snake worship. Obeah is an affair of charms, of love-potions, of the laying on of curses. It is a nuisance, but not more than that.

The last chapter of *Where Black Rules White* is called "Can the Negro rule himself?" It is a question that has perplexed Europe and the United States from the time of emancipation until today; and the importance of Haiti lies in the partial answer that it offers to that question.

Pritchard liked the Haitians. He found them kindly, hospitable, good-hearted, song-loving and cheerful. He found them ignorant, lazy and superstitious, disastrously addicted to the consequences of serpent worship. But he could only find one answer to the question in terms of Haiti. The Haitians had the most fertile and beautiful of the Caribbean islands; they inherited a made country; they had the advantages of the *Code Napoléon* as a model for their legislation; they were given the best of opportunities in a prosperous territory. Yet, after a hundred years, government had degenerated into a farce; houses and plantations had been reclaimed by the forest; there was no stability, no security for the individual. At the turn of the century it appeared to Hesketh Pritchard that Bryan Edwards' prophecy had been fulfilled.

CHAPTER XV

The Century's Close

Gently, imperceptibly, the nineteenth century neared its close. In contrast with the high drama of the preceding three hundred years, there had been, since Waterloo, for the majority of the sugar islands, a bloodless period of decline, in some areas a period of decay. But others had the promise of rebirth. The sun had shone, the rain had fallen, hurricanes had blown, houses had shivered under the impact of earthquakes. Little by little, one by one, the islands licked their wounds, recovered their composure and began to prepare themselves for the place that they would eventually occupy in the world of trade. The phrase "rich as a Creole" belonged now to the past, yet in recompense a man could sleep at night without fear of being woken before dawn, to face the cutlasses of a slave revolt or the musketry of an invasion. One by one the various islands adjusted themselves to their changed allegiance; St. Lucia and Grenada realized that they were British; Martinique and Guadeloupe were at peace in their return to France; Dominica, housing the Caribs, her peasantry speaking patois, was still a little puzzled, uncertain whether she belonged to the Leewards or the Windwards, wondering, with the high mountains of French islands to the north and south, whether in fact she could ever belong to anyone except herself; St. Vincent, the long conflict with the Caribs ended, was entering into competition with the brother and sister islands that had a start on her. She had two particular products that encouraged her to be optimistic, arrowroot and sea island cotton.

To the north, the Danish islands of St. Croix, St. Thomas and St. John were slipping from the fortunate position that Labat had noted. Steam had taken the place of sail. It was no longer so important to meet the trade winds first, and what was the use of being a neutral when there was little likelihood of another war? The residents, on the whole, regretted that they had not been taken over by the United

States after the Civil War. They hoped that another opportunity would arise.

To no island had the century brought greater changes than it had to Trinidad. At the close of the eighteenth century, Trinidad had been one of the most neglected possessions in the Spanish empire; now, although the Caribbean was the least cherished section of Britain's expanding economy, it was rapidly becoming one of the most important islands in the area, and by the introduction of indented East Indian labor it had acquired an atmosphere and population very different from those of the other islands.

Holland had turned her attention to her East Indian possessions, to Java and Sumatra; she had little time to devote to the interests of Saba, Curaçao, Aruba, St. Eustatius and half of St. Martin. Curaçao was no longer important as an *entrepôt* for illicit trade; its only value lay in the liqueur made from its oranges, whose peels were originally dried in the sun and soaked in Jamaican rum, and later were shipped to Holland, unsoaked, for treatment there. Saba was described by Labat as a natural and impregnable fortress. It has no foreshore, no flat cultivated land at the mountain's base. It is an extinct volcano, and the Sabans have perched themselves round the lip of the crater. There are many uninhabited islands, and it must be assumed that the only reason why a settlement was made here was because Saba presented complete immunity at a time when wars were constant. In those days, the settlements round the crater could be reached only by a single passage cut in the stone, too narrow to admit more than one person at a time. The Sabans heaped stones over the passes in such a way that by the pulling of a string an avalanche could be catapulted onto an invader. Saba was able to survive and build up its own personal way of living, while its richer neighbors were the victims of attack and siege and plunder.

In Labat's day, Saba was inhabited by forty to fifty settlers and some hundred and fifty Negro slaves. The plantations were small and well cultivated, the whitewashed houses pretty and well furnished, the settlers living, as it were, in a large club and frequently entertaining one another. Labat was received, he said, very kindly. The principal trade in his day was in boots and shoes.

It is a curious community that has grown up there; one of its most surprising features being the lack of intermarriage between the descendants of the original settlers and the original slaves. Sabans are pure African or pure European. The two races live on terms of the greatest amity, dividing the cooperative duties of administration, but inhabiting different sections of the island. The Africans live inside the crater, in the section that is known as The Bottom, although it is eight hundred feet above sea level, because they prefer the warmth there, while the whites have perched themselves on the outer and exposed edges. Another curiosity of Saba is that, in spite of its being a Dutch island, scarcely one of its families has any links with the Netherlands, and the purest English in the Caribbean is spoken there. Saba is a social and architectural curiosity, with its houses on the windward side built so close together and on so steep a slope that it has been said that you step from the front door of one house onto the roof of the one below. That is an exaggeration, but it gives an idea of what the village looks like. Curious though Saba is, its possession is not a responsibility that has seriously disturbed the colonial administrators at The Hague.

During the nineteenth century, the islands repaired the damage that had been inflicted on them during the eighteenth. There was a great deal of damage to repair. Those of the towns that had not been destroyed by enemy action and civil war had been the victim of fires, hurricanes and earthquakes. Usually the forts guarding each harbor were the only survivals of the original colonization. Havana looked more Spanish than Spain itself, but otherwise, in the whole Caribbean, with the partial exception of the capitals of the Danish islands, there were only two cities that bore unmistakably the stamp of their first founders—Willemstad in Curaçao and Saint-Pierre in Martinique.

Curaçao had had a special history. When the navigation acts of Britain and France drove the Dutch to regard their Caribbean possessions as trading bases rather than colonies, Curaçao was advantageously placed to conduct illegal traffic along the Spanish Main. The Spanish governors, fettered by the bureaucrats of Seville, found the proximity of Curaçao's harbors not only useful but lucrative. They did nothing to hinder its activities. It became a smuggler's paradise, a black-market slave market, a rendezvous for revolutionaries and various stormy petrels. The Dutch did their best to maintain their neutrality. For the most part they succeeded. On the two occasions when they failed, Curaçao was fortunately sited geographically. She did not interfere with the belligerents. In the American War of Independence she avoided the fate of St. Eustatius; twenty-five years later, in the Napoleonic period, she slipped easily and painlessly into British hands. There was no fighting.

In another way, too, Curaçao has been lucky geographically. It is a low, flat island that has not attracted storms and has lain out of the path of hurricanes, so that the modern traveler, when his ship swings round toward the harbor to a pontoon bridge, guarding an entrance so narrow that the sentries can talk across it, finds himself a few minutes later looking down on a succession of Dutch eighteenth-century houses, pastel-colored with white scrolls upon the rounded gables, with steep tiled roofs, chunky dormers and baroque parapets. He will imagine himself in The Hague or Amsterdam; but to reassure him that he is actually in the tropics he will hear spoken in the streets a language that bears no relation to anything he has heard before. It is called Papiamento and it is a pepper pot of a language—a mixture of Spanish, Dutch, Indian, African and Hebrew. All these races have at one time taken root here; the first real settlers were, in fact, the Jews who had been expelled from Portugal. The Jewish cemetery, started in 1650, is the oldest Caucasian burial ground in the Americas, and the synagogue, with its stout mahogany pews, is one of the most impressive buildings in the city; but there are also stern Dutch churches and there are señoras in black mantillas, their prayer books in their hands, returning from morning mass. That was Willemstad in the last decade of the nineteenth century, that is Willemstad in the middle of the twentieth.

Eastward and northward, on the other side of the Caribbean, lay during those days the one other city that had survived disaster—Saint-Pierre in Martinique. The fighting, fierce and consistent though it had been in Martinique, had been concentrated upon Fort Royal, whose name was later changed to Fort de France. Fort Royal was the capital of the island; it was fortified; it had a harbor, whereas Saint-Pierre was unfortified on an open roadstead. The French often had two centers in their islands; a capital, the administrative center and the official residence of the governor, and a secondary, commercial center; Saint-Pierre was that, but it was much more than that; it might be the business center, it was also the social center.

Set on the leeward coast, thirty miles north of Fort Royal, in an amphitheater of towering hills, under the shadow of Mont Pelé, Saint-Pierre was the loveliest city in the West Indies. The loveliest and the gayest. All day its narrow streets were bright with color; in sharp anglings of light the amber sunshine streamed over the red tiled roofs, the lemon-colored walls, the green shutters, the green verandas. The streets ran steeply, "breaking into steps as streams break into waterfalls." Moss grew between the stones. There was no such thing as silence in Saint-Pierre. There was always the sound of water, of fountains in the hidden gardens, of rainwater in the runnels, and through the music of that water, the water that kept the town cool during the long noon heat, there throbbed ceaselessly, from the hills beyond, the murmur of the lizard and the cricket. A lovely city, with its theater, its lamplit avenues, its *jardin des plantes*, its schooners drawn circlewise along the harbor. Life was comely there; the life that had been built up by the old French *émigrés*. It was a city of carnival. There was a culture there, a love of art among those people who had made their home there, who had not come to Martinique to make money that they could spend in Paris, and who had not had their traditions destroyed during the Revolution. The culture of Versailles was transposed there to mingle with the Carib stock and the dark mysteries of imported Africa. Saint-Pierre was never seen without emotion. It laid hold of the imagination. It had something to say, not only to romantic intellectuals like Hearn or Stacpoole, but to the sailors and the traders, to all those whom the routine of livelihood brought within the limit of its sway. "Incomparable," they would say as they waved farewell to the *pays des revenants*, knowing that if they did not return they would carry all their lives a regret for it in their hearts. Such was Saint-Pierre as the century waned.

CHAPTER XVI

Cuba—The Ever-Faithful Isle

For the Caribbean area as a whole, the nineteenth century was a period of gradual decay, but for one island it was a period of growth and drama; and that island, contrarily, was the very one that had been least affected by the turbulence of the seventeenth and eighteenth centuries. Cuba's history is curious, its destiny lying apart from that both of the Spanish-American empire and the Caribbean islands.

After its discovery by Columbus there had been a brief period of prosperity, when its mines were believed to be the repository of fantastic wealth, but the discovery of real wealth on the Central and South American mainlands soon depopulated it of men, horses and money. Its value for Spain lay from then on in the port of Havana, where the silver fleets could assemble. The mainland was neglected, with Santiago serving as a smugglers' base. So neglected indeed was the eastern section of the island, that it might well have been taken over by the French or British and split into a divided ownership, as Hispaniola was.

The African slave trade, as far as Spain was concerned, was based on Havana, but Cuba itself had little need of slaves, being occupied with cattle, and those of the original Indians who had not perished in the mines were declared free. The economy was allowed to disintegrate, the officials quarreled among themselves, and such little prosperity as the island enjoyed was the outcome of illegal traffic with privateers. In 1655, indeed, the colonists presented the King of Spain with a shipload of goods, to purchase his pardon for their smuggling offenses.

Until the eighteenth century, its only commerce was in hides and skins. Then tobacco was cultivated and bees were imported from Florida. But the tobacco trade was so hampered by trade monopolies that there were two uprisings, in 1717 and 1723. For a period, Havana served as a shipbuilding center, but Spain stopped the trade because it interfered with her other interests. As the eighteenth-century sugar boom increased, the development of coffee and sugar estates began, but in such a restricted form that when the British captured Havana in 1762 the island only possessed thirty-two thousand slaves.

In another aspect, too, Cuba differed from the other islands; its climate was far more temperate than that of Jamaica, Hispaniola and the Lesser Antilles. In Havana, the temperature never reached 100°; in January it went below 50°, and the average temperature during the four hottest months was 80°. This, as has been previously pointed out, made it possible for Europeans, particularly for Spaniards who were accustomed to the heat of Andalusia, to perform manual labor; a capacity that was to prove of great importance when the cigar trade was developed, since slave labor could not have acquired the technical skill that was needed for the rolling of the tobacco leaf. Cuba was able therefore to offer employment to Spaniards who were destitute in their own country. When Froude visited Havana in 1880, he was astonished at the small proportion of Negroes that he saw in the streets.

It has been already pointed out that Cuba's course was redirected after its capture by the British in the Seven Years' War. The occupation only lasted for a few months, but during that time the British acquired a taste for the Havana cigar, and the eyes of the Cubans were opened to their own possibilities. They recognized the advantages of less restricted trading with European powers and also they obtained enough slaves to develop their own sugar estates. In 1760, Cuba exported thirteen thousand boxes of sugar, in 1770 fifty thousand, in 1789 seventy thousand, and in 1824 a quarter of a million.

During the last decade of the eighteenth and the first decade of the nineteenth century, circumstances combined to hasten Cuba's prosperity. Cuba had always presented a refuge to certain types of European. A number of Irish, after the Battle of the Boyne, took rank in the Spanish army and made their homes in Cuba, founding families with such surnames as O'Reilly, O'Donnell, O'Farrell and O'Lawlor, and there was now a considerable immigration both of capital and personnel. Soon after the outbreak of the French Revolution, the Spanish section of Hispaniola was ceded to the French, and many of the Spanish planters sought refuge in Cuba, just as they had done a hundred and forty years earlier when Jamaica was captured by the British. Later, when the slaves rose against the French, many of the survivors crossed to Cuba. Settling mainly in the southwestern section of the island, they brought with them their experience and skill as agriculturists, and the province of Oriente was soon rich with coffee. Cuba at this point also offered a satisfactory refuge for Spaniards at odds with their own government. A couple of liberal-minded governors provided scope for the Cubans to develop their own industries without excessive government interference; and when Simon Bolivar lit the fires of rebellion in Central and South America, Cuba did not follow the example of Colombia and Venezuela. In consequence, many conservative Spanish planters who did not approve of the new regimes emigrated to Cuba, and when Napoleon set his nephew on the throne of Spain, Cuba remained loyal to the royal house, earning the title of "the ever-faithful isle." Cuba seemed more contented with its lot than any Spanish-speaking territory in the New World, though it must be remembered that the fact of its being an island made it very difficult for the revolutionaries to attack it. The colonies on the mainland were far more vulnerable.

In 1815 Cuba was in a fate-favored position, and in fact her prosperity did mount progressively through the century. In 1851, for example, she produced six million hundredweight of sugar, whereas all the British West Indian islands put together did not export three million hundredweight; and in addition to sugar she had her tobacco crop and, in a lesser degree, coffee, until the competition from Brazil became too great. She was better equipped than any of the other islands to meet the slump caused by the end of the slave trade and the subsequent emancipation of the slaves, because though the slave trade had been forbidden, and Spain had been paid a substantial recompense for her losses through its closure, she used her compensation money to purchase from Russia five ships-of-the-line and eight frigates, and she continued to transact steady business with the illegal traders. The Havana customs house records the entrance of 116,000 slaves during the second decade of the century, and statisticians estimate that between 1811 and 1825 very nearly 200,000 slaves were admitted. Nor did Spain later follow the example of her European neighbors in emancipating the slaves. The population at the turn of the century was estimated at 275,000. But the census of 1817 gave 290,021 whites, 225,259 slaves and 115,091 free colored, and these figures should probably be increased by twenty-five percent, since census figures are unreliable, and a planter's taxes were based on the number of his slaves.

In addition, Spain imported a number of Chinese coolies. They came without proper contracts. They were sold to the planters for four hundred dollars each. They received four dollars each a month for eight years' service. Their masters presumed that by the time their eight years were up they would be so heavily in debt that they would have to stay on as long as they possessed the power to work. They did not bring their womenfolk with them, so that there was no possibility of their settling in the island. It is not surprising that the Jamaican sugar planters looked enviously across the water, complaining that they were subjected to unfair competition.

And indeed, the paper profits of the island soared prodigiously throughout the first half of the century. At the same time, the island itself was in a constant state of ferment, industrial and political, for which the disturbed condition of Spain herself was in large part responsible. The bare details of Spain's history over this period speak for themselves.

Spain has not been lucky in her kings, and Ferdinand VII, who occupied the throne when Napoleon was turning his attention toward the Iberian Peninsula, was one of her least creditable. His country was at the time disturbed by a persistent conflict between the resolve of the court to rule despotically, with a truncated *Cortes* presenting a semblance of constitutional authority, and the growing popular demand for a more democratic form of government. Ferdinand, thinking that he could exploit Napoleon's interest in Spain to his own advantage, begged the Emperor for a Bonaparte bride. "I venture to say," he wrote, "that this union and the public announcement of my intentions which I will make to Europe if Your Majesty permits, will exercise a salutary influence on the destiny of Spain and deprive a blind and angry people of the pretext for deluging their fatherland in blood, in the name of their prince, the heir of their ancient dynasty, who has been converted by a solemn treaty, by his own choice and by the most glorious of all adoptions, into a French prince and a son of Your Imperial Majesty."

Napoleon, however, preferred to place his nephew on the throne of Spain, and Ferdinand became a king in exile; in which situation, to rally his subjects to his defense, he issued in 1812 a new constitution that was later to become one of the chief points of issue between the contending parties. No sooner had British arms, with the gallant cooperation of Spanish patriots, driven the French out of Spain and restored the monarchy, than Ferdinand revoked the new constitution and Spain was split in two. In 1815 the Congress of Vienna confirmed Ferdinand's reaccession, but the country was already divided against itself, and committed to a condition of civil war that at the time of writing must still be regarded as being not dead but dormant. Within five years, a minor revolution made Ferdinand a prisoner in the hands of the *Cortes*, and the chaos was so complete that France and Russia decided, in the name of the Holy Alliance, to intervene on his behalf. Ferdinand promised a liberal government if he was restored to power, but no sooner was he his own master than, under the protection of French bayonets, he delivered himself to an orgy of reprisals. The general who had led the usurping government was dragged through the streets in a basket, at a donkey's tail, before being hanged and quartered as a felon.

Ferdinand lived until 1853, and he was to leave behind him a politically inflammable situation. His first three marriages had left him without an heir, and his brother Don Carlos was heir presumptive; but a fourth marriage, contracted a few years before his death with a very young woman, produced two daughters; the succession of the elder daughter led to the Carlist wars.

The issue turned on the Salic law, by which a woman was not allowed to ascend a throne. That law had never been operative in a country which owed so much to Isabella of Castile. Philip V, the first Spanish Bourbon, had limited the succession to male heirs "by pragmatic sanction," which meant by his own order. This enactment was irregular, was never registered by the *Cortes* and was protested by the council of Seville. Carlos IV, the father of Ferdinand, revoked the enactment, but never published his revocation, when several sons secured the succession. Ferdinand published his father's revocation, but when his daughters were born the extreme clerical party urged him to restore Philip V's enactment. In a moment of extreme ill health he agreed to do so, and Don Carlos was accepted by him and the nation as his heir. But on the recovery of his health he revoked the Salic law and appointed his wife, Doña Maria Christina, as the regent. The consequent Carlist wars lasted intermittently for thirty-five years.

The young princesses were brought up in a curious atmosphere. Their mother had been a dutiful and loyal wife, but she was still a young woman, and within a few weeks she had contracted a morganatic marriage with a private soldier. The union produced four children, but as the law did not allow her to remarry, she could not officially be pregnant. She had to display tact, courage and discretion to carry out her official duties, as she did, punctiliously, through this period.

In 1843 Isabella II assumed the power of the throne, and the intrigues of European diplomacy to find appropriate husbands for the two sisters figure in history as "the case of the Spanish Marriages." Louis Philippe was anxious that his son Montpensier should be her consort, but Britain opposed the match. Louis Philippe's failure to effect this marriage was a contributory cause to the loss of his own throne. Had Isabella married his son, it would have been better both for her and Spain, and possibly for Europe. Eventually she married an effeminate, weak, degenerate Bourbon, Francisco de Asis, Duke of Asis. Isabella was disgusted at the choice that had been forced on her. "What," she complained, "shall I say of a man who, on his wedding night, wears more lace than I?" When many years later they paid a state visit to Paris and were received in Versailles by Louis Napoleon, the Duke, ignoring the court that was gathered to honor him, anxiously inquired, "Where is Lambert?" Lambert had been the Duke's valet on an earlier informal visit. *Où est Lambert?* became one of the jokes of the boulevards. Doña Maria Christina told him that he was not worthy of lying in her daughter's bed, but in point of fact this privilege was soon denied him, and Isabella consoled herself with a succession of lovers. One of the later ones, a lieutenant of Engineers, Antonio Perez Motlo, is believed to be the father of the son who became Alfonso XII. On one occasion, when the Queen was closeted with her lieutenant, with the door guarded by her Prime Minister and her A.D.C., the King and the Minister of War demanded access to the royal suite. Access was denied them, and a duel ensued in which the A.D.C. and the Minister of War were killed. The deaths were reported as being from natural causes. And all the time the Carlist war was draining the reserves of the country, like a running sore.

Eventually, in 1868, Isabella left the country and signed an act of abdication, in favor of her son. There followed a confused period of massacres and mutinies, with generals issuing *pronunciamentos*; there were regencies; there was a republican interlude; an Italian prince, the second son of Victor Emmanuel, sat briefly on the throne but soon resigned. It was not till the accession of Alfonso XII in 1874 that the country saw any order. By then, as far as Cuba was concerned, it was too late.

Sixty years of domestic chaos had had their inevitable repercussions on the only important colony that was left to Spain. In the uncertain period that followed Waterloo, several European nations had their eyes on Cuba. When Spain ceded Florida to the U.S.A., Britain, who had once owned Florida and had yielded Cuba in 1763 in exchange for it, felt that she should now be given Cuba as a recompense. Russia and France, when in the name of the Holy Alliance they restored Ferdinand to his throne, had an idea of suppressing some of the new Central and South American republics and themselves administering Spain's colonial possessions, but the U.S.A.'s concern over Cuba's welfare was more insistent. Cuba was her special problem. Jefferson had often asserted that Cuba lay too close to the mainland of the United States to be left with safety to a European nation. John Quincy Adams had termed its annexation "indispensable to the continuance and integrity of the Union itself," and when Russian and French interference in the Caribbean appeared imminent, Adams, as Secretary of State, drafted for his President the policy that became known as the Monroe Doctrine, namely, that "any attempt by a European power to extend their system to any portion of this hemisphere would be regarded as dangerous to our peace and comfort." That was in 1823, and six years later the U.S. ambassador in Madrid asserted that Cuba must belong to nobody but Spain. Eventually Europe accepted this doctrine; Spain, after all, could no longer damage them. The only interests that she was now in a position to damage were her own peace and comfort, and that she did in very ample measure where Cuba was concerned.

A great deal has been written about the tyranny to which Cuba was subjected during the nineteenth century. Much of this writing was of a biased propaganda nature, conducted partly by expatriate Cubans anxious to overthrow the regime and partly by Americans anxious to justify their own intervention; and it can be scarcely questioned that Spanish colonial maladministration reached its zenith in Cuba during the nineteenth century. Each victorious revolution sent out its supporters to govern the island, and each new governor undid his predecessor's work. Between 1837 and 1874 as many as twenty-six different captain generals were sent out to Puerto Rico.

Spain did her best according to her lights, and it can be argued that from the days of Isabella onward she had been the best intentioned of the colonizing powers. Her regulations for the management of slaves were, for instance, so humane that when Britain captured Trinidad, her planters wished to adopt the British regulations, as giving them greater powers, but were prevented from doing so by the antislavery committee. Spain always meant well, but a colonial system that was barely effective under a master bureaucrat like Philip II could only lead to chaos in the hands of narrow-minded, arrogant administrators who had been trained to believe that political office existed for the benefit of the officeholder. Spain had now become a third-rate power, with her empire diminished to an area of a few square miles. Yet her pride was as inflated as it had been in the days of Charles V. She behaved toward Cuba as though she were the recipient of a sacred mission.

Under Ferdinand VII a stringently reactionary policy was enforced. The Cubans had no democratic institutions. Absolute power was placed in the hands of the captain general, who, so the royal warrant affirmed, was "fully vested with the whole extent of power which by the Royal addresses is granted to the governors of besieged towns." Cuba was, in fact, treated as though it were in a state of war. The government was run from Spain. The Cuban had no vote, and no redress. No public career was open to him. He could not be a magistrate or hold a commission in the army or police force, nor could he enlist in the army as a private, as a black man could. He had to maintain through taxation the full cost of the Spanish administration, its army, its navy, its civil service and its priesthood. Judges could be deposed by the military chief. Spain encouraged its retired officers and officials to marry and settle in the island, to strengthen the occupying power. As conditions grew more straitened in Spain, the number of immigrants increased, many of them Catalan mechanics and small traders.

The fortunes of the Cubans depended on the whim of the captain general, one of whom informed his subjects that he was not here to promote the interests of the Cuban people, but to serve his master, the King. Much depended on the kinds of orders that were dispatched by that King and master, but more depended on the spirit with which they were interpreted by the man upon the spot. In point of fact, that particular governor, General Miguel Jacon, was not unpopular with the Cubans. He embellished Havana and laid out the Prado. He also had a sense of humor that appealed to the Spanish temperament; a sense of humor that was exemplified by his treatment of a wealthy count who had abducted a local girl, to the indignation both of the girl and of the man she had hoped to marry. Jacon summoned the pair to his presence and made the count marry the girl right away. He then ordered the count to return to his estates alone, having arranged that on his way back there he should be murdered; his wife therefore became a rich widow and was able to marry the man of her choice.

So omnipotent were the captain generals that as late as 1843 the

captain general of Puerto Rico was able to issue as reactionary an
edict as this.

"I, John Prim, Count of Reus, on account of the critical circumstances of the times and the afflictive condition of the countries in
the neighbourhood of this island, some of which are torn by civil
war and others engaged in a war of extermination between the white
and black races, find it incumbent on me to dictate efficacious measures to prevent the spread of these calamities to our pacific soil. I
have decreed as follows: All offences to be judged by court martial.
Any individual of African race, whether free or slave, who shall offer
armed resistance to a white, shall be shot if a slave and have his right
hand cut off by the public executioner if a free man. The owners of
slaves are authorised to correct and chastise them for slight mis-
demeanours without any civil or military functionary having the
right to interfere. If any slave shall rebel against his master the latter
is authorised to kill him on the spot."

There are those always who benefit from a rigid totalitarian regime, whether of the left or right, and the planters were far from dissatisfied with this subservience to Madrid, since it secured their own
survival, which was imperiled by the liberal and nationalistic ideas
that were in the air. They did not want an independent Cuba, which
would involve a freeing of the slaves. There was the example of Haiti
across the water. Many of them had come originally from Santo Domingo. They might grumble about the excessive level of taxation, but
they felt safe.

And indeed, for those who had property and position, the anach-
ronistic existence of the plantocracy was extremely pleasant. Many
visitors to the island testify to the beauty of Havana and the elegance of the life that was enjoyed there. Richard Henry Dana wrote
of the palaces in which the merchants conducted their affairs. The
staircases were as stately as that of Stafford House, the rooms were
high and floored with marble, the walls paneled with porcelain tiles.
Froude, too, was immensely impressed. Kingston had not one fine
building in it, but Havana was a city of palaces, of wide streets and
plazas, of colonnades and towers, of churches and monasteries.
"Whereas the English," he said, "had built as though they were passing visitors, wanting only tenements to be occupied for a time, the
Spaniards built as they built in Castile, built with the same material,
the white limestone, which they found in the old world as in the
new. The palaces of the nobles in Havana, the residence of the governor, the convents, the Cathedral are a reproduction of Burgos or

Valladolid as if by some Aladdin's lamp a Castilian city had been taken up and set down unaltered on the shore of the Caribbean Sea; and they carried with them their laws, their habits, their institutions and their creed, their religious orders, their bishops and their inquisition. . . . Whatever the eventual fate of Cuba, the Spaniards have taken root here."

There were, Froude said, ten times as many Spaniards in Cuba as there were British in the whole West Indies, and Havana itself was ten times larger than any city in the Caribbean. Most of the Spaniards lived in Havana itself; they called the rest of the island "the interior." The original coffee planters, many of whom were French refugees, had laid out their plantations as gardens, since coffee requires shade, and lived on their estates, but two hurricanes, in 1843 and 1845, and the competition of Brazilian coffee, coupled with the English free-trade policy, decided the planters to sow sugar instead; it is a crop that does not require shade, so the groves of fruit trees were cut down and the planters went to Havana.

The life that was lived there was completely Spanish, or at least Castilian, and most of the residents spoke Castilian. The visitor and resident of substance was called early for a light breakfast consisting of oranges and coffee. The coffee was taken without milk, since it was believed that milk was injurious when taken with oranges and bananas. Mass, which was attended by many, was at eight; breakfast was taken at ten; it was a heavy meat meal, preceded by sherry and accompanied by red Catalonian wine. An omelette was invariably served; the rice was excellent. Dinner was at three in the afternoon. Very similar to breakfast, it was followed by a siesta. The cool of the evening was devoted to pleasure-driving. At eight o'clock a band would play for an hour, and the streets round the main square were lined with carriages, in which ladies reclined to receive the compliments of their masculine admirers. It was not considered proper for a lady of quality to walk in the streets. The late evening, when the music ceased, was devoted to shopping and paying calls. Windows were deep and large, with wide gratings and no glass. In the chief room of the house, rows of chairs were placed, facing each other, three to five in each row, at right angles to the street. Women sat opposite the men. There was no supper, though occasionally coffee and cakes would be served last thing at night.

Cockfighting was one of the town's main diversions. Meals in restaurants and hotels were interrupted by the importunities of lottery-ticket vendors. The rewarding of beggars was made awkward by the absence of small coins. There were no streetwalkers.

It was a leisured and gracious way of living, and the richer planters accepted the strict regulations that were imposed on them as the price they had to pay for this leisured graciousness. They would regard as a salutary warning to the masses the chain gang which passed regularly along the streets, each man with an iron band round his ankles, another round his waist, a chain fastened to each wrist, so that every movement clanked. The prisons might be foul, the standard of education low, but the conditions of the proletariat were no concern of theirs. There was a law insisting that no stranger could be the guest at a friend's house without permission of the magistrate; they considered this precaution prudent. On the sugar estates the male slaves outnumbered the women by four to one, and during the sugar season the slaves were worked harder than they had ever been on the British and French plantations. They were allowed only four hours of sleep, with an hour off for dinner and half an hour for breakfast. The night was divided into two equal watches. Work never ceased. But there was little flogging. Solitary confinement on bread and water was the most serious punishment.

It was a way of life that might have been maintained had not Spain herself been in such a disordered state, had not the proximity of the United States and the concern that the United States very naturally felt over Cuba's fortunes been a constant source of complication. The United States had indeed ample occasion to be concerned.

In 1836, when the Carlist wars were raging, the Queen Regent, Christina, in her desperate need for funds, nearly sold Cuba, Puerto Rico and the Philippines to France. The agreement had been indeed drawn up and was ready for signature when Louis Philippe tried to haggle for a better bargain. The Spanish ambassador, in a fit of wounded pride, tore up the document. Had it been signed, its implementation would have been a violation of the Monroe Doctrine, and would have placed the U.S.A. in an extremely awkward position. The fact that it had been prepared made the State Department acutely aware of how very inflammable a situation existed ninety miles from its own boundaries.

For the next sixty years it was a problem that Washington was never permitted to forget. Though the rich planters of Cuba, apart from certain amply justified reservations, might be well enough content, there was a large and growing dissident majority. The many Cubans who did not own profitable estates resented the illiberal regime. A Masonic lodge, *Soles y Ravos de Bolivar*, fanned their discontent. A secret society called The Black Eagle had its headquarters in Mexico. The example of the Central and South American republics inspired them to action. The slaves were well aware that their fellows in the neighboring islands had been freed. The one section of the Spanish administration that was efficient was the security branch of the police. It acted swiftly and ruthlessly. In 1844, on the merest suspicion that a revolt was being planned, a number of slaves were tortured and, on the strength of the confessions wrung from them, there was an intimidating series of executions.

A number of Cubans fled to America, many of them to become citizens, and from this base a war of propaganda was directed against the Spanish authorities. The most prominent of these exiles was Narcisso Lopez, a Venezuelan, who had risen to high rank in the Spanish army, had married a Cuban and planned to settle there, but was so irked by the autocracy of the regime that he emigrated to the United States. He was a vivid, dramatic personality; dashing, handsome, electric. Women found him irresistible. He claimed that he could press a horse to death between his knees. He was not content to fulminate on paper. His aim was the launching of a rebellion, and he toured the country, appealing for arms and money. Finally he sailed from New Orleans with eight hundred American adventurers. He made a landing and captured a railway station and a small town, but the Cubans did not rise to welcome him as he had expected, and he was forced to reembark.

His exploit created a diplomatic issue between Spain and the U.S.A., and on his return to Florida he was arrested. He had become, however, a national hero, and was soon released to continue his private war against the country of his first allegiance. He toured the United States appealing for arms and volunteers, and soon had another mission ready. This time he was prevented from sailing by federal officers. But he was not deterred, and in 1859 he was again ready to sail, this time with a young American, W. E. Crittenden, a graduate of West Point who had been decorated during the Mexican war. The security of this expedition was lamentable. Lopez was outwitted by the Spaniards at every point. They misled him as to the amount of support he could expect; they sent him forged letters, purporting to come from dissatisfied Cubans, advising him to land in the west instead of the east. The Spaniards prepared the trap and baited it. They knew the hour of his sailing. He coaled at Key West and landed at Bahia Hondas. He left Crittenden on the shore, with half his force, and went inland with the remainder. He was accorded the welcome of Holofernes. He was hospitably received, well dined and wined, and while he slept messengers were sent to the nearest military authorities. His men were shot and he was garroted. Crittenden, on the shore, receiving no news from Lopez, assumed that the landing was a failure and set out to sea in open boats. He was captured and he and his men were shot. Crittenden met his death bravely. He refused to kneel with his back to the firing party. "I kneel only to God," he said.

His execution roused the American public to indignation. But there was nothing that Washington could do. Spain was within her rights. But Crittenden's courage and the brutality of Lopez' killing alienated public opinion in the U.S.A. to an extent that Spain could ill afford.

Public opinion had already been strained a few months earlier, by the incident of the *Black Warrior*, a cargo boat that plied between Mobile and New York. In Havana its master had failed to submit the right kind of manifest, and the Spaniards threatened to confiscate the cargo. Technically, Spain was within her rights, but she was, once again, quibbling over a technicality, and the master of the *Black Warrior* was following the general custom of the trade in not submitting a manifest in the manner stipulated by the regulations. After diplomatic representations, the *Black Warrior* was allowed to proceed upon its business. But the incident aggravated the state of tension.

The U.S. ambassador in Madrid who made these representations was a Louisianian, Pierre Soulé, and it was Soulé who a little later drew up, in company with the U.S. ambassador to Britain and James Buchanan, the U.S. ambassador to France, a document that was known as the Ostend Manifesto, recommending that the U.S. should offer 120,000,000 dollars for Cuba, and that if this offer was refused, appropriate the island in terms of "the manifest destiny" of the U.S.A.; France and Britain were engaged in the Crimean War and the opportunity seemed appropriate.

Spain indignantly rejected the proposal, or rather the prospect of the proposal, and the Secretary of State also dismissed it as "a robber doctrine I abhor." But its drafting was to have important repercussions. The President at the time was Pierce, a Republican. Tension between the north and south was mounting; the parties were mustering their forces; and the Democrats were toying with the idea of enlisting the support of Cuba as a slave-owning state. A number of Cuban planters were attracted by the idea. Could not a free Cuba follow the example of a free Texas? Buchanan, by endorsing the Ostend Manifesto, proved to his fellow Democrats that he was in favor of the annexation of Cuba. This was to stand him in good stead in the Democratic convention in Charleston. Up till this point, Douglas had seemed the favored candidate. Douglas was a man of parts and power who had first attracted attention by his championing of Andrew Jackson and his insistence on the restoration to Jackson of the fine that had been imposed on him after the battle of New Orleans. But at the Democratic convention, in the changed climate of approaching conflict, he was outmaneuvered by Buchanan. Buchanan won the nomination and was elected. He was not a failure as a President; an obese bachelor, he was socially a great success, and entertained the future Edward VII in a manner that that exacting gourmand thoroughly appreciated, but he was not the man of destiny that the hour required. Four years later he retired from the public scene. No one can tell to what heights a man may rise if circumstance "puts the sword into his hand"; if Douglas had won the nomination, he might have held the fort for the Democrats in 1861. Had he done so, the course of history would have been different. At this point, as so often in the past, the politics of the West Indies affected the drama of a larger stage.

For the four years of war between the States, Cuba's concerns lay outside the story of the U.S.A. Cuban interests lay with the Confederates, and her harbors were extremely useful to them; so useful that the State Department felt that it must have some protection for its trade in the Caribbean, particularly after the episode of the *Alabama*. There was serious talk, after the war, of her purchasing the Danish Virgin Islands. The Danes believed, indeed, that the deal was going through, and proclamations from Charles X were posted in the streets of St. Thomas, St. John and St. Croix, announcing the conditions of the take-over, but, under a new administration, Congress did not endorse the bargain, and once again the Cuban issue filled the center of the stage.

It was to remain there till the century's close. In 1868 a revolution broke out in Spain and Isabella was deposed. This was the signal for a revolt in Cuba, and a civil war began that was to last ten years. It was a war of murder and destruction as ruthless as the 1936–1939 civil war in Spain. The rebels freed the slaves, without compensation to the owners, not on humanitarian grounds but to swell their own ranks. There was no quarter on either side. Women enlisted as soldiers in the

Cuban army because they felt that that was the safest place for them to be. The Spanish forces greatly outnumbered the Cubans; they were better trained and better armed; but the government made the mistake of sending out infantry instead of the cavalry, which would have been better suited to the terrain. Spanish generalship was also at fault in organizing a series of defensive zones which involved the splitting up of their forces into small groups which provided easy targets for the Cuban guerrillas, who were expert horsemen and wielded their cutlasses with pitiless skill. A smaller army might have done better. The Spaniards were, moreover, more vulnerable to tropical diseases than the Cubans, and a fifth of their casualties were due to fever. The governor, Valmaseda, was as fierce as any of his conquistador predecessors. He issued a series of proclamations as a warning to civilians; any unoccupied house was burned, any occupied house had to fly the white flag of surrender.

The contest was watched with the closest attention in the U.S.A. With the war between the States ended, the Southerners no longer needed a slave-owning state as an ally, but Cuba lay too close to the United States for its concerns to be ignored. The sympathies of the country lay with the rebels. There was the long tradition of support for any colony striving to free itself from the overlordship of colonial masters. The Spaniards were slave owners. A number of exiled Cubans toured the country appealing for arms and funds; a number of Americans enlisted in the Cuban army, while the more prudent lined their pockets with the proceeds of blockade-running. Relations between Spain and the U.S.A. grew strained. Nor can it be denied that Spain had many causes for complaint. It was estimated that during the ten years of war thirty thousand Cubans emigrated to the U.S.A. and changed their nationality; many of them then returned to Cuba, demanding protection as American citizens. The American authorities were clearly making no attempt to prevent their nationals from supplying the rebels with arms, money and supplies. Spain announced that she would treat as pirates any gunrunners that she captured, and was soon provided with an opportunity of showing that she was not threatening idly.

During the war between the States, a British firm had built two sister ships as gunrunners, the *Virginius* and the *Tornado*. The *Tornado* was bought by Spain. The *Virginius* was sold in the United States, apparently to a private trading company. With her papers seemingly in order, she sailed out of New York in 1871, with an American captain and crew, and flying the stars and stripes. Two years later she was chased in the open sea by the *Tornado*. Her speed should have been equal to her sister's, but it was many months since she had been overhauled, and her engines were in a faulty state. She jettisoned much of her cargo; lacking fuel, she plied her engines with fried fat, the smoke from which facilitated her pursuit; eventually she was caught before she could reach a neutral harbor, and was brought back a captive to Santiago.

She was flying an American flag; her master, Captain Fry, was an American, so were the majority of his crew. She was carrying a hundred passengers. She was ostensibly plying between Curaçao and Jamaica, but her cargo contained arms and contraband. Her papers were not in order. It was evident that she was operating under instructions from the Cuban rebels. According to the instructions that he had received from Madrid, it was the duty of the officer in charge, General Burriel, to treat her as a privateer.

The case aroused the greatest excitement. The U.S.A. was in a difficult position. Captain Fry had been trading illegally, but he was captured on the open sea, and it was the laws of the U.S.A., not of Spain, that he had infringed. But Burriel was not the man to be deterred by a legalistic quibble. The trial was perfunctory; the crew was sentenced to be shot. They were lined up on their knees, with their backs to the firing squad; Captain Fry, whose sentence was not to be carried out till the following day, walked along the line, bidding each member of his crew farewell. When the shooting was over, the heads were severed from the bodies and impaled, while the trunks were trampled on by horses. G. W. Sherman, of the *New York Herald*, was imprisoned for four days for attempting to sketch the scene, and Ralph Keeler, a well-known writer who had gone down as a reporter, disappeared and was never seen again. It was generally believed that the Spaniards had had him murdered.

That night Captain Fry wrote a farewell letter to his wife that, although obviously written for posthumous publication, is not unmoving. "Calmly seated on a beautiful moonlight night in a most beautiful bay in Cuba," it began.

Next morning Captain Fry marched calmly with his fellow officers to his execution. He was fortunate in that the first volley proved mortal for him, since the marksmanship of the firing squad was vacillating and most of the victims had to be finished off by an officer's revolver. Among the men who marched with Captain Fry was the second engineer, who had assured his captors that he had meddled with the engine so that the ship might be overtaken by the

Tornado. He was promised his freedom, but was told that in order to prevent his fellows from learning of his treachery he should march with them to the point of execution. But either through bad shooting, carelessness, faulty orders or official contempt for treachery, he met the same fate as the others. He died protesting violently.

A number of passengers, and a few members of the crew, still awaited sentence, but at this point a surprising intervention occurred. Admiral Lorraine, a British naval officer in charge of the squadron at Jamaica, brought a man-of-war into Santiago and assured the authorities that he would shell their city if there were any further executions. He eventually secured the release of the survivors. On his arrival in New York he could scarcely be given an official welcome, but in private he was treated as a hero, and the wild men of Nevada sent him from the Comstock mines a silver nugget with the message, "Sir, you are a brick."

Throughout the U.S.A. there was an outburst of indignation; the Spanish Minister of State rejected the U.S.A.'s first protest with "serene energy," but eventually Madrid disowned the action and paid an indemnity of eighty thousand dollars to the families of the victims. It refused, however, to make any reparation to the Stars and Stripes, which the U.S.A. claimed had been insulted. Spain argued that it was Captain Fry who had insulted the flag by using it as a cover for surreptitious and illegal trading. Eventually the matter was allowed to drop, and the *Virginius* was released. She was not, however, to reach American soil. A hurricane struck her east of Florida. She perished, but without loss of life. Spain, though she had officially disowned General Burriel, promoted him.

Before the ten years of war ended, another incident was to lower the prestige of Spain. The grave in Havana of a pro-Spanish editor was desecrated, and forty students were suspected of the outrage. They were brought to trial, but there was no evidence against them and they were acquitted; this did not, however, suit the military authorities. The captain general ordered their rearrest; they were tried by a court-martial and found guilty. Every fifth one was shot as a warning to the community. The U.S.A. began to feel that it was more than uncomfortable to have so close a neighbor with so little regard for the laws of justice.

The civil war followed its course, with varying fortunes, with neither side quite strong enough to subdue the other. At last an uneasy truce, the outcome of boredom and exhaustion, was concluded.

The liberation of the slaves was confirmed, under a time clause. Cuba was promised representation in the *Cortes* and some share in the administration of its own affairs. There was an amnesty for the rebel leaders. On paper it looked a reasonable compromise, but Spain made little attempt to fulfill her obligations. Technically, Cuba was represented in the *Cortes,* but the voting was so manipulated that the seats were held by the puppets of the captain general. The level of taxation was maintained. When a Cuban received a prepaid letter, he was liable for additional postage. The island contributed twice as much per capita to the interest on Spain's national debt as a Spaniard did. Trade was so hampered by duties and restrictions that it was cheaper to send a sack of flour from Mississippi to Spain, pay duty on it there, then ship it back to Cuba, than send it straight to Havana. A trade agreement with the U.S.A. was signed in 1891 but withdrawn in 1894. And all the time, refugees from Cuba were working up anti-Spanish propaganda. Even though the Spanish throne itself seemed relatively stable, most visitors to Cuba felt that beneath the calm prosperity of its cane fields and tobacco plantations danger waited.

It came unexpectedly, without warning, and for no special cause in 1895. At first the Spaniards took the revolt lightly, and one officer complained that it was a bore having to hunt mountain goats, but the opposition was stronger now than it had been in 1869. The Cubans were convinced that Spain was resolved to deny them a fair constitution. Spain had not counted on the amount of ill feeling that she had engendered in the U.S.A. She also did not know that at the close of her tenure in the Caribbean she was to be opposed to a buccaneer every bit as ruthless as any of those who from Tortuga had harried her silver fleets.

In New York, William Randolph Hearst was in the saddle, and he was ready to exploit to its full the mounting clamor in the country to be rid of this menace on its doorstep. Grover Cleveland was at the White House; he had said that "Cuba is so close to us as to be hardly separated from our territory." But Cleveland was a Democrat, and opposed to war. Theodore Roosevelt describes him as having "no more backbone than a chocolate éclair."

Hearst was concerned with the publicity of his newspapers. He sent down Richard Harding Davis as his chief reporter, and Remington to illustrate his stories. The Spaniards were waging the war with a brutal ruthlessness. General Weyler's little finger was thicker than Valmaseda's loins. He organized a system of concentration camps

*—recontentrados—*into which the inhabitants of whole areas were herded and allowed to perish of hunger and neglect. In his search for suspects, neither sex nor race were respected. Hearst double-headlined as the truth each fresh rumor of atrocities. Pulitzer watched with alarm the rise of the *Journal's* sales, and harried his reporters on the *World* to outdo his rival. Had there been no Hearst, Pulitzer might well have used his influence in favor of peace. The journalists were in a most difficult position. They were not allowed to visit the front; they had to stay in a hotel in Havana, relying on official handouts and rumors from insurgents. The censorship was extremely strict. At one point Remington cabled Hearst: "Everything is quiet. There is no trouble here. There will be no war. I wish to return." Hearst cabled back: "Please remain. You furnish the pictures. I'll furnish the war."

Eventually Remington sent up a picture, portraying three young women being stripped naked in the presence of gloating soldiers. The picture was accompanied by a story under Davis' signature, explaining that the women were suspected of carrying secret information and that the search had taken place on an American ship. The public was indignant, but not nearly as indignant as the three young ladies were on their arrival in New York when they were shown the picture. They had been searched, they protested, in the privacy of their cabins, and by female policewomen.

Pulitzer made the most of his rival's slip, but Hearst was not deterred. He was soon exploiting the predicament of a Cuban Joan of Arc, who had been flung into prison because, Hearst maintained, she had resisted the advances of a Spanish colonel. In vain did the Spaniards protest that the woman was a baggage anyhow. The spirit of American chivalry was roused. Hearst scooped Pulitzer and his other rivals by sending down a commando raid to rescue her from prison.

The war followed its guerrilla course; once again, neither side was strong enough to subdue the other, but this time neither side was prepared to compromise. Weyler, "the brute," was recalled and a more humane captain general was appointed in his place; but the system of *recontentrados* was continued. The tempo of Hearst's editorials grew more belligerent, while a *World* journalist was screaming, "American citizens are imprisoned and slain without trial. Blood on the roadside, blood in the fields, blood on the doorsteps. Blood, blood, blood."

For many years, lawlessness had thrived in the country districts, and no man had ridden there unarmed. Now even the towns became unsafe, and the U.S.A., to protect the lives and properties of its citizens, sent down one of its men-of-war, the *Maine*, on a friendly mission to anchor in Havana harbor. On the night of February 15, 1898 she was blown up, and 286 sailors were drowned. No explanation of this disaster has been found. Spain immediately sent a message of sympathy to Washington, and the American consul at Havana cabled that "public opinion should be suspended until further report," but Hearst and Pulitzer were baying for blood and McKinley was now at the White House. The politicians in Washington were as much in the dark as the journalists in Havana. Senators, indeed, relied for their information on "eyewitness" reports written from hotel lounges. The American ambassador in Havana was anti-Spanish. Spain was ready to compromise to a point deeply humiliating to her pride, and the American ambassador in Madrid pleaded her case with Washington. But Madrid was many thousand miles away. The Senate was almost equally divided, though the pro-war majority in the House was overwhelming. Had McKinley been firm, he might have won over the four senators whose votes would have turned the scale. But McKinley was weak, and Hearst got his war.

It was a comic-opera kind of war, as far as any operation can be described as comic in which men are being killed and maimed. If the Cubans and Spaniards had been left to fight it out between themselves, the war might have dragged on for twenty years, but Spain, from a distance of three thousand miles, was ill-equipped to match "the might, majesty, dominion and power" of the United States. She fought, however, with her traditional pride and courage. In the far Pacific, Admiral Dewey in a single morning and with the loss of seven lives destroyed the batteries of Manila and the ships at anchor in the harbor, but the Spanish fleet under Admiral Cervera, which was based on home waters, was to cause a good deal of trouble. When war broke out, it was refueling in the Canaries, and for several days the American fleet was uncertain of its whereabouts. The eastern seaboard was considerably disturbed. A hostile flotilla was capable of inflicting heavy damage upon unprotected towns. Rumor succeeded upon rumor, but at last it was learned that the fleet had eluded the protective cordon and slipped into Santiago. The Americans did not know how powerful a fleet was to be opposed to them, and one of the most daring and skillful exploits of the war was undertaken by a young naval officer, Victor Blue, who landed down the coast, alone, climbed the hills above the harbor, and brought back the news that five cruisers and two torpedo boats were anchored there.

As a countermeasure, the admiral in charge of the U.S. fleet conceived the ingenious idea of sinking an anchored coaling ship across the narrow 350-foot entrance to the harbor, thus imprisoning the Spanish fleet. It was the same device that the Spanish had practiced against Drake three centuries before in Puerto Rico, and he entrusted this mission to Lt. Richmond Hobson, a twenty-seven-year-old officer born in Alabama, youngest member and head of his class of '89, who later was to propose and conduct a postgraduate course in naval architecture at Annapolis. It was a most dangerous mission, the chances of survival were small. Hobson, with six companions, wore underclothes, life preservers and revolvers at the waist. The ship, the *Merrimac*, was loaded with coal. It was Hobson's plan to shatter the hull with small torpedoes as soon as the ship was anchored across the entrance. He started immediately after moonset.

Every battery in the harbor opened fire on him; the steam launch of the *New York*, which had followed to pick up survivors, was forced to retire. The rudder and stern anchor of the *Merrimac* were shot away. It was impossible for Hobson to anchor her where he had intended. The ship drifted past the narrow neck.

Hobson and his crew had been instructed to leap from the deck as soon as the ship began to sink, and make for the rowboat, but the fire was so intense that he felt that it would be unwise for them to show themselves. He therefore ordered his men to lie on their faces on the deck, to go down with the ship, and when they were flung to the surface out of the whirlpool of eddying waters, to swim to the life raft. By a combination of luck, tenacity and skill, every man reached the raft, where they lay waiting for the daylight.

In every particular the mission failed, but its execution was the most dashing exploit of the war. It fired the imagination of the public on both sides. In the quick-risen daylight of the Antilles, Hobson saw a steam launch bearing men in uniform. He shouted to it, "Is there an officer on board to receive the surrender of prisoners of war?" The officer on board was Admiral Cervera. Later in the day, Cervera sent under a flag of truce a message to the American admiral, announcing the safety of Hobson and his crew. "Daring like theirs," he wrote, "makes the bitterest enemy proud that his fellow men can be such heroes."

The excitement in America was prodigious. Hobson became a national hero. He was tall and handsome, with elegant mustaches. On a subsequent lecture tour, young women flung their arms round his neck. In Denver he was kissed by three hundred debutantes, and a brand of chocolate called "Hobson's Kiss" was put upon the market. Many years later, Hobson remarked cryptically that the man was unfortunate who tasted success too young.

It would have been better for Cervera if Hobson's mission had been successful. A few weeks later, in accordance with instructions from Madrid, he slipped out of the harbor, to meet destruction in the open seas. As one of his ships went down in flames, the crew of an American ship began to cheer. Their captain stopped them. "Don't cheer. There are men dying there." The traditions and courtesies of chivalry had not yet died.

It was in keeping with her history that the United States should be readier to go into action with her fleet than with her army. In most peaceloving countries the general staff opens a new war in terms of the tactics of its predecessor. Under the compulsion of the press, to the slogan of "Remember the *Maine*, to hell with Spain," recruits rushed to the colors, but there were few arrangements for their accommodation; there was a shortage of arms, barracks, uniforms; there was no training cadre, but the national spirit of enterprise was in the ascendant. Theodore Roosevelt was at the time Assistant Secretary to the Navy, and his duties clearly lay in Washington, but he was not the man to sit at a desk in wartime; his spirit called him to the battlefield. He resigned his post and was soon busily organizing at Tampa, under the command of Colonel Wood, a body of elite troops called the Rough Riders. Wood was in his fifties; he commanded his men with a Harvard accent and a Bowery vocabulary. While the federal troops were being fitted with woolen tunics which would have provided admirable protection against the frosts of the Adirondacks, Wood asked for stable uniform, of light, dun-colored cotton, and wide-brimmed Western hats that were admirably suited to the damp heat of the semitropics. The Rough Riders were handpicked. Any recruit whose stomach measurement was larger than his chest was rejected. Wood and Roosevelt welcomed Oyster Bay aristocrats when they could get them, but they wanted fighters first.

> We're rough, tough, we're the stuff.
> We wanna fight and we can't get enough.

As a young man, Wood had served in the Confederate army, and he occasionally got confused as to which war he was fighting in. "Come on, boys," he shouted. "We've got the damned Yankees on the run." Wood was a wangler, a *debrouillard*; he got men on trains that had been reserved for other troops. His Rough Riders went into action before the troops that had been earmarked for the assault, and it was at their head that Theodore Roosevelt, waving his saber, charged up San Juan Hill.

On July 25, Santiago surrendered, and on July 26 the French ambassador sued the United States for peace, in the name of Spain.

As the clouds of war dispersed, Washington found itself faced with a problem that it had not anticipated, the island of Puerto Rico, which had never until that moment presented a problem to anyone, so placidly had it followed its uneventful course outside the current of Caribbean politics. The third largest island in the Caribbean, it was for centuries one of the most neglected. It had offered no problem to the United States; it had offered no problem to Spain; it had offered no problem to itself. Yet when the United States found themselves at war with the Spaniards in Cuba, they were automatically at war with the Spaniards in Puerto Rico. So eventless had its history been that the war correspondents who hurried to the public library to "read it up" could find practically nothing about it in the English language.

On sighting the harbor of San Juan Ponce de Leon had exclaimed, "*Ah, que puerto rico!*" ("What a rich port!") And it was prophetic of the island's destiny that that name should have been chosen, its subsequent importance to the Spaniards being simply its value as a port. It had no rich minerals, but the prevailing trade winds gave it a strategic value, and the citadel that had resisted Drake was strongly fortified. Though Cumberland held it for a little while, fever soon killed off his troops. During the long wars of the seventeenth and eighteenth centuries, the Spanish flag flew from its ramparts. It became the Gibraltar of the Caribbean. But nothing was done to develop the interior of the island. In the middle of the seventeenth century a priest was to report that, while it had many cattle farms, there were only seven sugar mills. Ginger was one of its chief commodities. It also exported tobacco and hides.

The workers were very undeveloped. The priest stated in his report that: "They scarcely know what implements are; they bring down a tree, principally by means of fire; with a saber, which they call a machete, they clear the jungle and clean the ground; with the point of this cutlass, or a pointed stick, they dig the holes or furrows in which they set their plants or sow their seeds. Thus they provide for their subsistence and when a hurricane or other mishap destroys their crops they supply their wants by fishing or they collect edible roots.

"Indolence rather than want of means makes them confine their cultivation to the level lands which they abandon as soon as they perceive that the fertility of the soil decreases, which happens very soon because they do not plough nor do they turn over the soil, much less manure it, so that the superficies soon become sterile; then they make a clearing on some mountain side. Neither the knowledge of the soil and climate, acquired during many years of residence, nor the increased facilities for obtaining the necessary agricultural implements, nor the large number of cattle they possess that could be used for agricultural purposes, nor the government's dispositions to improve the system of cultivation, have been sufficient to make these islanders abandon the indolence with which they regard the most important of all arts, and the first obligation imposed by God on man—namely the cultivation of the soil. They leave this to the slaves, who are few and ill-fed and know no more of agriculture than their masters do. . . . Their great laziness, together with a silly, baseless vanity, makes them look upon all manual labour as degrading, proper only for slaves, and so they prefer poverty to doing honest work. To this must be added their ambition to make wealth quickly, as some of them do, by contraband trading which makes good sailors of them but bad agriculturists.

"These are the reasons why they prefer the cultivation of produce that requires little labour. Most proprietors have a small portion of their land planted with cane, but few have made it their principal crop because of the expense of erecting a mill and the greater number of slaves and implements required; yet this industry alone, if properly fostered, would soon remove all obstacles to their progress.

"It is useless, therefore, to look for gardens and orchards in a country where the plough is yet unknown, and which has not even made the first step in agricultural development."

At this time the capital was the only authorized port open to commerce, so that there was smuggling all along the coast.

A century later the position was very much the same. A commission sent by Charles IV in 1765 reported: "To form an idea of how these natives live and still live it is enough to say that there are only two schools in the whole island. Outside the capital and San Germán, few know how to read; they count time by changes in the Government, by visits from Bishops, and by the arrivals of *situados*. They do not know what a league is. Each one reckons distance according to his own speed in travelling. The principal ones among them, including those of the capital when they are in the country, go barefooted and barelegged. The whites show no reluctance at being mixed up with the coloured population. In the towns (the capital included) there are few permanent inhabitants beside the curate; the others are always in the country, except Sundays and feast days, when those living near to where there is a church come to hear Mass. During these feast days they occupy houses that look like hen coups, which consist of a couple of rooms, most of them without doors or windows and therefore open day and night. Their furniture is so scant that they can move in an instant. The country houses are of the same description. There is little distinction among the people. The only difference between them consists in the possession of a little more or less property and perhaps the rank of a subaltern officer in the militia.

"The priest Abberd wanted the population increased by distributing unoccupied lands among the *agregades* or idle hangers-on: the convicts who have served their time and do not want to return to the Peninsular, the freed slaves and deserters from ships. Their numbers are so small and the soil so fruitful that they generally have an abundance of bananas, maize, beans and other food. Fish is abundant. They are rarely without a cow or two. The only furniture they have and need is a hammock and a cooking pot. They make plates, spoons, jugs and basins out of bark. A saber or machete is the only agricultural implement they use. They can build a house in a day or two."

It had not, in fact, greatly altered in over a hundred years, nor was it to alter greatly in the next seventy. In 1830, a visitor, Captain Flinter, was to say: "If some perfect stranger were to be dropped from the clouds as it were on this island, naked, without any other auxiliaries than health and strength, he might have married the next day and maintained a family without suffering more hardships or privations than fall to the lot of every labourer in the ordinary process of clearing and cultivating a piece of land."

The leaders of society at this time were the Spanish civil and military leaders who married rich, Creole women and made the island their home, as well as the merchants and shopkeepers who did not marry and who returned home as soon as they had amassed sufficient money. The tradesmen and artisans were Creoles. In addition, there were a number of adventurers who came and went. There were also a quantity of ex-convicts who settled with their colored families. It was probably on account of them that Puerto Ricans enjoyed at this time a bad reputation in the French and British islands. Horse racing and gambling were their chief amusements. In San Juan there was a gambling house in every side street. "Let them gamble," said one of the magistrates. "While they are at it, they will not worry about politics, and if they ruin themselves it is for the benefit of others."

The descendants of the early settlers who had spread through the interior had cleared themselves pieces of marshland that no one wanted. The peasants, called *Jibards*, were sickly and anemic in consequence of the insufficient quantity and innutritious quality of their food and the unhealthy conditions of their homes. Rice, plantains, sweet potatoes, maize, yams, beans, salted fish composed their diet. They wore no shoes; their damp clothes dried on their backs. Their two-roomed rectangular huts, raised on posts two feet from the ground, were made out of cane, trunks of coconut palm, bark of trees. They were wracked by fever. They usually had many children.

"Civil in their manners," Captain Flinter was to continue, "they are so acute in their dealings that they are sure to deceive a person who is not very guarded. Although they would scorn to commit a robbery yet they think it only fair to deceive or over-reach in a bargain. Like the peasantry of Ireland, they are proverbial for their hospitality and like them they are ever ready to fight on the slightest provocation. They swing themselves to and fro in their hammocks all day long, smoking their cigars or scraping a guitar. The plantain grove which surrounds their houses and the coffee trees which grow almost without cultivation afford them a frugal subsistence. If, with these, they have a cow and a horse, they consider themselves rich and happy. Happy indeed they are; they feel neither the pangs nor the remorse which follow the steps of disappointed ambition nor the daily wants experienced by the poor inhabitants of northern regions."

Puerto Rico was a garrison, no more and no less than that; a fact that explains the distinctive nature of its population. Only a small proportion of its natives have marked African features—the crinkled hair, thick lips and nose—that you will find in Guadeloupe, Antigua and Jamaica. The average Puerto Rican has a darkish skin, but straight black hair and delicate European features. This cannot be due to the original Indian strain, for here, as in Hispaniola, the Indians were eliminated within a few years of the occupation. Very few Spanish women came out during the first decades, and it must have been with imported Africans that the Spanish troops formed their alliances. But as the plantation system was not developed, the number of slaves imported was limited to the needs not of an agricultural community but of a garrison. Its population in 1765 was thirty thousand, of whom only five thousand were slaves. In consequence, the Spanish strain predominated over the African.

Puerto Rico was always given favored treatment. Its value was not to be assessed in terms of a credit and debit balance sheet. Spain did not expect it to pay dividends. Its value lay in the protection that it gave her shipping. Its successive governors appear to have been more liberal than those which were appointed to Peru and Mexico. It was not till 1815 that Puerto Rico was raised to the status of a colony. From this time on her population and prosperity increased. Hither, as to Cuba, came many of the landowners from South and Central America who wanted to retain their links with Spain. Sugar was planted. Relations with Madrid were cordial. There was little civil disorder, little resentment against the government. In 1870 Puerto Rico became a province of Spain. In the very year that the Spanish-American war broke out, Spain, through the diplomacy of Luis Muñoz Rivera, the father of the governor who in the late 1940s launched "Operation Bootstrap," was on the point of ratifying a constitution that granted the colony a high measure of autonomy. The majority of Puerto Ricans were as contented with their lot as any group of mortals in an imperfect universe. They had no particular wish to become Americans, but they had no alternative. Spain had no longer any standing in the Caribbean. The island could not be administered from Madrid. It could not stand on its own feet. It could not federate in a joint parliament with Cuba. It had to come under the protection of the United States. The caprice of history had ordained for Puerto Rico a surprising destiny which is still very far from settled.

An armistice was declared at the end of July, but it was not till the end of the year that peace was signed. Under the best conditions, Spaniards are leisurely negotiators, and there were many points at issue. It was recognized from the start that Puerto Rico should be handed over to the United States and that Cuba should become an American protectorate, but Spain was reluctant to cede the Philippines. The United States were adamant, however. The security of the Pacific seaboard depended on their retention; there was at this time no Panama Canal. The talks in Paris progressed slowly. Spain had much to worry her. The Carlists were causing trouble once again. The national finances were desperate. Spain had received no money for the loss of Cuba, yet she was not relieved of the Cuban debt. The bondholders were indignant. And all the time disbanded Spanish soldiers were being landed in Málaga, penniless and homeless. Letters were written to the London *Times*, pleading their distress.

In Cuba itself, conditions were no more comfortable. The Cuban army, numbering thirty-five thousand, was under arms, without pay or food; it was in a disgruntled mood. Its troops had been fighting consistently for three years and intermittently for thirty, so that their flag should fly from the mastheads of Havana; instead of that, the stars and stripes were fluttering in the trade wind. Their war for freedom had become the Spanish-American War. They were delighted to see the Spaniards go, but this was not quite what they had wanted. In the meantime they were hungry.

Moreover, the maintenance of order in Havana itself was proving difficult. The Spanish police, like the married Spanish officers, were exiled from their homes, without their savings and without their wives and families. The city police—a force recruited from the Cubans—was disbanded under tumultuous circumstances. They demanded their savings, which they had been forced to deposit, but no money was available. They mutinied, and a general ordered his troops to fire on them. The troops refused, and next day the troops were shipped back to Spain. There were a number of shooting affrays. Spanish soldiers stood about in pairs or wandered about in groups of eight. Toward the end of November, American troops began to arrive. On the tenth of December the treaty was signed; the take-over was fixed for the first of January.

The ceremony took place at noon. Very few people attended to watch the control of Cuba being handed over to the U.S. general. It was not what the Cubans had wanted when they went to war, but they accepted the inevitable in a spirit of acquiescence. The Spanish residents remained indoors. The royal flag of Spain was lowered, the stars and stripes run up, and a salute was fired. The Spanish general retired to the throne room to bid his officers farewell. Tears were in his eyes. "Men, I have been in more battles than I have hairs upon my head, and my valor has never failed me except today. Goodbye. Goodbye." He then marched to a Spanish transport. The U.S. military band played the Spanish royal march. The ship drew away from the quay, and the last symbol of Spain's majesty and power passed, after four hundred years, from the area that she had found and won and ruled. The twentieth century had begun. The first volume of West Indian history had closed.

Epilogue

1

The end of one story is the beginning of another. The Victorian novelist, after the peal of wedding bells had faded from the village steeple, would round off his three-decker romance with an epilogue beginning "And now dear reader, you will want to know what happened to the other characters in our story . . ."; and it is not perhaps inappropriate that this history should conclude with a brief résumé of the chief events during the last sixty years.

For the British and French West Indian colonies, the first half of the twentieth century has been a period of slow growth and change, with the administrative power passing out of the hands of the white plantocracy, and the descendants of the African slaves coming to recognize their former prisons as their own proud heritage. Martinique and Guadeloupe are now departments of France, as much a part of France as Normandy and Provence, equal in status with the Var and Seine-et-Oise, sending their own representatives to the House of Deputies and the Senate. Jamaica and Trinidad, on the other hand, have become independent countries within the framework of the Commonwealth, while at the moment of writing (October 1963), Barbados is in process of merging with the Windward and Leeward Islands into an independent federation, also within the boundaries of the Commonwealth. These changes have been brought about without riots and bloodshed, through constitutional procedure. The account of how it has been achieved in the British islands has been fully and effectively told in the concluding chapters of Sir Alan Burns' history, which is, in its full, wide scope, required reading for any student of the area. Year by year, decade by decade, it may well have seemed that nothing very much was happening in the islands, but in the long perspective of half a century, it can be seen how much the stream of progress was effecting.

Change deals gently with tropical countries. The rhythm of the weeks follows an unaltering sequence. There are the months of heat, when day after day an unclouded sun shines out of a metallic sky; when the grass withers and goes brown; when the earth crumbles and splits under its unbroken radiance; when eyes grow dazed under its steady glare; when each night, as you toss tired and damp and sleepless under the transparent lawn of the mosquito net, you can visualize out of your memory of the past the exact course, detail by detail, of the hours that await you when light has returned in unwavering brilliance to the horizon's rim.

By an hour's measure you can judge the coming of the temperate months. And by an hour's measure you can judge the return of the wet months; when the skies are gray, when the rain thunders with a steady drumbeat upon iron roofs and stone-faced gateways; when the dead palm fronds are torn from their browned roots and swept whistling to the ground. With the succeeding seasons the green shoots of cane strengthen and grow tall; the soft, green coconut grows brown and hard; the sweet, cool milk within it sours, thickening into the hard rind that the traders dry and ship.

Along the hills, the scarlet flower of the *immortelle* protects the cocoa plant. And as the seasons and the crops succeed, to man, cherishing, guarding, guiding that succession, drawing his sustenance and profit from it, life has a seeming permanence. The forces of nature at work upon the fields and hills are part of an eternal process. Cities, which are the expression of man's changing taste, in cold latitudes with their long record of man's struggle against nature, wake in a man's heart the sense of man's importance, of human destiny, of the value of personality. But in the warm countries of rapid growth, where the earth is fertile and abundant; where man is born to plenty; where man's function is only to direct, with the minimum of effort on his part, this facile opulence to his use, it is easy for man to accept the Nirvana of unchangingness; difficult for him to recognize the currents and the drifts of change.

Each individual island has had, however, over this period its own special landmarks. Although the area is considered climatically one of the most pleasant in the world, there remains the constant menace of the hurricane. Every West Indian child has learned the doggerel:

> June too soon,
> July stand by,
> August you must
> Remember September,
> October all over.

Every prudent West Indian family sets itself on its guard in August. The earliest records enumerate the warning signs—the heavy atmosphere, the red aspect of the sun, the rumbling subterranean grunt, the stars shining through a kind of mist that makes them seem larger though less bright; the northwest horizon clouds, and often there is a sulfurous exhalation from the sea. In spite of the weather being calm, there is a heavy swell on the sea, and sudden changes of the wind from east to west. Horses neigh, cattle bellow, there is a general restlessness among the animals, and a faint rise in the barometer before its steady fall. In that way, before the existence of meteorological stations, the islanders recognized the approach of danger. Most of them in their lifetime have been the witnesses of a hurricane; can describe how they had noticed the first fine wisps of cirrus clouds, with the air calm and sultry, till they were dispersed by a gentle breeze that was soon supplanted by the full fury of the gale. Each island dates personal events in relation to the particular hurricane that has struck it.

Nor must it be forgotten that the islands are of volcanic origin. St. Vincent has suffered greatly from the devastations of Soufrière, and it was during this century that Martinique endured one of the worst tragedies in the history of the world. On May 8, 1902, within forty-five seconds, the entire city of Saint-Pierre was destroyed.

The story has been often told. For years the inhabitants of Saint-Pierre had joked about the rumblings of the extinct volcano in whose shadow their city had been built. There was "old Father Pelé muttering in his sleep," they would say. They ignored the warnings that they were given during that last doomed spring. Smoke plumes rising from the crater's mouth encouraged the young people on Sunday afternoons to clamber up its steep sides and peer over the edge, just as their grandparents had done. Even when cinders were mingled with the smoke, and the vegetables that the women brought from the hills to market were dark with ashes, even when the rumbling noises became explosions, and the river to the north of the city was swollen with a torrent of boiling mud, tearing down the Guerin factory, even then the inhabitants, as a whole, refused to believe that there was any danger. That old monster of the mountain! What harm could he do now? Had he not growled and grunted in his sleep longer than any Carib legend could recall?

Dramatic irony hangs over all that happened during those last days. The authorities in Fort de France, disturbed when a few timid families began to desert their homes—it might cause a housing problem in the south—sent a committee of scientific experts to make a report on the spot. The committee confidently announced there was no cause for alarm, and on the afternoon before the disaster, the governor drove out from Fort de France to take up residence in Saint-Pierre, to allay the fears of the inhabitants and to prove by his presence his complete faith in the verdict of his experts. The next morning was Ascension Day. He did not want anything to interfere with the town's traditional enjoyment of its *jour de fête*.

It was on a gray afternoon that he arrived. A film of dust lay over the red-tiled roofs, over the plane trees of the *Grande Rue*, over the moss-grown runnels. Many windows were shuttered and the shops were closed. The front page of the local newspaper was mainly concerned with the eruption. There was a scientific leader explaining why it was not serious. There was a catalogue of the subscribers to the fund for those whose homes had been destroyed. There was a list of those who had been killed when the *Rivière Blanche* was flooded. There was an article about the governor's visits. But there was no atmosphere of gloom, and when night fell and the avenues were bright with lamps, Saint-Pierre was her habitual gay-hearted self.

That night there was a heavy thunderstorm. For hours the rain lashed over the amphitheater of the city's hills. But it was into a sky blue and cloudless that the sun rose next morning. The rain had washed clean the roofs and plane trees; the stale smell of grit had vanished from the air; from the *jardin des plantes* came the scent of flowers. The market was filled with chattering groups. On all sides the business of preparation for the fête had started.

The governor, taking his coffee on his balcony, was very likely thinking how in a few hours' time under the high sun there would be the rich parading of the streets, the bright dresses, the carnival masks; the laughter, the dancing and the music. And then, shortly after eight, two loud explosions thundered from the hills, and sailors from the decks of the ships at anchor saw a large white cloud emerge from the crater of Mont Pelé—it looked as though one side of the mountain had fallen away—and roll upon the town like an Alpine avalanche, engulf it and then swing out to sea. Of the ships at anchor only one escaped—the *Roddam*. She was under steam, ready to sail, and her captain managed to slip her cable. Her deck was covered with lava, she nearly capsized under the impact, her ropes were charred, members of the crew lay dead among the ashes, but she managed to limp her way across the channel to St. Lucia, bearing the sole eyewitness account of the disaster.

A European cannot picture in terms of any tragedy that is likely to come to him what that tragedy meant for the survivors of Martinique. It did not mean simply the death of twenty-eight thousand people or the loss of property and possessions, the curtain for many years upon the prosperity of the island. It meant the cutting of their lives in half, the loss of half their friends, half their families, half their possessions. In 1929, in Fort de France, a man on the brink of fifty talked about it.

"I left Saint-Pierre on the seventh," he said. "I was to be married on the ninth. I had come into Fort de France, leaving my *fiancée* behind to make some last arrangements. I cannot express the excitement with which I woke on that morning of the eighth. I was twenty-four. She was three years younger. It was the first time that either of us had been in love. And that was the last whole day, I told myself, that I should ever spend alone. It was so lovely a morning, too. Bright and clear. And after one of the worst nights that there can have ever been. Thunder and lightning and unceasing rain. The sunlight was a happy omen. Never had I known, never shall I know, anything like the happiness with which I dressed and bathed and shaved that morning. And then, just as I was finishing my coffee, there came those two explosions. They were terrific. They shook the entire island. But I wasn't frightened. Why should I be? What was there to connect them with Pelé? I went on, as the rest of us did, with what I had to do.

"For a while that morning, life went on in Fort de France in its ordinary way. But soon you had begun to notice a worried look on people's faces. The sky was dark; a thin dust in which pebbles were mingled was falling over the town. Rumor had started. There was no news coming through from Saint-Pierre. The telephone line had been cut suddenly in the middle of a message, at the instant of the two explosions. Since then there had been silence.

"You know how it is when a rumor starts in a small place. The most fantastic stories get about. A *porteuse* from Carbet had reported that a fisherman had seen flames behind Saint-Pierre, and no one asked how a *porteuse* could have done the twenty-eight kilometres from Carbet in two hours.

"I tried not to feel frightened. It was absurd to be frightened. No one had been frightened in Saint-Pierre the afternoon before, when I had left it. Earlier they had been frightened, yes; when those cinders had been falling in the streets, when lightning was flickering about the crater's mouth; when the day was dark with clouds; when the sugar factory by the *Rivière Blanche* was being swept away by boiling mud. They had been frightened then. But the scientists had told them there was no need to be afraid. The governor and his wife had come out there themselves. The cinders had practically stopped falling. It was old Pelé amusing himself again.

"That was what I told myself. But you know how it is when panic catches hold of a place. By eleven o'clock our nerves had gone. Three hours and still no news, with the wildest rumors flying round; not one of us could work. We sat in the club, forgetting our rum punches, one thought only in our minds. I shall never forget that morning: the suspense, the terror, the uncertainty. Midday, and still no message had come through. The boat that had been sent out to make enquiries had not returned. We sat and waited. It was not till one o'clock that we knew."

He paused and shrugged his shoulders.

"It's twenty-six years ago," he said. "That's a long time. One can forget most things in that time. One thinks one's heart is broken. But it mends. One thinks one's life is over. But it isn't. One goes on living. One makes the best out of what's left. I've not had a bad best, either. I've had a happy marriage. I'm proud of my children. I've made a position. But," he again shrugged his shoulders, "I don't know that since that day I've felt that anything mattered in particular."

It was believed at first that there was not a single survivor, but on the third day a search party heard yells from beneath the bank of rubble that once had been the prison, and they discovered in an underground cell a felon who had been imprisoned a few days earlier for a minor misdemeanor. He had been scorched by the hot air that had passed over his head, but he had not been seriously hurt. He had been woken by the noise, but he had no idea what was happening. He was hungry and indignant, demanding of his rights. The remainder of his sentence was remitted as a compensation for his three days' discomfort, and he subsequently was exhibited in a circus in the United States as sole survivor.

2

The outbreak of the First World War had little effect upon the Caribbean except that it produced an era of prosperity by sending up the price of sugar. Germany possessed no Caribbean colonies, Britain and France were allies, and the Netherlands and Denmark were neutral, so that no campaigns were launched as they had been in the Napoleonic Wars. The only form of belligerence that Germany could take was through her submarines in the Atlantic, and that did not affect the day-to-day routine of life.

The only island to become seriously involved was the one island that could have been expected to stand outside and above the battle —the independent republic of Haiti. During the first decade of the century, the ramshackle conditions described by Hesketh Pritchard had steadily deteriorated. The currency was debased. The interest was not paid on foreign loans. The island, rich though it was in natural resources, meager though the standard of living was that it maintained, was not able to pay its way. The cultural links with France had been maintained in spite of the political break, and many of the richer families sent their children to Paris for their education. There was probably more intellectual conversation in Port-au-Prince than there was in Fort de France, and Haiti produced its poets—in particular Oswald Durand—but this small educated class was not strong enough to keep power within its hands. It could not keep pace with modern methods of business, government and finance. The gangsters, the opportunists, the racketeers obtained control; and brigands in the hills sold their services whenever revolution threatened.

The speed of deterioration quickened. In August 1911 the eighteenth President was deposed by a revolution. By March 5, 1915 he had had six successors. Three were deposed by revolutions, one was blown up in his palace, the fifth was poisoned. The United States observed this deterioration with, in diplomatic phraseology, "grave and growing concern." It could not welcome anarchy on its doorstep. It had financial commitments in the island. American lives and property might be imperiled. Moreover, it was afraid that some European power would intervene to protect its interests. Germany had in 1912 sent a gunboat to collect the interest on a loan. Germany was also taking steps toward acquiring a customs control and building a naval base at Môle St. Nicolas. It was at this point by no means certain that Germany would lose the war. She might well, at the eventual peace conference, demand a special status in regard to Haiti. Such a prospect was far from being agreeable to Washington. The Monroe Doctrine was at stake. Washington was prepared to take action on the first major provocation. That provocation was soon to come.

On November 7, 1914, Davilmar Theodore was elected President for seven years. He was destined to rule for three and a half months. Conditions in the north were chaotic, and the American bankers there were afraid that the gold assets in their banks would be confiscated. They requested Washington to send troops to carry this gold to safety, and shortly before Christmas, five hundred marines landed and took half a million dollars in gold back to New York. To enforce order, Theodore sent to the north as his delegate General Jean Vilbrun Guillaume Sam, a man with presidential hopes. After a cursory examination of the situation, this officer informed the authorities of Cap Haitien that a revolutionary army which he was not strong enough to resist was threatening the city. The army entered the city unopposed and proclaimed Sam the wielder of official power—*chef du pouvoir executif.*

Sam was now ready to launch a revolution. For several months a U.S. warship had been patrolling Haitian waters in defense of foreign interests, and it was in keeping with the comic-opera atmosphere of the average Haitian revolution that the American admiral of this ship should instruct Sam as to how his revolution was to be conducted. The admiral had no intention, he asserted, of questioning the sovereignty of the Haitian nation or of maintaining any but a neutral attitude toward the contending factions. He must, however, insist that no fighting take place in the town of Cap Haitien and that contending factions fight their battle well clear of the town.

Sam proceeded to move south, and at each main point of pause along the way, an American naval officer was on hand to ensure that he followed the admiral's instructions. H. P. Davis in *Black Democracy* describes the campaign as a "personally conducted" revolution. Theodore offered no resistance; on February 22 he escaped in a Dutch boat to Jamaica. On March 9 Sam was installed as President.

In the north, however, Sam's revolution was only partially accepted, and the original insurgents were making trouble under Dr. Rosalus Bato, who had been minister of the interior under Theodore, to such an extent that on June 19 a French cruiser landed marines to protect its consulate and bank. Sam, in Port-au-Prince, realized that his position was precarious. He acted promptly and ruthlessly, ordering the arrest of some 170 of his chief opponents. The foreign legations were filled with refugees. Once again a revolution moved toward Port-au-Prince. Sam was far from being a coward, but believing he had no support, he fled to the French Embassy, and the commandant of the prison promptly ordered the death of every political prisoner in the jail. Such prisoners, including members of the best and most influential families, were, without trial and in cold blood, massacred and mutilated in their cells with cutlasses. This was the provocation that Washington required.

It is uncertain whether or not this slaughter was the outcome of a direct order from the President. In the pocket of the prison commandant, who was subsequently shot, was found a note from Sam, written in the French legation, complaining that he had been misled as to the military position, and ending with the words, "as regards yourself take such measures as your conscience shall dictate. Too much to say." That could have meant anything. But it is hard to believe that the prison commandant could have acted so brutally without authority. In any case, the indignant populace were not in a mood for legal "pretty points," and when they saw the smoke of an American warship within their harbor, they realized that unless they acted quickly their chances of dealing with their President were slight, and the mob surged to the French legation. "A small body of well-known citizens after courteously explaining to the French minister that the people were no longer to be balked of their revenge, entered the house, dragged Sam down the stairs and threw him over an iron gate to the mob." His body was cut to pieces, and the trunk was being paraded through the streets as the American marines marched in. The independence of the first Negro republic was temporarily at an end.

The subsequent story has been often told, but nowhere better, in the opinion of the present writer, than in H. P. Davis' *Black Democracy*. The next twenty years were the most prosperous, in fact the only prosperous years that the island has known since the fall of the Bastille. Under American control, order was achieved, the finances straightened out, health services installed, roads improved, hotels organized; a law was passed allowing foreigners to own property.

By the middle twenties, Haiti was in the news. A number of excellent books had been written about it: there were Frank Crane's *Roaming through the Caribbean*, and Blair Niles' travelogue; then John Vandercook's fine novel, *Black Majesty*, about Henri Christophe; finally there was William Seabrook's sensational *The Magic Island*, with its stories of cannibalism and voodoo. Articles about the citadel at Cap Haitien appeared in the American papers and a great many tourists were anxious to see it for themselves. The tutelary period ended, however, in the middle thirties, and the country gradually slipped back toward anarchy and chaos. The tourist trade from the U.S.A. continued for a while; there was a market for Haitian wood carving, particularly for salad bowls, there was a vogue in painting for

Haitian primitives, and a number of avant-garde American artists and writers went down, a parallel with their predecessors who, after the First World War, had settled on the Left Bank in Paris. But the difficulties and the cost of living became too great; the insecurity and lack of order, the insolence and rapaciousness of the Haitians became too irksome. At the time of writing, this distracted community would seem to be about to dissolve once again in chaos.

In the meantime, a very different destiny had marked the fortunes of the Spanish section of the island. During the eighteenth century, what is now known as the Dominican Republic had been as much neglected by the Spaniards as Trinidad had been. There had been no large importation of slaves. Its population had been small, and brown had predominated over black. During the nineteenth century it had for long periods been overrun by the Haitians, and it was only the collapse of order in Haiti that restored it to independence. Its finances foundered, and in 1905 the U.S.A. took them over. A president was assassinated in 1911 and in 1916 the U.S.A. assumed military control. The occupation did not prove popular, and eight years later it was withdrawn. The country drifted again toward insolvency until in 1931 General Trujillo assumed command.

Opinions are divided about the merits of his regime. His military dictatorship was tyrannical and ruthless. There was no liberty of opinion and it was corrupt to the extent that he and his friends appropriated large quantities of public funds. Yet at the same time order was maintained, works of reconstruction were undertaken, and the "common man" was better off than he had ever been.

During this period, relations with Haiti deteriorated. In the national census only eleven percent of the population was classified as being completely Negroid, and the Dominicans scoffed at the "inferior African culture" of their neighbors and denounced the lower salaries that they accepted. This led to friction on the border, where the frontier was not clearly marked and where Haitians were in the habit of crossing over to help the Dominican farmers gather in their harvest. In protest against this custom, Trujillo's troops in 1937 rounded up and slaughtered several thousand Haitians. International pressure alone prevented a war, and the Dominican Republic agreed to pay an indemnity of 750,000 dollars to the families of the victims. Only a part of this sum was actually paid, however. In 1961 Trujillo was, in his turn, assassinated, and at the time of writing, chaos is firmly reestablished.

3

In 1917 the U.S.A. entered the First World War on the side of Britain, France and Italy, and it was presumably her involvement with European politics that forced her to reconsider her own defenses. During the Civil War, she had been concerned over the ease with which European ships had traded with the Confederate south, and she had almost concluded arrangements for the purchase of the Danish Virgin Islands, so that her eastern approaches might be protected. Congress, however, had failed to ratify the deal. Now negotiations were resumed, and in return for a cash settlement, the islands of St. Thomas, St. Croix and St. John flew the stars and stripes from their mastheads.

Two years later the Volstead Act became the eighteenth amendment to the Constitution of the United States, and the manufacture and sale of alcoholic liquids became illegal. This measure had an unfortunate effect on the prosperity both of the United States' new possessions and the recently acquired Puerto Rico. Rum was one of the chief products both of St. Croix and Puerto Rico, and a West Indian island that did not offer its visitor the opportunity of resisting the midday heat with the cool, mellow and fragrant sustenance of a rum punch stood little chance of attracting tourist trade.

To many individuals, prohibition brought substantial subterranean wealth, and the harbors of Bermuda and the Bahamas, and the beaches of the French islands, St. Pierre and Miquelon, served as important bases for the rumrunners. But Cuba and Jamaica were the only West Indian islands to profit from this trade. The Windward and Leeward Islands, Trinidad and Barbados lay too far to the south. Indeed, during the 1930s, the Caribbean was as a whole a depressed area; houses were crumbling, sugar factories were abandoned, plantations were turned over to casual husbandry, but in all that area the American possessions were among the most depressed. President Hoover was to describe them as a "poor house," a remark he was not permitted to forget.

Wars, by and large, bring prosperity to those whom they do not actually destroy. In August 1939 a team of West Indian cricketers was touring England. They canceled their last two matches and sailed for home. They were very wise. Within a few weeks, the Atlantic was infested with submarines. Throughout the war a great many of the ships that sailed from West Indian harbors did not reach their destination, and the *Lady Nelson,* one of the four smart Canadian passenger ships that had for the last ten years linked the smaller islands with Boston and Montreal, was sunk in St. Lucia harbor. But these sinkings did not impoverish the British West Indians themselves, since the ships and their merchandise were insured. There was also, of course, an improved market for West Indian produce.

In the summer of 1940 Winston Churchill and Franklin Roosevelt made a deal, which the governments behind them ratified, to exchange for fifty Liberty ships and a million rifles, bases on a ninety-nine years' lease at St. Lucia, Antigua, Trinidad and Bermuda. Whether this deal was legal, whether, that is to say, the British government had the right to cede West Indian territory to a foreign power without the permission of the local legislatures was not considered at the time, and there has been a certain amount of argument in recent years in relation to the base at Trinidad. But the Liberty ships were extremely welcome to Britain at the time, and so to the West Indians were the American dollars that were poured out freely at the bases. St. Lucia has rarely been so gay socially as it was at that time.

The situation in the French islands was very different, since the officer in command there, Admiral Robert, remained loyal to the Vichy government. When the Battle of France began, Martinique and Guadeloupe were protected by a patrol squadron, headed by a cruiser and an auxiliary cruiser. In mid-June an aircraft carrier started from Halifax for France with 105 planes. Halfway across the Atlantic, she was ordered to sail to Martinique. At the same time the *Banque de France* decided to transfer across the Atlantic its reserves of gold, estimated at 250 million dollars. The Canadian authorities in Halifax tried to get the gold transferred to Montreal, but the commander of the ship, the *Emile Bertin,* dodged the Canadian customs and sailed —it has been said on his own initiative—to Martinique. The gold was transferred to the vaults of Fort de France, and its presence there immeasurably increased Admiral Robert's power and prestige.

After the armistice, British agents tried to persuade Admiral Robert to rally to the Free French cause, but Admiral Robert was resolute in his loyalty to Vichy, and an attempt to produce a pro-Gaullist *coup d'état* misfired. The French islands presented, therefore, a permanent problem, not only to the British but to the U.S.A. Washington was naturally resolved to prevent these islands being amalgamated with the Third Reich, and a conference was held of Latin American governments in which it was resolved to prevent any change of ownership in Caribbean colonies. In the meantime, Britain, who was allied militarily with the exiled government of the Netherlands, landed troops in Curaçao and Aruba to protect the oil refineries, and imposed a blockade on the French islands, nominally to prevent ships and planes being transferred to Germany, but actually to watch the store of gold. All mail was stopped and the cable to St. Thomas cut.

The position of Martinique and Guadeloupe soon became highly serious. They lacked medical supplies, they were short of food, they could not conduct trade. On humanitarian grounds it was agreed that the neutral U.S.A. should intervene. In December, President Roosevelt made a tour of the islands; he did not receive Admiral Robert officially, but it was presumed that they had met at sea, since Admiral Robert left the island within an hour of the President's arrival at Fort de France, and shortly afterward the British abandoned the blockade and the French agreed to accept the authority of a U.S. destroyer patrol. The French called these ships "the guardian angels," since they did not stop foodstuffs and medical supplies. Moreover, commerce with France was reestablished on a minor scale.

Even so, the residents of the islands, particularly of Guadeloupe, suffered great privations. Robert insisted that his troops and the police should be well fed in order to ensure their loyalty. This meant that the workers in the cane fields were undernourished.

A number of them escaped to Dominica to enlist with the Free French Army, not out of loyalty to de Gaulle, but because they were hungry. By the regulations of enlistment they were entitled to a regular diet of meat meals. This involved Dominica in a cattle shortage that lasted for a number of years after the war. Dominica, as on so many other occasions, fared unfortunately during this war. Lacking a suitable air base, she was cut off from the general atmosphere of the war. She received none of the mental stimulus of being allied with great events, and had to accommodate several thousand refugees.

After December 1941, when the U.S.A. came into the war, the position of Martinique and Guadeloupe became more constrained. It worsened in the winter of the following year, after the North African landings, with the whole of France under Axis control. The full story of what happened during the two grim years that followed has never been told, officially or fully. It is still not known to what extent, if any, the islands were used as refueling bases for German submarines. The American and British authorities were apparently in doubt as to what action they should take, and residents in St. Lucia assert that at one point an invasion of Martinique was planned but at the last moment was called off. The full story will be, no doubt, told some day. In the meantime, it can be truly stated that the four years of June 1940 to August 1944 were for the actual residents among the most harassed that those two islands had known during their dramatic lives. But the four years passed for them, as the hurricanes and earthquakes do, and by the late 1940s, these two great islands were living once again, happily and hopefully, in the future as in the present.

4

A new existence started for the family of islands in 1945. It was not simply that peace had followed war, but that a new medium had added a dimension to the area. Air travel had brought the islands within a few minutes of one another and a few hours of the metropolitan mainland. Pan American was their fairy godmother: other lines have followed, BWIA in particular; but Pan American was the forerunner. The tourist potentialities of the area became apparent; at the very time when the climate in the northern hemisphere was at its worst, that in the Caribbean was at its best. When rain and snow and sleet held captive the cities of the north, the golden beaches were a few hours away. Hotels opened everywhere—even on the barren desert of Aruba. Once wealth had flowed away from the West Indies; now it flooded back. Prosperity returned; and all the time, while the tourists were spending their money at the bars and beaches, at the galas and gaming tables, the inhabitants of the islands were working out their own basic problems of self-government. It is a story that cannot yet be told, because it is only now being evolved. Another historian will tell it at the century's close. The story that this book set out to tell ended on the first day of the twentieth century.

Index